Command of the Seas

Other Books by
John F. Lehman, Jr.

Making War
Beyond the SALT II Failure (with Seymour Weiss)
Aircraft Carriers: The Real Choices
The Executive, Congress and Foreign Policy
The Prospects for Arms Control (editor, with J. E. Dougherty)
On Seas of Glory

Command
of the
Seas

John F. Lehman, Jr.

BLUEJACKET BOOKS

Naval Institute Press
Annapolis, Maryland

Naval Institute Press
291 Wood Road
Annapolis, MD 21402

First Bluejacket Books printing, 2001

Library of Congress Cataloging-in-Publication Data
Lehman, John F.
    Command of the Seas / John F. Lehman, Jr.
        p. cm. — (Bluejacket books)
    Originally published: New York: Scribner, c1988.
    ISBN 1-55750-534-9
    1. Lehman, John F. 2. United States. Navy—History—20th century. 3. United States. Marine Corps—History—20th century. I. Title. II. Series.
    VA58.4 .L44 2001
    359'.00973'09048—dc21

                                                                                        00-052447

Printed in the United States of America on acid-free paper ∞
08 07 06 05 04 03 02 01   8 7 6 5 4 3 2 1

Quotations from *Supercarrier*, by George Wilson, copyright © 1986 by Macmillan Publishing Company, a division of Macmillan, Inc., are reprinted with permission of Macmillan Publishing Company.

To my wife,
Barbara Thornton Wieland Lehman,

my father,
LCDR John Francis Lehman, Sr., USNR (Ret.)

and my mother,
Grace Constance Cruice Lehman

Contents

Part IV: A Summing Up

Figures

Preface to Bluejacket Edition

When I left the navy in 1987 we were but eleven ships short of the 600-ship objective, and it was an extremely ready, high morale and fully modernized fleet.

Before I resumed my business career, I resolved to set down my thoughts on the experiences while the facts and passions were still vivid. *Command of the Seas*, published in 1988 was the result.

Since *Command of the Seas* was written in 1988, the grand purpose of the efforts and events described in it have been accomplished. The building and deploying of the 600-ship navy was part of a bipartisan effort led by President Reagan to rebuild America's armed forces and its leadership of the free world. The impact of that rebuilding upon the leadership of the Soviet Union was accomplished as intended. It set in train events, however, that moved much more rapidly and decisively than any of us had expected. I cannot claim to have foreseen the end of the cold war. No one did. We knew, of course, that the Soviet Union had weaknesses and the essence of our strategy—indeed the essence of any strategy—was to exploit those weaknesses. Yet the contingent factor in history, the role of leadership, altered the pace and scope of events. Ronald Reagan led a resurgence of the West, and Mikhail Gorbachev, forced to compromise with restored U.S. military power, unleashed a fatal dosage of reform upon his very well armed but otherwise crippled empire. George Bush skillfully managed its final disintegration. In the absence of these men and their supporting casts the story cannot be told. As for the end, it can be described simply enough: Democracy won. Dictatorship lost. The Soviet Empire was no more. The cold war was over.

In preparing a paperback edition of *Command of the Seas* for the Naval Institute, I have made some additions, some deletions, and a very few revisions. The additions come in the form of an afterword at the end of each of the four parts. In the twelve years since the book was written much has happened that has served to validate many and invalidate a few of the policies and actions that are described in the book. The afterword of each part provides that commentary. The deletions from the first edition are primarily material that is no longer relevant or of interest to today's reader. The few revisions that I have made are of accounts of events where new facts have come to light.

In this memoir of the late cold war period, the alarms and excursions of the time may have a certain quaintness seeming as they are so far in the past. I have left that perspective unchanged. Overall, I was pleasantly surprised to find how well the book has stood the test of time.

In preparing this edition for the Naval Institute I am grateful once more to Dr. Harvey Sicherman, who helped me on the original manuscript and provided insightful suggestions for the revisions to this edition. I am grateful also to Don Price who provided very helpful suggestions. George Sawyer, who was Assistant Secretary for Shipbuilding during my tenure, has provided particularly helpful analysis of the lessons of our shipbuilding and procurement policies which are included in the afterword for that part. Mark Geier handled flawlessly the administration and mechanics of making and keeping track of the revisions.

September 1, 2001

Preface

Once in a while a person has the good fortune to participate in grand events that make a real difference. Being asked by President Ronald Reagan to lead the rebuilding of the U.S. Navy was a breathtaking opportunity. It commenced a six-year adventure in applying theory and commitment to an elephantine bureaucracy and byzantine political arena. Each week was filled with excitement and peopled with earnest strivers, chancers, fancy dans, sturdy comrades, and a few warriors and statesmen.

This book was written in the belief that the story of these experiences, and of what was accomplished, has useful lessons for the future. It is not an autobiography. I have included a selection of anecdotes from my early life that will help the reader understand how I accumulated the interests and convictions that guided me as secretary of the navy.

Nor is the book a chronicle or history, strictly speaking. Of the hundreds of decisions, policies, and crises during my watch, I have dwelt on those few whose lessons are most important. During my watch, I made my share of mistakes and bad calls. The reader no doubt will forgive the scant attention I give them, as others have already given them so much.

Hoping to avoid being too professional, I nevertheless suggest lessons from each experience—indeed, that is the fundamental purpose of the book—to show that if, in Theodore Roosevelt's words, people are willing to step into the arena, and mar their faces with dust and sweat and blood, it is still possible to know, as today our sailors do, the thrill of high achievement.

In writing this book I am deeply grateful to Dr. Harvey Sicherman for combining friendship with editorial criticism and intellectual challenge. This book is much better in content and clearer in prose because of his talented help. Edward T. ("Ned") Chase, senior editor at Macmillan/Scribners is a master and delight to work with, though I must work further on his political views.

Others of my friends ploughed through early drafts and helped me greatly. I thank them.

Janis Grimes, Barbara Majett, Vikki Ravinskas, and Elizabeth Kelly all worked hard on the many transcripts, and each was flawless.

I am especially grateful to Dr. Ronald Spector, historian of the navy, and to Judy Short and others of his staff for their professional support.

Command of the Seas

Introduction

Rickover and the Navy Soul

"Mr. President, that piss-ant knows nothing about the navy." The admiral turned toward me and raised his voice now to a fearsome shout. "You just want to get rid of me, you want me out of the program because you want to dismantle the program." Shifting now toward President Reagan, he roared on: "He's a goddamn liar, he knows he is just doing the work of the contractors. The contractors want me fired because of the claims and because I am the only one in government who keeps them from robbing the taxpayers."

As I sat there in shock, the previous year of careful orchestration of Admiral Hyman Rickover's hoped-for *graceful* retirement flashed before my eyes — and cratered in flames!

The maneuvering had begun during the pre-Inaugural transition in 1980, when I told the secretary of defense designate, Caspar Weinberger, that one of my first orders of business as secretary of the navy would be to solve, at last, the Rickover problem. Rickover's legendary achievements were in the past. His present viselike grip on much of the navy was doing it much harm. I had sought the job because I believed the navy had deteriorated to the point where its weakness seriously threatened our future security. The navy's grave afflictions included loss of a strategic vision; loss of self-confidence, and morale; a prolonged starvation of resources, leaving vast shortfalls in capability to do the job; and too few ships to cover a sea so great, all resulting in cynicism, exhaustion, and an undercurrent of defeatism. The cult created by Admiral Rickover was itself a major obstacle to recovery, entwining nearly all the issues of culture and policy within the navy.

Taking on Rickover and his culture would, I knew, be a grueling task. But I had by then experienced some epic Washington combats and had the confidence earned by those scars. Nothing, however, had prepared me for what was happening in the Oval Office. For a relatively young secretary of the navy, new to the job in 1981, it was most discomforting to be in the presence of the president of the United States and the object of Admiral Rickover's legendary temper and vocabulary. As the bureaucrats say, such experiences can be "non–career-enhancing." I rarely have a drink during the week, but as I poured a double whiskey that evening, I told my wife, Barbara, that I had wished that a hole could have yawned open there in the Oval Office floor into which I could have quickly leaped. Not only was I embarrassed and shocked at the president being subjected to such *lèse majesté*, but also my immediate boss, Cap Weinberger, was glaring daggers at me. He had strongly opposed scheduling this meeting, which I had initiated while he was on an extended trip. While he was away, I had assured Frank Carlucci, his deputy and the acting secretary of defense, that Hyman Rickover had calmed down and accepted his fate in the several months since we had told him that he must retire. We recommended strongly that the president meet the admiral to honor him. Cap and I had also worked out with the White House staff a new job for him in the executive office of the president, as nuclear science adviser to the president.

I had provided President Reagan with a detailed briefing paper for the meeting in which it had been proposed that the president thank the admiral effusively for his historic contribution, expressing the gratitude of the nation; offer him the job as White House adviser; and then ask for his reflections and lessons learned from his sixty years of government service. The president had immediately agreed and the meeting was set for Friday, January 8, 1982. I fully expected it to be a straightforward, cordial meeting. It was instead the most incredible meeting I had ever experienced.

I arrived at the White House reception room at 11:10 A.M. to find Admiral Rickover already there, seated on the couch. We had not seen each other since the day in Cap's office last November when we had informed him that he must retire.

While I hardly expected a warm embrace from him, I had been assured by the sachems of the nuclear tribe, including Admirals Bob Long and Jim Watkins, that although his attitude toward me was one of great disdain, he was reconciled to a dignified retirement. Was I in for a shock.

I walked over and, with a smile, extended my hand to him. He looked up with great surprise and said, "What the hell are you doing here?" I replied that

I had been asked by the White House the day before to come to the meeting. He said, "You have a hell of a nerve after you fired me!" He then launched into a stream of vituperation against me that left me only slightly less stunned than the receptionist and three other guests waiting in the reception room. I began to suspect that the meeting with the president might not go all that well.

He said, "You know that everybody in the navy is saying about you, they know what you're up to. Everybody in the navy is talking about you, and I intend to tell the president all about it."

Trying to hush him up, under the saucer-eyed gaze of the strangers in the room, I replied, "You are welcome to tell the president whatever you like, but I would suggest that you bear in mind the best interests of the navy—"

Rickover interrupted me and said with a hiss, "What the hell do you know about the navy?!"

Gasps from elsewhere in the room.

"—and the best interests of the president . . ."

"What the hell do you know about the president!"

Now everyone in there, including the receptionist, had gotten up from their seats.

". . . and the best interests of the country. . . ."

I looked around the room trying to give these strangers a smile that said, "Heh, heh, only joking, only joking."

Doing my best to stay cool, I said, "Bear in mind, Admiral, that you have an obligation to do what you can to use your time to help the president in his responsibilities whatever you say, and not to use the time to vent your spleen."

"You have a hell of a goddamn nerve!" replied the admiral.

At this point, Chuck Tyson of the White House staff walked into the reception room to inform us that the president was now ready to see us. We walked down the corridor past the Roosevelt Room and into the Oval Office, with Admiral Rickover leading the way. Cap Weinberger, Jim Baker (the president's chief of staff), and Bill Clark (the national security adviser and an old friend of the president) were in the room with the president as we entered. Two White House photographers had accompanied us, and there were several minutes of shaking hands and posing for photographs with the president. The admiral behaved impeccably, smiling and making small talk with the president and the others while the photographic session proceeded. I was immensely relieved at his behavior after the performance in the reception room.

The photographers were ushered from the room, and the president led the admiral over to the fireplace, which was crackling. The Oval Office has two comfortable chairs placed at forty-five degrees to either side of the fireplace. Next to each of these chairs are end tables with lamps, and next to them two long couches face each other perpendicular to the fireplace. The president seated the admiral in the chair on the east side, and he took the chair on the west, with Secretary Weinberger sitting next to the president on the west-side couch, and I sat next to Weinberger. Judge Clark and Jim Baker sat on the opposite couch, next to Rickover. It was very cozy.

The president began by telling Admiral Rickover how much he personally had admired his accomplishments over the years and what a debt the country owed him. He really started to warm to the theme as he followed generally our briefing paper. He could not have been more cordial.

After about three minutes of this, Admiral Rickover broke in and said, "Well, if all that is so, then why are you firing me?"

The president, somewhat jolted, paused a moment and then said, "Well, I'm certainly not firing you, it's just that the Pentagon has recommended that it is time for a transition."

Admiral Rickover said, "If that's so, then they [pointing to Cap and to me] are lying; they told me that you ordered me fired. Secretary Lehman told me that specifically."

I immediately responded with what I think was composure. "Mr. President, that is absolutely not true."

Secretary Weinberger said, "We had concluded that it was time for an orderly transition and that there was no intention to fire the admiral."

It was at that moment that Admiral Rickover seemed to turn a switch within him and suddenly raised his voice quite a few decibels as he called me a piss-ant and started his tirade against me.

As this tirade went on, I looked across at Judge Clark and Jim Baker, and they were dumbfounded. The president was wide-eyed and perplexed. Rickover was carrying on so violently that I genuinely feared we would have to restrain him physically. After about five minutes without a breath, Rickover paused and the president tried to begin to calm him down, but only got into half a sentence before Rickover turned on him and began attacking the pres-ident in the same strident shout. "Are you a man? Can't you make decisions yourself? What do you know about this problem? These people are lying to you. You won't get away with this. You won't get away without this hurting you. Don't you think that people aren't already using this against you? They say you are too old, and that you're not up to the job either. I have never seen anyone treated like I have been treated. No one has even told me why I'm being fired;

no one has ever told me that I am not doing the job. Do you know how I first learned that I was being fired?"

The president said, "No. How?"

He said, "I read it in the paper. No one even had the decency to tell me before it was announced."

I said, "Mr. President, that is not true. We had several meetings with Admiral Rickover before it appeared in the paper."

Now, the president is such a good-natured person that, instead of kicking the guy out of his office, which is what I would have done, he was genuinely concerned and sympathetic to the admiral. He tried very hard to pacify him and make peace. He said, "Well, Admiral, I share your frustration at leaks. I would like to know how we could find a way to stop the leaks out of this White House."

Admiral Rickover then repeated in detail his tirade that he was being fired by me, and by Weinberger, because the contractors demanded we do so.

At this point Admiral Rickover took out an envelope and pulled out some papers and said, "Mr. President, I want you to read these papers. They are on a number of subjects, and this one here is on how to run the presidency. I have given this paper to President Nixon and he liked it very much, and I gave it to President Carter and he liked it very much."

President Reagan took the papers, thanking the admiral.

The admiral then resumed his tirade. He said, "Mr. President, you're too smart to be taken in by all this. You're a decent man, that's why you've been elected by the American people. Would you tell me right now why I am being fired?"

The president said, "Admiral, you're not being fired, it is really my hope that you will be able to come to work to help the administration—"

Admiral Rickover interrupted, "Aw, cut the crap!"

At this point, suppressing the urge to leap up and grab Rickover by the throat, I said, "Mr. President, we've made arrangements for Admiral Rickover to have an office and a staff at the Navy Yard so that he might continue to be available and involved to help you and all of us at the Pentagon." With the agreement of the White House, Cap and I had made the offer to Admiral Rickover of the job of counselor on nuclear power issues. His response was, in effect, "You can take your job and shove it." Before this meeting, however, we intended that the president repeat the job offer directly to Rickover, with the expectation that he would, of course, accept. I interjected the Navy Yard office (instead of the White House job) at this point in the meeting in order to head off the president actually making the job offer. If he had done so, I am sure the admiral would have told the president himself to cram it.

The admiral continued his tirade, developing the theme that Cap and I were obsequious toadies to the defense contractors. Feeling that the president had enjoyed about all of this that he could stand, Judge Clark rose from the sofa, attempting to bring the meeting to an end, and was joined by Jim Baker. I also stood up, but the admiral continued without pause to berate the president.

After three or four minutes of this tableau, Rickover stopped and threw a contemptuous glance at Clark, Baker, and me, then turned to the president and said, "Are you a man or not? I thought this was to be a meeting between you and me. I want to speak to you alone."

The president looked at me and I gritted my teeth and nodded a firm negative. He then looked at Weinberger, who did the same. The president looked quite perplexed, but motioned for us to leave the room. With great reluctance we all filed from the room into the president's secretary's office, leaving Rickover alone with the president. As I walked out of the Oval Office, I thought that if fisticuffs broke out, the president lifted weights every day and could take care of himself. I was more concerned about the verbal violence I was about to receive from Weinberger for having set this meeting up.

It was really comical as we all stood around in the little office just off the Oval Office. At first everybody was silent, straining to try to hear what was going on, but of course we could not. Judge Clark and Jim Baker, both shaking their heads, gasped in amazement that they had never seen such a meeting in their entire careers. I took the blame for recommending the meeting, saying that I had been completely hoodwinked by Rickover, who had indicated that he just wanted to give the president some helpful advice in his farewell call. I said in defense, "This may give you some idea of what we in the navy have had to put up with from Rickover over the years." All heads nodded in agreement. Jim Baker then sent his assistant in to get Rickover out after ten minutes, but apparently he was rebuffed by the president and came back empty-handed. Cap was furious, as I expected, and told Baker he never would have allowed the meeting to go forward had he known about it. After another five minutes, Jim Baker went into the Oval Office to get the admiral out.

As the door to the Oval Office opened and Admiral Rickover walked out, I was standing in the corridor that leads directly to the Cabinet Room. Rickover walked over to me with a smile and said in the very chummiest way, "Can I give you a ride back to the Pentagon?" I declined the offer. Still in a state of shock,

I went straight back to the Pentagon and dictated a verbatim record while it was still reverberating in my mind.

Later that afternoon, I went down to see Weinberger about the meeting and decided what action, if any, was needed. Cap told me that the president told him that when he was alone with Rickover, Rickover had again threatened that his firing would be used against the president because he, Rickover, was older than the president, but he was in far better shape than the president was in. He said that the president had also told him that Rickover had attacked Dr. Harold Agnew, whom the president said he had never heard of, but Rickover said that it was Agnew who was the mastermind behind engineering his firing.

Dr. Harold Agnew was the distinguished nuclear physicist who had been the director of the Los Alamos Nuclear Laboratory in New Mexico. He had been one of the brilliant young scientists on the Manhattan Project, and had been a moving force in the nuclear field ever since. It was known that Agnew had been a friend of mine since the late 1960s, when we were introduced by Scoop Jackson. Agnew had crossed swords many times with Rickover and was well known as a critic. While it was certainly true that Agnew had contributed to my overall view of Rickover during the preceding ten years, his had been one of many inputs, and he had done nothing to lobby me directly to fire Rickover since I had become secretary of the navy.

I later found out that what had precipitated the attack on Agnew was a letter he had sent to me on August 17, 1981, in which he said, "About ten years ago we at Los Alamos and here at General Atomic tried to introduce some new propulsion technologies, nuclear and nonnuclear, and were tossed out by Rickover. If he continues to have absolute rule over your nuclear and nonnuclear propulsion systems for submersibles, it will be very difficult to implement the type of Navy you would hope to have in the future.

"He doesn't want us to manufacture his fuel either, so the DOE will have to spend about $300M instead of allowing General Atomic to do it at a fraction of the cost. . . . P.S. Have you had an eye-to-eye conversation with Rickover recently? I believe at times he is further along than most people realize." A copy of this letter was passed to Rickover by one of his many disciples in the Navy secretariat.

Cap and I agreed that I would watch Rickover's behavior very carefully during the days ahead, in case his immediate removal might be necessary, but otherwise we would leave him in place for the remaining three weeks until his scheduled departure on the thirty-first of January. Further extension on active duty after that date was unthinkable. Cap directed that he would be extended only the courtesies required in the way of a transition office at the Navy Yard that were equivalent to those given any other retiring four-star. Later he relented and okayed my recommendation that we go a bit farther and give him a car and driver and a secretary, and that his office at the Navy Yard be given to him on six-month extensions for an indefinite basis as long as he wished it, assuming he behaved responsibly. About six months later these special privileges were added to legislation by his congressional friends in one of the final exercises of the classic Rickover touch.

Paradox: The Sweet and the Bitter

In one of the many eulogies delivered following Admiral Rickover's death on July 9, 1986, he was described as a "paradoxical visionary." His vision was a nuclear-powered navy second to none, and paradox characterized every aspect of his quest to achieve it.

Born on January 27, 1900, in Makow, Poland, a village close to Warsaw but then part of Tsarist Russia, he came to the United States with his parents at age six. Educated in public schools in Chicago, he entered the Naval Academy in 1918 on a congressional appointment. From all accounts, his experience at the Academy was not a happy one. Jews in the navy at the time were a great rarity, and when Hyman Rickover chose a naval career in the 1920s, he could hardly have expected to advance free of the anti-Semitism that prevailed through so many American institutions of the day. As Rickover recalled years later, he had endured more than his share of hazing "because I was Jewish."

Long gone was the time when the navy listed in its ranks a Commodore Uriah Phillips Levy, who served on the *Argus* during her daring raids against English Channel shipping during the war of 1812 and served a spell in Dartmoor Prison for his trouble; or Ezekiel Salomon, son of the Revolution's financier Haym Salomon; or Joseph B. Nones, who served under Decatur in the campaign against the Algerian pirates. In fact, the navy seems to have been a popular choice for many adventurous sons of the Sephardic Jewish "aristocracy" that dominated American Jewish life until displaced later in the nineteenth century by the German and later Russian immigrations that included Rickover's family.

By the 1920s, when the future father of the nuclear navy first entered the service, official and unofficial quotas denied Jews admission to leading American universities; social and business discrimination were widespread; and no less a figure than Henry Ford had tried to popularize the notorious forgery *Protocols of the Elders of Zion*, postulating a global Jewish conspiracy behind wars and social strife.

Rickover was commissioned an ensign in June 1922 and went to sea on four-stacker destroyers and the old battleship *Nevada*. After getting an electrical engineering master's from Columbia, he became a submariner and by June 1937 was assigned to the U.S.S. *Finch*. Later that year he became an engineering duty officer (EDO), a separate restricted line community within the navy. He remained an EDO for the remainder of his career. During World War II he worked in the Bureau of Ships in Washington and later commanded the Naval Repair Base in Okinawa. After the war he joined the Manhattan Project, beginning his historic vocation in nuclear power.

In 1949 he was assigned to the U.S. Atomic Energy Commission, where he became chief of the Naval Reactors Branch. He remained in that job in the AEC, and then the Department of Energy, until his retirement over thirty years later. The ability to maintain this anchor to windward outside the Department of the Navy proved to be the most important cause of his longevity, independence, and success. In that same year he assumed a second hat as director of the Nuclear Power Division in the Bureau of Ships. That position grew into the Office of deputy commander, Nuclear Power Directorate, Naval Ship Systems Command, with the rank of four-star admiral. Despite his rank, he was four echelons below the secretary of the navy. Rickover reported to the commander of the Naval Sea Systems Command (NAVSEA), who reported to the chief of navy materiel, who reported to the chief of naval operations (CNO), who reported to the secretary of the navy.

Rickover's accomplishments under these two hats are legendary. By 1951, the first land-based prototype naval reactor began operations, and today the naval nuclear propulsion program runs over 150 nuclear reactors. Nuclear ship operations have compiled a record unblemished by a single serious incident. Rickover instilled a discipline and professionalism in the nuclear navy that is unmatched in any military service in the world.

One of the most laudatory descriptions of Admiral Rickover's virtues was given to me in a memorandum on February 15, 1985, by Jim Watkins, then the CNO. He remained a loyal friend to Admiral Rickover and his wife, Eleanor, and gave a moving eulogy at his memorial service. The following is excerpted from his memorandum to me:

"I have never met a man who worked harder or evidenced less interest in material possessions than Admiral Rickover. His life was devoted to the job.

"He worked long hours in spartan surroundings, shunning fancy clothes, cars, and furniture. He had no stewards. He traveled tourist class.

"Admiral Rickover could have retired in 1952 at three-quarters pay and made a fortune in the private sector. But he stayed on serving his country for another thirty years. That's when he designed and built the nuclear propulsion plant for *Nautilus* and for all the ships that today comprise 40 percent of our major combatants. . . .

"Long before the terms 'waste, fraud, and abuse' became fashionable, Admiral Rickover was on his own campaign. This stemmed not only from his sense of duty to country but also from his conviction that technical discipline and financial discipline go hand in hand."

Admiral Rickover is unquestionably the father of the nuclear navy. Some of his critics within the navy maintain that it would have come about anyway and that his conservatism has made it twice as expensive as it otherwise would be and prevented much more dramatic breakthroughs in nuclear technology. But the "zero defects" system (that precludes mistakes or compromises in safety) that is the standard of the nuclear navy is not found in any other institution in the government. It is hard to believe that it could have been achieved or could now be maintained without the obsession with conservatism of design and absolute discipline of training that are the hallmarks of the Rickover nuclear navy. Whatever his critics may say, Rickover made the nuclear navy.

In his lifetime, Admiral Rickover earned deserved honor. He was twice awarded the Congressional Gold Medal for exceptional public service. He was presented the Presidential Medal of Freedom by President Carter in 1980 for his contribution to world peace, to name but a few of his hundreds of medals and awards.

The reality of his accomplishment of the nuclear navy will survive his critics. But the navy has paid an enormous price. Rickover's legacy in design philosophy, in contracting and procurement policy, in personnel policy, in his philosophy of education and training played a role in virtually every problem, policy crisis, and decision I faced in six years as secretary of the navy.

Design Philosophy

From the original *Nautilus* prototype built in 1951 until the current propulsion plant now under development for the new SSN-21 Seawolf class submarine, the design of our naval nuclear reactors has undergone a steady if conservative evolution. The advantages of nuclear power to submarines are overwhelming. Heat is produced in a reactor through the fission of uranium atoms. There is no internal combustion and no need for air or for exhaust. Nuclear submarines, like many warships for the past hundred years, are propelled by steam turbines. In a nuclear submarine, however, the steam is not produced in boilers but in steam generators. In the *Nautilus* prototype, the heat produced by the reactor was carried to the steam generator by pressurized water that circulated through the reactor to cool it and to carry the heat to the steam generator where, in transferring the heat to produce the steam, the pressurized water is cooled and returned to the reactor, where it repeats the cycle.

For high speed requiring more steam, a higher rate of fission, and the generation of more heat, more pumping must be used to speed the coolant water through its cycle. In Rickover's later designs, at lower speeds primary pumps are not necessary because natural circulation is designed into the reactor. The natural circulation approach is very desirable for operations because pumps make noise, which can reveal a submarine's location to enemy detection. But it has an even greater benefit in its inherent safety. Unlike designs requiring mechanical circulation of the coolant, if there are electrical, mechanical, or catastrophic failures, the reactor remains cool and safe through natural circulation.

Water, however, is not an ideal medium for heat exchange, requiring much more volume than alternatives. Using a liquid metal, for instance, enables the same cooling to be done in a far smaller volume. The second nuclear submarine prototype reactor used this design concept, with liquid sodium as the coolant. The advantage of liquid metal coolants is a much greater power density, enabling a smaller reactor weight and volume for a given power output. That is immensely important in a submarine, because the reactor size dictates the minimum size of the submarine itself.

Admiral Rickover rejected this design approach after the experience with the second prototype. Liquid sodium proved to be highly corrosive and very difficult to deal with in a practical maintenance and overhaul environment. Most decisive, however, in rejecting the approach is the requirement that liquid metal must be actively circulated. Thus, if there is a mechanical or catastrophic failure in the circulation system, the liquid metal in parts of the reactor will cool and solidify, and all circulation and hence cooling can cease. That could then result in a meltdown of the reactor.

Rickover never again experimented with exotic approaches, and our newest advanced design for the Seawolf class remains an evolution of the proven design. Rickover and the navy have been criticized periodically by military reformers, armchair strategists, and some quite respectable physicists and design engineers for refusing to explore new and innovative design approaches that would yield much smaller and more efficient reactors and hence enable the navy to move to much smaller and less expensive submarines requiring fewer people.

I believe that Admiral Rickover's conservatism in reactor design, and the continuing conservatism of his successor, Admiral Kinnaird McKee, are justified. The undeniable payoffs of more radical designs could never compensate for just one nuclear accident, which might very likely spell the end of our nuclear navy in a peacetime environment.

The foundation of Admiral Rickover's power was his responsibility, established in the law creating his office, for maintaining the safety of nuclear reactors. Over the years he was able to extend this power to every aspect of the design of nuclear ships from stem to stern, rather than just the propulsion plant. The same conservatism he applied to reactor design is to be found in all other aspects of our current attack and ballistic missile submarines. If a visitor is taken through the *Nautilus* today in its permanent home as a museum in New London and views the nuclear plant control station and then goes aboard the very latest Trident submarine, he will find very little different. Indeed, the bank upon bank of analog gauges would not really cause much of a surprise if they were seen in a steam plant at the turn of the century. Virtually nothing is automated. Every part and aspect of the propulsion plant is monitored twenty-four hours a day by very high-quality and highly trained enlisted personnel. They in turn are constantly watched by experienced chief petty officers, who in turn are under the constant supervision of commissioned officers.

Aircraft propulsion plants and combat systems were essentially operated manually until the Second World War. From that time forward, however, progress in aviation has come by constantly increasing the automation of every aspect of flight. The same evolution took place in commercial ships, though delayed in the United States, where featherbedding and subsidization of the unions and operators forestalled the investment needed to bring about innovation. The most modern supertankers and container ships today carry crews of only about twenty people, and their propulsion plants require a maximum of eight.

In the U.S. Navy, Rickover's conservatism in the nuclear power program came to dominate the entire Naval Sea Systems Command. Thus the evolution in advancing technology that took place in the aviation world, and in the commercial shipping world, essentially passed the ship navy by until very recent years. Instead of eight people a U.S. combatant ship the size of a carrier today will average about 600 people just for the propulsion plant. Instead of the four people it takes to man a B-1 bomber, a 688 submarine needs 110.

Because Rickover demanded and achieved a dominance not only of the propulsion plant design and construction but also of every aspect of postwar submarine design, the same philosophy of no automation came to be applied to command and control, ship operations, and weapons systems. Here was a unique instance of the influence of a powerful figure pervading almost every aspect of navy policy.

I first went to sea as a visitor aboard one of Rickover's submarines in the early 1970s, and I have been aboard them many times since, including most recently on a trip under the polar ice near the North Pole. As an outsider, I am invariably struck by the same impression. First, the uniformly high quality of the sailors, chiefs, and commissioned officers; second, the monastic atmosphere—austere, disciplined, with a deep reverence toward the reactor within the holy of holies, and for its high priest and prophet, Admiral Rickover. Third, I am struck by the anachronism of manual control of everything and an untrusting hierarchical supervision of almost every function by extra personnel. I accept the judgment of the professionals to the effect that this conservatism is justified for the security, the safety of the nuclear reactor. Yet as an aviator, I have been perplexed at why this approach, established by Rickover, is still applied in actually controlling and fighting the ship. The commander of a submarine operates and fights his ship through a surprising chain of command. For turning left or right, for instance, there are aircraft-type controls operated by a sailor. To go up or down, there are a separate set of controls operated by a different sailor. Both of these are monitored and supervised by a chief petty officer of the watch. He, in turn, reports to the commissioned officer of the watch, who in turn reports to the captain. If the captain wishes to turn, the order proceeds down this chain of command to the sailors at the controls, and a confirmation proceeds back up to the captain via the same route. All of these gentlemen are in the same compartment separated by, at most, ten feet. Each of the other functions for controlling speed, depth, and trim have similar hierarchies. The weapons systems have yet another set of people and a chain of command to the captain.

In a modern tactical or strategic aircraft, all of these functions plus more are all automated and brought together in cathode ray tube (CRT) displays, head-up displays, buttons, knobs, and cursors, all under the busy fingers of the commander himself, or the commander and his weapons system operator or, as in the case of the B-1, the commander assisted by three other crew members.

The reasons given by the Rickover establishment for not automating are not persuasive. For example, consider safety: Modern technology allows quadruple redundancy in fail-safe control systems. Automatic controls for the operation of nuclear reactors are no more difficult than other complex systems. The mathematical probability of error in the current system can be equaled with modern technological systems. Or consider the argument that a large crew is needed for damage control in combat—one can never have too many well-trained hands in combat. Of course, the B-1 commander, too, would like to have a hundred well-trained people aboard when the shooting starts, or if he takes a hit. Only the nuclear submarines get to indulge that unjustified luxury. A large crew requires a large sub, and size drives the cost up.

But change and innovation in such a tight, well-disciplined priesthood cannot be done by diktat. We have in fact made significant evolutionary progress in submarine design philosophy. As it happened, Admiral Rickover's successor, Kin McKee, agreed with me, as did Jim Watkins, and they both made efforts to press the system in that direction. They have achieved real improvements in the new SSN-21 Seawolf class design, to be operational in the mid-1990s. While it will be a much larger and far more capable and quieter submarine, it will still carry about the same crew as the current Los Angeles class. That, at least, is some progress. But the greatest volume of a submarine is taken up by living space and life support for its crew. If through automation the crew of a submarine was reduced to say, fifty, the submarine itself could be reduced dramatically in size, though not by 50 percent. Its power plant could be much smaller and the cost of each submarine of a given capability reduced enormously.

Contracting and Procurement Policy

As Admiral Elmo Zumwalt's memoirs, and the accounts of other former chiefs of naval operations attest, Admiral Rickover held CNOs in small regard and paid them heed only when it suited him. Held in even lower esteem were secretaries of the navy. When testifying about the claims and overrun mess in nuclear shipbuilding, Rickover usually laid heavy blame on various navy secretaries. His testimony before the House Defense Appropriations Subcommittee on May 5, 1981, was typical: "Through lax contract enforcement and liberal claims settlements, the navy itself bears considerable responsibility for the claims-oriented environment that has grown up in the shipbuilding industry. With each new administration arrives a new navy secretariat comprised of civilians from other walks of life." His attitude was "Ya seen one, ya seen 'em all."

In the year that we overlapped I received only two communications from him. The first of these was a classic. It was unclassified, unsigned, and unaddressed, and titled only "Notes on the Naval Nuclear Propulsion Program," dated May 1, 1981. I knew that it was authentic only because I had been warned for several days before by his office and some of his disciples that I soon would be honored by a direct communication. Being unsigned, unaddressed, and unclassified, his unwritten message to me was clear that I was not the only one to receive the memo. The first five paragraphs were a reminder to me that the unbroken record of safety in naval nuclear reactors was because of his authority enshrined in law to assure the safe operations of these plants and that that, in turn, was part of his Department of *Energy* responsibilities, over which I had no authority. He advised me that such responsibility included total control of the selection, qualification, and training of all nuclear naval personnel, and that his budget of about a half a billion dollars a year in R&D was not subject to the navy's control but was provided from Department of Energy funds. The seventh paragraph was a discussion of the urgent need for new officers to enter the nuclear power training program.

The meat of the memorandum to me, however, was his discussion of shipbuilding policy. He began by warning me: "In the past, shipbuilders have managed to deal directly with the secretariat in contractual matters, thus bypassing the Naval Sea Systems Command. This makes NAVSEA ineffective, hurts morale, and overloads the secretariat. In cases where high-level meetings involving the secretariat are necessary, the responsible NAVSEA official should be present."

This was precipitated because I had put together a management team to get to the bottom of the Electric Boat mess and educate me on it, and to develop options for solving it.

The remainder of the memorandum was a recitation of the problems at Electric Boat and the shortcomings of the alternative builder, Newport News.

A few days later Admiral Rickover expanded at length in congressional testimony, which typically was not shown to anyone in the navy in advance. In that testimony he issued a major call for returning to building nuclear submarines in naval shipyards. This had long been his objective. His dealings with corporate shipbuilders were always a battle, whereas he had total control of the yards owned and operated by the navy. Navy-owned yards had built nuclear subs in the early years of the program, but at a cost 40 percent higher than the corporate yards. In his testimony, Rickover smote the corporate shipbuilders hip and thigh.

The testimony went on in lengthy detail, recounting the practices of "buying-in" (an age-old abuse wherein contractors bid unrealistically low to win, knowing they can make their profit when the customer makes changes to the project) that had become so prevalent in the navy shipbuilding program. He repeated his vigorous attacks on the settlement that had been negotiated during the Carter administration for $2.7 billion worth of claims for the contractors. He repeated his years-long campaign against lawyers: "Some law firms now specialize in contract claims—particularly shipbuilding claims against the navy. Many former government attorneys fill their ranks. These firms are the 'ambulance chasers' of the Washington bar, and they guide shipbuilders in preparing and prosecuting their contract claims against the navy. Rather than promoting justice as officers of the court, many claims lawyers use their skills to cloud issues, harass the government, and frustrate prompt resolution of disputes—except on the client's terms."

Much of this was, of course, the old Rickover trademark, diatribes against the defense industry that had earned him such devotion from Senator Proxmire and others in Congress. Much of what he said was, in fact, quite true and agreed with the findings of my management team, but it was only half of the story.

In going over his testimony in June, one of his accusations led George Sawyer, assistant secretary of the navy for shipbuilding, to an idea for ending the thirty-year practice of massive claims litigation. I almost shouted "Eureka!" when I heard it. It did, in fact, become the most important key to what we finally achieved, which was the ending of all shipbuilding claims and the running of our shipbuilding program for six straight years thereafter without the submission of a single claim.

The discovery was simple. Rickover pointed out that every time Electric Boat or Litton or Newport News submitted a huge claim to the navy, they then listed this as an account receivable on their balance sheet and, hence, on their reports to stockholders. No matter that the claims might ultimately be settled for only thirteen cents on the dollar, the company lawyers could assure that ultimate resolution would take many, many years, during which the claims could be booked at full value.

When I read this in Rickover's testimony, I could not believe it was so, and I asked our lawyers to verify it. They assured me that this was perfectly legal and, in fact, was the practice by all defense contractors. It was therefore obvious to me that we would never solve the problem of claims, buy-ins, and overruns because it was like free money to the contractors as a cost-free way of boosting their stock prices. The answer seemed to me obvious. If contractors could lash us with claims, why shouldn't we lash them right back with counterclaims? If we submitted claims that were not frivolous but based upon at least as much substance as the contractors', then would they not have to list those claims as contingent liabilities on their balance sheets? The lawyers hurried off and returned with the answer that, indeed, the SEC would demand that they do so. I immediately instructed the late Walter Skallerup, my very wise general counsel, to begin at once to build a litigation strike team in his organization to use the claims process against the contractors precisely as it had been used against the navy. How this became the key to our success is recounted in more detail in Chapter Eight.

In addition to Admiral Rickover's quite justifiable war against the abusive practice of claims, his other great war was against excess profits in the defense industry. In 1981 he attacked Newport News Shipbuilding for earning an average of 21.7 percent in profit on seven submarine repair contracts with a total price of $42.6 million. In another case he blasted U.S. Steel for receiving profit percentages on contracts ranging from a low of 27 percent to a high of 40 percent profit on six different purchase orders. Those figures alone, however, were meaningless without knowing the risk, investment, and price performance of the contractor. But to Rickover, profit was inherently evil, while *costs*, which were the real cause of price escalation, he largely ignored.

While Admiral Rickover's concern about excess profit was occasionally justified, his focus was on the wrong issue. Until recently, the guidelines for profit in Pentagon contracting were based on a percentage of costs. And since virtually all of the contract types in shipbuilding in those days were cost-plus, obviously the contractor had every incentive to maximize costs, since it was on those costs that his profit percentage was calculated. We set out to break the link between amount of profit and total cost, and instead to link profit to capital investment, risk, and performance rather than cost.

But in this issue we see the fundamental paradox of Admiral Rickover's influence on navy contracting policy. Admiral Rickover demanded total control over his contractors just as he did over his subordinates and the naval shipyards. In the contractors' yards as in the naval shipyards, the power of NR (naval reactors) was absolute. If these officials said that nuclear safety required that a stove in a galley be moved three feet, that was not subject to appeal—it was moved. Because of this approach, construction and overhaul of nuclear ships were accompanied by thousands upon thousands of change orders. Such customizing and absolute authority on the part of the customer could not be accommodated by a contractor on a fixed-price basis, only on a cost-plus basis. Where they did sign fixed-price contracts, they did so with the unstated intention of getting well on change orders and claims for the cost of those change orders; thus, the infamous "buy-in."

Because of Admiral Rickover's uncompromising standards for quality control (in the view of his admirers) and/or his arbitrary and capricious demands (in the view of his detractors), nearly all the competition had been driven out of supplying components to the nuclear shipbuilding program. In key components such as pumps and valves, there ended up only one supplier willing to put up with the Rickover system and, as a result, as with every monopoly, the prices paid for components were often astronomical. Even where there was more than one source—for instance, for nuclear reactor components—the shares were allocated rather than competed for. Thus, even when we were eventually able to achieve true competition on 688 class attack subs between Newport News and General Dynamics and started achieving real cost reductions and savings, much of the cost was immune to the pressures of competition, since both yards had to buy many components from the same monopoly supplier.

Thus the quite awful abuses of some contractors in excess profits and bogus claims were in no small measure the results of Rickover's own policies over the years in contracting and procurement.

This situation would be difficult enough were it confined to just the construction of nuclear ships. But in fact, as in so many other areas of the navy, Rickover had managed to impose his philosophy and practice through most of the procurement system. Until we abolished the Naval Materiel Command, the chief of naval materiel, a four-star admiral, was responsible for overall procurement policy for everything—ships, beans, bullets, airplanes, and missiles. The last three chiefs of naval materiel were nuclear submariners, and the Rickover doctrine during the 1960s and 1970s came to be universally applied. Thus by 1981 we found that thirty thousand suppliers had been driven from navy procurement, and competition overall had dropped to only 15 percent of all navy procurement. The Rickover philosophy that excess profits were the problem and that all contractors were out to rip off the government pervaded the navy bureaucracy. There was no recognition of the role that the absolutizing of requirements, change orders, and engineering with no balancing of costs played in bringing that situation about. In fact, there was some profit gouging, and it needed to be dealt with. But allowable *costs* were much larger than profits, and they were running wild.

With a special measure of vindictiveness, Rickover had accused some of the major shipbuilders of criminal fraud and had pressured the Naval Investigative Service and the Justice Department to pursue criminal investigation. This may have been warranted by some of the evidence in some cases, but certainly not for every shipbuilder that disagreed with Rickover. Moreover, he succeeded in getting a criminal investigation begun on my Democratic predecessor, Ed Hidalgo, as soon as the administration changed. This proved, of course, to have absolutely no foundation and was shortly dropped, to Admiral Rickover's great disappointment.

The second and last communication I ever received from Rickover, and the only one with his signature, was dated May 11, 1981, and was part of his careful plan to move steadily toward complete independence from the private contractors for all nuclear maintenance and construction. The subject of the memorandum was a "water pit facility" costing $50 million, which everyone questioned except the nuclear brotherhood. Its only utility is in building or refueling nuclear aircraft carriers. As of this writing, it has never been used, and it will probably be used only once this century, for the refueling of the U.S.S. *Nimitz* in 1991. Because it is unclassified, and the only signed communication I received from the admiral, I reproduce relevant parts of it here:

MEMORANDUM FOR THE SECRETARY OF THE NAVY
SUBJECT: Water Pit Facility for Refueling Naval Aircraft [*sic*]
Dated May 11, 1981

As I explained over the telephone this evening, it is extremely important that we get going on the water pit. It is essential for refueling nuclear carriers at the Puget Sound Naval Shipyard. As we need to perform an aircraft carrier refueling in 1984, we need to begin construction by the middle of this year. Thus, the reprogramming action needs to be completed by May 22nd, when the current bids expire. . . .

I discussed this with Senator Jackson this afternoon. He said he would help. He also asked that I advise you of the situation, because you have an "in" with the Republicans in the Senate.

[*signed*] H. G. Rickover

Largely through Senator Jackson's efforts, the reprogramming was approved later that year.

Personnel Policy

Rickover's greatest contribution to the navy was entwined with his most malevolent and damaging. That was his influence over the personnel policies of the navy. As he reminded me in his memorandum of May 1, he had, in the earliest years, achieved absolute control over the "selection, qualification, and training of operating personnel." His objective was no less than the creation of a kind of new socialist man for the nuclear program. His biographers and his disciples have written much about his "quest for excellence," repeating Rickover's constant refrain, "Why not the best?" One of his apostles, President Jimmy Carter, used it to title his autobiography, crediting the question and the challenge to his mentor.

Over the years Rickover did, indeed, achieve a level of excellence in his personnel that is in no small measure responsible for the superb quality of the nuclear navy today. The molding of these "new nuclear men" began in the careful screening by his staff of applicants from the Naval Academy, the NROTC, and OCS. They demanded extensive grounding in mathematics, hard sciences, and engineering, and very high class standing. Only rarely was a humanities major chosen.

After initial screening the select candidates were brought to Washington for the now legendary interview with Admiral Rickover himself. Many accounts have been written about these interviews, the most extensive being Admiral Zumwalt's account in his memoir *On Watch*.

Admiral Rickover said that his criteria for selection in these interviews were based on a combined number of subjective elements but without a set formula. He looked for intelligence first and then judged the person to see "what kind of a guy he is." "I'll talk to a guy . . . and see how he thinks. I pose questions to him and see how he answers them. You don't have to be any superman. If he's the kind of guy that tells you what you want to hear, you kick the guy out of the office after one or two questions."[1]

Admiral Zumwalt and others, however, found it a humiliating and intimidating experience. Variously they had been forced to sit on chairs with two legs sawed off short, thrown out of the office, and made to sit for hours in confinement before returning for more intimidating and personal invective. The common thread running through these accounts was an attempt by the admiral to instill from the beginning in those selected a realization that they were of little consequence and that their hope to become someone of worth lay in submitting themselves to the vocation of the Rickover program. By the time he retired, Admiral Rickover had personally interviewed more than fifteen thousand candidates, rejecting about 60 percent.

For those selected, their novitiate begins in a most austere nuclear monastery in Orlando, Florida. There, for six months, the new acolyte undergoes his initiation, spending twelve hours a day studying advanced mathematics, nuclear physics, fluid dynamics, nuclear plant systems, and radiological control. Nothing is left to personal initiative. Above all, here "The Rickover Way" is established. Everything is by the numbers and by the book. The text and course outline for each course given was either written or edited by Admiral Rickover himself. It specifies exactly what must be taught and how much time must be devoted to each aspect of the subject. The classroom instruction is regularly monitored by people from the Division of Naval Reactors (NR). The novice is there not for inquiry but to receive the way and the truth. Six hours are spent in the classroom each day, and there are approximately six hours of homework each day, designed to keep the students at the reference books with essentially no free time. Anyone who falls behind in his grades is called before a review board. Normally he is given extra remedial work and a second chance. Nevertheless, that faltering stays a part of the man's record the rest of his life.

Upon successful completion of the six-month classroom training, the graduate goes on to another six months at one of the landlocked reactor prototypes owned by the Department of Energy. A Trappist monk would feel at home in the austerity of these establishments.

As Rickover expanded his power he was able to establish the requirement in the mid-1970s that *every* naval officer assuming a major sea command, nuclear or nonnuclear, must take at his desert monastery the Senior Officers Ships Material Readiness Course, several months long, to be indoctrinated in "The Rickover Way." The course is conducted at one of the Department of Energy land prototypes near Craters of the Moon National Monument in Idaho. The site was chose by Rickover to get as far away from regular navy influence as possible. Over the years this indoctrination has had an enormous impact in embedding "The Rickover Way" in the entire navy culture. In "The Rickover Way" the age-old military paradigm "Do not question higher authority" is raised to a higher level of purity; all the answers are to be found in the book, and the book and the checklist must be followed—a philosophy essential for nuclear safety, but grotesque when extended to every aspect of one's profession.

Following nuclear power school for the new officer is sub school at New London where, for twelve weeks, the basics of submarine warfare are taught in a framework of absolute Rickover orthodoxy. Immediately following graduation from sub school the young officer is assigned to sea duty aboard a nuclear submarine. Here he enters a world very different from that of the rest of the navy. While discipline and procedures aboard our nuclear submarines are largely the same as those aboard all naval ships, there is a major difference. The submarine community is not just an elite, but also a kind of religious brotherhood. Within the naval service there is the separate nuclear "vocation." Rickover himself often spoke of it as such. "Man's work begins with his job or profession. Having a vocation is always somewhat of a miracle, like falling in love."[2] The nuclear pope remains a brooding presence on every nuclear submarine. Having been personally accepted into the program in the interview with the almost mystical figure (and now his less mystical successor), the next level of holy orders comes upon selection of command of a nuclear submarine. Each candidate must take a three-month course at NR, followed by a written and an oral exam. Thereafter, upon assuming command, each commanding officer had to write a personal letter to Rickover every two weeks while in the yard or home port, and once per quarter while operating. He had to report in writing problems encountered and personal errors made, along with actions taken to correct both.

The new "nuke" very soon learns that the zeal of the faithful is not in itself enough. On every nuclear ship there is a parallel chain of command. "Each nuclear submarine is commanded by two people: its captain and the director, Division of Naval Reactors," is how one submariner described the process. "Monitors" from Admiral Rickover's office regularly visited all nuclear ships as a kind of Roman curia or commissariat, carefully inspecting procedures and conditions and reporting back to no one but Admiral Rickover, and now his successor.

The great strength of the naval service is that, unlike so many of our other government institutions that have become paralyzed by bureaucracy, line accountability remains strong, based on the ancient naval principle that a captain is master of his ship and will be held accountable absolutely. This principle exists also in the nuclear navy, but it is qualified by the shadow command line to "NR."

While this duality is mild when the ship is actually at sea, when it returns to port or is in the shipyard, the Naval Reactors Regional Office (NRRO) assumes a position that in some ways is superior to that of the commanding officer. Operating totally external to the chain of command, in a style that has occasionally been described as "Gestapo-like," NRRO personnel do not limit themselves merely to reactor safety. Unlike the rest of the navy, the NR office holds a veto over who will be assigned to each of the important billets under the commanding officer, as well as who gets selected for submarine command and for postcommand assignments such as squadron commander. The ubiquitous role of Admiral Rickover and his "monitors" was recognized as having a greater effect on one's career than the operational chain of command. Thus the ultimate allegiance of all nuclear-trained officers was conditioned from the first ship assignment to lie with NR rather than the operational navy.

While the numbers have fluctuated over the years, normally six of ten trained nuclear officers leave after their first obligated tour. Still others leave after their second or third. I was particularly struck by the pattern of these cases. The following excerpts from a 1982 report on one fine commanding officer who left the navy is representative:

> Commander felt his request for relief from command was the only realistic way of persuading you and CNO that the nuclear submarine service is on a disastrous course because of the aging, anachronistic leadership of Admiral Rickover. In his view the situation in the fleet is deteriorating to a very dangerous level. . . .
>
> Commander believes that Admiral Rickover's mistreatment of nuclear submarine officers has led to the alarming attrition rate in the submarine service. In the words of Commander, "Faced with constant scrutiny, and threat, on the nuclear propulsion side [from the NR monitor] he [the commanding officer] must sacrifice the possibility of a reasonable home life and 90 percent of all non-engineering aspects of submarining to devote the necessary hours in the day to confront this continuous challenge to his command.

Thus through personal selection, monastic indoctrination, and a commissariat outside the Navy chain of command, NR (Rickover) gained effective control of the assignments, promotions, and destinies of all nuclear-trained officers (about 8 to 10 percent of the officer corps). Through this control he soon established a religion of engineering excellence, an obsession with unquestioning adherence to mathematical certainty, approved procedure, and the almighty checklist.

From the very beginning Rickover was able to establish policy in the Bureau of Naval Personnel that no one could be executive officer or commanding officer of a nuclear submarine unless he had been through the Rickover program and was a nuclear engineer. This effectively eliminated a career path from diesel submarines. Defenders of this system have argued that the executive officer and commander of a nuclear submarine must also be the chief engineer of the submarine and must understand every aspect of the propulsion plant. By contrast, the Royal Navy, which has had an equally safe record of operating nuclear-powered submarines, maintains separate career paths for engineering officers aboard the ship responsible for the reactor plant and propulsion, and the deck officers, including the executive officer and captain, who are responsible for fighting the ship. The executive officer and commanding officer of Royal Navy nuclear submarines are almost never nuclear engineers.

As in any religion, there are many degrees of piety. I have known many truly superb men who have risen successfully through the Rickover system, playing by its rules, who have not been fundamentally changed by it. Others, however, have submitted to the system with a complete devotion. When placed in a position of conflict between the tenets of the nuclear community and those of the rest of the navy, or the Department of Defense, or the U.S. government, they unswervingly follow the dictates of the nuclear community. A third group simply cannot tolerate the cultlike allegiance demanded and leave the Navy as part of the 60 percent resigning after their obligated service or, like the commander quoted earlier, after fifteen years of service. These include some talented and creative officers who would otherwise have enormous potential in the naval service. There is, however, no option of simply leaving the nuclear community and remaining in the Navy as an unrestricted line officer in another community. The navy promotion system ensures that any apostate from the nuclear community has little chance of promotion after his defection.

Education and Training

Like all spiritual leaders, Admiral Rickover knew instinctively that to obtain total allegiance he must gain control of the education of the young recruit. He moved immediately after being appointed head of naval reactors to obtain total control of the nuclear education and training of everyone in his program. But he knew that to achieve "the new nuclear man" the process must begin earlier, at the entry level at the Naval Academy. A core doctrine of the Rickover religion was that empirical truth is found only in the physical sciences and mathematics. His acolytes like to point out that Rickover himself was very well read in the classics, in history, literature, and the humanities, and indeed his writing and testimony are laced with such allusions. But with regard to the social sciences and humanities, Rickover was once described to me thus: "He is a man who knows everything and understands nothing." His attitude was that philosophy and the humanities were things that every successful officer should read in his spare time—of which there would be

none, if he got his way—but they were definitely not education. He summarized it very well in a letter he sent to President Carter on October 6, 1977,
in which he said in part:

Dear Mr. President,
    This is in further response to your discussion with me concerning the edu-
cational aspects of the U.S. Naval Academy. I have also discussed this matter
with Dr. Brzezinski. . . .
    My recommended changes aim the midshipman into the engineering dis-
ciplines. . . . If a midshipman . . . is interested in acquiring a deeper understanding of history, law, international relations, etc., he should pursue this on
his own. . . . I firmly believe that each midshipman should have a solid foundation in history, English, economics, and political science. My objection has
been that the Naval Academy has been allowing midshipmen to major in
these types of subjects and in so doing creating the false impression that the
Navy needs ensigns who are experts in these fields. . . .

    [signed] *H. G. Rickover*

Unfortunately, his low regard for the arts, the humanities, all the "soft sciences" was but an extreme view of what had become navy orthodoxy. In the
transition from sail to steam and to mechanical technology that took place in
the nineteenth century, the navy concentrated very hard on mechanical and
engineering skills in training and education. Secretary of the Navy George
Bancroft established the Naval Academy in 1845 to prepare officers for the
increasingly technical demands of the industrial age.
    In other navies and merchant fleets of the world, as the requirement for
engineering mastery aboard ship increased, there evolved two career fields:
engineering and deck duty. Those in the former were educated and trained
engineers charged with propulsion plant and weapons systems, while the
deck officers were trained in seamanship, navigation tactics, and strategy.
These dual professions exist to the present day in all merchant fleets and
most navies.
    The U.S. Navy, however, evolved differently. At about the turn of the cen-
tury, the two specialties were amalgamated in the "unrestricted line officer"
category, but in fact everyone became an engineering officer. Thus the Naval
Academy has always been primarily an engineering school, and in this century at least, naval officers have suffered from a syndrome best described by
Winston Churchill: "The seafaring and scientific technique of the naval

profession makes such severe demands upon the training of naval men, that they have very rarely the time or opportunity to study military history and the art of war in general."[3]

Gradually Rickover succeeded in gaining control of the doctrine and much of the machinery of the naval education and training establishment. By 1975 his control over the curriculum at the Naval Academy became total. The vice chief of naval operations, Admiral Harold Shear; the chief of naval personnel, Vice Admiral Watkins; and the superintendent of the Naval Academy were finally all nukes. The leverage Rickover used was his absolute authority over personnel policy for nuclear safety. With graduating classes at the time of about eight hundred students, his program needed about a third of the class.

Except for rare exceptions, he would consider only math, science, and engineering majors. Since he would not accept more than 60 percent of those eligible who wanted to enter the program, that meant that at least 80 percent of every graduating class must be in the technical majors. He was, therefore, able to impose a hard requirement that 80 percent of every class must major in math, science, or engineering. He then drove through a major reform of the admissions system to a mathematical statistical "whole-man-score" system. That, in turn, was driven by aptitude and probability of success in the hard-science and technical majors. Thus, by 1980 the system was complete. The admissions system was grossly skewed to accept only those mathematically and technically inclined, and faculty hiring and course offerings became totally dominated by those disciplines. In 1981 there were eighty full professors of engineering and only one part-time professor of philosophy, who taught a total of twenty-four students during the whole year. The academy dropped any requirement for a core curriculum of humanities subjects.

The curriculum at the Naval Academy by itself is important. But it also reflected the much larger change in the values and culture of the naval officer corps itself. Driven by Rickover's obsession, we have raised a generation of naval officers who have been well trained in technology and engineering, but of whom a great many are essentially illiterate in the conceptual disciplines and humanities. In six years as secretary of the navy, I never once received a staff paper from the uniformed bureaucracy that got the mathematics wrong, nor did I ever receive a staff paper that even approached conceptual elegance or literate expression. There are, of course, many individual officers having those cultivated skills, but they have achieved them in spite of the system. When they launch an elegant paper up the hierarchy, it usually is shredded and recast in clumsy bureaucratese, a medium in which clear thinking is quickly choked to death.

One of the toughest wrestling matches I experienced with the nukes was in changing the academy curriculum to restore balance after Rickover. Using a distinguished blue-ribbon-panel report as a basis, I was determined to reestablish a humanities core, quality humanities majors, and abolition of the 80 percent science/engineering major quota. We could not have succeeded without the leadership of Admirals Watkins and Holloway. The Rickover establishment fought the reforms tenaciously, but those reforms are now in place, though for how long remains to be seen.

Integrity, Ethics, and Culture of the Naval Service

In balancing the scales of the Rickover legacy, the heaviest negative was undoubtedly his distorting influence on the ethical values and integrity of the naval service.

The fact that he was unfairly denied promotion to admiral by two successive navy promotion boards in 1951 and 1952 and gained his first star by order of Congress made Rickover's career a standing refutation of the navy promotion system and its chain of command. From that day forward his personal allegiance was shifted from the navy to a shifting coalition of outside political supporters, who protected him from his wrathful superiors.

Once he had established independence of the military and civilian control of the navy, Rickover flaunted it. He then used that independence to establish his own chain of command outside the navy hierarchy, and he made sure that all within the nuclear community understood where there fortunes lay. Four chiefs of naval operations (Moorer, Zumwalt, Holloway, and Hayward) and six former secretaries of the navy (Anderson, Nitze, Korth, Claytor, Hidalgo, and Chafee) have told me that they were routinely ignored by Rickover and, whenever it suited him, he simply flatly disobeyed direct orders or instructions. Elmo Zumwalt wrote in his memoirs, "Rickover brazenly—though seldom openly—challenges the duly constituted authority of every CNO, and indeed, every secretary of the navy, every secretary of defense, and every president."

In retrospect it is possible to say thank God he did challenge his superiors and the bureaucracy, for if he played by the rules the bureaucracy might never have produced the nuclear navy so essential to our security. Probably true. This is much more an indictment of the navy and its promotion system than it is of Rickover. To have succeeded despite the system, however, is very different from

setting up a parallel system and showing by example that duly instituted authority exists to be ignored, deceived, and flouted. That was Rickover's way, and that
was intolerable if the navy was ever going to be put back on an even keel.

For the first century of our military history, many of our military leaders, such
as George Washington and John Paul Jones, were active Freemasons. The system
for selecting their replacements bears many similarities to the election of members to a secret lodge. Selection boards are made up only of generals or admirals, and they take oaths of secrecy. By and large, they are as fair as their civilian
counterparts, and as unfair. The real standouts and the unqualified usually are
dealt with quickly. It is in selecting from the "middle of the bell curve" that all of
the human frailties of bigotry, cronyism, spite, and horse-trading come into play.

In such circumstances, loyalty to the lodge and adherence to the system
and its standard career paths usually determine the outcome. Rickover would
never meet those criteria.

Against persistent attempts to overrule him, Rickover would simply go to
Congress and have the proper phone calls made from the appropriate committee chairmen, or if that was not sufficient, simply have an appropriate prohibition slipped into law. Not only was this kind of maneuvering not hidden
by Rickover, but also many in the nuclear community, from the newest ensign
to four-star admirals, chuckled proudly at each occurrence.

My own first experience with Rickover was illustrative of how he operated. In 1970 I worked for Henry Kissinger on the National Security
Council staff as his congressional relations adviser. In this capacity I was
introduced to a number of Rickover's staff by Senator Jackson and by the
chairman of the House Appropriations Committee, Congressman Mahon,
Rickover's two most important supporters on the Hill. After that they con-
tacted me directly on a number of issues, passing information to me from
the admiral to get to Kissinger, information they felt was not being properly
handled by their superiors in the navy and the Defense Department. One
of the first issues was the sharing of submarine technology with the Netherlands.
The Pentagon and the State Department were actively discussing this sharing, and favored it for foreign policy reasons, but Rickover was categorically
against it. Rickover used me to get the issue before Kissinger, who agreed
with him and blocked the transfer. Rickover was right, and State and
Defense were wrong.

The most active role I played as Rickover's pawn was in getting him promoted to four stars. The navy had opposed every congressionally mandated
promotion that Rickover had received since captain. In 1972 Rickover was

a three-star vice admiral, and no one in the Pentagon supported his ever being promoted beyond that. But in 1972 the administration, as part of the SALT agreements, became very heavily committed to getting authorization for the Trident submarine program. This was very expensive and controversial and faced a strong uphill battle in the dove-dominated Senate of the time. As the battle was joined I was subjected to a sudden blitz from Rickover's people and from Senator Jackson, Chairman Mahon, and our other leaders who were carrying the Trident fight. They said that it would be essential to the campaign to get Trident through, that the president make a grand gesture and promote Admiral Rickover to four stars. I was persuaded of that argument since we were scratching for one or two or three votes in Congress that would decide the issue. Accordingly, therefore, with Rickover providing the documentation, I did the staff work and recommended to Kissinger that he get the president to approve the four-star promotion. I called Bud Zumwalt, who was then CNO, told him what I was doing, and asked him to support it. He tried to talk me out of it, but he admitted that the vote was very close and a very few votes could make a difference. Zumwalt had become the intellectual leader and chief lobbyist of the effort to get the Trident approved by Congress, and he had waged a brilliant campaign on the Hill. He reluctantly acquiesced in the fourth star for Rickover, and the president approved Kissinger's recommendation.

After Rickover was gone, one of the best of the nukes wrote me the following in a letter:

> I don't see what you did to achieve 600 ships as much different [from the way Rickover operated], you worked the Hill for your program, you made speeches not cleared [with Weinberger], you had little time for anyone who did not support your view, you strongly supported those who did.

While not fully accepting that charge, I must nevertheless add that that was my job as the President's political appointee, while Rickover was a serving officer in uniform, assigned neither to lobby Congress nor to set up a devastating parallel chain of command. Even that would have been tolerated if he hadn't insisted on control of the selection, education, training, and career paths—and ethics—of the service.

That such contradiction coexisted for more than thirty years with the proud tradition of integrity and honor promulgated at the Naval Academy, and all naval institutions, had a most unsettling effect on the morality and ethics of the naval service. If such wanton disregard of higher authority was okay for the father of the nuclear navy, and if his disciples were, as claimed, the brightest and the best, the elite of the navy, then what indeed and where was the place of integrity and obedience to authority? The example of Rickover provided a misleading standard, and I have seen grave dishonesty and hypocrisy from some of his prominent disciples.

Admiral Kinnaird McKee, appointed to succeed Admiral Rickover, while continuing "the Rickover Way," has brought a return of integrity to the job, but the effects on the navy of thirty years under Rickover will not be undone in a short period of time.

Retiring a Legend

When I was sworn in on February 5, 1981, as secretary of the navy, some of the press commented that I hit the ground running, with a clear-cut agenda. One of these was to retire Admiral Rickover respectably but immediately. I set about it at once. Having experienced firsthand the Rickover method when I was at the White House in the 1970s, I had no illusions that I would have a free hand in retiring him. The president would have to approve the decision, Congress would have to acquiesce, and the secretary of defense would have to make the formal recommendations to the president.

President Reagan himself had no strong feelings one way or the other about the admiral, but I knew that Vice President George Bush was ready to see him retire. President Carter's warm admiration for and identification with Rickover had not predisposed the Reaganauts toward his cause. Among the defense contractors, General Dynamics, like most big companies, had contributed heavily during the campaign and had good access to White House political advisers, access that no doubt would be used to pee in the admiral's well. I was confident that when the recommendation arrived at the White House the president would approve the admiral's retirement.

Several days after my swearing-in, Cap Weinberger and I held a long conversation about our priorities for the navy, which included the subject of Admiral Rickover's retirement. Although he made no commitments, it was clear that he was not a member of the Rickover fan club.

Therefore, the key became, as so often in the past, Rickover's supporters in Congress.

Although Rickover had a great many admirers in Congress, I knew that a small number would determine the outcome. In the Senate, Senators Proxmire, Jackson, Nunn, Tower, Stennis, Warner, Goldwater, and Thurmond, in the House, Congressmen Price, Bennett, Whitten, Stratton, and Edwards. With the exception of Senator Proxmire, all of these gentlemen had considerable influence in the Reagan White House.

In the ensuing months, I met with all of them except Senator Proxmire, and quite a few times with the most influential for the decision, Tower, Jackson, and Stennis. Most eventually agreed with the case for an orderly and dignified transition, but no one wished to support his retirement openly. A few opposed it, but not with great vigor.

Getting all these ducks lined up took most of the spring and summer of 1981. By August, however, it was clear that Congress would not prevent Rickover's retirement. The uniformed navy was a different matter. The chief of naval operations, Admiral Tom Hayward, a carrier aviator and not one of Admiral Rickover's admirers, applauded my intentions. I told him to begin at once to prepare a transition plan and to prepare a list of potential successors. The vice chief of naval operations was James Watkins, a nuclear submariner whom I later recommended to become chief of naval operations the following year. He, too, agreed, and he applauded the intention. There was, however, a kind of institutional smirk on the uniformed side because they didn't really believe I could pull it off. Even to the most senior officers of the navy, Rickover had a certain mystical and untouchable aura. As the year wore on and they came to see that I was indeed serious, they began to get cold feet. Ultimately, when it became clear I was about to do it, the formal recommendation from Admiral Hayward was to extend Admiral Rickover's term for an additional two years. Hayward and the uniformed establishment argued that if Admiral Rickover was retired, the five or six top key civilians would resign out of protest and the NR organization would collapse.

As on all the issues of our shipbuilding program, my key adviser throughout this period was George Sawyer, my assistant secretary for shipbuilding. A graduate of Yale, the NROTC, and a nuclear submariner for ten years, George ably refuted all the arguments that the senior admirals deployed for keeping Rickover. Frankly, it surprised me that I found no support among the three- and four-star admirals for Rickover's retirement. They all said, "Next time." (Rickover could be extended on active duty only two years at a time, by law.) Some of them, I believe, just did not want to go on record against Rickover for fear of his retribution, because they believed I couldn't pull it off.

In mid-September Cap agreed to a transition plan that included the following elements: (1) Admiral Rickover's successor would be named prior to the expiration of his most recent extension, on January 31, 1982. (2) Admiral Rickover would be asked to stay for two months further on active duty to assist in his successor's transition. (3) Admiral Rickover would be offered a position as nuclear science adviser to the president. (4) The term of Admiral Rickover's successor would be limited to eight years to avoid a repeat of the Rickover/J. Edgar Hoover problem of long continuity in office. (5) The current dual-hatting arrangement with the Department of Energy would remain exactly as before. (While this would lessen my control of his successor, it would strengthen his hold over safety.)

We agreed that Admiral Rickover's tremendous contribution to the nation should be highlighted and that every effort be made to avoid discrediting him in any way. We drafted a letter for the president's signature that was fulsome in its praise and that offered a very prestigious and logical position as nuclear science adviser. We agreed that "things that are to be done are not to be spoken of" and that nothing would be put in writing until Cap would have a chance to talk to the president and get his approval.

In the meantime, I had been spending considerable time getting to know as much as possible about candidates for the job. Bill Wegner, Rickover's former civilian deputy and heir apparent in the 1970s, rated highly. He had broken with Rickover but nevertheless remained on good terms with him. Wegner was one of a number of Rickover deputies who were thought to be heirs apparent over the years. They all came to the same end: As they grew in stature and gained their own following, Rickover gave them the ax. While we never reached the point of a concrete offer, I had several discussions with Wegner, and he asked not to be considered. On balance, I was persuaded by Tom Hayward and Jim Watkins that it would be a mistake to put a civilian in charge of NR, and so, from that point on, only military officers were considered. Since there was enough on the plate in just replacing Rickover, civilianizing the job was more than the market would bear. In the future, however, this option should be considered. It would have the effect of limiting the powerful role of NR to what it was originally intended to be—the guarantor of nuclear safety and quality control, rather than the Vatican of a military priestly order.

My choice was Vice Admiral Kinnaird McKee, a very bright Kentuckian who had a distinguished record in the submarine community and who had been one of the few members of Bud Zumwalt's team who had survived the great reformer's retirement. (These saturnine purges are, unfortunately, a long tradition in the naval service and have led to the loss of superb talent in periods following strong naval leaders. It happened after both of the Roosevelts, after Ernie King, after Zumwalt, and after my departure. Indeed, some have even accused me while I was secretary of the navy of encouraging the premature retirement of some identified with policies I was seeking to replace.) McKee was well thought of by Rickover, but not his first choice, which suited me fine. McKee was strongly recommended by Jim Watkins and Tom Hayward and strongly opposed by no one. I was impressed with McKee because he frequently disagreed with me and was a very tough customer to deal with. His record as superintendent of the Naval Academy, however, showed a human touch that was much needed in the personnel responsibilities of Rickover's replacement.

Admiral Rickover had been through the cycle now so many times that he was confident it would be repeated. I heard nothing from him through the spring. I received my first communication from him in May. As had happened in the past, beginning in May the president started to get letters from his supporters in Congress, of which Strom Thurmond's of May 25, 1981, was typical. He said, in part, "We simply cannot afford to lose a man of Admiral Rickover's vision, integrity, and skill, and I believe the very great majority of my colleagues in the Congress, and most of our citizens would agree we should keep him on." Letters from Warner, Addabbo, Bennett, and others followed in June and July. Some sent me a courtesy copy, but Admiral Rickover, of course, had them all.

Through August, Rickover's disciples were confident his term would be renewed. When I had canceled the award of four submarines to General Dynamics' Electric Boat Division in the spring, an action Admiral Rickover had strongly supported, it was interpreted by many as a vote of confidence in him.

On June 7 *The New York Times* reported that Admiral Rickover probably would be reappointed. "The decision is nominally up to Mr. Lehman, but he apparently lacks the political stature to make a ruling stick. Secretary of Defense Caspar W. Weinberger has the stature but he also has enough political savvy to know that retiring Admiral Rickover could set off a struggle that he does not need. . . ."

On August 19 I made a speech at the National Press Club in which I blasted the arrogance and negligence of the management of General Dynamics' Electric Boat Division, a point with which Admiral Rickover certainly agreed. Again, his supporters mistakenly viewed this as confirmation that his position was assured. Admiral Rickover had his hands full at the time, dealing with what appeared to be a full-scale effort to dislodge him waged by David Lewis, the chairman of General Dynamics, and Takis Veliotis, the manager of the Electric Boat Division. Through the spring and summer they lobbied heavily against

Rickover's reappointment. Their efforts on the Hill were also wearing down the intensity of his support. Accounts designed to portray him as incompetent and senile were circulated of Rickover's behavior on sea trials. While even his supporters admitted that he had slipped, he was by no means senile or incompetent.

Early in November everything came together well. The acquiescence of the necessary congressional satraps had been secured. Cap approved of Kin McKee as Rickover's successor, and at Cap's request the president had agreed to the complete transition plan. We decided to act swiftly. I had prepared for Cap's approval a press release and a talking paper, and we agreed that Cap would call Rickover into his office on Friday morning, November 13, and together the two of us would tell him it was a *fait accompli* and ask him for his cooperation and help in the transition. We agreed that the announcement would then be given in a press release a couple of hours later. Once I had begun talking to candidates, of course, Admiral Rickover knew he was in trouble, and a last-ditch effort had been mounted. On November 9 the decision leaked out of the White House, and Scoop Jackson and Congressman Sam Stratton went through the motions of having a "save Rickover" meeting, but they all knew it was a done deed.

On the tenth I called Rickover to my office and told him as nicely as possible that I had recommended to Cap and the president that he be retired. It did not seem to surprise him. He asked why and I told him it was time to start a new regime and get new leadership into NR. There was no point in further elaboration, because neither of us wished to debate the issues with the other. The meeting was brief. He didn't view my position as all that important. He knew that only the president could make the decision.

On November 11 we had the awkward situation of having to launch the long-delayed and overrun U.S.S. *Ohio,* the first Trident submarine. Vice President Bush was the keynote speaker, and on the podium with him, in addition to me, was Admiral Rickover; Admiral Hayward; Admiral Train, commander of the Atlantic Fleet; and Admiral White. Everyone knew what was going on, and it was a most awkward couple of hours making chitchat and small talk between the events. In introducing Admiral Rickover, Admiral White gave a speech that portrayed him as a blend of George Washington, Albert Einstein, and Mother Teresa. Admiral Rickover was dignified and polite throughout, never once mentioning anything about the pending decision.

False hope had been kindled the day before, when President Reagan had a press conference and was asked whether Admiral Rickover was too old to be continued in the job at age eighty-one. The president responded, "You're asking me?" He then followed by saying, "Mr. Gladstone reached his height in England at eighty-three."

The morning of our meeting with Rickover in Cap's office *The Washington Post* had an article headlined "Betting Line Favors Rickover, Whose Future Is Now in Reagan's Hands."

At seven-fifteen on the morning of November 13, I joined Cap in his office, and at seven-thirty Admiral Rickover joined us. Cap outlined the president's decision and made every effort to sugarcoat it. He made a sincere effort to urge Admiral Rickover to accept the president's offer of a job as White House nuclear science adviser. Rickover, of course, knew what my recommendation had been, so the outcome did not surprise him, and he was very calm throughout the meeting. He kept asking why was he being replaced, that no one had accused him of not doing his job, that he worked twelve hours a day and on weekends, and that no one had given him any reason why he was being fired. Cap kept repeating the arguments that it was time to do an orderly transition while Rickover was still fully competent to help set the new course. He responded that he had a thorough physical examination every year and that the doctors at Bethesda had certified him fully fit in every respect for continued active duty. He said, "If everyone were replaced on an actuarial basis, then everyone over the age of sixty-nine, which is the current average life span of American men, should be replaced." It was, to say the least, a difficult meeting, and Admiral Rickover was clearly not reconciled to his fate. He behaved in a most gentlemanly fashion, however, throughout, and departed with due courtesies. Later that afternoon I held a press conference in the Pentagon press room to announce the impending transition.*

---

*Immediate release, November 13, 1981, #523-81
*Admiral Rickover Asked to Serve as
Presidential Adviser on Nuclear Science*
    The president has asked Admiral H. G. Rickover to move from his present position to serve as a presidential advisor on nuclear science. The president feels that this is the proper time to plan and carry out an orderly transition of a successor to Admiral Rickover.
    Admiral Rickover's extension on active duty will expire on January 31, 1982. The secretary of the navy has reported that Admiral Rickover be extended on active duty for the time required to have an orderly transition to his successor prior to taking up his new responsibilities.
    The president has expressed his appreciation and admiration for Admiral Rickover, and the nation owes an unending debt of gratitude to the admiral for his contribution in leading the free world to superiority in nuclear propulsion and reactor safety. The president hopes that Admiral Rickover will agree to bring this great expertise to bear on the national problems of the civilian use of atomic energy.

In the press conference I stressed that the decision was based on the need to begin the transition to his successor now, that the successor would retain the same powers, and that the admiral's help was needed in the transition. While he would definitely not get a two-year extension, we wanted him to continue on active duty "for the time required to have an orderly transition to his successor prior to taking up his new responsibilities." I was at great pains in the press conference to avoid appearing as the smart-ass youngster. When Admiral Rickover took on his powers as head of NR, I was seven years old, and my father was seven years old when Admiral Rickover entered the Naval Academy. He had done a lot of good and some bad. He had stayed too long.

PART I

A Naval Vocation

Chapter I

My Early Life

One of the 317,000 naval officers who won the war in the Pacific was John F. Lehman, Sr. A "ninety-day wonder," my father was given command of a new LCS right out of Officer Candidate School, where he was commissioned lieutenant (junior grade). *LCS-18* was a very heavily armed amphibious assault ship with a crew of 120 officers and men. My father and his crew put it in commission where it was built, in Boston, and took it through the Panama Canal to the Pacific. They were with the first wave in the Okinawa invasion and saw a great deal of combat from then until the end of the war. Though my father never considered making the navy a career, leaving active duty for the reserves as soon as the war was over, he loved the navy and what it stands for.

Dad's admiration for the navy was infectious. Although he was not really a strict disciplinarian, my sister, my three brothers, and I grew up in a "tight ship." We had to "hit the deck" every morning for school, "muster on the fantail" for Saturday chores. If we didn't behave well, we were told to "shape up or ship out."

Like so many World War II reserve officers, my father had a kind of affectionate condescension toward officers in the regular navy, the Naval Academy "ring-knockers." The World War II ratio of reserve to regular officers was seventy to one. He was a great admirer, however, of Admiral Arleigh "Thirty-one-Knot" Burke for his courage in combat and in Washington. A career in the military was something that no one in my father's family had ever considered. From their arrival with William Penn, there is no record of any member of my father's family ever having served as a careerist in the military, though a great many of them served on active duty during every war.

A good example was my father's grandfather Dr. Joseph V. Kelly. In a fit of patriotic fervor he joined the 114th Zouave Regiment of Volunteers in 1862. After a serious dose of infantry combat in the Battle of Fredericksburg, where the colorfully uniformed Zouaves made a bayonet charge that saved the day for the Union Army, he was taken seriously ill and spent a month in Chestnut Hill Hospital in Philadelphia recuperating. Upon recovery he traveled to the Brooklyn Navy Yard in New York and passed the examination for surgeon's steward. He was assigned to the Union gunboat *Commodore Jones* and was soon in active combat supporting McClellan's Army in the Peninsula Campaign. After nearly a year of active combat in the Virginia Tidewater area, *Commodore Jones* was blown up by a mine in the James River at Deep Bottom. Kelly was one of a very few survivors and spent a month recuperating in Portsmouth Naval Hospital. He spent the remainder of the war as an assistant ship's surgeon on the *Shokoken* and other ships. At the end of the war he resigned from the navy and returned to Philadelphia where he completed medical school at Jefferson Medical College. After graduating he spent a long career as a practicing physician and professor of medicine at Jefferson.

The first Lehman to arrive in Philadelphia was Philip Theodore Lehman who was secretary to William Penn. Lehman remained in Philadelphia working for Penn after the latter returned to England, despite the fact that Penn once described his secretary's fees as "lewd and extravagant." In 1733 Lehman's younger brother Godfryd joined him in Philadelphia along with his son Christian. Christian had a son named George born in 1753. As a young physician George joined the Continental Army and served with George Washington at Valley Forge at the Yellow Springs hospital and stayed with him for the next four years. With fighting at an end in the north, in 1780 George Lehman shipped out with Stephen Decatur, Sr., as ship's surgeon on the most famous privateer of the Revolution. *Fair American* took a great many prizes between 1780–82 and made all of her officers and owners rich men including Lehman. Unfortunately, in 1782 *Fair American* was captured by the Royal Navy ship *H.M.S. Garland* and Lehman found himself first in the infamous *Jersey* prison hulk in New York, and eventually in the Old Mill Prison in Portsmouth, England. Lehman was able to bribe his way to freedom and return to Philadelphia where he became a prominent physician. He married and produced five children one of whom was William. William had a son George, and George had a son James who had a son Joseph who became a physician and professor of medicine. Joseph had a son named John and John was my father.

When my father left the navy, he returned to a career as an industrial engineer but kept a very active and lively interest in world affairs and politics. Our dinner table conversations were always active on the issues of the day. Both my mother and my father were strong supporters of Franklin Roosevelt, Harry Truman, Dwight Eisenhower, Richard Nixon, and Ronald Reagan. They never participated in party politics, but their views and interests no doubt provided me with my basic frame of political reference. To this day I find my father's insights and salty commentary on foreign policy and politics much more valuable than those of most of the professional pundits. And from my mother's unflagging compassion for the underdog, I take my only strain of liberalism.

On September 14, 1942, I was born in Philadelphia in my grandfather's hospital, the second child after my sister, Patricia. We and my three younger brothers grew up in a stable, happy home in a suburb called Glenside. I did all the usual things—Cub Scouts, baseball, and a paper route—while attending St. Luke's parochial school. While there I was occasionally addressed by some of the good sisters of St. Joseph as "a bold, brazen article." I went from there to an excellent private school run by the Christian Brothers, LaSalle College High School. At LaSalle I took up rowing, a sport I have loved ever since.

I went on to my father's alma mater, St. Joseph's College in Overbrook, where the Jesuits were able to find my intellectual light switch and turn it on. In philosophy and political and economic theory I found subjects as exciting as rowing and beer. I was put in the honors program in international relations, and by the end of my freshman year I knew I wanted a career in government and foreign policy, though I never was able, even at graduation, to answer my father's question: "That's nice, but how are you going to make a living?" (After fourteen years of government salaries, I still didn't have an answer for him.)

My director of studies then and good friend now is Jim Dougherty. He introduced me to the classical tradition of political theory: Socrates, Plato, and Aristotle; Cicero and Seneca; Ambrose; John of Salisbury; Marsilio of Padua; Aquinas; Machiavelli; Hobbes; Locke; Hume; and Burke. Captivating Jesuits like the late Ed Gannon used the heavy requirement in philosophy to build a devotion to rigorous logic. Immersion in classical theory and philosophy gradually built a method of disciplined conceptual thinking and integration of disparate bodies of knowledge that has been the most valuable acquisition of my entire education. It left me with a lifelong satisfaction in logic and disciplined intellectual debate and rhetoric and with a contempt for those politicians and commentators who disregard and debase the rules of logic. (My criticism of the Rickover educational philosophy and its effect on the navy was its treating of the quantifiable disciplines of math, physics, chemistry, etc., as the only true legitimate education, while the nonquantifiable disciplines of history, jurisprudence, philosophy, and political theory were mere luxuries to dabble in, in one's spare time. At the Naval Academy they were called "bull courses." The true value of a balanced liberal arts education is to learn the humane virtues of Western civilization, to conceptualize the unquantifiables of human nature, and to integrate in rational thought both quantifiable and unquantifiable knowledge.)

It left me also with an impatience for one of the great heresies of our time, of which Rickover and former secretary of defense Robert McNamara were disciples—the heresy of bureaucratic empiricism. The rise of computers in the 1950s gave a new life to an old bad idea—that the only reality was the quantifiable. It gave rise under McNamara to the cult of system analysis, to the practice of decision-making by computer modeling and statistical analysis, to body counts and cost-based, sole-source procurement.

When the empirical doctrine was grafted upon a navy already obsessed with engineering thanks to Rickover, it created a generation of officers comfortable in thermodynamics but illiterate and tongue-tied in conceptual and policy debate.

Through Jim Dougherty I was introduced to the great Robert Strausz-Hupé and his "school" of realist foreign policy scholars at the Foreign Policy Research Institute (FPRI) at the University of Pennsylvania. The Viennese-born author of Geopolitics had gathered a group of brilliant intellectuals at Penn. More than any other think tank of the 1950s and 1960s, the FPRI provided the intellectual foundations of the foreign policy of Jackson Democrats and conservative Republicans. Strausz-Hupé's elegant writing and riveting lecture style utterly charmed me. I dropped plans to go to law school and sought to join his "school." Though I was accepted into Strausz-Hupé's Ph.D. program at Penn, my entry was delayed until January 1965 so I could work in Barry Goldwater's presidential campaign.

To be a conservative Republican during those times was to enjoy the pleasures of a distinct minority. Like all 1960s campuses, St. Joe's was overwhelmingly liberal Democrat, and it was loaded with the sons of Irish and Italian politicians. After joining the Conservative Intercollegiate Studies Institute, I found intellectual succor for my minority views. The college paper, The Hawk, gave me space for a political column, which I wrote in the style of H. L. Mencken, to whose books I was addicted and to whom I still repair regularly for cynical refreshment.

Perhaps the strongest influence on the direction of my intellectual interests was my great-uncle George Kelly. He never married, and my mother and his other nieces were his only family. He was a major family presence. He was at once the most intellectually provocative and the funniest man I have ever known, and from the time I was about ten he held me spellbound until he died in 1971. He had achieved great fame as a Broadway actor (his first hit was as the lead in *The Virginian*), director, and playwright. He had received many honors, including the Pulitzer Prize in 1926 for *Craig's Wife*, and had traveled the world and knew it well. Every visit by Uncle George was a performance. Before, during, and after dinner he would alternate mimicking old Philadelphia neighborhood characters, Irish maids, thugs, cops, and movie stars like his one great romantic partner, Tallullah Bankhead. (She once said on *The Jack Paar Show* that George Kelly was the only man with whom she had ever been in love.) He would have to stop after a while because we had tears and cramps from unremitting laughter. I still remember almost wetting my pants as he recounted in lilting brogue about a great-aunt who ran a hotel in Atlantic City in the 1880s. One day this stern matriarch was disturbed by a fourth-floor guest playing lively Irish reels on his fiddle. She sent one servant after another up to tell the old Irishman to stop playing and disturbing the peace of the neighborhood. He took the part of each of the different maids and waiters, and of Aunt Mary, dispatching each with stern warnings. None returned, and finally there was none left to send—and still the fiddling continued. Furious, she climbed the four sets of stairs to deliver terrible justice. As she entered, there was the fiddler (Uncle George now looking just like a leprechaun sawing the imaginary fiddle), and there were all the servants all dancing jigs, "And saints preserve us if the divil himself didn't take hold of me feet and set them to dancin', and off I went even as I was shouting at the girls, and them with their skirts in their hands!"

When his audience truly couldn't continue from too much laughter, he would make a point and illustrate it with a scene from Shakespeare in which he would take every role from memory. His entire person was transformed with every character. And the force of his Lear or Macbeth still makes my hair stand. (He refused to do *The Tempest*, which he called "Shakespeare's only mistake.")

Through my college years I visited with him frequently. I would tell him over lunch about some moral or political issue we were studying and then he would talk and I would listen for hours and hours, spellbound. He would start on the issue and explore it with a combination of detachment and passion. Religion and philosophy, mysticism, the New Deal, existentialism, all were alive to him. To illustrate a point he would say, "In such-and-such a play [often one of his own] the character X is caught in just such a dilemma." He would then proceed to act out the entire play, taking every part. I have never experienced anything like it since. He was hypnotic. I was absolutely carried by him into the life of the play, the issues, the personalities. He took on twenty different personalities and intellects in a day, and every one complete. It was almost as if he were a medium through which other real people spoke.

More than any other person, he introduced me to the life of the intellect, and as a side effect moved me steadily to a foundation of conservative politics. He abhorred politicians as a class, but he had special contempt for left-wing ideologues. His political principles came from Burke, Santayana, and William James, and his prejudices from the famous "roundtable" at the Algonquin Hotel, where he was a welcome member for thirty years.

Uncle George was one of the ten remarkable children of John and Mary Costello Kelly, two Irish immigrants from County Mayo.

The oldest son, Patrick Henry ("P. H."), succeeded at a young age, founding a general contracting company that built many of the elegant buildings lining Philadelphia's Benjamin Franklin Parkway. Simultaneously, his younger brother Walter, who had started as a draftsman at the Newport News Shipbuilding and Drydock Company (which, along with the *Commodore Jones* episode, gave me a good line for all my ship-launching speeches there), became a huge success in vaudeville and later in Hollywood as "the Virginia Judge." He was a good friend of Theodore Roosevelt and went with him on his year-long African safari in 1911. P. H. and Walter's financial success eased the way for the younger children.

After working for P. H., younger brother Jack (Princess Grace's father) launched his own brick contracting firm while winning three Olympic gold medals in sculling in his spare time. Younger brother George and sister Grace gained entrée into the world of the theater through Walter. George was an immediate success as an actor in high comedy but Grace's very promising talent was cut short when she died of pneumonia at age twenty-two.

Younger sister Mary went to work as bookkeeper for P. H.'s company and soon became chief financial officer—a highly precocious position for a woman in those days (1912). She married Joseph Cruice and reluctantly gave up her career after their second child, Grace Constance, my mother, arrived. Mary Kelly Cruice was a formidable woman in the Irish matriarchal tradition. She ruled benevolently but with an iron hand. We grandchildren knew well, because we lived under her suzerainty every summer until she died. She raised her four daughters in comfortable circumstances with live-in help. Every summer was spent at Ocean City, New Jersey, Philadelphia's longtime seaside resort for upscale lace-curtain Irish.

When my mother and her sisters married and began families of their own, Uncle Jack bought a large Victorian house of seven bedrooms on the beach at Ocean City so that my grandmother could house all her daughters, sons-in-law, and eventually thirteen grandchildren together for summer vacations.

In our family my father wore the pants (as they used to say) and was used to command at sea. But when he and my uncles-in-law joined us on weekends, we kids took due note that the men were definitely second in command when "Ma" Cruice was on the bridge. But we also knew what a soft touch she was for ice cream or money for the boardwalk.

She was also wise enough to know that teenage boys would not fit well into the Victorian order of her summer household. As the first of us ten boys approached adolescence, a western-style bunkhouse was built away from the main house, and all boys over ten were exiled. Over there the regime of "the big house" rested lightly upon us, we soon learned, as long as we didn't become too outrageous. As one of the oldest, I assumed responsibility for establishing a new political order in our microcosm, and we soon had a functioning executive and judicial system that remained intact for a decade until the whole establishment was swept away by the great storm of 1962. As it happened, that occurred one month after my grandmother's death, and none of us questioned that the one was a natural consequence of the other.

The bunkhouse bums, as we soon came to be called, were a very talented bunch of lads. We reflected the contending interest of the older Kelly generation. The jocks idolized Uncle Jack, the Olympic gold medalist, and the intellectuals Uncle George, the Pulitzer Prize winner. Both men were heroes to us, tall, handsome figures who had conquered the world and who dispensed $20 bills to each of us when they visited. The senior jock, Bob Smith, later an outstanding end on the Boston College football team and a Marine Corps officer, had us all competing fiercely on the beach in football, stickball, surfing, running, and wrestling. It was no place for sissies. Everyone had to compete, and every single day. But the intellectuals ruled on rainy days and after dinner, and here again there was no option of dropping out and losing face. Learned debates on sex, books, politics, and religion (half of us were Catholic and half Episcopalian) went long into the night. The quick riposte, the bon mot, the verbal thrust were as essential for survival on rainy days as a strong arm and a good eye were on sunny days.

Later in our high school and college years, we all had summer jobs usually, like me, as a hod carrier for the Kelly Construction Company, and we joined the bunkhouse only on weekends. Despite its Irish heritage, Ocean City was and remains today a dry island. But just across the causeway on the mainland was a place called Somer's Point, which was a kind of rock 'n' roll Dodge City, made up of three blocks of bars, each with rock 'n' roll bands or jukeboxes. The crowd was college, and it went from dusk till dawn. What a fun place it was. All of the early rock 'n' roll greats played at the three main joints, Bayshores, Tony Mart's, and Steel's. Bill Haley, Bo Diddley, the Isley Brothers, etc.

Some of us rowed competitively for the Vesper Boat Club in Philadelphia, so we never broke training until the season ended, usually in mid-July. The bunkhouse competition changed a bit in those days, and we often crept in as the sun crept up.

The bunkhouse was a part of a family culture that created lasting bonds. Of the eight cousins who formed the bunkhouse bums, all finished college, and then seven took advanced degrees, two served in the marines, three in the navy, and one in the army. Four served in Vietnam. One, Tony Goit, died tragically of an LSD-induced suicide at Dartmouth College. The rest of us are all happily married (two for the second time) and have, as of this writing, fathered nineteen children. We all have a reunion every year at my parent's beach house at Ocean City, and this year my son, John III, asked me when he and his cousins Brian, Robbie, Jody, Chris, Derek, and Kent could move out of "the big house."

Grace

Another person who influenced me enormously over the years was another devoted disciple of George Kelly, Princess Grace. Grace's father was John B. Kelly, George's younger brother by two years. Jack had saved George's life when they were both soldiers in France during World War I, but their careers went in opposite directions and they had little sympathy for each other's pursuits. Grace, however, adored George and from her earliest years wanted to pursue a career in the theater. Although Jack put no obstacles in Grace's path, it was George whom she looked to for encouragement and help. It was he who provided the initial introductions in the theater world just as his brother Walter had done for him. As "George Kelly's niece" she was looked at carefully by those who counted in New York. George was very proud of Grace and of the role he had played in getting her started, though he never spoke of it. Her first acclaim in the press came from her performance in George's play, *The*

Torchbearers. They were always very close, sharing especially a unique sense of humor and a great sense of theater with a small "t." George was an immediate favorite of Prince Rainier and his father, Prince Pierre, after Grace's marriage, and was a frequent visitor to the palace.

When Grace was growing up, my mother lived only a few blocks away, in East Falls, Philadelphia, and was the favorite baby-sitter of Grace's mother, Margaret. Grace was the flower girl for my mother when she married, and later she was occasionally my mother's baby-sitter at Ocean City. When I was growing up, I saw her at funerals and weddings. When she first hit the big time in New York (in *Lux Video Theater*), I remember all of the bunkhouse bums walking down the beach to the Kelly house to receive autographed photos from her during a weekend visit. We came back and told the "grownies" at the big house that we had met some smarmy guy named "Ollie" Cassini, who was chasing her. We gave him a big thumbs-down.

In 1995 my brothers and sister and I were polished up and taken to the Kelly house on Henry Avenue for a family party to meet Prince Rainier. I came away awed that the first and only monarch I had met actually knew more about American baseball than I did. When I came to know him in later years, I found that in addition to baseball he understood American politics and government better than most of my professors. His grasp of world economic and political affairs remains today quite extraordinary.

After Grace married I saw her about once a year at Ocean City, where she always returned for a summer visit. While there in August 1965 I told her I was leaving soon to go to England to attend Cambridge University (where I eventually received B.A. and M.A. degrees), and she invited me to stay at the palace in Monaco for the Christmas holidays. During my first term at Cambridge, I read up on royal protocol and court routine and arrived on schedule a week before Christmas. It was quite a holiday. I was lodged in apartments in the newer seventeenth-century courtyard and had some awkwardness adjusting to the ever-present footmen, valets, and household officials, but otherwise was made to feel right at home. Following Grace's schedule every day was a challenge filled with many events. I was surprised to find that everything at court revolved around the children: Caroline, then eight years old; Albert, her younger brother; and newly arrived Stephanie. While Rainier had government meetings and ceremonials, he rarely let them interfere with events in the children's lives. Around the children's schedules there was for Grace a constant round of charity events, hospital visits, state lunches and dinners, formal balls, and glamorous galas. The business of being a prince and a princess, I found, could be very hard work indeed. But she clearly loved it, and she knew how to make it fun. There was a social event at the palace or the opera house or the sporting club nearly every night during the holidays.

After that first visit, I was invited back repeatedly for holidays and for special events. It was a wonderful experience, with many long conversations with exiled kings, crown princes, cabinet ministers, movie stars, famous rogues and roués, poets, and maestros. But of all the personalities I met there, none was really in the same league with Grace and Rainier.

She was one of the finest human beings I have ever known, with a subtle intellect and an exquisite sense of humor. She was able to apply an iron will to discipline her talents to achieve great things, but unlike so many in her profession, she never let that ascetic drive harden and dominate her personality. Her unique accomplishment was a perfect balance between disciplined achievement and strength of character on the one hand, and caring, warmth of spirit, and compassion on the other hand.

Grace grew up in a tough, competitive family, but a stable and loving one. Those values served her well breaking into the theater and later the movies. As Cary Grant once explained it to me at 4:00 A.M. one morning after a ball at the palace: "Grace had a reputation in those early days as a kind of ice-cool icon. She would not bend to the prevailing culture and sleep with producers, moguls, and leading men. She was great fun socially, but she chose her friends with care, and without regard to what might help her career."

After she had made it in Hollywood, she remained aloof from the tawdry culture and life-style of the place (although she loved to go back for visits). With constant prying by investigative journalists throughout her career, not one credible hint of scandal ever touched her for a simple reason: She never did anything scandalous.

One of her earliest friends while she was studying at the American Academy in New York was Paul Newman, who became her lifelong friend. Despite her virtues, she apparently was not a very great talent scout. Newman once told me that he went to her for advice when they were both students at the American Academy, and Grace advised him that he ought to go back home, get a job, and settle down, that there probably was no future for him in acting. They often had a laugh over that.

My first meeting with Newman was not quite so humorous. One evening in the late 1970s at a party at the palace, Grace had to intervene and break up a degenerating argument among Newman and me and the Sixth Fleet Commander, Admiral Jim Watkins. Watkins, whom I later recommended as CNO,

was visiting Monaco aboard his flagship, the cruiser *Albany*, and was one of
the guests. Newman, in chatting with Watkins, told him that he had read about
a new titanium submarine built by the Russians, and Watkins explained that,
yes, it could go deeper and faster than any U.S. sub. Newman said: "That's a
lot of baloney. It is just another fabrication of the Pentagon to get more
money." Watkins and I leaped in and lashed him with arguments till his
shoelaces danced. We soon gathered in a large crowd, and I was really warm-
ing to it when Grace led us away.

Grace's views, on the other hand, were sound. She was notorious in Europe
for her outspoken defense of U.S. policy, and once in 1967 gave Averell
Harriman a public tongue-lashing at a formal dinner at the American embassy.
Harriman was loudly ridiculing President Johnson and American foreign policy in general. He was reduced to shocked silence. Grace's views were heavily influenced by Prince Rainier on political and diplomatic affairs. I have
found his grasp of the subtlety of world events to be impressive, a wisdom evidenced by the success with which he has handled the delicate relationship of
Monaco with France.

Grace devoted enormous amounts of time to charity. While she made significant contributions to the arts, such as founding the School of Ballet in
Monaco, her most characteristic work was in helping families and individuals.
Hardly a single Monegasque who experienced tragedy or hardship did not benefit directly from her attention. I remember once in 1966 while I was visiting,
there was a terrible accident on the Corniche, in which a Monegasque father
of twelve was killed. Grace went immediately to the widow and took all twelve
children to the palace to care for them, while providing someone to help the
widow with arrangements. Grace never permitted publicity for such actions,
and she did them all the time.

No other person in my experience had such a fiercely loyal circle of friends
as did Grace. It was because she chose her friends with care, and for them she
had great affection. She was the source of great strength and never was too busy
to help when trouble hit them. When it did, very often a call would come from
Grace inviting them to come to the palace or to Roc Agel, their ranch in the
mountains above Monaco, or to Paris.

Princess Grace and Prince Rainier have always been very special favorites
of the U.S. Navy. While Prince Rainier had been schooled in England and
Switzerland, he served with distinction in the Free French Army in World War

II, and he had been a liaison officer for a period with the U.S. Army. He has always been very pro-American. During the height of Charles de Gaulle's anti-Americanism in the 1950s and 1960s, Rainier's pro-American attitudes were conspicuous. When de Gaulle kicked the American fleet out of Villefranche and refused requests for liberty visits, Rainier went out of his way to make American sailors welcome in the port of Monaco. When an American naval ship was in port, Grace and Rainier always invited the captain and some members of the crew for social events at the palace.

One of her old friends who became one of her secret charities was Josephine Baker. The great black expatriate singer had a roller-coaster personal life typical of so many entertainers. Grace helped her personally and financially to pull herself together. Josephine came back, and she started an orphanage in which she was the administrator and the mother. I met her on the night of one of her greatest personal triumphs. Grace had encouraged her on the long road back to aim for a comeback on the stage as a way to ease the constant financial problems of her orphanage. She succeeded, and in August, Josephine Baker starred in the Red Cross gala in Monte Carlo. Despite her years, she gave a magnificent performance and brought the house down. Sitting with Grace during the performance, I wondered why she was so emotional. At supper back at the palace after the performance, Josephine told me, with equal emotion, that it was Grace who had inspired her and stuck with her to bring about the personal, professional, and financial recovery. Grace never told anyone. In Grace's life there were dozens of Josephine Bakers.

As a chanteuse, Josephine Baker's trademark song was *"J'ai deux amours"*— I have two loves, America and Paris. The same could be said of Grace; she loved Monaco and its people, and she loved the United States.

After events like the Red Cross gala, Grace usually would insist that her lady-in-waiting and close friend, Virginia Gallico, wife of writer Paul Gallico, and any of her close friends who might be staying, come back to the private apartments for a nightcap to rehash the people and events of the evening. At first my eyes were wide as saucers listening to the stories told at these sessions about people who were legends, and just as frequently told by the legends themselves, such as Cary Grant, Frank Sinatra, Elizabeth Taylor, David Niven, King Constantine of Greece, and Maestro Rostropovich. There was never a touch of meanness in any of these stories, but they were certainly fun. We would laugh and laugh. Grace's humor and her laughter were infectious. It was always frustrating to me that I could never dine out on these stories back at Cambridge or

Washington, because of the confidences involved, and also because it would have to involve more name-dropping than anyone could tolerate.

Grace also really liked to get down and boogie. She and Rainier had built a disco on the ground floor and I brought her risqué posters from Copenhagen to help decorate it. After the big do's, if there was a good, lively group staying at the palace, she would lead us all down to the disco and out would come the Rolling Stones or Credence Clearwater. When that happened, we would dance till dawn. By the way, dawn in Monaco is a magnificent sight, with the white and beige buildings forming an amphitheater up the mountainside directly opposite the rising sun, which paints the town in brilliant shades of pink, rose, and orange.

I felt a bit like the old TV show *I Led Three Lives* while I was at Cambridge. During those two and a half years, for one weekend a month and two weeks at the end of summer term, I turned into an airman third class, took off my Cambridge gown and donned my Air Force uniform, and drove my Austin 7 at its top speed of thirty-seven miles per hour (with only two main bearings, that's the speed at which the crankshaft started to flex and the cylinders hit the valves) to RAF Lakenheath for duty with the U.S. Tactical Fighter Wing based there. As a hospital corpsman (with only on-the-job training), my main job was taking urine and blood samples. I got pretty good at both. I had spent four years in the Air Force ROTC to become an aviator, but disenrolled to enlist in the reserves. While my graduate study kept me deferred from the draft, I wanted to serve in the hope of getting my wings after graduate school. After graduating from Cambridge, I was commissioned an ensign in the navy and attended officer training at Pensacola.

In one of life's many strange coincidences, I returned as secretary of the navy in 1986 to that same Tactical Fighter Wing at Lakenheath to award them a navy unit citation. It was they who flew the joint air strike on Libya with our Navy A-6s in 1986.

The Truest Sport

I first joined "the navy" as a high school freshman in 1956. The navy in Philadelphia is The Schuylkill Navy, the 150-year-old association of rowing clubs along boathouse row in Fairmount Park, now renamed Kelly Drive in honor of the family. I went out for my high school rowing team because, in our family, one did. Grace's brother Jack had just made the Olympic rowing team for the third time, and he taught me to row. From the time he was born, Jack had been trained by his father to be a rowing champion. While John B.,

Sr., had won three Olympic gold medals, including both singles and doubles on the same day in 1928, a record that still stands, he had been denied the Henley Diamond Sculls championship in a most unpleasant incident. He was to race the British champion, Jack Beresford, whom he had easily beaten in the Olympics, for the Henley crown. Before the finals, Beresford lodged a protest with the Henley stewards based on the fact that Uncle Jack had worked as a bricklayer for his brother's farm and hence was not a "gentleman." The Henley stewards upheld the protest under the rules of the day and gave Beresford the cup by default.

In 1946, Jack, Jr., was able to avenge his father by winning the Diamond Sculls at Henley. Jack, Sr., triumphantly made a gift to the king of his son's Kelly green cap. Jack, Jr., won the Diamonds again in 1947 and 1948.

In 1966 Beresford was a steward in the judge's launch for my race at Henley when I stroked the Caius College Cambridge eight in the "Ladies' Plate" Race. I thought all the way down the course watching him how much I would love to stick my tongue out at him when we won, but unfortunately we lost by half a length to a London University crew.

Despite the fact that at five-nine I was rather small for rowing, I really became hooked on that magnificent sport. It teaches self-discipline and a self-knowledge in the most indelible way. As you learn the skills of rhythm, balance, and finesse of bladework, you are able to take your body farther and farther in physical performance—many times what you thought were your physical limits. As in yoga, the concentration of your mind and will in mastering the body pays back a direct return in performance, and once past a certain threshold, physical pain fades into an almost mystical satisfaction.

In no other sport is one more alone than in single sculling. The race is two kilometers and takes seven to eight minutes. In a typical race, after an all-out sprint to gain position, you hit the first pain barrier. On the famous Philadelphia course in Fairmount Park that was about when you went under the Strawberry Mansion Bridge. I always used to imagine and long for a rope ladder hanging from the bridge so I could escape the agony. Then you rowed through that barrier, settling to a lower rate while striving for a winning rhythm. By the halfway mark, a six-man race usually was down to a two-man duel. Here psychology plays a strong role. As a single sculler, you must balance internal concentration to row your own race, with external strategy in dealing with your opponent. Should you spend scarce energy early by upping the stroke to gain water on him? Or will it be too soon? If he starts a sprint, should you match him stroke for stroke, or count on his peaking too early? Should you try to break him now, or wait for the all-out final burst in the last quarter mile? There in front of the grandstands with the cheering crowds and the adrenaline pumping, it is possible to push through the last pain barriers and really go beyond your limit, to come face to face with your own rock-bottom endurance. It is in those ultimate seconds in a close race that you come really to know and understand your inner self.

In rowing eight-oared shells, less finesse is required, but the same inner challenge dominates. Successful eights achieve a genuine group sense that operates in a different psychological dimension. In the higher levels of competition among experienced crews a level of team consciousness and commitment has to be achieved for success. The great eight from our Vesper team that won in the Tokyo Olympics in 1964 was the last world champion eight produced by the United States. After that, the club and college team system, built around team loyalty and communal spirit, was abandoned by the United States and replaced by the national team system, which was based on selecting the best individual oarsmen by empirical engineering methods—by ergometers and computers; and then training them by the same methods, eliminating the human dimensions of heart and character, which cannot be assigned numerical values. We haven't produced a winning Olympic rowing team since adopting it.

While I won a few pots and medals during my twelve years of competitive rowing, the height of my accomplishment was winning the national intermediate double sculls championship with John Miller in 1963. Later, at Cambridge, I was elected captain of my college team, Gonville and Caius, and spent the two most interesting and satisfying years of my rowing career. As the first Yank ever elected captain in 146 years, I had great fun performing the role expected of me: the brash, colonial iconoclast. I introduced to Caius the radical Vesper/German training methods of interval wind sprints and weight training, leading to a rowing rate ten strokes higher than the traditional racing rate, which did not fit well into the archaic rowing traditions that made Oxford-Cambridge rowing unique in the world.

In retrospect it was an unusual presaging in microcosm of my later experience as secretary of the navy. My first task as captain was to rid the team of the old boatmen who, like Rickover, had a corrosive influence and a death grip on the team. Boatmen are venerable Oxbridge institutions, combining coach, boat repair craftsman, and butler not lightly to be challenged. It took me a full year of lobbying the college authorities to bring about the change, but it was the key to success. We had a great team and did very well, but when we went to Henley we had no boatman. All of the Oxbridge boatmen boycotted us. I was able to get our work done, however, because one by one, the boatmen came to me on the sly and offered to do the needed work on the boats, which they did late at night. While maintaining outward solidarity to their guild, they all felt, as the Trinity boatman told me, "You done right, Mr. Lehman, sir, that bloke 'e was a real sod, 'e was."

Captain of boats at an Oxbridge college is a fascinating job. One is coach, manager, treasurer, strategist, and psychologist. In addition to rowing in the first eight, usually at stroke, he also must arrange the selection and training of the second, third, and backup teams and deal with the college and university authorities. It is a challenge, to say the least. When the captain is a Yank with an agenda for change, then it really gets fun. And fun it was. I have never had a more satisfying job. I came to England two weeks early, at the request of the rowing team. I found myself among the most delightful assortment of characters, with whom I shared the same sense of humor, passions, and prejudices. All Brits, except me and one South African, six of these gents have remained among my very closest friends, and every one is a considerable personal and professional success. While I soon had other circles of friends at Cambridge, these were the hard core, and it was the experience of rowing and of forging ourselves into a winning team that bound us together. Oxbridge rowing is exactly what intercollegiate athletics should be: intense competition, a high level of skill and competence, serious discipline, keen team spirit, but never taken beyond the point of common sense. One of the primary duties, for instance, of every college boatman was to ensure that there was always a properly tapped keg available in the locker room so that everyone could have a pint or two after each day's workout. Nor would any of us have dreamed of missing an all-night ball just because we happened to have a race the next day. More than once key members of the team, and indeed even the captain himself, arrived at the boathouse for a morning race or workout still in a dinner jacket.

Higher Learning

It was indeed through rowing that I decided to apply to Cambridge. I was sold on it by a Vesper clubmate, my friend Boyce Budd, who rowed at Cambridge after Yale, and prior to winning his gold medal at the Tokyo Olympics. My course, however, was already set to enter the Ph.D. program in international relations at the University of Pennsylvania, and I had put even that off for a semester to work in the 1964 presidential campaign.

Through Robert Strausz-Hupé, who was adviser to Barry Goldwater, I had been offered a job as a flunky on the Goldwater campaign staff. My first assignment was to work for Steve Shadegg at the Republican Convention at the Cow Palace in San Francisco in the summer of 1964. It was a gaudy show and quite an initiation into power politics. I was given credentials as a page on the convention floor by Shadegg and was assigned to monitor the Pennsylvania delegation, led by Senator Hugh Scott. Scott was the key strategist for the Rockefeller forces, who were supporting Pennsylvania governor William Scranton in an effort to stop Goldwater. Scott and the Rockefeller forces were furiously trying to corral votes on the floor of the convention, and my assignment was to hover around them and monitor which delegations they were targeting. That was very easy to do, and I would then go to one of the Goldwater floor managers with the information and he would relay it by radio directly to Shadegg, who was in a trailer outside the Cow Palace in a command center. Shadegg would then see that Goldwater forces smothered the Rockefeller targets before they could waver. It was pretty heady stuff for a country boy from Philadelphia. I used to remind Goldwater of this service to him later when I was secretary of the navy, but I never could get him to vote for the navy.

After the election was over, I started at Penn in January 1965. Strausz-Hupé strongly encouraged his students to spend at least one year out of the three-year requirement abroad. I was nominated by him for a Weaver/Earhart Fellowship for study abroad, and I applied to study international law at Cambridge and was accepted by the university and by Gonville and Caius College (most recently of *Chariots of Fire* fame).

Going over to England on the old *Queen Elizabeth*, I found myself among fifty or so Rhodes and Marshall scholars all going to Oxford. I was the only Cantab. They were an obnoxious lot and would often say, "Oh, Cambridge? Pity you couldn't get into Oxford," to which I would always reply, "Yes, it is a pity I couldn't be admitted because, you see, my parents are married." Or I would point out that were it not for the stupidity of the three Oxford men in George III's cabinet—North, Shelbourne, and Grenville—we could never have won American independence, while the enlightened Cambridge men like William Pitt were strong supporters of America; or I would quote sir John Coleridge, who said, "I speak not of this college or of that, but of the university as a whole: And gentlemen, what a hole Oxford is."

I found my first year at Cambridge enchanting. The tutorial system is the best possible teaching method. With a faculty-student ratio of nearly one-to-one, the system is based on direct face-to-face personal contact. Subjects are assigned in each week's tutorials upon which the student must study and write, bringing an essay with him to the following week's tutorial. Regardless of what subject the tutorial may be, everyone majors in English composition, with the emphasis on elegance of style and clarity of logic. Even if the facts are all there, it will not meet with favor if it is not well written and well said. Even at our best American universities, this standard is often ignored. Far more effective than examinations or quizzes, the prospect of having to sit through two hours with your tutor not having done any work is too awful, and therefore the work was nearly always done. There are three or four of these tutorials a week, and in addition, a rich offering of lectures where no roll is taken. There are no quizzes or exams, only the final exams at the end of the year, upon which everything rides. These are three or four grueling all-day sessions of answering essay questions.

Perhaps more important to the learning process than this excellent system is the diversity and excellence of the quality of the students themselves, and of the dons. Since everyone must live together in the semicloisters of the college, the educational dialogue goes on round the clock in college rooms, dining clubs, pubs, and boathouses. It is a world where diversity and eccentricity are prized—as long as they are marked by excellence, or at least style. The intensity of every activity is at a very high level, whether in tutorials, ballrooms, or boathouses.

In addition to rowing, my interest in things naval was heightened at Cambridge by my discovery of Samuel Pepys. Pepys was a Cambridge man and bequeathed his library intact to his Cambridge college, Magdalene. The Pepys Library at Magdalene College is a time capsule from the day its owner died in 1703. The Pepys diaries are perhaps the most valuable existing insight into the life of seventeenth-century London, and most people are familiar primarily with his accounts of the London plague and the great London fire. What those who have not read all eleven volumes of his diaries may not appreciate is that he was, effectively, the first secretary of the British Navy. As secretary to the Admiralty Board under Charles II, it was Pepys who really created the Royal Navy as an organized, uniformed service. I found his library fascinating, filled with his books, notebooks, diaries, and maps. I read his diaries with fascination then and, upon rereading some of them now, I find his descriptions of his problems with his workers in naval shipyards and with shipbuilders and admirals little different from what I experienced three hundred years later.

Some things, however, have changed. Pepys got quite rich in the job, and as he described it in his entry of August 16, 1660, " . . . It was not the salary of any place that did make a man rich, but the opportunities of getting money while he is in the place."

Nor could I necessarily condone all the circumstances given in his entry for March 9, 1666: ". . . Music and women I cannot but give way to, whatever my business is."

Midway through the year I decided that one year was not enough and that I would stay and complete a degree. The decision was cemented when, in the final term, I was elected captain of boats for the next year. They were two wonderful years, at the completion of which I got a "two-two" honors B.A., and after the requisite five-year wait, an M.A., to which all those who earn a B.A. with "honors" are entitled, assuming they remain "of good character."

During my final term, after seriously considering staying in London, I received a letter from Professor William Kintner, the noted scholar on American foreign policy and deputy director of the Foreign Policy Research Institute at the University of Pennsylvania. He offered me a job as the administrative officer of the FPRI, which I could easily do while completing my doctorate there at Penn. I accepted and returned to Penn to resume my doctoral studies.

While a totally different environment than Cambridge, Penn was a very enjoyable experience. Despite the fact that the antiwar riots of the period were boiling, the FPRI was an academic island of sound thinking, and in addition there were some marvelous professors from whom I learned a great deal: Anthropologist Loren Eiseley, historian Hans Kohn, Strausz-Hupé, Kintner, Robert Pfaltzgraff, and Soviet expert Alvin Z. Rubinstein.

The FPRI was part of a network of institutes such as the Harvard Center for International Affairs, the new Georgetown Center for Strategic Studies, and others where the "realist" school of foreign policy flourished among both Republicans and Democrats. It was on this circuit that I met David Abshire and Richard V. Allen, the founders of the Georgetown Center, and Henry Kissinger, formerly an associate of FPRI and then a principal of the Harvard Center. It was through these associations that I found myself working as a part-time researcher on the Nixon foreign policy staff during the 1968 campaign. Dick Allen was the full-time foreign policy staffer for Nixon and after the election was named Henry Kissinger's principal deputy national security adviser.

After the election I took a leave of absence from Penn, having completed my course work, and went to work full-time on the Nixon transition staff at the Hotel Pierre in New York, working on the foreign and defense policy transition. While there I was offered a job as a member of the National Security Council staff by Allen and Kissinger. There was not really a vacant day among Cambridge, Penn, the Nixon transition, and the National Security Council. It seemed one natural continuum. But joining the government and moving to Washington was most definitely the start of an entirely new phase of my life. The earlier phase of my life came to an end during that first year in Washington. It was during that year that I met my femme fatale. Rendezvousing with my Cambridge pals at Zermatt, Switzerland, in 1969, I met Barbara Wieland of Philadelphia. Since she was in the company of one of my Brit pals, I wouldn't dare poach. But months later, when she was across the sea again, alone at college, I came a-courtin'. The pace of life with Kissinger did not encourage out-of-town romances, but we did fall in love, and, after I chased her for five years, we were married in an old-fashioned Philadelphia wedding.

Barbara's family had been in Pennsylvania for generations, but it had much deeper roots in Maryland and Virginia from earliest Colonial times. Her great-uncle Paul Dashiell had been a famous football coach at the Naval Academy in the last century. Her father, the late Alexander Wieland, was a Harvard lawyer and noted sportsman in Philadelphia, playing amateur ice hockey until he was seventy-five years old. Her mother, Virginia Thornton Dashiell Wieland, is a charming lady who is holding forth still in Chestnut Hill.

Barbara attended Springside School in Philadelphia and got her B.A. from The Moore College of Art, but nothing in her experience prepared her for the political world she entered when we married. Her first introduction was during our engagement in 1975: She traveled from Philadelphia to attend every one of my five confirmation hearings as deputy director of the Arms Control and Disarmament Agency. She was so appalled by the vituperation, the sleeping senators, and the staff intrigues that she urged me to reconsider spending a career in policy and government.

As an accomplished artist with a highly developed sense of aesthetics and proportion, her insights and advice on policy have been far more valuable to me over the years than any policy adviser's. She is at heart rooted in the best American tradition, distrustful of the government as a necessary evil and disdainful of the public attention that goes with high-level government service. Her own personal diplomacy on our official visits to China, the Philippines, Japan, Central America, Europe, the Persian Gulf, Africa, the Mideast, and Pakistan achieved as much as or more than my own efforts.

She remains my greatest love, my strongest supporter, my toughest critic, and my wisest counselor.

Earning Gold Wings

From the time I was eight years old I had wanted to be a naval aviator. Earning navy wings is very difficult and very time consuming in the best of circumstances. For me it was considerably more so. I took the exams for Pensacola when I was a sophomore at St. Joseph's College and scored extremely well. In my senior year, however, I received scholarships for graduate study at both the University of Pennsylvania and Cambridge University and my navy aspirations were postponed. After graduation from Cambridge I was commissioned an ensign in the naval reserve as an intelligence officer and promptly put in my application for flight training. While it was being processed I was offered a job working for Dick Allen on Henry Kissinger's National Security Council staff. I accepted the job with the intention of taking a leave of absence after a year or so to go to navy flight training. In the meantime I earned my private pilot's license. My application for flight training was eventually approved, but I was not actually able to take a leave of absence to pursue it until 1974. In the meantime I made four reserve active duty tours each of several weeks to Vietnam where I flew with naval units in my capacity as an air intelligence officer. There were some who criticized the fact that reservists like me, and there were many, who did temporary active duty in Vietnam were awarded Vietnam Service ribbons when they had thirty days in the combat zone.

Thus by the time I finally reported to Kingsville Naval Air Station for pilot training in March, 1974, I had already accumulated several hundred hours of flight time. I was first assigned to VT-23, flying the T-2 basic jet trainer, where I stayed until I was qualified safe for solo. I then moved on to VT-21 for training in the TA4J advanced jet trainer.

My training was once again interrupted in the summer of 1974 when I was recalled to serve as a delegate to the Force Reduction Negotiations in Vienna. While interesting, these negotiations went into recess for months at a time and during those intervals I returned to my flight training at Kingsville. Finally, in October 1976 I returned to Pensacola for the final three weeks of training as a bombardier/navigator. In November I took my final NATOPS exams and flight tests and was awarded my wings as a naval flight officer on November 19, 1976.

It goes without saying that this highly unusual piecemeal training program could not have been done without a senior mentor in the navy. Admiral James Holloway, who was vice chief of naval operations, was able to overcome the bureaucratic obstacles. Nevertheless, because of the unusual nature of my training, I was held to more demanding standards than the normal syllabus. Obtaining my wings on this non-standard timetable had advantages and disadvantages. On the one hand the two years it normally takes from start to final qualification to earn navy wings includes many months of wasted time in pooling and waiting flight assignments. There was no waste of time in my program, and every day that I was in training usually involved two training hops as well as the normal ground school. There were two significant disadvantages to balance, however. Because of the exceptions and waivers allowing the interruptions to the normal syllabus, I was always held to a brutally high standard in NATOPS flight checks. Everyone involved wanted to make sure that the record was replete with every requirement having been met and insuring that my skill level was well above the minimum required at every stage of the training. For each of my final check rides, for instance, an instructor was selected who was about to leave the navy, to ensure that there could be no whisper of going easy on me.

Another disadvantage was, as with Admirals King and Halsey who had gotten their wings mid-career, there were occasional whispers from those who were not my admirers to the effect that somehow I had not properly qualified. The reality was that not only had I accumulated almost twice as much flight time and training as required by the standard program, but I was held to a much more demanding standard in the flight checks that were required.

After earning my wings I was assigned in January 1976 to the A-6 airwing at Oceana, Virginia, where I then flew as a member of various A-6 squadrons for normally two weekends a month and three to four weeks of active duty training with the fleet. I continued in that status throughout my time as secretary of the navy and for several years after leaving the Navy Department.

After earning my wings as a bombardier/navigator, I continued my status of training as a pilot. I returned to Kingsville each year for continuing training in the TA4J. Finally, after I became secretary of the navy I had the chief of naval air training review my training jacket and my log books thoroughly and make recommendations for a training program to complete requirements for designation as a pilot. I requested qualification as a helicopter pilot and the training command designed a syllabus to complete that objective. From February until November 1981 I carried out that training syllabus at Quantico Marine Air Station completing the ground school and flying every weekend. In October I was sent to Pensacola for five days of rigorous final examinations and check rides. These final NATOPS check flights were given by the most experienced instructor available, a lieutenant commander who was retiring from the navy. He was selected because he had the reputation of being the toughest examiner and because he had absolutely no incentive or temptation to cut me even the slightest bit of slack. I passed all of the written and flying examinations and was awarded my pilot's wings on November 1, 1981. The chief of naval air training signed an affidavit declaring that "Upon his designation as a Naval Aviator Commander Lehman had greater proficiency as a helicopter pilot than that of a due course newly designated pilot."

For the six years that I was secretary of the navy I maintained my full qualifications as a helicopter pilot in the UH1N and AH-1J flying primarily with the Marine Corps. During that period I accumulated 600 hours of helicopter time. In that period I also maintained all of my qualifications as an A-6 bombardier flying primarily with the squadrons at Oceana, with the deployed carriers around the world and with Marine A-6 squadrons. The discipline of maintaining these qualifications was invaluable to me in carrying out my responsibilities as SECNAV.

Chapter 2

Kissinger, Vietnam, and the Uses of Naval Power

After a violent 4-G pull to the right, Charlie Ernest then reversed the stick to the left and back, putting the A-6 into a slow aileron roll. "What the hell was that?" I said, eyes like saucers, "a SAM?" "No. Look right there above you." I looked straight up, which, being inverted, was straight down at a dark blue sea and a large green island. There off to the left was a tiny round object growing larger as it seemed to float up toward us. "What is that?"

"An 85mm [antiaircraft shell], but don't worry, we are out of range."

"Oh."

"We have bombed the shit out of that island for seven years, but we've never been able to knock out those triple-A [antiaircraft gun] sites. They're dug back into caves and we just can't get at them. At least they don't try putting SAMs on them anymore," Ernest explained. The island below us was Cat Ba Island, in the entrance to Haiphong Harbor, in North Vietnam.

Naval officers in the ready reserve, in addition to weekend training, are required to do at least two weeks active duty each year, usually with the fleet. From 1969 through 1973, I, like may other reservists, did my annual duty in Vietnam. During each of my tours in 1969, 1970, and 1971, I had seen some action in the South, but this mission on July 8, 1972, was my first (and only) over North Vietnam. As Charlie put it quaintly, "When you first go up North, you tend to ruin a few parachutes before you learn to relax." I was flying as a lieutenant (JG) bombardier with attack Squadron 75 off the aircraft carrier U.S.S. *Saratoga* on Yankee Station. We were flying in a massive daylight "alpha" strike against Haiphong, and our A-6 was assigned the role of SAM suppression. We carried the standard ARM (antiradiation missile) designed to home in on SAM radars. The main strike on the harbor complex was a complete success, and we lost not a single aircraft. Nor did we have to fire our ARM, since not a single SAM radar came on line. Knowing that we were airborne with an ARM, the North Vietnamese switched instead to their less effective backup visual targeting system for their Russian-built SAM. As Winston Churchill said, there is nothing quite so exhilarating as to be shot at without effect.*

Flying in the left seat of the A-6 Intruder was the squadron commander of VA-75, "The Sunday Punchers." Commander Charlie Ernest was typical of the leaders of the naval aviators who fought in the Vietnam War. He was a graduate of Auburn University, Class of 1955, with a graduate degree in physics. He had served a tour as a systems analyst on the whiz-kid staff of the secretary of defense,* and by the time I got to fly with him he had already flown more than 350 combat missions over North Vietnam and was on his third carrier deployment to Yankee Station.

As we sat on the deck waiting our turn, we watched the Phantoms and other A-6s, each loaded with eighteen bombs, being shot off the catapult toward Vietnam. We chatted after we had gone through all the takeoff checklists. "Charlie, after all that you've already done with 350 combat missions, with the brilliant record you've achieved already in your career, with a master's degree in physics, why are you back here for a third tour on the *Saratoga*?" After all, I said, most other aviators have done their year of combat duty out here and that was it, and of course there are, as we both know, those favored ones being groomed for flag who won't ever have a tour over here. We then had to taxi forward and take our position on the catapult. I unfolded the wings and completed the checklist on the right side of the cockpit while he did the power and control checks prior to catapult. As we both put our heads back on the headrests ready for the catapult stroke, he turned to me before he gave the salute that signals the catapult officer to shoot, and he said through the intercom, "You're right. What the fuck am I doing here?" For some reason we both thought that was very funny, and we were laughing into our masks as we accelerated down the catapult track and into the air. He was, of course, joking. He was a warrior and would never be anywhere

---

*Few realize that as the office of the secretary of defense (OSD) has expanded, more and more active-duty military are on the staff doing the work of civilians. As of this writing there are 658 military personnel on the secretary of defense's staff.

but where the action was. Unfortunately, it is often the meek who inherit the peacetime armed services.

Four months later, on November 28, 1972, Charlie was killed off that same No. 2 catapult. As his A-6, loaded with bombs, accelerated down the catapult track, the cathode-ray display, directly in front of the stick, on his instrument panel broke loose because of defective bolts and landed in his lap, jamming the stick back. The jet did an immediate hammerhead stall right off the end of the catapult track, and with the huge box in his lap, Charlie was unable to eject. The bombardier was able to eject the split second before the aircraft hit the water. Another great warrior, Admiral Jack Christiansen, was watching from the flag bridge, and it was he who presented posthumous awards to Charlie's son, Brad, months later. He accepted his father's three Silver Stars, seven Distinguished Flying Crosses, the Bronze Star, thirty-two air medals, and various other awards and ribbons.

Charlie Ernest was one of more than a hundred navy squadron commanders, executive officers, and wing commanders who were killed in Vietnam, a terrible loss of talent for today's navy. The deeper tragedy of their loss and the loss of the thousands of other airmen in the war was that they were used so foolishly by the bureaucrats in the uniformed chain of command in Washington. In every year of the war except 1972 the targets they flew against were by and large meaningless and stupidly selected: suspected truck parks, ferry landings, and others with absolutely no military utility, picked by faraway staff officers pursuing the academic game theory approach of "sending messages" with "surgical strikes" and "measured responses." Every day, men like Charlie Ernest saw their roommates die or be taken prisoner after attacking such nonsensical targets, while they were prohibited from striking targets that could have indeed hastened the end of the war—such as the SAM assembly sites, military staging areas, headquarters, the famous dikes, power plants, and infrastructure of the North Vietnamese economy. When restraints were finally taken off during 1972 by President Nixon and mining of harbors was authorized, the effectiveness of the air force and navy strikes brought the North Vietnamese to capitulate before the end of the year. How sad and tragic that it was not done in 1965.[1]

The entire war, of course, was surreal and full of strange juxtapositions. In July 1971 I was flying with VAL-4, a navy attack squadron that was using borrowed marine OV-10 turboprop aircraft as World War II dive bombers. Vietnamization had removed the last U.S. ground forces from the Mekong Delta region, and we were assigned to give close air support to a South Vietnamese unit that was engaged with a North Vietnamese unit in Dinh Tuong Province. While we were

circling awaiting our turn to be assigned to a South Vietnamese forward air controller, we had the ADF radio turned to Radio Australia. We were quickly assigned
a target that turned out to be a North Vietnamese platoon that was in an exposed
position between two clumps of forest. Just as we started our first dive run the
soothing notes of Debussy's "Claire de Lune" began and played throughout our
four strafing runs as we machine-gunned and fired Zuni rockets at the North
Vietnamese soldiers scattering below us. It was a different war.

In 1972 I spent a week with the 8th Division of the South Vietnamese
Marines with a small U.S. advisory team led by marine major Don Price,
another outstanding warrior. Despite constant ridicule in the American press,
the South Vietnamese were very effectively defeating the North Vietnamese
Army (NVA) and retaking all the ground lost in the initial Easter offensive
begun in April of that year. By the fourth day after I had arrived, the 8th
Marines, who had the sector along the coast, had actually gone past Quang Tri
City, the provincial capital several miles inland. The city was still held by the
North Vietnamese Army. We paused for a day for the other sectors to catch up.
Just offshore the navy destroyers and cruisers were providing massive naval gunfire on the North Vietnamese positions. Since the NVA was ten miles inland,
the naval guns were using rocket-assisted projectiles. We watched for hours
atop an armored personnel carrier, sipping coffee as the naval shells ignited
their rocket boosters, spreading an infernal red glow just under the high cloud
layer as they fired directly over us into Quang Tri City.

There is not a single American adviser who served with the South Vietnamese
Army and Marines during their counterattack in 1972 who was not immensely
impressed with their courage and their effectiveness. Never, however, was an
accurate picture portrayed by the American press. And small wonder. Saigon
was full of VC disinformation agents. There were also many civilians who
appeared to be in sympathy with the North Vietnamese cause, including a few
in the American embassy and U.S. Information Agency (USIA) staffs.

On every one of the five trips I made to South Vietnam I was approached
during the few days I spent in Saigon by various Americans who, knowing I
was on Kissinger's staff, wanted to introduce me to Vietnamese who would tell
me what was "really" going on. Usually the meetings took place in some bar
or in the Caravelle Hotel, and generally the Vietnamese were minor officials
in the South Vietnamese government. Always the pattern was the same: tales
of corruption in the Thieu regime; cowardice in the South Vietnamese Army;
and a plea to reduce support for Thieu. One visit in 1972 was illustrative of
them all. On Tuesday, July 11, before going on active duty, I spent a day in

Saigon with Bud Krogh of the White House staff, who was investigating the problem of drug smuggling. We were asked by two Americans working for the U.S. Customs Service to accompany them to meet with one of their informants. We met with him in Cholon in a bar that looked like a set from a Charlie Chan movie. The informant claimed to have documents proving that General Dzu and President Thieu and a number of other high South Vietnamese government officials were heavily involved in the drug traffic. He offered to turn these documents over to us if the Customs agents would agree to place two members of his "political club" in the Ministry of Customs in the metropolitan police. After an hour's discussion, during which the informant castigated Thieu and one by one extolled each of the seven points currently then being offered by the North Vietnamese at the Paris peace talks, there was no doubt in my mind that the informant was Viet Cong. Our bureaucrats, however, fell for it hook, line, and sinker, as had so many other civilians in the American embassy staffs before them. We spiked that particular effort, but many others succeeded. It was indeed a different war.

While debates over policy issues in the Reagan administration have been at times rather sporty, they are genteel indeed compared to the brawls between the Nixon administration and the Senate in the early 1970s. It is hard to describe today the deep bitterness that characterized the ferocious debate between hawks and doves that Vietnam brought to Washington. By 1969 the Senate had become polarized, and the doves, led by Senator Fulbright of Arkansas, were dedicated to forcing the administration into an immediate withdrawal from Vietnam. With President Johnson being of the same party as the leaders of the House and Senate, there had been some restraint. But now with the Republicans in control of the White House, the Executive felt the full fury of a Democratic-controlled house and senate. The overarching issue was, of course, Vietnam, but foreign aid, strategic programs, defense readiness, and all of defense policy were treated simply as subsets. All these issues coalesced in fundamental challenges to presidential power and a reopening of the most fundamental constitutional issues over which branch of the government was to control foreign and defense policy. Between 1969 and 1974 I worked on 240 different legislative battles involving the president's foreign policy and defense powers.

By the end of my first year on Kissinger's staff I was well stuck in the legislative maelstrom, though I had never intended to be thus occupied. I began as Dick Allen's junior staff member when he was appointed as Kissinger's deputy. Dick is one of the sharpest foreign policy experts I have ever worked with, and he has an intellectual toughness that is very rare in government. I really enjoyed working for him. Unfortunately, those attributes coupled with his personal association as national security adviser to Nixon during the campaign made him a marked man with Kissinger. As an outsider from the Rockefeller camp, Henry could ill afford to have a deputy with closer ties to the president than he had.

Kissinger is without a doubt one of the most effective wielders of bureaucratic power that modern government has seen. He moved with lightning speed to establish total control over the president's national security policy. To do this he had to establish himself as the one and only channel to the president on national security issues. He was able to establish even before the Inauguration that no piece of paper and no human being could reach the president on an issue of national security policy without going through Kissinger. In the earliest weeks he was able to establish with Bob Haldeman and John Erlichman, Nixon's chiefs of staff, that there would be no discussion of any national security issue without Kissinger present. In a conversation once with Bryce Harlow, chief lobbyist in the Eisenhower White House and now counselor to President Nixon, Bryce told Henry that he should not be so obsessed worrying about his access to the Oval Office. Kissinger responded, "You don't understand, Bryce. If I'm not in there talking to the president, then someone else will be."

In constructing his staff he purposely selected people without any ties to Nixon or his campaign organization for the same reason he didn't want Allen as his deputy. The two exceptions to that were Dick Allen and me.

He moved at once on Dick. He ensured that Allen could not have an office in the West Wing with the inner circle, but instead killed him with kindness, giving him the largest, fanciest office on the third floor of the Executive Office Building (EOB), where the rest of the NSC staff was lodged. Unbeknownst to Dick, he then deleted his name from all meetings with President Nixon that took place in those early weeks. At first Nixon asked "Where is Dick Allen?" But after the first month or so, he stopped asking. Kissinger also cut him off from the flow of all important documents. Henry immediately assigned Dick to vast projects, to begin rewriting the entire strategic strike plan, and to take over a total review of worldwide military basing. Realizing what was going on, Dick made a major effort to reestablish access through Bryce Harlow, Erlichman, and Haldeman. Kissinger was smart enough never to oppose any specific request, but it soon became apparent that Henry was in total control and would never let Dick become a functioning deputy. By April 1969, Colonel Alexander Haig, who had been selected by Henry as his military aide, and having no ties to Nixon, was in fact the functional deputy. Dick Allen, to his credit, decided to leave rather than bog down the new administration in a power struggle. He was gone in August.

In the meantime, through the base study, I had been dragged into the battles on the Hill. Senators Fulbright and Symington began major new investigative hearings on U.S. commitments abroad and were deluging the new administration with requests for classified documents. Dealing with that had dragged Allen and me into a full range of other issues with Congress because there was simply no one else on the staff who worried about them, and at the time there was no member of the NSC staff who worried about Congress at all.

When Dick resigned in the summer of 1969, I was suddenly left as the only junior staff member without a senior staff member. At the time the hierarchy on the NSC staff was more formalized than it is today. The policy professionals, of which there were about thirty, were of three ranks: junior staff members and staff members, who worked for six senior staff members. Instead of assigning me to another senior staff member when Dick left, Haig had me report directly to him and to Kissinger because, more and more, events on Capitol Hill were of direct and growing concern to them.

Thus, without either me or Kissinger or anyone else planning it, I became the legislative strategist and had the good fortune of becoming a de facto senior staff member at age twenty-six. I got the title of senior staff member in 1972. The Nixon-Kissinger policy to end the war in Vietnam was pretty well established by the time of the Inauguration (see Kissinger and Nixon memoirs). Its slogan was "Peace with Honor," and its strategy was to begin immediately to turn over the fighting to the South Vietnamese. We were all a bit amazed to find that this had been done in only the most perfunctory way during the Johnson administration. The strategy in the Johnson administration was to have the army secure the countryside, with the Vietnamese essentially standing aside. The pacification program, headed by Ambassador Robert Komer, was aimed at winning the "hearts and minds of the people," but there was very little effort to arm and equip and train the South Vietnamese Army to take on the North Vietnamese Army and the Viet Cong. The new policy of Vietnamization, begun in Johnson's last year, was promulgated very early in the Nixon administration in its first national security policy document, NSSM-1. It was later broadened as a generic policy in the "Guam Doctrine" announced by President Nixon in the summer of 1969.

While I did not think so at the time, in retrospect it was clear that Nixon and Kissinger missed the opportunity to conclude the war in the first year. He had only a brief window to act in order to avoid the Democrats' war from

becoming Nixon's war. If he had ordered the mining in 1969 instead of waiting until 1972, a settlement would in my judgment have come three years earlier. He could have guaranteed the observance of a peace settlement through
the threat of resuming mining and bombing of real targets—a threat he had
the power to carry out before Watergate.

But as in every administration, Nixon underestimated the bureaucratic
entrenchment of existing policy. He also shared the common misperception
that the huge Joint Chiefs of Staff (JCS) bureaucracy could be counted on to
put forward the strongest case for the best use of military force. In my twenty
years of working with them the JCS has nearly always resisted the use of force,
and getting effective contingency plans from them is next to impossible. In this
case the JCS bureaucracy in particular resisted a major policy change, and no
mining options or any other fundamental changes in policy were ever put forward. By the end of 1969 the opportunity had passed, the administration had
embraced the bureaucratic tar baby, and it was now the Republicans' war.

On May 14, 1969, President Nixon announced his decision to withdraw
incrementally all U.S. combat ground forces. It began on July 8, 1969, with
no deadline established for completion, but the process was to be inexorable.
After Saigon fell in 1975, some critics said that the entire Vietnamization program was simply window dressing for a decision by Nixon and Kissinger to cut
and run. That was not the case. Haig, Kissinger, and Nixon all believed that
it was vitally important not to pull out without having first given the South
Vietnamese a fair chance to defend themselves.

It wasn't long before Vietnam policy and the war all became all-consuming
to most of us on the staff, taking on an emotional content in response to the passionate attacks of the antiwar activists in the media and in Congress. Those on
our staff who were basically agnostic on the war at the beginning of the administration became crusaders as Vietnamization unfolded. It was infuriating for
those people on the staff traveling back and forth to Vietnam, seeing the enormous efforts being made by the South Vietnamese, and their success in gradually creating an effective armed force, to see the gross unfairness with which the
American media treated the effort. There were, of course, abuses and corruption
in the Thieu regime, Vietnamization was far from totally successful, and the wisdom of our involvement was indeed debatable. But by 1970 the media became
more and more polemical participants instead of accurate reporters of fact.

In August 1971 I spent three days with John Paul Vann, one of the genuine
heroes of the war. Vann had been a lieutenant colonel and had been forced
out of the army by his strong opposition to the "search and destroy tactics" and

the overall army strategy in fighting the war from 1965 to 1969. He had really been the guiding prophet of the Vietnamization program and had been brought back as a civilian with Kissinger's support and put in charge by General Abrams, the new senior U.S. Army general of the II Corps area in Vietnam, including the Central Highlands, which had defied pacification throughout the war. A former B-29 pilot, Vann flew his own helicopter, and without any set plan we traveled from South Vietnamese unit to South Vietnamese unit throughout the Central Highlands. The North Vietnamese were in the middle of a periodic surge and had attacked several of the fire bases we had visited. Without exception the South Vietnamese had defeated the attacks, including one fortified hamlet we visited just hours after the North Vietnamese had been beaten back. The readiness and the spirit and the success of these South Vietnamese units really was impressive. After getting a debriefing of the fight that had ended just two hours before, we went to see the Montagnard chief in the village outside the fortified hamlet. The chief didn't have much to say, but he gave me a good lesson in Montagnard cuisine. As we were squatting in his hut speaking with him through a South Vietnamese translator, a three-inch cockroach scuttled up the bamboo wall next to the chief. Without taking his eyes off me, his hand shot out, grabbed the cockroach, and he sucked it dry, throwing the husk out the window. I lost my appetite for several days.

Vann always liked to fly in his stocking feet, and, as we departed, he kicked off his Weejun loafers and left them on the deck of the helicopter. As we took off, he banked steeply and circled the hamlet to gain altitude before flying out over the area where the North Vietnamese were still lurking. I told him to be careful that he didn't lose his shoes through the open door. He said thanks for warning him, because exactly that had happened to him the previous week. He looked down and noticed one shoe missing. He immediately reversed course and headed back to the village. His interpreter said, "John, you're not really gonna go back to try and find that loafer, are you?' As the helicopter arrived back over the village, he kicked out the loafer and said, "Hell, no, but the poor son of a bitch who finds it ought to have a matched pair, at least."

As we started to fly out over the North Vietnamese-controlled territory, I heard what I thought might be engine compressor stalls in the jet ranger, or what we in the navy call "chuggs." With a certain amount of concern I said, "John, sounds like we've got an engine problem. Do you hear those chuggs?"

Cracking his chewing gum, he replied, "Nah, relax. The engine is fine. Those are AK-47 rounds. That's the noise they make when they pop through the rotor wash." That really relaxed me!

How depressing to find upon my return to Washington that the press accounts of those North Vietnamese attacks on the sites we had visited portrayed the South Vietnamese as inept cowards who ran every time. The accounts were false and must have been written in the bar of the Caravelle Hotel in Saigon.

More than any other single person, Vann was responsible for the success of the Vietnamization program. Haig and Kissinger always listened to him when he occasionally came to Washington, and all of us were deeply grieved when he was killed in action in 1972. With the initial North Vietnamese onslaught in the Easter offensive of 1972, the South Vietnamese Army's 22nd and 23rd divisions, which Vann had built, were badly beaten and demoralized by a far superior force. With President Thieu's approval, Vann took command of both divisions, fired all the corrupt and inept officers, rallied and rebuilt the divisions, and marched them back to victory at Kontum and Pleiku. It was in the final stages of his victory in retaking Pleiku that he flew his helicopter into the ground on a pitch-black night on his way into the fighting in the city. The president awarded him the Medal of Freedom posthumously.

Things were difficult enough in 1969 and 1970 in holding sufficient support to carry out the Vietnamization program. Then, on April 30, President Nixon ordered the attacks on the North Vietnamese supply lines and staging areas across the border in Cambodia. That sensible military action triggered a new wave of student protests all around the country. The worst possible thing happened. Four students who happened to be near an antiwar demonstration on the Kent State University campus in Ohio were killed by ill-trained and panicky National Guardsmen. This outrage lit a fire storm around the country and on Capitol Hill. Americans had killed Americans. Was this a price worth paying for the war in Southeast Asia? screamed the editorials. Students from all over the country rushed to Washington.

It was too bad they didn't have minicams in those days, because I wish I had a record of the scenes of my daily trek to work at the White House. To protect the White House from siege, the police had rented hundreds of buses, which they put end to end entirely around the White House complex down Seventeenth Street, over E Street to Fifteenth Street, and up Fifteenth Street and back across Pennsylvania Avenue. The White House was literally surrounded by protesters and under siege for several weeks. During that period I had to dress like a hippie every day to work my way through the crowds to the buses, and then crawl underneath a bus, flashing my White House pass just before I was clubbed by a cop on the other side. Then into the EOB, where it was an obstacle course climbing over soldiers in full battle dress sitting in the hall-ways. It was an incredible time.

Emotional opposition to a war that had cost by then nearly fifty thousand American lives in pursuit of a no-win political strategy was understandable, particularly since the public did not have an accurate picture of what was really transpiring, neither from the media nor from the government. At about this time I got my first introduction to the unreliability of the huge bureaucratized U.S. intelligence system. The decision to attack the VC marshaling areas in Cambodia was based in part on the intelligence community's assessment that virtually all of the supplies to the Viet Cong and North Vietnamese in the southern part of South Vietnam came down to the Ho Chi Minh Trail through Laos and Cambodia. But when the Cambodian government of Prince Sihanouk was overthrown and a pro-American government took power in Phnom Penh, we found that over 90 percent of the Communist supplies to the southern part of South Vietnam had always come through the port of Kampong Som and were driven to the border areas in Cambodian Army trucks, with fees being paid to the Sihanouk government.

The last U.S. ground combat forces were withdrawn from Vietnam on August 12, 1972. The president had announced that U.S. air support and naval support and military assistance would be provided to South Vietnam for as long as it was needed. Seeing that Vietnamization had succeeded in the South, and knowing that the war could not be won on the ground unless it was won in Washington, the North Vietnamese launched a massive offensive with their regular army on March 30, 1972: the "Easter offensive of 1972." It was the greatest mistake the North Vietnamese made in the entire war. After substantial success in the early weeks of the offensive, they pushed back the South Vietnamese Army and took Quang Tri, reaching to within artillery range of Hue City. They took Kontum and Pleiku in the Central Highlands and temporarily gained control of the western half of the III Corps area in the South. But after the initial shock, the South Vietnamese Army counterattacked with great success.

President Nixon reacted to the invasion immediately by taking off all restraints from the bombing of North Vietnam and, most importantly of all, authorized the mining of the entire North Vietnamese coast. By the end of the summer North Vietnam was totally defeated in both North and South, and it offered terms. Kissinger prematurely made his famous "peace is at hand" announcement on October 26, 1972, before the last issues had been settled. The North Vietnamese then quickly hardened their position and wouldn't budge. The result was the "Christmas bombing" of December 1972, which, using B-52s and aircraft carrier strikes, utterly flattened the last remaining targets in North Vietnam. They then accepted Kissinger's terms, and the peace settlement was signed on January 27, 1973.

The terms of the settlement were very controversial on the NSC staff. Sven Kraemer, one of the most dedicated and brightest public servants and a personal protégé of Kissinger, accused Henry of a sellout. Kraemer believed that once the treaty was signed and the last U.S. support withdrawn, Congress would never fund the military assistance necessary to enable South Vietnam to continue to deter the North. Kissinger countered that if the North violated the agreements and began infiltrating again into the South, we would resume the bombing and the North Vietnamese knew it. Kraemer responded that the president would never again be able politically to resume the war and it was a hollow bluff.

Kraemer proved to be correct, but when Kissinger negotiated the terms, Watergate had not yet broken. Shortly after the agreement was signed, the Watergate scandal began its rapid destruction of the president's power, and when the North Vietnamese began blatantly to violate the agreement and started building highways and infiltrating forces back into South Vietnam, the president refused to resume the bombing. And then as the presidency collapsed, the bitter foes of the administration, led by Fulbright, Church, and McGovern, were successful in passing a cutoff of funds to the South Vietnamese. When I returned to Vietnam in late 1973, it was a heartbreaking situation. A total of 60 percent of the South Vietnamese Air Force was grounded for lack of spare parts, and fire bases everywhere were rationed to a hundred rounds per month. In the following year, 1974, the last of the military assistance and direct economic assistance funding was killed by the Senate Foreign Relations Committee.

After so many lives had been lost and so much suffering endured, after a smashing military victory in 1972, the U.S. Congress imposed defeat on the South Vietnamese with their funds cutoff. It was then I first learned the meaning of the term "contempt of Congress." This experience seared into the military establishment a determination to avoid in the future any use of military force without full congressional commitment. It dominates the advice of the JCS to this day.

There were, of course, hundreds of other issues we worked on simultaneously, and because Congress was always involved one way or another, I was able to participate in all of the interesting policy issues. It was the most exciting possible life for a bachelor who was a foreign policy junkie. For the first two years we worked seven days a week, fourteen hours a day, with a half day on Sunday. My colleagues were a very high-powered group of interesting people, and there was never any question that they were all tightly under control of Haig and Kissinger. But it was a control that gave everyone a lot of leeway as long as they were carrying out Kissinger's policy direction.

Kissinger had carefully picked the staff, and it was made up of about half career government professionals and half appointees from academia and business. There were many holdovers from the Kennedy-Johnson years and very few conservative Republicans. The overall cast was basically centrist to conservative, but the political appointees on the White Houses staff considered Henry's staff to be a fifth column filled with Democrats. We were therefore all kicked out of the White House dining mess and kept pretty much separate from the rest of the White House staff. That suited Henry just fine. While we resented it at the time, it was a godsend in protecting any taint of Watergate from touching Kissinger's staff.

It was pretty heady stuff for someone my age to be spending his days sitting in on meetings with the president and congressional leaders or taking notes at private meetings between Kissinger and the key Hill barons. Kissinger was a tough taskmaster and had a habit of losing his temper twenty times a day.

When Henry moved to the State Department, he complained to Haig that his office was too big. At the White House, when he would burst out of his office in a rage, there were always people to scream at, but at the State Department his office was so big that by the time he got across to the door, he had cooled off. If you had a tender skin, such outbursts could be humiliating, and they drove some to leave the staff. Many's the time I had Kissinger call me an idiot and worse as he threw one of my papers back at me. But the storm was always over quickly and often was followed by a bit of sly humor, and having just dismissed your recommendation with a tirade, he would then say, "Do you really think that's what we should do?" And get on with it. When once admonished for the harsh language he used when he blew his top at his staff, Kissinger replied, "Since English is my second language, I didn't know that 'maniac' and 'fool' were not terms of endearment."

It really used to bother some of the prima donnas on the staff that Henry would never let any of their names appear on any memorandum, and rarely would any of us on the staff be included in meetings with the president, except occasionally as notetakers. But that was one of the ways in which Henry kept total control over policy direction, and it was exciting enough for me to have my words occasionally signed by Kissinger and acted on by the president of the whole United States.

Al Haig was far more even-tempered, and I would always stumble into his little office outside Henry's to lick my wounds after a wire brushing from Henry. Haig's reputation for coolness under pressure was no myth. In four years working for him, I saw him get rattled and lose his temper only once, and that was after three straight nights without sleep during the Cambodia incursion. They were a great team, and if I failed to convince Kissinger on the first try and if Haig agreed with me, then he would await the right moment and take the paper back in and get it signed.

In my view, loyalty to both superiors and subordinates is one of the most important dimensions of integrity. Both Haig and Kissinger were always loyal to me. I had a particularly bad month in November 1970. Kissinger and the president had been increasingly concerned with the leaks of sensitive information that were pouring out of the Foreign Relations Committee under Senator Fulbright. White House concern with leaks grew to a paranoia that later resulted in the setting up of the infamous "plumbers" under John Ehrlichman to fix the leaks. At a dinner meeting sponsored by the Foreign Service Association, I lamented this hemorrhage of classified documents finding their way immediately into *The Washington Post* and *The New York Times*. The next morning there was a headline in *The Washington Post* saying, "Kissinger Aide Accuses Fulbright of Leaking." Fulbright was furious, and the State Department loved it. By that time, Kissinger and his staff had become highly unpopular with the foreign service establishment, and they loved to see one of us step on our crank. When President Nixon was told about it that afternoon, Bryce Harlow told me that he exclaimed, "Good for Lehman," but the issue got bigger and bigger in the next couple of days. Finally the State Department came over to the president, saying they had negotiated a deal that Fulbright would be assuaged if I would be quietly fired. Knowing that Kissinger was determined to try to keep good relations with Fulbright, I thought I was going to be thrown off the sled. Haig called me over to receive what I expected to be the bad news. He told me what I already knew, that State had made the recommendation to the president. "And what was Henry's reply?" I queried. Haig said, "Henry told State to stick it in their ear."

That flap had barely settled down when I really fell in the soup. I lived in a town house in Georgetown with two good friends, Jim Gidwitz, who worked on the White House staff, and Joe Henwood, who was an active duty Navy pilot. We cohosted a party that was a black-tie *sans pantalons*, continuing an old

Cambridge tradition. There was a maid at the door checking the men's trousers, and everyone wore outrageous shorts. It was all very proper, with no lewd or saucy behavior, but someone stole the guest list, which included some very prominent names, and gave it to Maxine Cheshire, *The Washington Post* gossip columnist. Her headline read "Black Tie, but No Pants." The column was syndicated all over the world, and the White House was deluged with outraged letters decrying the moral decay and carnality in the White House. William Loeb denounced me as a Communist spy in a boxed editorial on the front page of the *Manchester Union Leader*. This time I was sure I was done for.

On Saturday morning I got the inevitable call from Haig. "Henry wants to see you." I marched across West Executive Avenue for what I was certain would be my last meeting with Kissinger. Haig waved me into Kissinger's office with a stony face. When I saw the look on Henry's face I was sure I was dead meat. Without cracking a smile, he said, "Lehman, you are going to have to make a hard choice." Then a long pause. "You are going to have to either keep your mouth shut or your pants on. You don't have to do both." I won't say which one I chose.

The National Security Council was established in the 1947 National Security Act establishing the Pentagon. It was really conceived by Secretary of Defense James V. Forrestal to ensure that the president and his staff did not act alone. The NSC was composed of the president, the vice president, the secretary of state and the secretary of defense, with other officials included by invitation. There was also established a small professional staff of career military and civilian professionals. Truman resented its establishment and never used it until the Korean War. Eisenhower expanded its use and its staff and depended heavily upon it. By then the term "NSC" had become interchangeable, meaning the members or the staff.

Kennedy changed the NSC staff to be part of the White House staff under McGeorge Bundy, bringing to it many noncareer political appointees, and Johnson continued it under Walt Rostow, though the use of full meetings was gradually dropped.

Nixon pledged a reemphasis on the NSC, promising regular meetings and a high-powered staff. He selected Nelson Rockefeller's longtime adviser Henry Kissinger to head the staff and be his national security adviser.

The system really did work extremely well for Kissinger, primarily because he understood power and how to use it, and he shared with Nixon a very clear conceptual view of the world and what American foreign policy ought to be. Events, wherever in the world, were dealt with in a coherent conceptual framework and not as unrelated episodes, in the manner of administrations that followed. There was a realistic direction and consistency to national security policy. Eventually, however, based on their estimate that a troubled America needed détente to recover its balance, they got into a collection of bad deals with the Soviets on arms control, trade concessions, credits, and embassy construction.

Thus it was that Kissinger uncharacteristically found himself talking the pieties he dismissed with intellectual contempt in years prior and years since. To hear him argue that subsidized credits, increased trade, and scientific cooperation and sharing of technology would fundamentally change the nature of the Communist state was—well—embarrassing. Only a year before, he was fond of quoting Lenin: "The West are wishful thinkers, we will give them what they want to think."

Henry was able to keep the bureaucracy basically though not totally on track because he had a very sharp staff and he backed them up. The whip was cracked if anyone went off on forays of his or her own, and an Iran-contra fiasco would have been inconceivable under Henry's rule. He was proud of his staff but rarely ever gave anyone credit. Once when I happened to be in his office when Nelson Rockefeller stopped by, Rockefeller made a remark complimenting Henry on the quality of his staff. Henry replied, "Many people say that, but it's not really true. Look at Lehman here, for instance—an Irishman with a Jewish name—if it were the other way around I would really have something."

On reading the biographies of the Roosevelts and of Harry Truman, one is struck by the huge change that has taken place since Truman's day in the nature of presidential government. As late as 1950 the president had fewer than fifty people on his White House staff. The president spent his day in important policy deliberations and decision-making, not with faceless staff aides and advance men, but with his cabinet officers. Men like Forrestal, Acheson, and Lilienthal were the principal daily influences on the decision-making of the president.

One reads the accounts of Watergate, of the Carter administration, and of the Iran-contra scandal with a sense of shock at how much has changed. The secretaries of defense, state, and of the Treasury, and the director of the CIA have become distant figures, separated across town and by layers of vast new unaccountable bureaucracy around the presidency. Presidents since Truman's time have spent their days in policy deliberations with former advance men, public relations experts, political pollsters, and junior officers. It is a major event for the secretary of state or the secretary of defense to travel across town for a scheduled meeting with the president. There is no opportunity for day-to-day, spontaneous interaction between the president and these men. They have been supplanted by the president's staff aides. One might ask what difference that makes. There is a very large difference in that men and women appointed to seniormost positions in the administration are people of accomplishment, with long, proven records of experience. The emergence of television and the media as the determinants of presidential politics, however, has meant that the presidential candidate is surrounded by imagemakers, pollsters, and advance men, men and women whose interests often are alien to serious policy. They are process people and not substance people. With campaigns now running for years, it is of course natural that, once elected, a president brings with him the entourage that chased his lost luggage and handled the unruly press corps on the campaign trail, the functionaries who saw to it that the balloons were released on time at the rallies during primaries. And, as bad money drives out good, process people drive out substantive people. I have watched it at close quarters in the Nixon, Ford, and Reagan White House. The Carter White House was exactly the same. Instead of fifty people, the president's staff in the executive office of the president now numbers over three thousand. And of these not more than two or three are persons of what the British call "real bottom."

For his own reasons, Kissinger moved immediately to isolate his National Security Council staff from the rest of the White House staff. Bob Haldeman and John Ehrlichman ran the vast White House staff for President Nixon, and they had come from the ranks of advance men and PR experts. They distrusted the NSC staff and resented the intrusion of Kissinger's efforts to keep the president focused on the substance of foreign policy rather than day-to-day image-making and photo opportunities.

In November 1970 I had carefully arranged with Dave Abshire, a founder of the Georgetown Center for Strategic Studies and now the assistant secretary of state for congressional relations, an important meeting for the president to meet with the senior congressional leadership at the White House to get their support for a critical vote on the defense bill, which included essential support for the Vietnamization program. We had done a great deal of spadework, and the president's participation was essential for legislative victory. Two days before the meeting I was notified by one of the scheduling flunkies that it had been decided that there were more important things for the president to do involving a large number of photo opportunities, so they had canceled the meeting. I immediately ran over to tell Haig, and he exploded. He said, "What the hell do a bunch of goddamn account executives from J. Walter Thompson know about running this government! You mark my words, those advance men are going to bring this president to ruin." He then took me in to talk with Kissinger, who reacted the same way. Kissinger immediately went down the hall, saw President Nixon directly, and got the meeting approved. It took place on the eighteenth of November and was a smashing success. Despite Fulbright's determined efforts, we carried the day and got the supplemental funding approved. Although they could not have predicted Watergate, Haig and Kissinger were convinced that the advance-man-dominated White House staff was going to bring about disaster.

When the story broke, none of us on Kissinger's staff believed that the reports of the Watergate break-in that had appeared in *The Washington Post* on September 7, 1973, could be true. Surely even these advance men were not that dumb. Henry Kissinger has related in his own book his shock when on Saturday, April 14, 1973, the president's counselor Leonard Garment confided to him that his "second-rate burglary" had the most far-reaching ramifications.[2] On that same day, *The Washington Post* had broken another sensational story, this time about "hush money" being paid to the defendants in the Watergate break-in—money transferred from the Committee to Reelect the President and traceable to the White House, if not to Nixon himself.

It was in this atmosphere and innocent of the real facts that I walked over that same Saturday morning to see Kissinger about an offer I had had from the assistant secretary of defense, Bob Hill, to become his principal deputy over at the Pentagon. When I walked into the office with my assistant, Trip Mosbacher, Kissinger was holding the morning *Washington Post* with its huge headline about hush money.

I told Kissinger what a great opportunity the job offer was, and that as much as I enjoyed working for him I wanted to accept it and go over to the Pentagon. Kissinger said, "Did you read this story in the *Post* this morning?" I said, "Yes," but I really did not see what bearing that had on the issue. Kissinger said, "This is the end of Nixon. He cannot survive. It is only a matter of time. That means that we are going to have to hold everything together here at the NSC. God knows what the Soviets might do as the presidency disintegrates. I have to hold this place together, and I am going to have to have your help. I can't let you go over to the Pentagon." While I was flattered by his devotion, I was mightily upset at losing the opportunity. I was sure Kissinger was grossly exaggerating what could happen and that he simply did not want me to go join the ranks of his bureaucratic opponent Melvin Laird. But he foresaw what was to unfold.

War Powers

Well before Watergate, however, Congress and the Executive were heading into a constitutional impasse. As legislative point man, I found myself on the grinding edge of a brutal struggle for control of foreign policy, a struggle waged in the midst of a war abroad and a presidential crisis at hand. It has been said that the Constitution is the last resort of an outargued politician. Much of the bitter debate in Congress over Vietnam gradually crystallized into a constitutional issue over war powers, and the division of responsibility between Congress and the Executive over control of military commitments. Opponents of the war resorted early to constitutional arguments, contending that there was no congressional sanction for the policies pursued by the executive in Indochina. They dismissed the twenty-odd authorizations and appropriations statutes facilitating the actions, as the nearly unanimous passage of the Tonkin Gulf Resolution, as the same meaningless "approval" given to Theodore Roosevelt to bring back the White Fleet he had already sent halfway around the world.

More accurate, however, was the view stated by Barry Goldwater:

> The fact is, Congress is and has been involved up to its ears in the war in Southeast Asia. It has known what has been going on from the start, and has given its approval in advance to almost everything that has occurred there. Far from being the innocent dupes of a conspiring Executive, Congress has been wholly involved in the policy decisions concerning Vietnam during the entire span of American commitment there.[3]

Nevertheless, legislative proposals began to appear in 1970 affecting war powers. This in fact has been the normal practice of Congress when they get into political differences with the president on foreign policy issues. It is invited by the vagueness of the Constitution on the distribution of war powers.

War has been identified as that situation in which a nation prosecutes its rights by force. Under that definition, contrary to the popular wisdom, war normally does not involve declaration or the legal formalisms of customary international law.

A scholarly study of the involvement of the United States in war identified 149 cases of the use of force by the United States between the undeclared war with France of 1798 and Pearl Harbor. A more recent study done by the Library of Congress identifies 165 cases of the use of U.S. armed forces abroad between 1798 and 1970. During this same period, however, the United States has actually declared war only five times, and four of those were made only after hostilities were already in progress.[4]

Looking at the intention of the framers of the Constitution does not really provide much help. It is generally accepted that the prevailing view was expressed by Madison: ". . . Those who are not conducting a war cannot in the

nature of things, be proper or sage judges whether a war ought to be commenced, continued or concluded." The power formally to place the nation
in a state of "solemn" war was undoubtedly intended for Congress alone.[5]

But it is equally clear that it was intended, in Hamilton's words, that "If,
on the one hand, the legislature have a right to declare war, it is, on the other,
the duty of the executive to preserve peace."[6] Also, the powers to do so ". . .
ought to exist without limitation, because it is impossible to foresee or to find
the extent and variety of national exigencies, or the correspondent extent and
variety of the means which may be necessary to satisfy them."[7] It is the president alone who is held constitutionally responsible for the nation's readiness
to meet any enemy assault.

Between these two principles, the answers to questions about war powers are
really left for events to decide. What is the meaning of "the power to repel sudden attacks"? What of hostilities such as the war with Tripoli, the insertion of
marines in Lebanon in 1958? In 1983? Of the bombing of Libya in 1986? Of
the escorting of Kuwaiti tankers in 1987? What is Congress's power over the
movement or deployment of the armed forces that it may provide, maintain, and
make rules for—in time of hostilities and in time of peace? These issues offer
so many complexities, such infinite variety, and such inconsistent precedent in
the history of our nation that there cannot be said to be any clearly settled division of power. Congress has sometimes interfered enormously during major hostilities, and sometimes it has not. The 1801 action against Tripoli, the Boxer
Rebellion in 1900, the Panama action in 1903, the Mexican Expedition of 1915,
the Russian expeditions of 1918 and 1920, Nicaragua in 1926, the occupations
of Greenland and Iceland in 1941, Korea in 1950, the Bay of Pigs in 1961, the
Dominican Republic in 1965, Beirut and Grenada in 1983, as well as scores of
lesser measures were actions of war undertaken by the Executive with no formal
and usually no informal authorization or censure from Congress. In nearly all,
however, there were strong criticisms and often direct interference by Congress.

The most infamous example was the Congressional Joint Committee on
the Conduct of the Civil War, set up in December 1861 after the defeat at First
Bull Run. Lincoln called this a "vigilante committee to watch my movements
and . . . obstruct military operations."[8] Robert E. Lee observed after the war
that this committee was worth about two divisions of Confederate troops.

As Watergate destroyed President Nixon's power during 1973, Congress passed
the War Powers Act, which Nixon promptly vetoed. Congress immediately over-
rode his veto, and the War Powers Act is now law. Under this legislation, American
military forces that are deployed in "hostilities or into situations where imminent

involvement in hostilities is clearly indicated" must be withdrawn after ninety days unless Congress acts to approve it. The act on its face seems a clear violation of the powers of the commander in chief, but every president since Nixon has gone out of his way to avoid a test case. Clearly, the escorting of Kuwaiti tankers in 1987 without meeting the notification requirements of the legislation was in violation of it. Congress reacted, however, by continuing to support the escorting.

The year 1973 became increasingly unpleasant as the paralysis of Watergate gradually spread through the American government. Kissinger's own effectiveness, eroded by the Vietnam "peace" settlement and SALT I treaty, dropped further when Al Haig left to become vice chief of staff of the army. He was replaced by another very able military staff officer, Major General Brent Scowcroft of the air force. Kissinger's effectiveness, however, had always depended on his working relationship with and backing from Nixon, and as Nixon became totally engrossed in Watergate, Kissinger was able to accomplish less and less.

The fun went out of the job of NSC staff member as the bureaucracy adjusted to the absence of Nixon's power and came to disregard the NSC staff.

In a major shuffle, Kissinger was able to get President Nixon to appoint him secretary of state in August 1974. For a while he was able to keep both jobs, as secretary of state and national security adviser, but finally under congressional pressure he had to relinquish the latter position. In so doing, however, he was able to get his deputy, Brent Scowcroft, named his successor, and that provided Henry with a very comfortable relationship for the rest of his tenure.

When Kissinger went to State he asked me to accompany him, and he suggested the position of director of political-military affairs, an assistant secretary-level job. It would have been a delight to accept but I was nearing the end of the five-year period allowed for writing my Ph.D. dissertation at the University of Pennsylvania, so I requested a six-month leave of absence.

Leaving the NSC staff in January 1974, I became a visiting fellow of the School of Advanced International Studies of Johns Hopkins University. While there, I completed my Ph.D. dissertation, successfully defended it, and received my degree in June 1974. Subsequently, the dissertation became a book that was published by Praeger, titled *Congress, the President, and Foreign Policy*. Its thesis was that the Constitution does not settle whether Congress or the president should dominate national security policy, but wisely leaves it for struggle to decide.

MBFR

When I had completed my dissertation, Fred Iklé, with Kissinger's approval, offered me the job as a delegate to the Mutual Balanced Force Reduction negotiations in Vienna. He and Kissinger had also agreed to ask me to become Iklé's deputy as the director of the Arms Control and Disarmament Agency, a post that was to become vacant in January 1975. I accepted the package deal. From negotiating with Congress, which in those years often seemed like a not-so-friendly foreign power, it was now my task to negotiate with the government that had always been the major danger to the free world: the Soviet Union. The issues were complex, daunting, and went to the heart of America's most enduring and costly postwar commitment: the defense of Western Europe.

For most of the period following World War II, the United States maintained a "temporary" garrison of about 400,000 troops in Europe. As part of the deal made following the Cuban Missile Crisis, the Kennedy administration embarked on a policy of détente, including withdrawal of the Thor intermediate-range ballistic missiles (IRBMs) from Europe and a gradual and unspoken withdrawal of troops. (The "Pershing II" IRBM was deployed in Europe in 1982, and then its withdrawal was negotiated in the INF Treaty of 1988.) By the end of the Kennedy-Johnson administrations, U.S. forces had been reduced to about 300,000. Characteristically, however, the Soviets, instead of following suit, as McNamara had confidently predicted, steadily increased their forces in Europe, from about 475,000 at the time of the Cuban Missile Crisis to 600,000 in 1969 (largely the result of the invasion of Czechoslovakia in 1967). The idea of negotiations to achieve reductions from these force levels had kicked around foreign ministries throughout most of that period. Outside of professional diplomats, however, there was no interest in the Soviet Union, the United States, or Europe to pursue actual negotiations.

When we were at the Pierre Hotel in New York during the transition in 1968 preparing the policy agenda for the Nixon administration, included in the briefing book sent to us by the Department of State were proposals to begin exploration of possible MBFR negotiations. Kissinger rejected them out of hand.

The political setting, however, was transformed by the world financial crisis and the collapse of the dollar in the spring of 1970. Senator Mike Mansfield used the political alarm in Washington about the fate of the dollar and the burden of the adverse balance of payments to reintroduce his resolution to withdraw unilaterally 60,000 U.S. troops from Europe. A preliminary vote count that I did with Tom Korologos in the White House legislative liaison office showed that Mansfield had a healthy majority of the Senate supporting his resolution. We then put together a strategy to mobilize public and press support. Kissinger invited Dean Acheson to head a bipartisan group of elder statesmen to undertake a major lobbying effort in the Senate. The possibility of MBFR negotiations was used as an argument against unilateral action by the Senate. After a long effort we managed to defeat the Mansfield proposal, but he and his supporters vowed to bring up the issue again, which he did in November. For a second time that year there was another bruising debate, and we again defeated him. Once again, the argument was frequently used that such unilateral action would undercut possible negotiations.

When the Ninety-second Congress convened in January 1971, I warned Kissinger that we were losing ground. John Stennis, chairman of the Armed Services Committee and upon whom we had heavily depended in the previous year's debates, announced that he would vote in favor of cuts, though he said he wanted a smaller size reduction than Mansfield. From that point on there was at any given time a majority of the Senate in favor of reductions. We were able to prevent a rapid enactment because we were able to keep them from coalescing on any given number. Some wanted 100,000, some wanted 60,000, others 20,000.

The Soviets were, of course, watching our debate closely, and thinking to exploit the opportunity, General Secretary Brezhnev on March 30, 1971, announced that he favored reducing armed forces in Central Europe. I seized on the statement and had it spread around the Senate, to reinforce the idea that negotiations were possible and therefore Congress should not cut unilaterally but let us use the offer of NATO cuts to get Soviet troop cuts, although Kissinger was very worried about my tactics actually having the effect of dragging us closer to such negotiations, which he thought would be very counterproductive to NATO solidarity. Brezhnev returned to the subject two months later in a May 31 speech at Tbilisi, where he asserted the readiness of the Soviet Union to begin negotiations on force reductions. This greatly strengthened the Administration's hand in the Senate, but Kissinger and other leaders of NATO were ever more skeptical about the prospects and dangers of actually undertaking such negotiations. There were, of course, many other developments on the diplomatic front, most particularly the Soviet effort to achieve a conference on European security. Nevertheless, the debate in the Senate continued to drive the process. On October 5 the NATO secretary-general, Manlio Brosio, was directed by the NATO ministers to begin exploratory talks with the Soviet government about beginning negotiations.

By early December, however, we had our backs to the wall again in the Senate, and were saved only by a presidential letter sent to John Stennis, that

Stennis read with great drama on the Senate floor on November 23. The letter read, in part:

> Passage of the proposed troop cut would, with one stroke, diminish Western military capability in Europe and signal to friend and adversary alike a disarray and weakness of purpose in the American government. . . . Sincerely, Richard Nixon

The letter dramatically turned the tide, and once again, by a hair-breadth, Mansfield was defeated.

In fact, the Soviets never did receive Brosio, to Kissinger's immense relief, but the process was moving inexorably. In President Nixon's visit to Moscow in May 1972, Nixon and Brezhnev agreed to begin negotiations on MBFR. Preparatory talks began in Vienna on January 30, 1973, and in November the first formal plenary session of the MBFR negotiations was convened in Vienna.

Large international negotiations are really quite a scam. The MBFR negotiations were typical, and it was a brilliant stroke to hold them in Vienna, which had set the style for such negotiations in 1815, when the Great Powers danced their way to a settlement of post-Napoleonic Europe, ending these deliberations at the behest of the Austrian finance minister, who could no longer take the expense. The normal session lasts for about six weeks and then goes into recess for two months. While the negotiations are in session, there is only one plenary session per week. For MBFR they were Thursday afternoon for about one hour. There is, in addition, an informal session lasting from one to two hours each week. There were also formal and informal sessions among NATO members prior to each formal and informal plenary session with the Warsaw Pact negotiators. We also had meetings of the American delegation several times a week. The remainder of the time was available for the cultural and social life of Vienna, of which, as a bachelor, I made full use: the Staatsopera, the Volksopera, the Musikverein, and the wine gardens, restaurants, and coffeehouses that make Vienna so charming. During the two long recesses, I was able to return to active duty with the navy to continue flight training.

During one of these periods I went on active duty with an A-6 squadron VA-176 aboard the U.S.S. *America*. I left Vienna and flew to Naples, where I boarded a navy C-130 to pick up the ship, then in port in the Greek island of Rhodes. This was during one of the many periods of anti-Americanism being whipped up by the anti-NATO elements in Greece, and we had been warned that the Communists were planning a major demonstration against the U.S. Navy during the port visit. As we landed the C-130 and taxied toward the terminal, we saw several hundred people waving at us, we thought in welcome. As we taxied toward them, suddenly the crowd started throwing rocks at the airplane. We immediately wheeled the aircraft and taxied rapidly to the other side of the field. We radioed out to the carrier in the harbor, and they sent a helicopter to pick several of us up. On the way out to the ship we circled around City Hall because we were told that the admiral's chief of staff, Captain Ace Lyons, later to be Pacific Fleet commander, was under siege by a crowd. Sure enough, there were thousands of people demonstrating and burning cars around City Hall. He was later extracted safely by helicopter.

Despite my best efforts in 1974, the negotiations proceeded without interruption and absolutely no progress was made from November 1973 until the date of this writing. The lack of progress is hardly surprising, since neither side was particularly anxious to engage in the negotiations. The negotiations were really the child of debate in the U.S. Senate, and from that perspective stymied any further efforts by Congress to force withdrawals of American troops from Europe for more than a decade.

Once in the negotiations, Soviet objectives were first to prevent any upsetting of the military status quo in Europe, which was much to their liking, and second to attempt to exploit the negotiations by isolating Germany if possible and decoupling the United States from the rest of the NATO allies at every opportunity. As the negotiations proceeded, the unexpected solidarity and harmony among the NATO allies, coupled with the lessening of domestic political pressures that the negotiations brought about in the Senate, forced the Soviets to make a choice between their two negotiating objectives. They could easily have driven a great wedge between the United States and its European allies by accepting a NATO proposal for unilateral withdrawal of 29,000 American troops in exchange for 68,000 Soviet troops. While the military balance would have been slightly improved to NATO's favor, the United States–only withdrawal would have begun a major unraveling of NATO solidarity. Interestingly, the Soviets refused to seize this opportunity because they were more committed to maintaining the military status quo than they were to taking political advantage of an opportunity to "Finlandize" the Europeans by achieving a United States–only withdrawal.

In broader terms, however, the fourteen years of negotiations are standing testimony to the fact that both East and West were generally satisfied with the political-military map of Europe, at least to the extent that both sides seemed to be unwilling to take any risks to change it. That assumption, of course, now bears rethinking in view of the INF Treaty, which once again involves a pending American withdrawal on the NATO side.

I returned from Vienna just before Christmas 1975 to announce my engagement to Barbara Wieland and to become deputy director of the Arms Control and Disarmament Agency.

Arms Control and Disarmament Agency

Like being made a delegate to MBFR after the role I had played in bringing the negotiations into being, there was considerable irony in my becoming deputy director of the Arms Control Disarmament Agency (ACDA). When the ACDA was set up in the Kennedy administration at the initiative of Hubert Humphrey, President Kennedy told Scoop Jackson that the purpose was "to put all the doves in one place where we can keep an eye on them." Kissinger used to say, "The ACDA is not an agency, it is a lobby." When I was nominated to be the No. 2 man in January 1975, the ACDA had an annual budget about the price of one fighter plane and a staff of only 250 people. It had bureaucratic power, however, because its director, or deputy director, sat as a member of the National Security Council whenever arms matters were on the agenda. They also had responsibility for administering all arms control negotiations. In fact, important negotiations like SALT and MBFR were run totally by Henry Kissinger. Fred Iklé had been appointed director in 1973. He is a brilliant intellectual from Rand Corporation and MIT and is one of the foremost strategic thinkers and theorists of the negotiating process. My two years working with him was one long seminar, from which I gained enormously.

The irony of my appointment derived from the role I had played in carrying out a restructuring of the organization in 1972. As part of the deal that Kissinger had made with Scoop Jackson to get his support for the SALT I agreements, Kissinger agreed to get the president to replace all the liberal Democrats in political appointments at the ACDA. Jackson blamed the influence of these disarmament zealots for much that he thought was bad with the SALT negotiating process and result. Gerard Smith, a Republican, had already submitted his resignation as director of the ACDA, but about fifteen political appointees below that level were holdovers from the Kennedy-Johnson administrations. Kissinger assigned me to work with the White House personnel office to replace these people with sound-thinking Republicans. It was done very efficiently and with great civility, despite the legends.

So-called "Schedule C" (noncareer political) appointees and presidential appointees normally resign at the change of administrations. From that perspective, the surviving Democrats in the ACDA had already had four extra years under a Republican administration. Nevertheless, we allowed them as much time as they requested to find jobs before going off the payroll. Fred Iklé was named by the president to replace Gerard Smith as director, and I worked with Iklé to build a very strong staff of conservative Republicans and Jackson Democrats, of a uniformly high quality. At the time I had no expectation ever to go to the ACDA, but when in fact I arrived three years later, I found myself among friends.

That was hardly the case, however, when I went before the Senate Foreign Relations Committee for my confirmation hearings. My old nemesis Senator Fulbright had happily been defeated in the previous election, but nevertheless he mounted a full-scale lobbying effort to defeat my nomination. His old friend Stuart Symington took up his cause and led what turned into a brutal fight to defeat me. He was joined by all the doves on the committee, including Church, McGovern, Pell, Clark, and Biden.

Rarely has the Senate seen such bitterness as all the pent-up bile from my five years as Kissinger's legislative quarterback came spilling out. The bruising battles over Mansfield amendments and end-the-war efforts obviously had left more grudges than I had realized. During five hearings over a period of three months, left-wing zealots on the Foreign Relations Committee staff exhumed everything I had ever written or that had ever been written about me. They sent gumshoes to the University of Pennsylvania to pore over my Ph.D. dissertation and interview the examining committee there in the hopes of finding some flaw. During every hearing I was grilled and cross-examined for hours.

The denouement came during the fifth and final hearing when, after failing to draw any real blood despite all the staff research, Symington made a last-ditch effort to undo me. In the fourth hearing he had declared that he had inside information from a member of Kissinger's staff that Kissinger did not really support my nomination because of my known skepticism about his SALT policies. At this, the chairman, Senator John Sparkman of Alabama, who had slept through most of the hearing, ordered the staff to send a cable to Kissinger—who was in the midst of his shuttle diplomacy among Israel, Egypt, and Syria—requesting clarification of his position on my nomination.

In the fifth hearing, Kissinger's reply, supporting my nomination, was read into the record by Senator Sparkman. At this, Symington, in total frustration, objected and asked that the cable be stricken from the record because there was no signature on it. Even the somnolent Sparkman had trouble with that one. He rebuked Symington, saying that obviously with Kissinger in Egypt, a cable could hardly be signed in Washington, and with that he called for a vote. I was confirmed on a 9–7 vote in which Senator Hubert Humphrey, who normally voted with the doves, spoke in my favor and voted for me. His was the decisive vote, and even after the vote was recorded there was a furious effort for about an hour by the staff and by Senators Symington and Church to persuade Humphrey to change his vote. He wavered for a while and notified the chief clerk that he was reconsidering, but then Senators Gale McGee and Scoop Jackson got to him and firmed him up.

Among the reasons for Senator Humphrey's favor was that he knew me personally not to be the monster of political myth. By good luck I had spent a day with him outside Vienna during my time at MBFR. Humphrey had made an official visit to the negotiations and wanted to visit an orphanage outside town, and I offered to drive him out there. It was, in fact, a very heartwarming day. Humphrey had been supporting this Austrian orphanage ever since World War II, though he never publicized it. I marveled at how happy he was spending the whole day playing with the children and talking with the staff. Behind his public image of a compassionate man was indeed a fine human being.

I never would have been confirmed at all had it not been for Scoop Jackson's strong lobbying behind the scenes and the magnificent efforts of Senator Gale McGee, a Democratic member of the committee from Wyoming. Not a single Republican on the committee would take up my cause, but Gale McGee became incensed at the first hearing at what he saw was a Fulbright-led derailment. He then was my counselor and my barrister throughout, although it actually cost him politically. He and Jackson were two of the finest men I ever worked with in the Senate.

My two years spent at the ACDA were occupied principally with the negotiating efforts to reach a SALT II agreement. The last two years of every president's administration since the SALT process began in 1967 had been characterized by an accelerating rush to achieve an agreement before the end of the president's term. Johnson, Nixon, Ford, Carter, and Reagan have been hooked by that political narcotic. The Soviets have become very adept indeed in using such frantic periods to extract inordinate concessions.

President Ford and President Brezhnev of the Soviet Union held a summit at Vladivostok in November 1974 and agreed on a framework to negotiate a permanent SALT accord to replace the SALT I interim agreement. Ford had agreed to put a ceiling of 2,400 each on the total number of intercontinental ballistic missiles, submarine-launched missiles, and heavy bombers. He had also agreed to a sublimit on the numbers of missiles that could be armed with multiple warheads, MIRVs. Of each side's total of 2,400, only 1,320 could be multiple-warhead. Kissinger and Ford ultimately failed to achieve an agreement, primarily because there was such deep division in their own administration and in Congress over the issues exempting the Soviet Backfire bomber and including a ban on sea-launched cruise missiles.

While Kissinger and I have remained loyal friends, our relations fell to a low state during Ford's last year. Iklé and I argued forcefully against the concessions that were made at the Vladivostok summit, and we joined forces with Secretary of Defense Don Rumsfeld and Admiral Jim Holloway, chief of naval operations, in opposing the drafted SALT II agreement.

One of Iklé's real accomplishments during that two-year period was to achieve the negotiation of a threshold test ban that for the first time included on-site inspection to verify the terms of the treaty. The Soviets agreed to accept American teams present at Soviet test sites, and we accepted the right of Soviet teams to be present at American test sites. Iklé did a masterful job of running those negotiations, and ultimately they were a complete success. Unfortunately, they were not ratified by the end of the Ford administration, and the Carter administration asked the Senate to put it aside because they wanted instead to negotiate a total test ban, something they utterly failed to do. At this writing the threshold test ban still awaits ratification by the Senate.

After President Carter's election in November 1976, I remained as acting director to oversee the transition until January 20, though I had submitted my resignation effective on that date. Paul Warnke was President Carter's nominee to be ACDA director, and as soon as he took office he purged Republicans down to the ribbon clerks. In an amusing example of the double standard of the Washington press corps, not a word was ever written about Warnke's purge, yet articles are still being written about my "purge" of the ACDA, though I replaced fewer than a third of those Warnke did. Republicans replacing Democrats is a purge, while Democrats replacing Republicans is "bringing in fresh, new talent."

Chapter 3

Why I Wanted the Job
and How I Got It

On January 19, 1977, I turned out the lights as acting director of the ACDA and walked out of the office (once described by Dean Acheson when he occupied it as "having all the charm of a salon on a North German Lloyd Steamer") for the last time. To avoid conflicts, I did no job-seeking until out of government. Strategic corporate planning for international aerospace companies appealed to me, and I borrowed a stake to open a consulting company at Eighteenth and K streets in Washington. Former ambassador Seymour Weis, retired air force general John Vogt, Dr. Haakon Lindjord, my brother, Joe, and, three years later, Richard Perle eventually joined up. These were talented and agreeable people. We focused especially on European marketing and joint ventures, and we grew steadily.

A few weeks after I left the ACDA, I broke my foot while jogging, and thus it was that Barbara assisted me up the hospital steps on March 11 on her way to delivering our first child, Alexandra Constance.

In my spare time, Bill Brock, chairman of the Republican National Committee, had asked me to chair the RNC Advisory Council on Defense, part of an excellent shadow government. (It is in many ways more fun to be in opposition than in power. Our polemics in those years smote Carter and Brown hip and thigh!) Periodically we issued white papers articulating the Republican alternatives to Carter policies. Senator John Tower asked me also to assist him as chairman of the Republican Policy Committee, in a continuing effort to back up Republican senators' efforts to improve the Carter defense budgets, and particularly to fight the administration's efforts to cut down the navy. I shared Tower's concern about the severe problems the navy faced, certainly not all the making of President Carter.

That it took nearly a full year of zealous effort, strategy, and coercion to retire Admiral Rickover illustrates how deeply rooted were the ills that afflicted the navy. They were decades in the making and by 1980 had really debilitated the institution. The decline began shortly after World War II.

In the years immediately following World War II, the navy basked in the deserved glory of the greatest naval victory in recorded history. The war in the Pacific had been a naval war. It had been brilliantly controlled by Roosevelt and commanded by Nimitz and MacArthur. The titanic struggle for the mastery of Europe was determined by vast armies and air forces. But the Allied victory could not have been accomplished without the achievement of total maritime superiority by the U.S. Navy, with major assistance from the Royal Navy. Hitler had failed in Russia not only because of a heroic defense by the Russian people but also because that defense was made possible by naval shipment through contested waters of the millions of tons of tanks, ammunition, and the logistics of war. It was made possible because 40 percent of Hitler's army was tied down uselessly around the entire periphery of Europe, defending against a maritime invasion that could come from any direction.

Ironically, it was the very magnitude of the navy's victory at sea that began its equally historic postwar decline. Franklin Roosevelt had spent eight years as an assistant secretary of the navy under Josephus Daniels and was a naval person through and through. During the war, his naval orientation so infuriated the army that at one point in a meeting at the White House, General George Marshall, chairman of the Joint Chiefs of Staff, exclaimed, "Mr. President, I must insist that you stop referring to the U.S. Army as 'them' and the navy as 'we.'" When Harry Truman succeeded Franklin Roosevelt as president, he brought with him an antipathy to the navy and marine corps that was at least equal to that of George Marshall. General Marshall produced almost immediately proposals long under preparation in the War Department to bring about substantial reduction of naval influence and resources. While there were many versions of the proposals, the version put forward to the president was an update of the Collins Plan, named for General Lawton Collins, who prepared it at the direction of General Marshall. Clothed in the rhetoric of motherhood and unification, it was sold as a final solution to the urgent need to end "interservice rivalry." It called for the consolidation of all of the military services in one department. While that was the rhetoric, the actual details of the plan simply abolished the Department of the Navy, with the component forces put under the War Department, renamed the Defense Department.

To gain the support needed to get congressional approval for such a plan, its advocates had to accept the paradox of going in the opposite direction by reluctantly granting the army air corps its long-sought independence and by offering the air force the added incentive of acquiring all naval and marine corps aviation.

The battle over unification occupied Washington even more than the cold war in 1946 and 1947. The establishment of the Department of Defense in 1947 was a compromise solution. Thanks to Secretary of the Navy James Forrestal, the navy had won very significant compromises in retaining some independence within the new department, but it had lost the bureaucratic war. When Forrestal died in 1947, after becoming the first secretary of defense, the navy lost its only strong spokesman in the administration. He was succeeded by Louis Johnson, who, with President Truman's blessing, went after the navy and the marine corps with a vengeance. The arena was the fiscal 1950 defense budget, in which President Truman set a ceiling of $14.4 billion, a reduction from the $21.4 billion proposed by the joint chiefs. While all of the services objected to the drastic reductions in the budget, the new balance of a two-to-one Air Force/Army versus Navy Department ensured that the overwhelming brunt of the cuts fell on the Navy Department. Strongest support was given to the air force and its defense strategy based on a nuclear air offensive against Soviet cities.[1] So drastic was his onslaught that it precipitated the famous "revolt of the admirals" in congressional hearings in October 1949. After the navy testified, Captain John Crommelin, Admirals Blandy and Bogan, and the CNO, Admiral Louis Denfeld, were all fired. The secretary of the navy, John L. Sullivan, had resigned the previous April when Johnson ordered the new carrier *United States* broken up on the building ways at Newport News. While one of the symptoms of the debate was the B-36 strategic bomber versus the supercarrier, it was really the much wider issue of naval versus land forces that was at issue.

JCS documents recently declassified show how complete the power shift to the army and air force was within the JCS. On January 24, 1950, against the navy's objections, the joint chiefs modified the overall defense plan from one of global focus giving high priority to Middle East oil and Far East strategic areas to one entirely focused on Europe. The January 24 revision eliminated the assignment of forces for the defense of Persian Gulf oil and earmarked them for Europe. In the policy papers leading up to the decision, the joint chiefs pointed out, "In their opinion, if the Western powers lose Western

Europe, they lose the war. On the other hand, the loss of the Middle East in the early stages of the global war would not in itself be fatal. The strategic defense contemplated for the Far and Middle East indicates that those areas are for planning purposes, now considered to be in a lower category than Western Europe."[2]

By 1950, the navy and marine corps share of the defense budget had dropped from half to almost a quarter. The fleet was slashed to less than a quarter of its size in 1945, and all but 6 of the 110 aircraft carriers had been ordered decommissioned. The naval officer corps had been decimated and billets shifted wholesale to the army and the new air force. In flag officers, the prewar ratio was shifted to a ratio of a total of 750 army and air force generals and 250 navy admirals, where it remains to this day.

The outbreak of the Korean War in June 1950 and an immediate trebling of the defense budget reversed the Truman disarmament, and many ships were pulled out of the breakup yards and hastily returned to sea.

President Truman was succeeded by General Dwight Eisenhower, who shared his predecessor's lack of enthusiasm for the naval service. Successive reorganization legislation in 1952 and 1958 consolidated the Marshall victory. While in theory the Department of Defense was created de novo, it was in fact the organization, structure, and bureaucracy of the War Department. The staffing from the very beginning was approximately a total of four army and air force officers to one navy/marine officer, a ratio that has endured to the present day.

The next five presidents after Eisenhower were all former naval officers, but the weight of the bureaucratic institution kept the balance the same. Unlike the army and the air force, the navy was required to deploy around the world on six-month deployments. In 255 crises since World War II, the navy was sent by the president as the principal arm of American foreign policy. The constant theme in navy testimony during the 1950s, 1960s, and 1970s was "We will have to do more with less." As peacetime budgets shrank, cold war and crisis management commitments steadily increased. Beginning in 1965, the navy entered a decade of ten years of wartime operational tempo off Vietnam. During that period, because for political reasons the administration would not ask Congress for the increased money actually being spent in Vietnam, money for shipbuilding, maintenance, and modernization was diverted to fund fleet operations on Yankee Station and in South Vietnam. By 1973 the backlog of ships requiring overhaul that could not be fixed for lack of funds had grown to seventy-five. The fleet itself had shrunk to about five hundred ships. The navy assumed that when the Vietnam war ended there would be a major period of rebuilding. The postwar wave of antidefense feeling in Congress, however, prevented that. The navy budget declined 22 percent in real terms between 1973 and 1980.

One of the most unfortunate side effects of the unification of the services within the Department of Defense has been the transformation of all of the service headquarters' staffs into budgeteers and programmers rather than war fighters and strategists. In his biography of Admiral Ernest King, CNO during World War II, Thomas Buell recounts that King spent a total of one hour on the entire navy budget during 1945. In *Forrestal Diaries* one looks in vain for discussions of budgetary maneuvering. Since their consolidation in the Department of Defense, the JCS and the secretaries of each of the services spend at least half of their time in the budgetary and programming process each year. The staffs of the military departments now each number about three thousand souls, of whom more than 80 percent are engaged in the planning, programming, and budgeting system (PPBS) process. The best path to success in each of the military services has come to be agility and effectiveness within the bureaucratic process rather than in operational and war-fighting skills. While we have had some superb leadership and war-fighting records among our last five chiefs of naval operations, four had spent their principal Pentagon tours as programmers.

Although Robert McNamara brought some much-needed budgetary discipline to the Pentagon process, he also brought one of the great heresies of our time, the cult of "systems analysis." Putting some tough restraints on the infinite desire of the uniformed services to develop quicker, slicker, and thicker weapons is one of the greatest management tasks of the civilian leadership of the Pentagon. The tools of empirical analysis can be very useful in providing a framework for making such judgments. Unfortunately, such useful tools once set in motion within the government bureaucracy are very often carried to absurd extremes, and this is exactly what happened to systems analysis in the 1960s and 1970s in the Pentagon. Instead of a tool, it *became* the decision process.

In self-defense against McNamara's whiz kids, each of the services created its own whiz kid staff of systems analysts, and the total focus of the service leadership within the Pentagon came to be consumed in these bureaucratic budgetary wars. The grafting of the systems analysis cult onto the navy had particularly unfortunate effect. Given the overwhelming engineering bent of the naval officer corps and the effects that Rickover's obsession with engineering were having throughout the navy, the seeds of systems analysis found naval waters most hospitable, and they grew like hydrilla, choking off strategic thinking.

The result of these trends was the disappearance within the navy itself of any coherent rationale for the navy and its historic mission. One looks in vain through the congressional testimony of the late 1960s and 1970s for a consistent intellectual case for the navy. There is much talk of cost-effectiveness, trade-offs of statistical trends in readiness in personnel, and chart after chart after graph. Things that could be quantified, put into statistics, and massaged by computers became the total product of the Department of the Navy headquarters. This took place in spite of the fact that there were very able and strong naval leaders at the time. They were, however, fully occupied with the dual challenges of fighting the escalating war in Vietnam and scrabbling for sufficient funds to keep the rest of the navy from being destroyed to pay for the war.

The Vietnam War wrought terrible strains in all the services. The corrosive criticism and ridicule in the American media, the divisive and bitter opposition from the Senate doves; and the refusal of the Johnson administration to fund the war effort adequately, forcing the services to destroy their infrastructure to pay for the daily bombs, beans, and bullets necessary to conduct the war—all had devastating effects on each of the military services. As if that were not enough, the racial tensions in American society, when placed in the crucible of a naval ship at war, created a special devil's brew.

In 1970 and 1971 the navy suffered its first real mutinies since the nineteenth century. On the *Hassayampa*, the *Kitty Hawk*, and the *Constellation* there were racial incidents that escalated into riots, sit-downs, and flat refusals to obey orders.

When I was on active duty for training aboard the carrier *Saratoga* on Yankee Station in 1972, no white officer would walk unescorted on the second deck, where the enlisted mess was. There were many incidents of racially inspired muggings and beatings by both blacks and whites and including some officers. In the enlisted mess itself, one never saw blacks with whites. It was totally polarized.

Admiral Elmo Zumwalt came in for some criticism for setting up a channel on racial matters outside the chain of command and other reforms loosening discipline. They may indeed have contributed to precipitating the crisis, but the real causes were much larger. Whatever mistakes he made, Zumwalt's determination to achieve real racial equality in the navy succeeded. Much credit belongs to him and to his successor, Admiral James Holloway. By personal leadership these men transformed the attitudes and practices within the navy that had given credibility to the charges of racial injustice and had helped to spark the problems. They dealt sternly with the bad actors, but they moved dramatically and at great political expense to themselves to rid the navy of the ingrained practices that were inherently prejudicial to minorities. As a result, the navy I inherited in 1981 had as healthy racial attitudes as any organization in the United States. Genuine equal opportunity had been established.

The Nixon administration came to office with one overwhelming defense priority, and that was to end the Vietnam War, to achieve "peace with honor." Nixon and his national security adviser, Henry Kissinger, were very well disposed toward the navy for its political utility. In my five years working for them both, I cannot recall a single crisis where the refrain was not heard, "Where are the carriers?" From the first crisis we faced, with the shooting down by the North Koreans of the navy's EC-121 in 1969, until the 1973 Yom Kippur War, time and time again the principal military tools used by the president were the navy and the marine corps. There was certainly no antipathy in the Nixon White House to the army or the air force and their essential and often less-well publicized roles, and indeed both received full support and consideration. The navy received inordinate attention by the simple fact of geography.

The appreciation of the navy was far less by the secretary of defense, Melvin Laird. He was a fair-minded man, but he was soon overwhelmed by the anti-naval bias of the entrenched OSD bureaucracy. Based on the same phony OSD systems analysis used before and since, he approved and carried out the reduction of the fleet from 950 ships in 1969 to 505 ships by 1975, and he reduced the aircraft carriers from 24 in 1969 to 13 by 1975. This took place despite the opposition of Kissinger, because Laird's strong congressional base enabled him to maintain far more independence from the White House than any other cabinet secretaries. One day in early 1973 I was talking to my friend Vice Admiral Bill Houser, the deputy CNO for air and a fellow alumnus of Ocean City, Somers Point. He lamented that Laird had just ordered two more carriers retired early, including the *Franklin Roosevelt*, which had at least another fifteen years of life. I immediately told Kissinger, and he got the president to overrule Laird. After a decent interval, Laird simply had the appropriations committees legislate the retirement of the carriers.

Because of Kissinger's concern for the decline of the fleet, one of the last studies he commissioned before relinquishing his title as national security adviser was a comprehensive review by the National Security Council of our naval force structure. This study, in which I participated, went on for two years and resulted in a national security decision memorandum that called for rebuilding the Navy to about 600 ships and 15 aircraft carriers. It was the thinking and reading I did during this study effort that was the real basis for the program I put together for my tour as secretary of the navy. This study formed the basis for the naval budget put forward by President Ford in his last budget, beginning a major rebuilding of the navy. It was, of course, a lame duck budget and, like Jimmy Carter's 5½ percent real-growth budget four years later, it was undoubtedly more generous than it would have been had it not been lame duck.

When the Carter administration came into office with Harold Brown as secretary of defense, the navy rebuilding died aborning. Though Carter himself was a Naval Academy graduate, he shared Rickover's view that except for nuclear submarines, the navy was of marginal utility. Brown, a former secretary of the air force, made no bones about his belief that the navy was of quite secondary utility. As a result, there was a major reduction in support for the navy during the Carter years.

At the end of the Vietnam War and the end of the draft, the Nixon administration embarked on a bold initiative to create an all-volunteer armed force. Huge increases in enlisted pay were enacted, but because of the post-Vietnam antipathy to military service, the initiative got off to a very shaky start. Through the rest of the 1970s none of the services was able to attract sufficient numbers of high-quality enlistees to meet its requirements. After the initial pay raises of 1973, there were no more pay raises until 1980. During that period we saw inflation grow to nearly 20 percent, which had the effect of pauperizing much of the enlisted career force in all the services. The navy was hardest hit because, in addition to the declining standard of living, sailors were subjected to more and more family separation. Despite the fact that the fleet was being cut in half, more and more commitments for fleet deployments were added by each administration throughout the 1970s. As a result, enlisted retention dropped by 1979 to the lowest ever recorded. The navy nearly had to resort again to press-gangs. Recruits were accepted who were illiterate, convicted felons, drug users, and worse. And, of course, the bad drives out the good, so the decline accelerated to the point where by 1979 the fleet was manned at only 91 percent, four ships could not sail that year because of undermanning, and the CNO, Admiral Thomas Hayward, testified that we had a one-and-a-half-ocean navy for a three-ocean commitment.

Even more disturbing than these sad things, however, was the collapse of self-confidence in the naval officer corps itself. The negative developments had seemed to have reached a critical mass. There was fragmentation into narrow communities: aviators, submariners, etc. Turning inward, debate centered on unimportant programmatic issues rather than the important issues of mission, purpose, and strategy.

With the navy leadership fully engaged in keeping the ship from sinking, there was no integrating vision that provided coherence and direction to the countless enterprises of operating ships, designing missiles, and training sailors.

Like Paul on the road to Damascus, I remember the exact moment when I suddenly decided that I wanted to be secretary of the navy.

On March 28, 1978, at the invitation of President Carter's secretary of the navy, Graham Claytor, I accompanied him to the annual secretary of the navy's Strategic Conference at the Naval War College in Newport. I sat in the audience with about three hundred naval officers from rank of lieutenant commander to admiral. The main speaker was President Carter's young assistant OMB director, Randy Jayne. Jayne's speech had me slack-jawed. It was a condescending attack on the navy. It was an accurate reflection of the reigning attitudes in the Carter administration. As the naval service was attacked as a service without a mission, with no coherent ideas, I began to fear for the man's personal safety. But as a I looked around me I was amazed to find that instead of gritted teeth and clenched fists I saw heads nodding in agreement. It suddenly dawned on me that here was a collapse of spirit; this crew was really whipped. It was the kind of cynical defeatism found in the French Army in the 1930s.

Then and there I thought, "This outfit is really in trouble, and I want to do something about it."

From that point on it became a kind of crusade for me to get the Carter administration out and the Republicans in before the navy reached the point of no return.

While I was handling congressional relations for Henry Kissinger, I also came to work closely with George Bush. Bush was a junior congressman from Texas but one of the most effective and active spokesmen in the House on national security issues, and we depended on him a great deal. We had worked together from time to time through the remainder of the Nixon and Ford years, and when he indicated in 1977 that he was going to make a run for president, I offered to help in any way I could. During the next four years I was one of his national security advisers, and I met with him from time to time to brainstorm various national security issues, particularly defense and SALT policy. Unlike most candidates, Bush used these sessions more to bounce his ideas off his advisers, using them to help mold and polish and integrate his policy thoughts rather than receiving positions from them. Bush's policy positions in the campaign were his own, and the sessions at his home in Kennebunkport and in Washington in which they were put together were very lively.

Shortly after the SALT II treaty's signing, Bush was called by the White House to come over and be briefed on the treaty. Bush was seen as the principal rival to Reagan. The administration, knowing Reagan was hard against the treaty, wanted to persuade Bush to favor it. As I was one of Bush's campaign advisers, he asked me to come with him to the White House briefing. We were ushered into the Roosevelt Conference Room, across the corridor from the Oval Office. It was my first return to the room since Carter took possession, and I was amused to note that the portrait of Theodore Roosevelt was gone along with the other bits of TR memorabilia. The briefing was given not by Carter or Brzezinski but by Brzezinski's deputy, David Aaron. Bush listened carefully. Aaron's briefing indicated that Aaron himself had not been accurately informed on what the treaty actually conceded to the Russians on heavy missiles, Backfire and Tomahawk, and otherwise he made a most convincing case. Bush had been a participant in the SALT process since 1969 and knew the issues in detail. He knew a bad deal when he saw one.

Bush had already formulated very well his thoughts on what was wrong with the SALT II agreement, and he opposed it vigorously during the rest of the campaign. His objections were that the totals of warheads and vehicles allowed by the Treaty were too high; that the Russian Backfire bomber was permitted in addition to the Russian allowance in the Treaty; and that the sea-launched cruise missiles, in which the United States had a great advantage, were banned in a protocol.

Bush felt even stronger concern about the Carter policies with regard to the navy. Bush had joined the navy as soon as he graduated from high school, and he became the youngest carrier pilot in the navy in 1943. He saw a great deal of action in the Pacific, and he was awarded the Distinguished Flying Cross after he was shot down by the Japanese over the Bonin Islands. He had a hair-raising escape from the Japanese and was rescued by a submarine, the U.S.S. *Finback*. He then spent the entire patrol aboard the *Finback* and was depth-charged several times. It is a very useful experience for any future leaders to learn early in life that there are forces and people in the world who are very mean indeed. George Bush has taken a realistic approach to national security because of his war experiences.

As CIA director he had watched with great concern the growth of the Soviet fleet and had participated and at times dominated the NSC navy study done during the Ford administration. Very early, we put together a six-hundred-ship navy program as a central plank of his 1980 campaign.

When Bush withdrew from the primaries in April 1980, Dick Allen asked me to join the Reagan team, and I became a member of the campaign's National Security Advisory Group.

Early in the spring, Senator John Tower was chosen as chairman of the Republican Platform Committee, and he asked me to be the draftsman for the National Security Subcommittee headed by Congressman Jack Kemp. In this capacity I attended the convention in Detroit.

To my great satisfaction the platform committee of some two hundred members and the full convention strongly supported a very tough defense section in which the modernization of the navy formed a central plank. As chief draftsman it was my pleasure to carry out the will of the convention.

The platform read in part: "Of all the services, the navy and marines suffered most from Mr. Carter's cuts. . . . We will restore our fleet to six hundred ships. . . . We will build more aircraft carriers, submarines, and amphibious ships."

When the campaign started in earnest, Ronald Reagan and George Bush each found that the defense plank, and particularly the navy theme, always got a strong audience response, and as the campaign wore on, it was stressed more and more. The theme of the deterioration to a second-class status of our military manpower and the sad state of our navy gained a great deal of credibility as the press gave more and more coverage to the human-interest stories of sailors' wives on welfare and ships that couldn't sail from Norfolk. The seeming powerlessness of the United States during the collapse of the shah and the subsequent hostage situation directed more and more attention to defense and to the navy. Our successful effort to defeat the SALT II treaty gave added strength to the issue. And the fiasco of the Desert I rescue operation, failing as it did in part because of inadequate training and equipment problems, increased public interest. (The Navy helicopters used in the rescue were from squadrons that were each short some fifty maintenance technicians, because of low retention, and had fewer than a third of their spare-parts allotment. Two of them broke down and had to be abandoned in the desert because of maintenance problems. The Marine pilots had almost no training on those Navy versions of the CH53 helicopters.)

By the time Election Day arrived, the navy and the defense issue had become very major parts of the mandate the president was seeking, and when he won by such a landslide, we began to carry it out with great enthusiasm.

Right after the election, David Abshire, the distinguished head of the Georgetown Center for Strategic and International Studies, and I were appointed cochairmen of the national security transition. We were charged with organizing and carrying out the staffing and the initial agendas for the

State Department, the Defense Department, the CIA, the National Security Council, and other agencies involved in foreign and defense policy. The transition office was opened on M Street in Washington, and we worked from early November until January 20 doing the staff work so that each cabinet secretary could hit the ground running and with an agenda that derived straight from the platform and campaign issues, and drawing up for the top policy jobs slates of people who had policy views congenial to the president's mandate.

There are about five hundred policy-level jobs in the national security area and, except for the glamour jobs, finding people of proper qualifications and policy orientation who can be persuaded to come into the government is not an easy task. Just before President Ford left office, he granted a 30 percent pay raise to Congress and the senior executives in the government. We then had four years of double-digit inflation, and when Carter was asked to do the same thing Ford did, he refused. Thus we had to persuade people in the midst of their careers with mortgages and tuition bills appropriate to their careers to move to Washington to live on a small fraction of their salaries in private life. This is less of a problem for cabinet officers, since most candidates are millionaires anyway, but for all of the essential subcabinet jobs it is a very serious obstacle to recruiting. Particularly for jobs in the Pentagon, finding willing people who have proven records in managing large enterprises is especially difficult. I took a very special interest in the staffing of the Pentagon, and by the time Secretary Weinberger was named by the president we had about five good candidates for every job in defense. Persuading them to take the jobs was another matter.

On behalf of the president-elect, Dick Allen asked which position in the administration interested me. I repeated what he had heard many times: secretary of the navy.

In the autumn of 1980 I had not, as the proverb goes, just ridden into town on a pumpkin cart. The navy was not quite the straightforward Boy Scout-pure institution described by my Pensacola drill instructors. Nor was the selection by a president-elect of his cabinet and senior subordinates quite the Athenian ideal of the civics books but, instead, usually was attended by swinishness, deception, and screams in the night. Nonetheless, even I was amazed at the chicanery that went on around my nomination to be President Reagan's secretary of the navy. The week after his election, Ronald Reagan told *The New York Times:* "My basic rule is that I want people who don't want a job in government."[3] I fit his bill. My consulting firm, Abington Corporation, was flourishing, I enjoyed the business world, and Barbara and I had two infant children. There was no denying, however, that eight years at the top of the policy process had left me with a kind of permanent addiction to national security policy. My deep concern for what was happening to the navy, and my certain conviction that I knew how to fix it shifted the balance. Barbara and I decided that I ought to try to become secretary of the navy.

Scoop Jackson once told me that the important jobs in Washington tend to seek the best people rather than the reverse. I have yet to see that happen in my time. Reluctant candidates are simply noncandidates. So, once I decided to seek the appointment, I went all out for it.

Transitions, as 1968 and 1976 had taught me, were like making sausage: not a pretty sight. Now, in 1980, there was occasion to reflect on the grievous harm done to the national executive government by the Twentieth Amendment to the Constitution. Prior to its adoption, a president had four full months between the election and his inauguration in which to select personally all his important policy subordinates. Since its adoption, the time available to a president to build his administration has been cut in half, but the size of the administration itself has expanded by nearly a hundred times. Instead of a few dozen presidential appointments, as in the last transition before the Twentieth Amendment became effective in 1933, President-elect Reagan had to select twenty-four hundred presidential appointees, of whom eighty-seven were on a top-priority list requiring personal presidential decision. In just two months a new president-elect must select his cabinet and his senior subcabinet and White House staff, and they, in turn, must then pick their principal subordinates. The top glamorous jobs are highly sought after and, as President Garfield found when he was shot by a disappointed office-seeker, feelings often run high.

For a variety of reasons, the office of secretary of the navy has always been one of the most highly prized. Within a week of the election there were fourteen strong candidates, including two former senators, three former governors, and a dozen multimillionaires. My selection by the president-elect to cochair the National Security Group in the transition put me in good pole position, but I was still a very dark horse indeed.

Not being a Californian, as a former Bush advisor and a callow youth of thirty-eight, I felt that my chances appeared slim. Nor did I have many friends in the Reagan "kitchen cabinet," the group of old friends convened by the president-elect to screen and recommend candidates.

There was another problem. The secretary of the navy position was considered to be a political plum and a nonpolicy job, definitely not a post for a

"Washington policy expert." For part of the history of this country, the secretaryships of war and of the navy were among the most important of the cabinet jobs, right up to and through the last Roosevelt administration. But Presidents Truman and Eisenhower were determined to reduce the power and influence of the Navy Department, and the succession of legislative reforms they got through Congress in 1947, 1949, and 1952, though in theory unified the services under one Defense Department, in fact put the Navy Department under the War Department, renamed Defense. The powers of the secretary of the navy were greatly reduced, and he became, in effect, a deputy to the secretary of defense. In 1958 the secretary of the navy was dropped from the cabinet, and very soon the job came to be seen more and more as a figurehead position to be used for political patronage. While there were notable exceptions, and some very able men to serve in the job over the past thirty years, most have had little interest in or credentials for taking on the burdens of actually running the Navy Department, preferring instead the role of a kind of head of state rather than head of government. The admirals, of course, were only too eager to keep such men booked up year-round with travel abroad and endless change-of-command ceremonies at home.

Presidents had come to view the jobs with disdain and, as President Nixon once said about a particular candidate for secretary of the navy, "It's a job anyone can do, and he can't do any harm over there."[4] Republican presidents especially are prone to a kind of childlike faith in generals and admirals more appropriate to the holy saints. President Reagan would get downright misty-eyed whenever the chiefs would appear in full-dress medals. Republicans and Democrats alike tend to believe that career military men are all secretly conservative Republicans. In fact, based on twenty-five years of working with career military officers, I have found that they fall in the same proportion as civilians along the political spectrum—if not from A to Z, then at least from C to X.

"The chief of naval operations really runs the Navy. Why do you want to be secretary of the navy?" This was a question I was often asked during the transition. We have, in fact, had in the navy some superb men as CNO over the short seventy-odd years that the job has been in existence, but we have also had some real mediocrities and a few jerks. The quality spread has been about the same as that found in secretaries of the navy. But the nature of the duties of the CNO and the path an officer must follow to reach the ranks of senior admirals make certain that he cannot run the navy as a chief executive. Inspirational leadership, perhaps, but management, never.

We have never once had a CNO with business management or acquisition experience, yet the Navy does nearly $100 billion of business every year and manages assets equal to the top seven Fortune 500 corporations. The CNO must travel worldwide about 25 percent of his time. He must spend endless hours every week in tedious JCS meetings, and he must entertain more than a hundred foreign CNOs who visit at least every other year. The best CNOs have provided real leadership and inspiration to the naval service and good professional advice to the president, but never have they operated as chief executive officers. When the secretary of the navy does not run the navy, the navy simply is not run. Procedures and bureaucracy carry it along, and usually very quickly right onto the rocks.

Thus, when I let it be known that that was the job I was after, everyone was incredulous. "What the hell do you want to waste your time with that? Haven't you seen enough parades?" said Dick Allen. "We need you to do something important, like ISA [assistant secretary of defense for international security affairs] or under secretary of state." Shortly after Al Haig was named to be secretary of state, he asked me to be his under secretary, ridiculing the idea of secretary of the navy as a "mere ceremonial job." Several weeks later it was seriously considered to put Dick Allen as Haig's deputy secretary of state and me as national security adviser under Ed Meese. I appreciated the flattery but insisted that if the position of secretary of the navy was unavailable, I would give all my support to the president from the private sector.

Reluctantly, Allen, Haig, Abshire, and Fred Iklé all agreed to support me for the job. While they were the most important players on the policy side of the president-elect's staff, they were not the inner circle. Except for Paul Laxalt and Bill Casey, those were all Californians. But other friends in the Reagan organization came to the rescue. In the kitchen cabinet, Anne Armstrong surfaced as my chief advocate. A former member of the Nixon cabinet, chairman of the Republican National Committee, and ambassador to the United Kingdom, she knew me from our work together in Kissinger days; Anne had a tough and astute grasp of foreign policy. She and her husband, Tobin, made perhaps the best team we have ever had in London. I had first made their acquaintance during pilot training in South Texas, where their historic ranch in Armstrong, Texas, adjoins the Kingsville Naval Air Training Base.

The vice president-elect supported me strongly for the job. He was deeply concerned with the state of the navy and agreed that the secretary of the navy was the key to fixing it.

Bill Timmons was the overall head of the transition staff, and his partner Tom Korologos was in charge of its congressional relations. Both are close personal friends from days in the Nixon White House and worked steadily on my behalf, as did Fred Fielding, counsel to the president-elect; and Ed Feulner, head of the Heritage Foundation.

Because my close friends Tina Karalekas, Jim Gidwitz, and George Smith all held key jobs in the transition personnel organization headed by Pendleton James, I was never out of date on where each horse was in the race.

Former chiefs of naval operations Arleigh Burke and James Holloway and Thomas Moorer were enormously helpful to me. "Thirty-one-knot" Burke, one of the finest CNOs in our history, had been what is known in navy jargon as my "sea daddy." I had met him when I was in college and worked with him on several studies while I was doing my graduate work. He persuaded me to transfer from the air force to accept a commission in the naval reserve in 1968. His advice and counsel have been invaluable to me right up to the present. He actively lobbied for my selection.

I first met Jim Holloway in Vietnam in 1970, when he was Seventh Fleet Commander off Vietnam and I was a lieutenant JG on active duty for training. He became chief of naval operations in 1974, and when I was appointed deputy director of the ACDA in 1975, we worked closely together on SALT policy and became very good friends. When President Carter was elected in 1976 and I resigned, Holloway made me a consultant to his office. During the 1980 transition Admiral Holloway became my chief strategist and worked tirelessly and with great effect to build support.

The judgment of Tom Moorer, former chairman of the joint chiefs of staff, was much valued by the president-elect, and Moorer became a strong supporter of mine during the Carter years, but it had taken some convincing to bring him around. He had been chairman while I was working for Kissinger, and he knew me as one of Henry's "whiz kids," a status in his eyes about equivalent to a car-repossessor. Former CNO Bud Zumwalt also was very helpful with advice and quiet support behind the scenes.

Of almost equal importance in matters of appointments to the views of the principal advisers and confidants of the president-elect are those of the chief sachems in Congress. Scoop Jackson, John Tower, John Stennis, Fritz Hollings, and John Warner began lobbying for me immediately. Once I threw my hat in the ring, Ronald Reagan heard directly and repeatedly from each of those senators and from Senator Sam Nunn and Congressman Charlie Bennett, chairman of the House Seapower Subcommittee.

With all my support coming from so many different quarters, the battle polarized almost immediately to Washington insiders versus the California mafia. All the candidates in the race quickly fell behind and were dropped from consideration except me and two Californians with strong ties to the Reagans: Verne Orr, Reagan's budget director in California and later secretary of the air force; and Robert Nesen, a Cadillac dealer, former assistant secretary of the navy, and later ambassador to Australia. Both were fine men and later served with distinction in the administration, but thanks to Dick Allen and Anne Armstrong, the kitchen cabinet was divided in their recommendation.

Nevertheless, the tide was running against me in late December, when the president-elect was to hold a reception at Blair House for congressional leaders. I called both Scoop Jackson and John Tower and told them it would take a last-ditch effort directly with Reagan to save the day. That evening Dick Allen, who was with the president-elect, and both Tower and Jackson each called me at home to recount what had happened at the reception. Tower and Jackson had together backed Reagan into an isolated corner and double-teamed him for fifteen minutes, describing me, in Tower's words, "as a combination of James Madison, Horatio Hornblower, and Francis of Assisi." Reagan made no commitments, but my best shots had now been fired. For two days, there was no word, and then my friends on the personnel staff told me that Verne Orr had decided after talking to the president-elect that he really wanted to be secretary of the air force. This was cheering. On Thursday, January 8, Jim Gidwitz called me from the personnel office, saying "Boy, you got problems. The decision has just been made to go forward with a decision memorandum recommending Bob Nesen, and it is being prepared by Helene von Damm, who is his very strong supporter."

I immediately called Dick Allen and said, "This is it. It's time to pull out all the stops." Now, Dick at this time was sore beset in trying to put together a strong National Security Council staff. The California inner circle wanted to downgrade the NSC because it symbolized to many of them the eastern establishment, liberal orthodoxy against which they had crusaded. Despite his problems, he had tracked the status of my appointment hour by hour, and he now dropped everything to work on it. He decided it was time to bring the issue to a head. The president-elect had just left Washington to return to California, where he would stay until coming to town for the Inauguration. Dick immediately called the president-elect and lobbied him hard. He then followed up with an urgent decision memorandum recommending that Reagan immediately name me as the secretary of the navy. I met with Dick the next morning at eight o'clock, and he told me that the memorandum had been sent. Shortly after that, Rich Armitage, working with Cap, called me to say that Weinberger and his designated deputy, Frank Carlucci, had agreed to my nomination. Within an hour, however, my cause was reported to be in deep trouble.

A horribly frantic day ensued, with several false starts and alarms until George Bush called me at six-fifteen. He sounded very ominous. He said, "You have a big problem." Then there was a long silence, and he continued, "Your problem is that the vice president's house is run by the secretary of the navy, and I've just been over to see it and the tennis court is in terrible shape." This released the tension of the past twenty-four hours, and we both had a great laugh. The vice president-elect then continued, "The president-elect had decided he wants you to be the secretary of the navy and I was authorized to tell you. Congratulations!"

The next hour and a half was spent on the phone calling everyone, starting with my wife, Barbara, and then my parents to tell them the good news. Then came calls to all of my supporters to thank them for having pulled me through. That evening Barbara and I went to dinner with our friends Doug and Marie-Pierre Bazata to celebrate.

No one with a weak heart or delicate digestion should seek the job of secretary of the navy. After a sound sleep, I received a call the next morning, Saturday, the tenth of January, at nine-thirty, from Helene von Damm: "President-elect Ronald Reagan has asked me to call you to tell you that there has been a terrible mistake; he has not decided to appoint you secretary of the navy but wants me to assure you that he would very much like to have you in the administration."

It took three excruciating days to piece together "who shot John." It was none other than Michael Deaver, who had personally promised the job to Bob Nesen. Deaver had gotten the president to rescind the earlier decision and to take "another look" before Inauguration Day.

The president-elect scheduled a meeting with his inner circle at Blair House for January 15 to resolve remaining cabinet-level appointments, secretary of the navy among them. Several of my friends reported that Deaver was telling friends that he had information that would kill my appointment. Thus we knew that Deaver would make an attempt to undo me with a smear at the meeting, but we had no idea what it was about. Dick Allen was to be in the meeting and was well prepared to do battle. The morning of Wednesday, the fourteenth, Dick called me to tell me that Deaver had succeeded in getting him excluded from the meeting because he was an "interested party." Meese, Lyn Nofziger, and Deaver were all included, and all were committed to Nesen. I was left with no supporter in the final decision meeting. I feared for the worst and was bemoaning my predicament to my old friend

Milt Pitts, the famous barber-counselor of presidents, as I sat getting a haircut. After commiserating with me, Milt said, "Well, you just better stick around then, because my next appointment is the vice president-elect, your friend Mr. Bush." I did just that, and when the vice president-elect came in and took my place in the chair, I unloaded my tale of woe. After hearing it, he said that he would modify his schedule for the next day and make sure he was at the meeting to try to thwart whatever it was that Deaver had up his sleeve.

Thursday morning, the day of the meeting, I got my first clue what Deaver was up to. I got a surreptitious call from an admiral friend of mine in the office of the CNO, Admiral Hayward. He said, "A certain congressional staffer is coordinating the campaign against you on Capitol Hill and for his friend Bob Nesen. Through his contacts in the navy he has got hold of a document from your navy personnel jacket that you signed indicating that you were flying E-2C's as a naval aviator in Norfolk, when in fact you have never done so."

So that was it! At the time and for four years prior, I was flying A-6s as a bombardier reserve augment at Oceana Naval Air Station in Virginia Beach. I was fully qualified to do so and had been exceeding all my training requirements. Though I was under a normal and official set of reserve orders, the actual selected reserve billet they had put me into for administrative purposes was an unfilled billet in a different squadron of E-2C aircraft at another base in Norfolk. All perfectly legal and proper. To use this against me indicated clearly that Deaver was not the sort of chap one would invite to one's club.

At five-thirty, shortly after the president's meeting adjourned, John Warner called me: Would I authorize the release of my training jacket and my full personnel file from the navy to the Armed Services Committee? Later I got a secondhand account of the meeting. I was told that, sure enough, when the secretary of the navy appointment came up, Deaver raised questions about my qualifications as a naval aviator. The vice president-elect was spring-loaded and, as a naval aviator himself, said that this was a very grave accusation indeed and that no decision should be made until it was ascertained to be true or false. He recommended that the president-elect ask the Armed Services Committee to designate some qualified persons to examine my records thoroughly to determine the validity of the charge.

The Armed Services Committee designated Admiral Moorer, former chairman of the joint chiefs, and Senator Warner, former secretary of the navy, to sit with the chief of naval personnel and review in detail all my officer records from commissioning in 1968 to that day. On Friday morning, naval couriers were dispatched to Pensacola, Florida, and Kingsville, Texas, where

I had undergone pilot and bombardier training, to my current squadron at Oceana, to the naval reserve unit in Norfolk, and to the Naval Reserve Command in New Orleans. Each document, flight log qualification, and fitness report was pulled together and compiled by the chief of navy personnel. The entire set of records was presented to Senator Warner and Admiral Moorer and gone over with a fine-tooth comb with naval personnel experts. I heard nothing until five o'clock on Saturday afternoon, the seventeenth, when I got a call from Frank Carlucci. He told me that the Armed Services Committee reported back to the president that I had been given a completely clean bill of health and that Admiral Moorer, himself a naval aviator, had high compliments for the thoroughness of my aviation qualifications and that there was absolutely no evidence of any impropriety. Frank said, "You should rest easier. You are about 90 percent in."

After the great celebrations at the Inaugural Ball on Tuesday, January 20, the first call I received at home on Wednesday was from John Tower. He said, "I talked to the president last night, and it looks like it is set. But they are looking for a spot for Bob Nesen." That was all nice to hear, but I'd had too many bumps to uncork the champagne just yet. The next afternoon, on Thursday, the twenty-second, at five-seventeen, Helene von Damm called. She said, "Could you please hold the line for President Reagan." The president soon came on the line and said, "John, I'd like you to be the secretary of the navy." I replied, "Thank you very much, Mr. President, I am deeply honored, and I'm delighted to accept." The president said, "Welcome aboard."

I never saw Deaver during this period, and for the entire time he remained at the White House we never once spoke.

In contrast to the five rambunctious confirmation hearings for the ACDA in 1975, my first confirmation hearings as secretary of the navy were scheduled immediately upon receipt of the formal nomination and were held on Wednesday, the twenty-eighty of January. The hearing was marked by high compliments from every member, Republican and Democrat, and I was approved, 15-0. The most controversial exchange in the whole hearing was when my son, John III, then one and a half years old, started squealing. Senator Goldwater said, "That child is making more sense than most members of this committee." After unanimous confirmation by the full Senate the following day, I took the family to Sun Valley for a skiing vacation.

The tempo of my new job became apparent when, the day after I arrived at Sun Valley, Senator Tower called to inform me that he had scheduled the navy's posture hearings for the following Wednesday, in the middle of my

week's vacation. I spent the next day preparing my maiden posture statement,
and I arranged to have an EA-6 jet based at Whidbey Island stop at Mountain
Home Air Force Base near Sun Valley and pick me up so I could get some
reserve flight time on my way back to Washington. Between Mountain Home
and Washington we stopped to refuel at Offutt Air Force Base in Omaha, headquarters of the Strategic Air Command. Because they get so many congressmen and distinguished visitors at SAC, they have perhaps the best-organized
and most efficient protocol office in the nation. While they were refueling our
jet, my fellow aviators from Whidbey and I were sitting in the pilots' lounge in
our G suits and flight gear having a Coke and a sandwich. A handsome group
of air force officers came rushing through the lounge. Over his shoulder one
of them said, "There's a Code 2 [cabinet-level] VIP who just landed here. Have
you seen him anywhere?" I couldn't resist saying, "He went thataway," point-
ing in the opposite direction. Back they rushed and were not seen again. We
took off and returned to Washington to lay before Congress for the first time
the new course we had charted for the navy.

Afterword

Rereading *Command of the Seas* has reminded me personally of just how
much my life was affected by what President Kennedy called the "long twi-
light struggle" of the cold war. I pursued an education in history and international affairs because I wanted to go into the government to help win the cold
war. In those days such a path had much more glamour to young undergrad-
uates than going to Wall Street or a law firm. In the post–cold war period this
no longer seems to be the case. Very few of my son's generation would consider
going into the government or the military. From that perspective, Part I of this
book already has a quaint period piece quality about it.

The events described in the introduction, regarding Admiral Rickover's departure and of his role within the navy seem also to be far in the past. The navy
nuclear power program and its personnel selection and training have continued
smoothly and effectively with no loss of safety or efficiency without Admiral
Rickover. That is due both to the rigorous disciplines that he instilled permanently in the service, but also to the talent and common sense of the admirals
who succeeded him. The personality cult has disappeared from the submarine
service without any loss of the excellence of the people and the program.

The legacy of Vietnam, and the events described in Chapter 2, has been
similarly long-lived but decidedly more mixed in its effects. There is still no
consensus on the lessons learned or the results achieved. With the perspective of

fifteen years since its tragic end my own conclusions have changed very little. The United States was wrong to pick up so readily the colonial legacy of the French but right in determining to confront the expansion of Soviet and Chinese supported communism and insurgency in Southeast Asia. We were wrong in sending regular army forces to Vietnam but right in finally turning over the effort to the Vietnamese with proper training and support in the Vietnamization program. We were wrong in counting so much on air power and technology and wrong in much of our assessment of the intelligence and of the results of bombing. We were right resisting the Khmer Rouge takeover of Cambodia and right in mining the harbors and removing the restrictions on bombing in 1973. It remains my belief that militarily we won the war in 1973 and that South Vietnam would have been able to maintain its independence had we continued to give full logistical and financial support to the government of South Vietnam and not cut it off as if they not the North were our enemy in 1974. Those successful Congressional efforts to seize defeat from the jaws of victory were of course the result of Watergate and the total paralysis of presidential power that resulted.

The political and economic depression that continues in South Vietnam and the genocide in Cambodia are strong testimony to the morality of our motivations if not of all of our methods. The dominoes that did not fall in Thailand, Malaysia, Singapore, Indonesia, and the Philippines are further testimony that despite the long and unsuccessful effort, many good things were achieved. Not the least of these was the infusion of nearly a million talented and resourceful new Americans fleeing communist takeover in South Vietnam, Laos, and Cambodia.

I'm not sure, however, that the United States has yet recovered from the Vietnam syndrome. The passage of time has eased the tension but underneath civil-military relations there lurks the old devil. Determined to speak with one voice and to avoid Vietnams, a new generation of officers have spearheaded the so-called Goldwater Nichols reforms, centralizing military advice in the chairman of the joint chiefs. A major motivation is to be able to present the civilian leadership with a single, authoritative military voice thereby somehow avoiding what many officers regard as the weakness and division of the Vietnam era military command. I doubt that was entirely the case but in any event, like most permanent solutions to temporary problems, this one has plenty of downsides of its own. In addition to depriving our leaders of multiple sources of military counsel, its worst effect is to encourage younger officers to see their service in joint staffs as their best route to promotion. The qualities of the warrior are put in the shadow of the bureaucrat.

September 1, 2001

PART II

A Navy Reformed

Chapter 4

Setting the Course:
Rebuilding a Naval Strategy

It was a great advantage to have been one of the first appointees named by the president. My nomination cleared all the hurdles of background investigation, conflict-of-interest and other screenings, and arrived in Congress within only a few days of the president's decision unlike those of later nominees, who were sometimes backlogged up to six months. By the time I arrived back in Washington on February 5, the Senate had already confirmed me, so as soon as I took off my flight gear I drove straight to the Pentagon and was sworn in by Coleman Hicks, the acting general counsel. The next day I appeared before the Senate Armed Services Committee with the chief of naval operations, Admiral Hayward, and the commandant of the marine corps, General Robert Barrow, to present the navy and marine corps' posture statement and to lay before Congress for the first time how we were going to rebuild our naval forces.

It really was a rare opportunity to hit the ground running. We had a well-thought-through program that I had pondered and crafted for years, the main parts of which were familiar to the president and vice president. The President had specifically called for maritime superiority in his principal national security campaign speech in Chicago in March 1980, and the six-hundred-ship objective was a plank in the Republican platform. The secretary of defense offered strong intellectual support, and the Senate and House Armed Services committees were equally committed.

The maritime strategy I had in mind was based mostly on sound principles long familiar to the navy; unfortunately, neither the navy nor anyone else had heard them for some time, and the very act of articulation was bound to be controversial in a town where systems analysis had been mistaken for strategy itself. We had to contend with a vast bureaucracy allergic to different thinking and jealous of its prerogatives. Finally, even if all of that could be overcome, would the navy system deliver: Could the Pentagon and the contractors actually build the ships and planes to the plans and the budget?

This three-front war I proposed to wage from a command post barely visible on the horizon. Fortunately for my own sense of proportion, my experience in the White House had led me to be wary of trappings. The secretary of the navy enjoyed many prerogatives: a spacious office decorated with the souvenirs of naval glory; saluting adjutants and staff; a car; and a mess with the best food in the building. And the secretaryship itself had a distinguished history. Until the late 1950s, the civilian head of the navy had a cabinet post. The long corridor of oil portraits of my predecessors was testimony that many of America's most able men had held the post.

In 1981, however, all that was in the past. The power of the office had atrophied from lack of exercise.

The navy bureaucratic apparatus put all policy decision-making under the chief of naval operations and his two-thousand-man staff, and the commandant of the marine corps and his eight-hundred-man staff. The secretary of the navy and his staff were generally not included in the debating and formulating stages but were presented with positions for approval from which dissenting views and issues had been eliminated and resolved.

This was a role incompatible with both my objectives and my temperament. I therefore took one of the offices of the E ring close to my own and had it renovated into a conference room, which we called "The Blue Room." Here a group would convene daily under my chairmanship that we called the Navy Policy board; its function was to settle the key issues faced by the navy and the marine corps. As the focus of decision-making, the membership of the group under my chairmanship were the under secretary and assistant secretaries of the navy, and the CNO and the commandant and their vice chiefs and deputies, depending on the agenda.

The first of those issues was strategy. There was only one good reason to build a six-hundred-ship navy, and that was to restore our maritime superiority.

Predictably, a Washington crowd long accustomed to the slumbering discourse of the systems analysts was taken sharply aback. Some commentators were shocked that an administration would actually use the word "superiority" because it might be newly provocative to the Russians. But this was nonsense. We were not breaking new ground, only recovering what had been foolishly thrown away.

Since the time of Teddy Roosevelt and his older contemporary Alfred Thayer Mahan, it had been naval and, indeed, national orthodoxy that the United States must have a navy superior not only to any other navy but also to any potential combination of naval adversaries. As the Soviet Union began its massive naval building campaign in 1962 and the United States its own unilateral naval disarmament during the 1970s, that naval superiority was lost. By the late 1970s the Soviet fleet had increased to some 1,700 ships, while the American fleet had dropped precipitously, from 950 ships in 1969 to 479 ships in 1979. While the United States had more tonnage, we had clearly lost ground on the real measure—which navy was likely to succeed in war, the United States in securing unfettered use of the seas or the Soviets in denying us that objective?

The annual official navy posture statements warned of adverse trends, but the illusion of superiority was officially maintained. Admiral Elmo Zumwalt was the first naval leader to break ranks after he left office, and he wrote in his memoirs that "none of us thought we had such a capability and all of us were under heavy pressure not to let on"; his public testimony was purged by the Pentagon of references to "adequate, marginal, or inadequate capability; to superiority or inferiority to the Russians, and to the odds on winning the war."[1]

When the Carter administration came to office, the secretary of defense, Harold Brown, and his staff of systems analysts took a fresh look and decided that the navy and marine corps were no longer as important to American security. It was part of a larger post-Vietnam attitude that disparaged, as President Carter said in his spring 1977 Notre Dame speech, America's "inordinate fear of communism."

Harold Brown appointed Ambassador Robert Komer as his under secretary for policy. Bob Komer was one of the most dedicated and colorful public servants of the 1960s and 1970s. He had been the architect of President Johnson's pacification program in Vietnam and was a long-time employee of the air force's think tank, the Rand Corporation. These experiences had left him with a professional obsession with land warfare. The defense doctrine that emerged from these men rightly saw the East-West confrontation in Europe as the fulcrum of the U.S.-Soviet military balance and set out to strengthen the army and air force capability to defend Western Europe. But they wrongly concluded that seapower could contribute little to that defense.

Under their scenarios of war in Europe, naval forces were relegated to "naval resupply . . . important after about thirty days,"[2] as Brown put it. Even while reorganizing the importance of defending NATO's vital northern flank and preventing a breakout of Soviet antishipping forces to prey on the vital convoy routes, the Carter team believed that offensive naval operations would be a diversion of resources. They reasoned that defeat of the Soviets at sea would not cripple the Soviet war effort, while an attack on Soviet naval or air facilities might threaten escalation in the early stages of a struggle. While this meant almost certainly far fewer carriers than the joint chiefs deemed desirable, the "navy as resupply" school comforted themselves with the idea of reinforcements for the Atlantic from the Pacific if necessary. Such "sequential operations" would focus our full naval strength on one theater and then another.[3]

It was ironic, of course, that these notions were obsolete even as they were being promulgated. It was certainly true that the defeat of the Soviet Union at sea would not guarantee a successful defense of NATO, but it was also true—and more important—that the loss of NATO's supremacy at sea would guarantee NATO's defeat. Our merchant marines had been shrinking rapidly; to allow the Soviets to seize the North and then prey on our convoys was a war of attrition we could not win. Finally, the massive growth of the Soviet Far Eastern fleet assured that the "sequential operation" to reinforce the Atlantic would grant the Soviets naval supremacy in the Pacific.

In short, the Carter naval doctrine would give the U.S.S.R. a free hand to seize NATO's northern flank, a huge advantage in attacking our convoys and a choice between abandoning either our Pacific or Atlantic allies at the outset of the war.

Apparently loath to take the doctrine to its most logical conclusion, the Carter administration changed its original target of just 6 carriers and finally settled on a force of about 450 ships and 12 aircraft carriers. But the navy itself was clearly downgraded, along with its mission.

No more large deck carriers were planned, to be replaced gradually with a new, smaller, nonnuclear class called a CVV. The marine corps was cut from two marine amphibious forces to one. To conform official doctrine with the reality of these naval cutbacks, in 1978 the chief of naval operations, Jim Holloway, was ordered by Brown's staff to drop the use of the term "maritime superiority." Holloway, to his credit, continued to urge the necessity of American maritime superiority throughout his congressional testimony.

The fundamental theory behind maritime superiority was very simple. At the strategic nuclear level the Reagan administration sought to achieve "parity," or functional equality. The objective was to restore a balance in strategic nuclear weapons, in which neither side had an advantage and neither side would have any incentive for a surprise attack, or first use. In ground forces, geography made the Soviet Union far more dependent on land-based forces than the United States. With all of her principal allies and resources on the Eurasian landmass, and all of the potential threats surrounding the vast periphery of Eurasia, the Soviet Union now maintains more than 180 divisions of active army forces, and some 20 million reserves in various stages of readiness. Only when fully mobilized can NATO come near to this balance, with some 140 divisions. In peacetime, the United States maintains 18 active and 10 reserve army divisions and the equivalent of about 5 active and 1 reserve marine divisions.

The United States, by contrast, is a "continental island," tied to its allies, trading partners, and resources by the great seas. The free world is an oceanic coalition. It follows, therefore, that the free world coalition must have unquestioned superiority on the seas if overall strategic parity is to exist—parity at the nuclear level, and inferiority in size and land force balanced by superiority at sea. We must be sure we can use the oceans in peace and in war if we are to survive. Equality applied to the naval balance would mean catastrophe for us because naval parity would bring stalemate, and a maritime stalemate would mean that the seas could not be used by the free world alliance. If our convoys could not get through to our European allies, then we would probably lose any conflict with the Soviet Union within weeks, and our survival would be in jeopardy.

Through the spring I testified repeatedly to Congress, using that fundamental theme, of which excerpts from my presentation to the Appropriations Committee are typical: "To restore stability to the international environment, to return again to an environment in which freedom can flourish and totalitarianism decline, America must regain that condition that Thucydides, Scipio, Sir Walter Raleigh, Lord Nelson, and Alfred Mahan have seen as indispensable to a maritime nation's survival, 'command of the seas.'

". . . we have seen the seas become a potentially hostile medium threatening our very shores in a few short years. More than half of our population lives within 150 miles of our coasts, and today Soviet missile submarines patrol off these shores within striking distance. Their long-range patrol aircraft regularly fly down our coasts, and Soviet spy ships intermingle with our sport fisherman off Norfolk and San Diego.

"Clear maritime superiority must be acquired. We must be capable—and be seen as capable—of keeping our access secure to areas of our vital interest. This is not a debatable strategy. It is a national objective—a security imperative.

"Maritime superiority does not mean that we must seek to be omnipresent on all oceans, nor to act as the world's maritime policeman. It means only that in those areas of our vital interests that we can prevail if challenged by the combined military threat of our adversaries. Geography, which strongly favors the United States and its allies, sets the parameters of our task. Besides our geographic advantages, we are also blessed with the firm partnership of history's great maritime powers, including the United Kingdom, France, and other NATO navies, as well as Japan and our Pacific allies. With the vital contribution of these friends and allies and the capabilities of our air force and army, the navy and marine corps have clear maritime superiority within reach."

Facts so obvious and logic so simple would seem almost a cliché, yet the phrase "maritime superiority" became the subject of astonishing controversy. Because of the entrenched antinaval orthodoxy of the two-thousand-strong office of the secretary of defense (OSD) bureaucracy, their opposition to this doctrine was passionate. If one could describe the OSD consensus, it would be a genuine belief that Central Europe was the only theater of life-or-death importance, that the army and air force were insufficiently funded to defend it, and that the navy was of no use in the theater and needlessly used funds needed more by the land forces. Totally dismissing the presidential policy behind the phrase, they gradually wore Cap Weinberger down to the point where he stopped using it in his public statements, and then in late 1982 his military assistant called my military assistant to direct that I no longer use the word "superiority" and substitute the phrase "naval forces sufficient."

Soon thereafter, I was asked by the president's staff to assist them in preparing a speech for the president to give at the recommissioning ceremonies in California of the first of our reactivated battleships, the U.S.S. *New Jersey*. I provided what I thought was pretty good stuff, but I informed the president's national security adviser, Bill Clark, who had by then replaced Dick Allen, that the secretary of defense had problems with the use of the term "maritime superiority" and that his staff especially felt very strongly against it. I recommended that he talk it over with Cap and that they reraise the issue with the president and the vice president. It was put to President Reagan and, as I expected, he strongly reaffirmed the policy. On December 28, 1982, the president journeyed to Long Beach for what was one of the more dramatic ceremonies of the administration. He said the following:

Though the Soviet Union is historically a land power, virtually self-sufficient in mineral and energy resources and land-linked to Europe and the vast stretches of Asia, it has created a powerful blue ocean navy that cannot be justified by any legitimate defense need. It is a navy built for offensive action, to cut free world supply lines and render impossible the support by sea of free world allies. By contrast, the United States is a naval power by necessity critically dependent on the transoceanic import of vital strategic materials. Over 90 percent of our commerce between continents moves in ships. Freedom to use the seas is our nation's lifeblood. For that reason our navy is designed to keep the sea lanes open worldwide—a far greater task than closing those sea lanes at strategic choke points. *Maritime superiority* for us is a necessity. We must be able in time of emergency to venture in harm's way, controlling air, surface, and subsurface areas to assure access to all the oceans of the world. Failure to do so will leave the credibility of our conventional defense forces in doubt.

We are . . . building a six-hundred-ship fleet, including fifteen carrier battle groups.

I could not have said it better myself.

Unfortunately, the bureaucracy does not pay much attention to a president, and for the remaining four years of my tenure the secretary of defense's staff refused to clear any naval document that used the term "Maritime superiority"— even when directly quoting the president. Because Cap himself—and the president—agreed with me, I simply ignored the OSD staff.

The Eight Principles of Maritime Strategy

To achieve maritime superiority, the very first priority must be to restore the self-confidence and sense of mission of the naval service itself, to dispel the cynicism and defeatism I had seen so vividly at the Newport Conference. The first step was to lay out the correct strategic principles and build a maritime strategy on them. From my first day after being sworn in, in hearings and in speeches, in press conferences, backgrounders, and interviews, I pounded away on principles I later codified as fundamental to maritime strategy. They are:

Principle I: *Maritime strategy is derived from and dependent on the overall national security strategy established by the president.* Establishing a maritime strategy cannot begin until the president has provided an overall national security strategy for the nation. Every administration begins its tenure with an exercise in updating the overall national security strategy. Perhaps the most famous was the NSC-68 of the Truman years. Each of these documents is a thorough statement of our national security strategy, set forward in the context of presidential policy. Every administration tries to combine enduring realities and vital interests with new policy directions and objectives. The initial exercise under Reagan was guided by the deliberations and discussions we had during the campaign in 1980, with both the president and the vice president providing broad direction and with Dick Allen, Al Haig, Cap Weinberger, and Fred Iklé and their staffs doing the detailed work. My own participation was through informal discussions with Dick Allen and formal position papers to Cap.*

Among the most important points we made:

- *Diplomatic and military alliances.* These are expressed in the web of more than forty treaty relationships that bind us to mutual defense coalitions around the world. Figure 1 (at the back of the book) illustrates their extensive spread.
- *Commercial interdependence.* Our economy today is more interdependent on overseas trading partners and suppliers than ever in our history. As noted elsewhere, the overall pattern of this trade interaction has shifted enormously in recent years, with the volume of trade in the Pacific Basin now being nearly 50 percent larger than with our Atlantic trading partners. A total of 95 percent of all this peacetime trade must travel by sea.
- *Energy dependence.* The United States first became a net importer of oil only in 1947. We are now once again approaching nearly a 50 percent dependence on imported oil. Here also, however, the global pattern of our dependence has shifted considerably in recent years, away from the Middle East and the Persian Gulf and to the Western Hemisphere.
- *Mineral dependencies.* We are now dependent on overseas sources for over 90 percent of the top eighteen strategic minerals on which our economy depends.

Principle II: *National strategy provides the Navy Department with maritime tasks.*

1. The navy is responsible for controlling diverse international crises. During the years of "violent peace" since 1945, naval forces have been deployed more than two hundred fifty times as direct crisis management forces. During my

---

*An unclassified version of the Reagan era assessment concerning the naval forces read as follows: "Maritime forces play a unique role in the supporting of our military strategy. Given the realities of our geostrategic position, fronting on two oceans, maritime superiority is vital to support our alliance relationships and our forward deployed forces." ("National Security Strategy of the United States" [Washington, D.C. The White House January 1987], p. 29)

five years with Kissinger on the NSC staff, I never once attended a meeting in the cabinet office or the Oval Office during a crisis where the first questions asked by the president and his national security adviser were not, "Where are the carriers? Where is the marine amphibious ready group?" During the Reagan administration the president employed the navy and the marine corps in crisis management in every theater of the world. At any give time the navy has about 110,000 sailors at sea all over the world engaged in peacetime presence, military diplomacy, and crisis management. In an average year the navy will visit more than a hundred countries for official and unofficial purposes.

2. The navy's role in deterring war: The fundamental task of all the armed forces is deterrence, to allow our national interests to be preserved in peace. Deterrence seeks to safeguard U.S. interests by convincing adversaries that we have the military capability to ensure that they will suffer more than they can possibly gain if they choose aggression against us, at any level—from individual acts of terrorism to all-out nuclear war. As President Reagan has often said, "A nuclear war cannot be won and must never be fought." Although there can be no "winning" an all-out nuclear war, it is the unpopular lot of the Pentagon to have to carry out the age-old paradox of deterrence, "If you would have peace, prepare for war." If the Soviets are to be dissuaded, then our threat to retaliate against a nuclear attack must be believable. A retaliation against civilian targets—when the Soviets, with sixteen thousand warheads, could reattack every U.S. city—is not believable. Hence, the Pentagon must think through the dynamics of factual nuclear war fighting and develop the weapons, fail-safe devices, and most importantly, the communications ("C_3") that will ensure that firm control can survive any attack. It must ensure that use of nuclear weapons can never be put on automatic and that if nuclear weapons are employed—by accident, miscalculations, or a third party—that conflict can be terminated rationally and as quickly as possible.

    Thus it was that Weinberger and his staff, particularly Deputy Assistant T. K. Jones, were required to testify repeatedly in 1981–82 about the dynamics of nuclear war fighting, to explain why it was necessary to spend so much of the defense budget (17 percent) on C_3 and new strategic systems such as the MX, Trident, and the B-1 and B-2 that reduced overall megatonnage from prior years but provided the capability to survive a Russian or third-party first strike. Among nuclear powers, any conflict carries the risk of irreversible escalation. Deterrence, therefore, must be a continuum. But it does not break into the discrete packages that academics prefer.

    The navy is tasked with being ready to deal with the full continuum of deterrence, from the *Achille Lauro* piracy at the lower end all the way up to strategic nuclear war at the high end, and every level of violence in between. This requires the maintenance of conventional forces that can operate anywhere in the world, under the sea, on the surface of the sea, over the sea, and projected ashore into any environment. It requires the maintenance of nuclear forces able to deter nuclear escalation at the tactical or theater level. Here again is the insidious task of having to plan to fight with nuclear weapons to ensure that nuclear war will never happen. Naval forces carry tactical nuclear weapons—Tomahawk torpedoes and bombs—in order to be able to retaliate against the use of tactical nuclear weapons by the Soviets, without having to escalate to strategic nuclear weapons, thus providing the incentive to terminate the conflict before it escalates to all-out nuclear war. All such naval tactical nuclear weapons are under the control of one of the joint theater commanders, the secretary of defense, and the president. This tasking also requires the navy to specifically maintain a completely survivable and instantly ready submarine-based strategic nuclear missile force. All these forces must be able to deter not only actual aggression but also coercion of the United States and its allies through the threat of aggression. As Winston Churchill observed in 1946, "I do not believe that Soviet Russia desires war. What they desire are the fruits of war and the indefinite expansion of their power and doctrine."

3. *If deterrence fails, prevent the seas from being used against us.* Today the Soviet Union maintains more than sixty operational strategic ballistic missile submarines and deploys some of them off our East and West coasts at all times. Their newer generation of ballistic missile submarines operate under the polar ice pack. We could develop the capability to break through the ice to fire missiles, but we have not. Other of the Russian ballistic missile submarines can hit targets in the United States from waters adjacent to the Soviet Union. The navy is tasked with being capable of destroying these submarines if ordered by the commander in chief. At the conventional level the Soviets now deploy nonmissile-carrying nuclear attack submarines in waters adjacent to our coasts, maintain bases in Cuba (and now they are building a similar base infrastructure in Nicaragua) to operate Soviet mining and bombing aircraft, and exercise regularly the capability to attack the United States with cruise missiles and to mine our harbors. The navy is tasked with preventing all these attacks, including attacks on our treaty allies, such as Norway.

4. *Deny the enemy use of the seas.* While the Warsaw Pact is a land alliance and the Soviet Union occupies the center of the Eurasian landmass, it is surprisingly dependent on seaborne transportation. There are only two rail lines connecting the western with the eastern Soviet Union, and it maintains a mer-

chant fleet of twenty-four hundred ships, which carry nearly 80 percent of its commercial tonnage, including internal waterways. Denying the Soviet Union use of this transportation, seizing its merchant fleet, and cutting off any seaborne communications with its clients in the Americas, Africa, and Asia is a major "tasking" to the navy. It is important to remember that our objective is to prevent use of nuclear weapons if war breaks out and to be able to bring a conflict to an end without use of them.

5. *Ensure unimpeded use of the seas by the United States and its allies.* A total of 95 percent of all commercial and military tonnage still must travel by sea. Free world merchant fleets have shrunk to very low numbers, and the loss of any significant percentage of those ships would defeat the free world coalition. During the first six months of 1942, for example, 450 ships, representing 1.5 million tons of Allied shipping, were lost. That damage was carried out by only fourteen of the fifty-seven U-boats operational that year. The Soviets maintain a force of 270 attack submarines, and thousands of aircraft with the range to strike the Atlantic and Pacific trade routes. In addition, the Soviets and their allies maintain the largest mine-laying force in the world.

6. *Ensure use of the seas to support the land battle.* In addition to the logistics support essential to carrying out any land defense of our European and Asian allies, the navy and the marine corps are tasked with support of the land battle through amphibious invasion, as in Normandy and the Pacific in World War II, providing air superiority, close air support, and interdiction bombing to land forces from aircraft carriers, and naval gunfire support up to twenty-four miles inland and precision strikes with conventional or nuclear cruise missiles launched from submarines and surface ships to ranges of up to fifteen hundred miles inland.

7. *Ensure use of the seas to carry the fight to the enemy and terminate the war on favorable terms.* The navy is tasked with ensuring that if the Soviet Union starts a war in a chosen theater, such as Central Europe, they cannot expect it will be limited only to the theater of their greatest strength. Command of the seas enables free world forces to be applied where Soviet forces are weakest and their vulnerabilities greatest, as in their Pacific territories and client states. The navy is tasked to ensure that the Soviets cannot have the luxury of fighting a war only on other people's territory, that the fight will be pressed to Soviet territory and targets with a primary objective of the systematic destruction of Soviet forces and their military infrastructure; the regaining of any lost territory; and the termination of the war at the earliest time on the most favorable terms.

It is this tasking in carrying the fight to the enemy, which may include the destruction of Soviet strategic missile submarines, that most appalled and horrified the liberal academics and journalists, some of whom now sought to discredit the entire idea of maritime superiority, calling it the "Lehman strategy." Thousands of trees have been sacrificed to provide pamphlets, articles, books, diatribes, and polemics against my supposed bellicosity. I explore their arguments in more detail below. I have enjoyed stirring the pot by stressing the controversy and lacing my testimony and speeches with quotations calculated to sound to these critics like fingernails scraping on a blackboard. "I mean to have nothing to do with a ship that does not sail fast, For I mean to go in harm's way" (John Paul Jones); "That overbearing power on the sea which drives the enemy's flag from it, or allows it to appear only as a fugitive . . ." (Mahan); "A Navy powerful enough not just to fend off the enemy, but to smite him down!" (Mahan).

Principle III: *Maritime tasks assigned to the Navy Department require maritime superiority.* This third principal is implicit in the tasks assigned the navy by national strategy, and as we have seen above, was made explicit in both Reagan strategy documents. For my very first hearing on February 6, 1981, before Tower and the full Senate Armed Services Committee, I stressed this principle as the primary objective of the Reagan navy recovery program, to regain clear "maritime superiority":

> Maritime superiority means that we must be capable—and be seen to be capable—of keeping our sea lines of commerce and communications secure in those areas of the world where our vital interests depend on them. If we are to survive as a free nation our access to our allies, our energy sources, and our trading partners cannot be hostage to the offensive power of any combination of adversaries. We must have the naval and marine corps power to defeat militarily any martial attempts to interfere with such access.
>
> In the coming months and years I shall be working with you to see that our efforts in personnel, in readiness, in research and development, and in procurement are brought into conformity with the pursuit of that single informing principle: maritime superiority.

Principle IV: *Maritime superiority requires a disciplined maritime strategy.* With the president having provided a national strategy requiring the Navy Department to reestablish maritime superiority, the first task was to reestablish the intellectual framework throughout the navy and the marine corps to guide our rebuilding of maritime strategy.

In Washington, imaginative daydreaming often masquerades as strategy. Our cottage industry of armchair strategists, as a kind of a chess game, spin out long hypotheses about how particular campaigns should be waged, how ships should be deployed, when the tanks should be used, and when and where massed firepower should be concentrated. This can be good fun, and in its proper sphere can produce a first-rate novel like *Red Storm Rising*, but it is not strategy. Strategy in that sense belongs to the combatant commander on scene and not anywhere within the Washington bureaucracy. Strategy simply is "the art of distributing and applying military means to fulfill the ends of the policy."[4]

Strategy as it falls to the president and his senior policymakers involves the rational ordering of global priorities, and deciding among competing strategic requirements, as Franklin Roosevelt did between the European and the Pacific theaters in World War II.

For the secretary of the navy and his principle subordinates, the CNO and the Commandant, strategy means simply addressing rigorous logic to the allocation of the scarce resources available to carry out the tasks assigned us by national strategy.

Many retired admirals believe that the secretary of the navy should stick to administration (whatever that is) and leave strategy and requirements to the admirals. It never occurred to me as secretary that strategy was none of my business. In fact, it *had* to be my business. Title 10 of the U.S. Code charges the secretary of the navy with ensuring the highest level of training appropriate to the responsibilities placed upon both the marine corps and the navy. He is charged also with developing and procuring goods and services, weapons, ammunition, equipment, and maintenance to ensure the best possible readiness of those services. That is what strategy provides and why it is the highest responsibility of the secretary of the navy. Strategy is the logical set of allocations and priorities that guide how the Navy Department spends its money and trains its people.

I began hammering away on strategy from the very first day. In April 1981 I made an important speech, "Hail the Return of Strategy," at the annual public strategy conference at the Naval War College. This was followed by a steady stream of interviews and articles elaborating the principles of maritime power. It gave me some pleasure to know that my audiences were not accustomed to hearing navy secretaries discourse on the subject, but after several months I realized that little was penetrating into the navy staff—the two-thousand-strong uniformed bureaucracy of the CNO called "OPNAV."

As noted in the introduction, Admiral Rickover had created an institutional obsession with engineering and hard sciences. Concurrently, the mechanistic religion of the McNamara managerial reorganization had raised systems analysis and the programming and budgeting process to the top of the naval headquarters organization. By the time I took over, programming and budgeting had displaced strategy and accounted for some 85 percent of the personnel on the navy headquarters staff. The navy had had to adjust to survive in the era of PPBS and the vast defense bureaucracy, but then when Harold Brown officially downgraded the navy and the marine corps, the collapse of self-confidence within the navy that I addressed in chapter 2 completed the demise of strategic thinking. The historical global conceptual approach to strategy, brought to the navy by Theodore Roosevelt, had disintegrated into a budget- and program-driven series of discrete doctrines for antisubmarine, antiair, antisurface, strike, mine, and amphibious warfare, with no integrated, coherent, intellectual framework.

While this decline was one of the strong motivations for my seeking to become secretary of the navy, I had not realized the extent of the trouble until I was on the job. Month after month I submitted requests to the OPNAV staff to be briefed on the overall naval strategy. It wasn't until May 1981 that it became clear why it was never put on my schedule: it did not exist! Graham Claytor and Jim Holloway were both strategic thinkers, and in the early years of the Carter administration they launched an effort to reestablish an overall strategy, which resulted in a study called "Sea Plan 2000." This was a good study and was intended to provide the beginnings of a reestablishment of an overall strategy, but it was received with such hostility by Harold Brown and his staff that it was never implemented. It never even took root within the navy because the navy headquarters had evolved into such a massive budgeting and programming staff that conceptual thinking and strategy simply had no place. There was, however, on the CNO's staff one office where the flame was kept alive—in the deputy chief of naval operations for policy and plans, OP-06. There was in this office a small subspecialty community of naval political-military strategic planners with very able minds.

Admiral Tom Hayward had been CNO for two and a half years when I became secretary of the navy. He had spent his tours in the Pentagon primarily in the systems analysis and programming staffs. As CNO he had done a first-rate job in fighting the navy's bureaucratic battles within an essentially hostile Pentagon during Harold Brown's tenure. As commander in chief of the Pacific Fleet he had directed a strategy for the Pacific that established his capabilities in that regard. It is no criticism of him that he did not take the lead in formulating the maritime strategy in the Reagan administration. He was in complete agreement with the effort, and he provided strong support for its formulation and implementation in the eighteen months that we worked together.

Before deciding on his successor (each CNO must retire after four years), I had extensive discussions with potential candidates about strategy. I was most impressed with the interest and grasp of the commander of the Pacific fleet at the time, Jim Watkins. That factor and others helped persuade me that he was the right man for the job. We were in total agreement on the principles that must guide maritime strategy, and the objectives of the Reagan administration. He took the maritime strategy, developed it, and implemented and promulgated it in fleet doctrine and in the bureaucracy. In this task he depended primarily on Admiral James A. Lyons, and on Lyons's able network of political-military specialists. Another major contributor was the Strategic Studies Group (SSG) that we established at the Naval War College in 1981. This elite group of midgrade officers, navy and marine, is selected from the fleet to spend a year working on the strategy. Each year a new SSG is formed, and changing perspectives help to keep the strategy from solidifying into dogma.

The process was well described by one of the primary action officers and naval strategic thinkers, Captain Peter M. Swartz:

> . . . the staffs of the chief of naval operations and the commandant of the marine corps—in conjunction with officers of their sister services and allies—had been tasked to develop for internal use a detailed description of the maritime strategy component of the U.S. national military strategy. This maritime strategy rigorously integrated into one clear, consistent document the following:
>
> - a number of long-held views of navy and marine corps senior officers
> - certain newly refined concepts developed in the fleet and at the Naval War College
> - agreed national intelligence estimates
> - the strategic principles articulated by Secretary Lehman
>
> Concepts developed by the navy's warfare communities and fleets, as well as by army, air force, joint, and allied commanders were examined and incorporated as appropriate. Where inconsistencies appeared, hard choices were made. Properly, the job was spearheaded by the strategic concepts group in the staff of the CNO, OP-603.[5]

While by 1984 we finally had one document containing a comprehensive maritime strategy, I was at pains to keep reminding the navy and the marine corps that, in the words of Sir Julian Corbin, "Nothing is so dangerous in the study of war as to permit maxims to become a substitute for judgment." The consolidated maritime strategy was never intended to be and must never become sacred script. Today one will search in vain for a navy "cookbook" that tells on-scene commanders when to move aircraft carriers, or how or where to move attack submarines or Aegis cruisers at any given point after a conflict commences. There must never be any such cookbook, and certainly it must never come from Washington. Those who criticize the maritime strategy for being the wrong cookbook, or for not being a cookbook, do not understand strategy.

Once we had established the maritime strategy, we set about relating and conforming everything else we did in the navy and marine corps to it. Planning; programming; budgeting; research and development; ship, aircraft, and weapons system design; and, above all, personnel and training policy all were reoriented to carry out this strategy.

We successfully established a process continually to test, refine, and update the strategy. Navy and marine corps senior operational commanders now review it individually and as a group. It is examined, challenged, probed, and refined at the international level by senior American and free world military and civilian officials. We test it repeatedly in war games and simulations, especially the annual global war games at the Naval War College in Newport, Rhode Island. It is used as the planning base for our major exercises—navy, joint, and multinational—and the exercises themselves become the crucible for testing its execution and challenging its assumptions. Each exercise provides useful lessons learned, which are fed back into the refining process.

In addition, lessons learned from every real-world crisis or conflict were applied immediately and integrated into our strategy. The Falkland Islands War, our own and Israeli operations in Lebanon, the Grenada intervention, the interception of the *Achille Lauro* pirates, the joint U.S. Navy/U.S. Air Force Strike on Libya, and our constant monitoring of Soviet exercises and deployments are all examples. Much of our budget request each year has been modified since the previous year by the lessons learned from intervening events as applied to our overall strategy. In December 1983, as a result of lessons learned from the Falklands, we accelerated installation of the Phalanx (a Gatling gun that shoots four thousand spent uranium bullets a minute and is very effective against Exocets and other cruise missiles) close-in cruise missile defense on ships serving in the dangerous waters off Beirut and in the Persian Gulf. As a result of the Grenada operations analysis, we have modified communications equipment to improve future interoperability with U.S. Army ground forces. The recent Libyan lessons highlighted the essential requirement for intelligence collection aircraft to support the battle group, and we immediately amended our budget to fund it. (See figure 2.)

Principle V. *Maritime strategy must be based on a realistic assessment of the threat.* The birth of the modern Soviet blue water navy may be clearly dated from 1962. Following the Cuban Missile Crisis and the diplomatic defeat of the Soviet Union by an American naval blockade, Admiral Sergei Gorschkov, the chief of the Soviet Navy, apparently won his argument for a considerably larger share of Soviet defense expenditures. Under his brilliant leadership an historic program was begun to build, train, and deploy a truly global navy for the Soviet Union. Gorschkov was able, through successive changes of leadership and coalitions in the Politburo, to maintain unwavering support and funding for this program.

Before 1962, the Soviet Navy was very large in numbers with a great many diesel submarines and small surface combatants. It had a large air arm, but that was entirely land-based. They had no aircraft carriers, no large-scale amphibious assault capability, and no infrastructure of command, control, communications, and logistics to support blue water naval operations distant from home waters.

By the time the Reagan administration assumed office, the Soviet Union had built a fleet of seventeen hundred ships, including as many cruisers and destroyers as we had in the U.S. Navy, half again as many fleet ballistic missile submarines, four aircraft carriers for vertical takeoff and landing aircraft, the beginning of a true amphibious assault capability, and a nuclear attack submarine force larger than our own. There was steady growth through the 1960s and 1970s in the communications, command, control, and logistics infrastructure, enabling operations farther and farther from home waters. For the first time we began to see massive worldwide exercises like Okeon '75 of great sophistication and effectiveness, including the employment of Backfire bombers against American battle groups and the integration of vertical takeoff and landing (VTOL) jets from the new Kiev class carriers into operations at sea. The acquisition of the American-built bases at Camh Ranh Bay and Danang in Vietnam gave the Soviets an enormously valuable new dimension to their operations in the Pacific, sitting astride the vital strategic choke points of all the sea lanes connecting the Pacific with Southwest Asia, the Persian Gulf, and the Suez Canal.

In the Americas, the Soviets had built a modern naval infrastructure and a modern navy in Cuba. Not only had they built a modern submarine base capable of supporting their own submarines in Cienfuegos, but also they had trained and equipped a Cuban submarine force with the most modern Foxtrot diesel electric submarines, and they had provided more than a hundred fast missile and torpedo patrol boats, new Koni class frigates, and an air force of some fifty modern aircraft. Taken together, this Cuban force is a formidable and effective block of the Caribbean choke points for American shipping. Nearly 60 percent of American commerce in peacetime must travel through the narrow Straits of Florida or the Yucatán Channel into and out of the Gulf of Mexico. There are no other routes in or out. In the event of a conflict anywhere in the world, 85 percent of Army resupply and reinforcement tonnage embarks from one of the Gulf Coast ports. This has added a very significant new dimension to NATO strategy because, while we can certainly secure these routes in time of war, it is not as easy as it may appear from looking at a map. It will take large naval forces, army divisions, and air forces, and a significant amount of time, to secure the routes effectively for free passage by merchant shipping. To emphasize that they intend to defend Cuba, the Soviet Union began in the 1970s regular deployment of a Soviet naval task force operating each year in the Caribbean and Gulf of Mexico waters.

By 1980 the Soviet and Warsaw Pact shipyards had achieved a steady momentum in shipbuilding far larger than that in the United States. They were outproducing us by two to one in major combatants and by five to one in submarines. They had begun initial construction of a large-deck nuclear-powered Supercarrier now completed, the *Brezhnev*, and were completing the third and fourth Kiev class VTOL carriers. They were completing the first of the huge Typhoon class ballistic missile submarines. They were building two new classes of cruisers, including the second of the Kirov class nuclear-powered battle cruisers, and two new classes of destroyer, the Sovremenyy and the Udaloy. There were no fewer than seven different submarine classes under construction. In between their organizing and demonstrating with Lech Walesa and Solidarity, the Polish shipyards were turning out an impressive stream of new amphibious warfare ships and repair ships for the Soviet fleet.

The U.S. Navy was deeply concerned as we observed closely the new Soviet sub classes at sea and how fast they seemed to be closing the technology gap. We did not know at the time that for ten years they had been reading our most secret fleet communications from ships and subs at sea, and from commanders and fleet headquarters—an advantage they would enjoy for five more years, well into the 1980s. They were also obtaining access to a great many of the most highly classified documents on our weapons systems designs and operational capabilities. The Walker spy ring had provided the Soviets with an invaluable window into the U.S. Navy. When the latest Akula class nuclear submarine began sea trials in 1986, we were aghast to learn that its "quiet level" approached that of the 688 submarines we were building just a few years before. The Akula class is now known in the navy as the Walker class.

The Walker case exposed the grave inadequacy of the navy security system. The sheer volume of sensitive communications in the satellite and computer age, where every ship receives about seventeen hundred classified messages per day, just overwhelmed the system. We made major efforts to close the door after the Walker exposure, cutting the seven hundred thousand security clearances in the navy by 46 percent and instituting tighter controls on the handling of material, increasing the number of investigators involved in counterespionage, and obtaining authority for wider use of random polygraphs. Another great frustration of the case was the inability to court-martial Walker for espionage, which had been dropped by Congress from the Uniform Code of Military Justice (UCMJ). It has since been restored. The case was handled by the Justice Department, and there the bureaucracy handled it like any other white-collar crime. Walker got a life sentence and will be eligible for parole after ten years.

In prior days, the penalty for treason was far greater. For instance, a typical sentence in 1803 was "That you . . . be hanged by the neck, but not until you are dead, but that you be taken down again; and whilst you are yet alive, your bowels be taken out and burnt before your face; and that afterwards your head be severed from your body and your body divided into four quarters. . . . And may God Almighty have mercy on your soul."[6]

Now the only issue is whether Walker will have to pay tax on his Soviet income.

In the mid-1970s there was great fluttering in defense reform circles about the deployment by the Soviets of the Alpha class submarine (see the discussion in the introduction). The navy kept quiet as it was raked over the coals by defense "experts" who did not understand the real nature of antisubmarine warfare. The Alpha class submarine, made of titanium, was capable of going faster and deeper than any American submarine. The Soviets are actually ahead of us in titanium metallurgy. We could build one of titanium, but the expense would be prohibitive. It was, however, as noisy as a freight train and often could be detected thousands of miles away. Thanks to the Walkers, this

ierability was revealed to the Soviets, their entire submarine build-
m was reoriented, and a massive effort was made to target American
Western technology to make their submarines quiet. That led
directly to the public furor over allegations that the Toshiba Company of Japan
and the Kongsberg Company of Norway enabled the Soviets to construct submarine propellers essentially as quiet as those of the Americans. It was alleged
that in pursuit of profit they actually went to the extreme of secretly providing
teams of technicians and software experts to set up and initially operate the
new machinery in the top-secret building yards in the Soviet Union.

More significant than the stream of new ships and aircraft to the Soviet fleet
were the steady improvements to the weapons and sensor systems in those ships
and aircraft. New missiles, naval guns, mines, torpedoes, radars, and sonars—
to name a few—were added at a steady pace, expedited by the continued transfer of Western technology, as in the Toshiba case. To his great credit, Cap
Weinberger very early set as a major objective the constricting of that flow, and
he set up a powerful office under Richard Perle and Steven Bryen. That office
has done much to strengthen the agreements with our allies to restrict such
technology transfer, but as Lenin pointed out, some capitalists will always try
to sell the rope to their hangman.

Whatever their motivation for the massive expansion in the capabilities and
sphere of operations of the post-1962 Soviet fleet, the U.S.S.R. has created an
offensively capable blue water force providing a global military reach in support of the expansion of Soviet influence from Nicaragua to the South Pacific,
from Vietnam to Africa. Daily, no matter where our fleet operates, our ships
and men usually are within sight of Soviet naval forces. Familiarity is breed-
ing a well-deserved respect on both sides; we see that the Soviets are good and
are getting better.

Soviet surface forces have long been making deployments to the vulnerable choke points around the world, and in the past decade in the Caribbean
and the Gulf of Mexico. Since their great expansion of the 1960s and 1970s,
we find the Soviet Navy able to maintain itself astride the vital sea lanes and
navigational choke points through which most of the free world's international
trade must pass. This constitutes a fundamental change in the global military
balance of power, surpassed in significance only by the advent of thermonu-
clear weapons, for these naval deployments embody the achievement of an
unprecedented Soviet global military reach. The nightmare of an earlier era
of geopolitical theorists, including Mahan, had been brought to reality: the
manpower and resources of the greatest land power joined to a blue water,

ocean-spanning fleet. (See figure 3.) The rise of the Soviet merchant marine has been an integral component of the unified Soviet concept of sea power and has taken on an even greater role in recent years in view of the precipitous decline in free world merchant shipping and building.

In determining what our response should be in restoring the naval balance, I was not too concerned that our buildup would lead the Soviets to do even more. They were already at full stretch. Their yards were operating essentially at capacity, unless they were to shift to a total wartime footing, which was highly unlikely. Naval intelligence was convinced at the time that we would see in the 1980s a leveling off in the building rates and a slight net decline in the size of the Soviet fleet as they retired older combatants and incorporated the much more expensive Western technology into their new combatants. When I departed the navy in 1987, that prediction had been totally confirmed.

Instead of quantity, we saw in the 1980s an increased emphasis on quality in ship construction and weapons systems. In addition to entry into service of two new classes of ultraquiet submarines in the Sierra and the Akula, the SSNX-21 "Tomahawkski" cruise missile appeared. The first 65,000-ton nuclear supercarrier, the *Brezhnev*, was launched in 1985, with the second being immediately begun on the same building ways. Work continued on the third and fourth Kirov class nuclear-powered battle cruisers, and series production of the Slava class cruiser and the Sovremenyy and Udaloy classes of destroyer. In 1986, Soviet shipyards alone delivered a staggering seventy-three combatants, of which only thirty-one were for export to their clients around the world.[7]

The capabilities of the Soviet task groups of the 1990s, when combined with continuing advances in the Soviet Navy's use of space for surveillance, communications, and navigation, will be an order of magnitude superior to the forces we now face. Maturing Soviet naval air power will be matched by an overall increase in fleet offensive and defense capabilities as the sophisticated ships of the 1980s replace the mass-production units of the 1950s and 1960s. The Soviet fleet of the 1990s will be slightly smaller than the current seventeen-hundred-ship fleet, but its submarines will be faster and quieter and will have better sensors and self-protection; its surface ships will have greater endurance, new generations of sensors and weapons, and greater survivability; and new aircraft will have greater endurance and payloads. The command, control, and communications network that binds together these forces will be far more responsive and redundant.

Principle VI. *Maritime strategy must be global in concept.* Water covers three quarters of the world, and the United States is, in effect, an island nation washed by the Atlantic and Pacific oceans. Our commercial, political, and military vital interests are spread around the globe. Now the threat to these interests, in the form of Soviet military power, is deployed everywhere in the globe where our vital interests exist. The development of these factors has eliminated the option of planning for a regionally limited naval war with the Soviet Union.

Unlike land warfare, should deterrence break down and conflict begin between the navies of the United States and the Soviet Union, it will be instantaneously a global naval conflict. Our fleets are deployed within hundreds of feet of each other every day in every major theater of the world. If war breaks out between us in Europe, at sea it will break out everywhere, and at once. Because the Soviet fleet is in strength in every theater, we no longer have the option of planning sequential operations theater by theater. If we "swing" naval forces from one ocean to reinforce another, we turn the abandoned theater over to Soviet domination.

Strategy for each theater is the responsibility of the combatant commander in that theater, and each will be different according to the geography and interests involved. In virtually every theater, geography favors the United States and its allies and is unfavorable to the Soviet Union.

Principle VII. *Maritime strategy must fully integrate all U.S. and free world forces.* In establishing strategy for each theater you begin with a base of free world forces in each. The navies of our allies are very good. In areas such as diesel submarines, frigates, coastal patrol craft, minesweepers, and maritime patrol craft, our allies have assets absolutely essential to us for sea control in war and in peace. Our allies, for instance, have approximately 140 modern diesel electric submarines. If they did not maintain these forces, we would have to build and maintain them ourselves. Similarly, they maintain about 600 minesweepers. In some regions, such as the eastern Atlantic and the waters surrounding the United Kingdom, our allies supply a majority of the antisubmarine capability to counter the Soviet threat. In fact, if we could not count on our allies, we would require a U.S. fleet much larger than 600 ships to deal with the 1,700 ships and submarines the Soviets can deploy against us. All but one of the world's greatest navies are on our side, and this gives a tremendous advantage to the U.S. Navy and significant cost savings to the U.S. taxpayer.

The integration of U.S. Air Force, U.S. Coast Guard, and U.S. Army forces into maritime strategy was essential for its success. In 1982 the secretary of the air force and I concluded a major umbrella memorandum of agreement to begin working groups for the active integration of air force and naval operations in mutual support of each other's strategies. Admiral James A. Lyons, when he became commander of the Atlantic strike fleet in 1981, immediately integrated Air Force F-15s, AWACs, radar surveillance aircraft, KC-10 tankers, and B-52 aircraft into his maritime strategy for the Atlantic. What were then seen as bold initiatives have now become standard integrated policy. Similarly, carrier aircraft and sea-based cruise missiles have now been integrated fully into land battle strategy in Europe, Korea, and elsewhere. In 1984 a similar umbrella memorandum of agreement was reached with the army to integrate and coordinate operations in maritime objectives and in establishing new equipment and procedures for interoperability where the army and the navy would operate together. The lessons learned from Grenada further refined this initiative. When Lyons became commander of the Pacific fleet, he pioneered extensive new joint air force-navy operations for a strategy to gain early control of the northeastern and northwestern Pacific, using land-based air force aircraft integrated with carrier battle groups.

Principle VIII. *Maritime strategy must be a forward strategy.* It is this strategic principle, along with the national tasking to carry the fight to the enemy, that has crystallized most of the criticism of our naval strategy. As Admiral Lee Baggett, supreme allied commander, Atlantic (SACLANT), has put it, "If the battle for the Atlantic is fought in the Atlantic, we will lose." With the global nature of our maritime tasks, the limited forces available dictate that our strategy must be a forward one, a strategy that identifies and exploits Soviet weaknesses such as inherently unfavorable maritime geography. It must force the Soviet Union to use its maritime forces, particularly its attack submarines, to defend its vulnerabilities rather than allowing the Soviets the initiative to prey on our vulnerabilities. In the Atlantic, for instance, if Soviet submarines are permitted to attack our strategic sealift, we are certain to lose. Geography itself dictates a forward strategy, since our allies, such as Norway, Turkey, and Japan, are themselves forward in waters adjacent to the Soviet Union. To defend them successfully in the initial stages of a conflict requires a forward strategy. Our adversaries must know that if they initiate hostilities, it is they who will be put on the defensive at sea. A forward strategy is necessary to destroy enemy forces before they are brought to bear, to keep pressure on the enemy's interior lines of communication, preventing his concentration of forces, and buying time for the capabilities of the industrial democracies to mobilize and come into decisive play. It will also prevent Warsaw Pact concentration of forces in Central Europe by forcing them to defend and distribute their forces against maritime vulnerabilities around the entire periphery of Warsaw Pact territory. Free world naval forces cannot allow the Soviets to choose the time and place of each engagement. Our strategy must assure that we fight on terms most advantageous to us, capitalizing on Soviet geographic disadvantages and keeping the Soviets concerned with threats all around their periphery.

Major changes in Soviet naval activity since 1986 suggest that the U.S.S.R. has been paying attention to the development of the maritime strategy and the renaissance of our fleet under the Reagan administration: While the deployment level of Soviet strategic "out of area" activity for other Soviet submarines and their surface forces has dropped markedly, major fleet exercises in 1986 departed from previous trends that emphasized far-ranging interdiction operations and instead were staged much closer to home, under the umbrella of land-based aviation. Overall, the Soviet Navy has continued to operate and to train, but activities have switched dramatically to their home waters. The net strategic result appears to us to be a Soviet fleet positioning and training to counter our new maritime strategy. That precisely was what we intended, to force them to shift from an offensive naval posture targeted against our vulnerabilities to a defensive posture to protect their own vulnerabilities.

The Six-Hundred-Ship Navy: Building to the Strategy

Applying the eight strategic principles in carrying out the maritime tasks assigned to the navy by national strategy enabled us to establish a disciplined maritime strategy as a conceptual framework for employing all assets to achieve those tasks. From that strategy, logic dictates the size of the fleet, the size of ships and weapons used, and the type and intensity of training and readiness.

Any view of the global disposition of the U.S. Navy and U.S. Marine Corps reveals that we must deploy them in peacetime very much as we would operate in wartime. For purposes of deterrence, crisis management, and diplomacy, we must be present in areas where we would have to fight if war broke out. Of course, the intensity of operations is different—roughly three times more ships needed in a given theater in wartime, as compared with peacetime. We also train as we intend to fight. A full-scale general war at sea rarely would find a carrier battle group operating alone. So we train often in multiple-carrier battle forces.

The six-hundred-ship-navy goal did not simply spring full blown from my brow, although critics liked to depict it that way. The size of the fleet is dictated by the maritime strategy and the separate requirements of each of the different geographic theaters: the Atlantic, the Mediterranean, the Pacific, and the Indian Ocean-Persian Gulf.

The Atlantic

The large Atlantic theater encompasses the North Atlantic; the Norwegian Sea; the northern flank of NATO, including the Baltic throat; the South Atlantic; the Caribbean; and the Gulf of Mexico. It includes the eastern coast of South America and the western coast of Africa—all vital sea lanes of communication. And it involves the Mediterranean and the Middle East. The U.S. Navy operates in the Atlantic theater with two fleets—the Sixth and the Second.

THE SIXTH FLEET

The Sixth Fleet, in the Mediterranean, is the principal fighting force of the NATO southern Europe command and provides amphibious strike capability, air superiority, antisubmarine capability, and close air support for the entire southern flank of NATO. In addition, the Sixth Fleet is the principal naval force that supports our friends and allies in the Middle East. The threat there is significant. The Soviets maintain a fleet in the Black Sea and a deployed squadron in the Mediterranean. In wartime we expect to see there also Soviet naval strike aircraft, a formidable number of diesel and nuclear submarines, and a full range of missile cruisers, destroyers, and other smaller combatants.

In wartime U.S. forces in the Sixth Fleet would have to include three or four carrier battle groups operating to meet NATO commitments. We also would need to deploy a battleship battle group and two under-way replenishment groups (a task force of supply ships that refuels and resupplies the combatant ships while under way). In peacetime we average over a year about one and one third carrier battle groups deployed in the Mediterranean.

THE SECOND FLEET

The Second Fleet is the heart of the Atlantic strike force for NATO. It is responsible for naval operations in the North Atlantic; Iceland; the Norwegian Sea; the defense of Norway; and the entire northern flank, including the North Sea and the Baltic throat. It must simultaneously accomplish any naval mission required in the Caribbean, where we now face a very large Soviet and Cuban naval interdiction capability; in the South Atlantic, where we have vital sea lanes; and along the West African sea lanes, where the Soviets now deploy naval forces continuously.

For the Second Fleet, in wartime, we must plan to have four or five carrier battle groups, one battleship battle group, and three under-way replenishment groups. Four carriers bring the equivalent firepower of forty World War II carriers and can deliver accurate strike ordnance on target equal to eight hundred B-17s every day. Most of our fleet training in the Atlantic occurs in the Second Fleet's operating areas. Today we have six carrier battle groups cycling between the Second and the Sixth fleets.

The Pacific

Our increasing commercial interests and security ties in the Pacific have significantly changed our naval planning. If we are to protect our vital interests, we must have forces available to deploy to the Atlantic and the Pacific theaters simultaneously. We cannot abandon one theater to deal with the other. A great paradox of the 1970s was the reduction of the fleet's size so it could be employed only in a "swing strategy"—just as that strategy was being rendered obsolete by trade, geopolitics, and the growth of the Soviet Navy.

THE SEVENTH FLEET

The Seventh Fleet is our forward western Pacific fleet, which meets our commitments to Japan, Korea, the Philippines, Australia, and Thailand, as in the critical straits of Southeast Asia as well as in the Indian Ocean. In wartime we would need to deploy five carrier battle groups to the Seventh Fleet, two battleship battle groups, and four under-way replenishment groups. In peacetime we average over the year the equivalent of one and one-third carrier battle groups in the western Pacific.

We do not have a separate fleet in the critical area of Southwest Asia, the Indian Ocean, and the Persian Gulf. In peacetime we have a Middle East force in Bahrain in the Persian Gulf reporting to a two-star task force commander afloat, who in turn reports to the Central Command, a unified command in Tampa, Florida, which also takes operational control of elements of the Sixth and Seventh fleets such as carrier or battleship battle groups when they enter the Indian Ocean. The disaster of the *Stark* and the mining of the Persian Gulf in 1987 illustrates now nonsensical the current command relationships are. The task force commander should report either to the Atlantic or the Pacific fleets rather than through a unified layered bureaucracy in Florida. The gulf warrants a joint task force commander who should be physically there. A huge unified command is unneeded and a hindrance. And its location in an office compound in Tampa is absurd.

In wartime we plan for two of the Seventh Fleet carrier battle groups to meet our commitments in the Indian Ocean, Southwest Asia, East Africa, the Persian Gulf area, and Southeast Asia. Notionally, a Seventh Fleet battleship battle group and one under-way replenishment group also would be assigned to operate in these areas.

THE THIRD FLEET

The Third Fleet has responsibility for operations off Alaska, the Bering Sea, the Aleutians, the eastern Pacific, and the mid-Pacific region. In wartime there would be considerable overlapping and trading between the Seventh and Third fleets. This happened in the Pacific during World War II. To cover that vast area, we must assign two carrier battle groups and one under-way replenishment group.

Strategic Submarine Force

Our national strategic deterrent posture depends heavily on the credibility and effectiveness of our strategic submarine force; therefore, its force level ultimately must be determined at a national level. The president has directed that we procure one Trident submarine per year until an ultimate force level is established. This level would be based on the military need to replace the Poseidon fleet and to take advantage of the enhanced firepower and accuracy of Trident in sizing the national strategic force. The outcome of current arms negotiations also may influence the force level requirement. At least twenty Trident submarines are needed to replace the aging Poseidon fleet.

Operational Tempo in Peace and War

These requirements compel us to deploy a six-hundred-ship navy. In peacetime, we deploy to the same places we must control in war, but at one-third the tempo of operations. This allows a bearable peacetime burden of six-month deployment lengths and 50 percent time in home port. Looked at either way, we require the same size fleet to meet peacetime deployments as we do to fight a global war. (See table 1.) Taken together, they add up to the following:

  15 carrier battle groups
   4 battleship battle groups
 100 attack submarines
      Lift for the assault echelons of a marine amphibious force and a marine
      amphibious brigade
      An adequate number of ballistic missile submarines

When escort, mine warfare, auxiliary, and replenishment units are considered, about six hundred ships emerge from this accounting—a force that can be described as prudent, reflecting geographic realities, alliance commitments and dependencies, and the Soviet fleet that threatens them. Unless Congress reduces our commitments or the Soviet threat weakens, there is no way to reduce the required size of the U.S. fleet and still carry out the missions assigned to the navy by the national strategy.

TABLE 1. CURRENT NAVY NORCE REQUIREMENTS

	PEACETIME MARITIME STRATEGY	WARTIME MARITIME STRATEGY
	6th Fleet	
CVBG	1.3	4
BBBG	.3	1
URG	1	2
	2nd Fleet*	
CVBG	6.7	4
BBBG	1.7	1
URG	4	3
	7th Fleet**	
CVBG	2	5
BBBG	.5	2
URG	1	4
	3rd Fleet*	
CVBG	5	2
BBBG	1.5	—
URG	4	1

* Includes forces in overhaul
** Includes Indian Ocean Forces
Note: CVBG = carrier battle group; BBBG = battleship battle group; URG = underway replenishment group.
Source: U.S. Department of the Navy, *Report to the Congress, Fiscal Year 1988* (Washington, D.C.: U.S. Government Printing Office, 1987).

Joint Training and Exercises

As the global maritime strategy has been continuously refined, it is directly applied to training. That training, like the strategy, is designed to incorporate not only navy and marine corps forces but also is critically dependent on those of other U.S. services and the forces of our allies. Only by eliminating needless overlap in total capabilities could we find sufficient funds for the essential programs. The past six years have seen major new agreements between the navy/marine corps and the air force, the army, and the coast guard. In addition, we have made extensive progress in multilateral and bilateral agreements with navies and air forces of our allies.

The fact that U.S. Air Force AWACS, B-52 bombers, and fighters are not integral parts of every significant naval exercise and theater strategy attests to the fact that while interservice rivalry is strong on the playing fields of service academies, it does not interfere with the effective integration of our operating forces. The unrehearsed yet fully integrated U.S. Navy/U.S. Air Force strike on facilities that supported terrorism in Libya in 1986 put the lie to the myth that the services do not work well together.

A uniquely valuable aspect of our maritime strategy is that the navy trains in the actual waters of expected combat operations, often with face-to-face contact with front-line Soviet surface, air, and subsurface forces. This active peacetime presence transmits a true deterrent signal to the Soviets and reassures our allies. In conjunction with this emphasis on training where we expect to fight, increased emphasis has been placed on multiple carrier battle group operations in the North Atlantic and Northwest Pacific, with annual exercises lasting months. The "northern wedding" exercises in the Atlantic, for instance, take place in an area stretching from the East Coast of the United States to the Baltic Sea and involve testing NATO's capacity to resist mounting Soviet aggression in the Atlantic Ocean and the Baltic and Norwegian seas. More than 150 ships and submarines and hundreds of aircraft operate for weeks in an intense multithreat environment, conducting carrier battle group operations, reinforcement convoy operations, and sea control operations in the Baltic approaches. The exercises usually climax with amphibious landings in Norway. Eight NATO allies furnish forces. The commander, Striking Fleet Atlantic, said in assessing "northern wedding '86":

> You've got to come up here and do it. You can talk about it all you want. You can sit around the table and plan it. You can war-game it. But until you put it all together, until you go to Norway and combine the four elements of the striking fleet—the carrier, the ASW, the amphibious and Marine strike forces—and coordinate with other NATO commanders, you really don't know if it will work. I think we showed it will work.

Fleetex-86 was a similar large, multiple battle group exercise conducted in the Pacific that demonstrated equivalent capability in the Bering Sea and approaches to the main Soviet naval fronts of Petropavlovsk and Vladivostok.

These exercises are expensive, but they are worth giving up other things to continue. They provide more real return in force effectiveness than any other expenditure.

Funding Priorities

Once we had our strategy in place and the process operating with feedback loops from exercises, commanders, planners, and war gamers, the navy very quickly derived a clear set of priorities for planning, programming, and budgeting that became the bases of our program for the remaining five years. Those priorities became:

- restoration of the quality, training, and morale of our personnel
- restoration of the overall readiness of the navy and the marine corps through adequate maintenance, repair, spare parts, and support
- modernization of our sea-based nuclear deterrent, the most survivable and enduring component of the U.S. strategic triad
- establishment of a shipbuilding, reactivation, and conversion program to increase the force with the right kinds of ships and to save an industrial base on the verge of collapse
- establishment of aircraft modernization and procurement program to restore aircraft numbers and quality to meet operational requirements
- building up stocks of ammunition and missiles to realistic objectives for sustaining combat

Thus, by the end of 1981, we had set the course for every aspect of the navy and the marine corps. All that remained was to carry it out. A piece of cake!

The Critics

After becoming secretary of the navy, I decided to emphasize the most controversial aspects of our new strategy and fight out the policy battles on these aspects while we still had the strong momentum of a newly elected administration. Every administration has a half-life, and I knew that the forces arrayed against the navy would gradually wear down the momentum in subsequent years. I therefore planned to go for the biggest, most controversial programs, such as more aircraft carriers, Aegis cruisers, and nuclear submarines, right away. Perhaps surprising to those who share the common view that the Pentagon is rife with interservice rivalry, very little opposition or criticism of the navy's plans came from the air force or the army. In fact, I never once encountered either service working actively against the navy or marine corps, although there were plenty of others outside the services who were. The critics of our maritime strategy fall into five categories: The OSD and JCS bureaucracy; the Europeanists; the reformers; the détentists; and the ad hominem critics.

The most threatening of all the critics were the OSD and the JCS bureaucracies. They are perhaps the most entrenched career bureaucracies in Washington and perhaps the world, and each number nearly 2,000 souls. Their opposition stems not from ideology but from the very permanence of their orthodoxy. The average civilian presidential appointee stays in his Pentagon position less than two years. The average OSD and JCS bureaucrat, civilian and military, stays thirty years. There is an overwhelming institutional smugness that says, "You, with your six-hundred-ship navies and new ideas, will come and go, but we shall be here forever." The orthodoxy itself is a rather shapeless mush of established attitudes based on the religion of centralization and "jointness." It inevitably takes its cast from the fact that 4 out of 5 of the 658 serving military staff officers in the "civilian" OSD staff are either army or air force officers.* On the JCS staff, 78 percent of the staff officers are either army or air force. Similarly, the civilians on both staffs share the same service ratio to the extent that they are retired military officers or serving reservists. The reason for this disparity is, of course, that the army and the air force together have 220,000 officers and the Navy has only 72,000 officers. The air force has a $4\frac{1}{2}$-to-1 enlisted-to-officer ratio, while the navy has a 7-to-1 ratio. Virtually every aspect of the new maritime strategy and the 600-ship-navy programs to carry it out were opposed virtually unanimously by the OSD and JCS bureaucracies throughout my tenure.

Another strong body of our critics were "the Europeanists," who cut across political parties and services, sharing a near-obsession with Europe and NATO as the center of all foreign and defense policy. Harold Brown and Bob Komer, the architects of Carter's policy making NATO policy the sole American defense policy, leaped into print early in the Reagan administration, taking on the maritime strategy. They and others, such as Edward Luttwak, sought to portray the maritime strategy as an alternative to the more traditional NATO-oriented "continental strategy." They were, of course, misusing the word "strategy" and creating a meaningless hypothesis. Maritime strategy is not an

---

*An immutable law of physics is that, once established, a bureaucracy grows. The OSD staff was originally limited by law to 50 people. One way in which such restrictions were evaded was by "detailing" military personnel to "assist" the civilian staff—hence the current total of 658. Many of the civilians are former military personnel who simply retired in place.

alternative, but it is a *prerequisite* necessary for any successful defense strategy for NATO. Maritime superiority alone may not assure victory, but the loss of it will certainly assure defeat—and sooner rather than later. Chronicles of warfare from the classical era forward attest consistently to the influence of sea power upon history. The singular lesson is that the great continental powers do not long prevail against an opponent with mastery of the seas. The Soviet Union seems to understand the experience of history, which has motivated their achievement of a blue-water navy. No maritime strategy, of course, can be a successful strategy for NATO without an effective land deterrent on the Continent itself. The choice, therefore, is not between a maritime strategy or some other strategy, but between maintaining a maritime strategy in defense of NATO or failing to do so—a failure that would prove fatal to NATO's survival.

To suggest that naval support of Norway or Turkey or Japan is too dangerous because it must be done close to the Soviet Union is defeatist. The argument rests on the presumption that ships cannot survive close to the Soviet Union. It ignores the facts that land bases are far more vulnerable in that they cannot move at thirty-one knots, are defended by far fewer defenses than the seven layers of a battle group, and indeed are deployed—especially in Norway—far closer to the Soviet Union than the carrier will ever go. If nuclear submarines and fully capable carrier battle groups cannot survive against Soviet Backfires and cruise missiles, how do such Europeanists expect that the army divisions and air force bases on the North German Plain will fare? In fact, both can survive if properly trained and equipped.

The principal new ideas of the reformers are that small cheap ships are better than big expensive ships, surface ships cannot survive, small lightweight fighters are better than big expensive fighters, and low-tech simplicity is better than high-tech complexity. Because our maritime strategy came to exactly opposite conclusions on every one of their favorite issues, we have provided them with a steady source of income from the think tanks, foundations, and defense contractors upon whom they prey.

A more serious stream of criticism comes from the liberal intellectuals and journalists who might generally be termed the "détentists." These critics, too, seem to grab on to the Norwegian aspects of the Atlantic part of the strategy, but for different reasons than the Europeanists. They see steaming the fleet into the Norwegian Sea as needlessly provocative of the Soviet Union, and likely to lead to escalation of the war by threatening attack on the Soviet Union itself. Implicit in this critique is that it's regrettable if the Soviets attack NATO, but NATO must not hit back on actual Soviet territory. To criticize the strategy on such a basis indicates the lengths to which some détentists will go to portray Soviet intentions as solely defensive.

Another aspect of the strategy that particularly upsets these critics is the intention and capability to operate under the Arctic ice, and if ordered by the commander in chief, to sink Soviet strategic submarines. On the one hand, this is part of the religious belief of détentists that civilian populations must be held hostage, and hence Soviet strategic offensive forces not be subjected to attack; and on the other hand, naïve ignorance of the mechanics of antisubmarine warfare. (They should read *The Hunt for Red October*.) Soviet missile submarines are very difficult to distinguish from other classes of Soviet attack submarines. Moreover, all their missile submarines carry antisubmarine torpedoes and sonars as well. If the Soviet strategic submarine is encountered by an American attack submarine once hostilities have begun, it will be taken under attack, if, indeed, it has not attacked the American boat already. An active campaign to hunt Soviet missile boats is another matter entirely. While a commander in chief could order this, it is not something that the maritime strategy would normally do because that would subtract SSNs from the primary conventional maritime tasks of the strategy.

The fifth and final category of criticism comes from a group that may be called ad hominem critics, or critics of John Lehman. While I remain convinced that I am a most agreeable — even lovable — person, once in a while an occasional person does not see me in such a light.

While there were plenty of critical articles on the maritime strategy in the press, I always felt that while I was secretary of the navy we got a reasonably fair shake and professional treatment on the merits.

By and large, the steady stream of criticism from these five directions was very helpful in keeping us on our toes and in refining and correcting certain flaws in the detailed logic of some aspects of the strategy. It also provided a great deal of fun in the various jousting sessions I had with them in TV shows, congressional hearings, and policy sessions. In these battles, just as in the maritime strategy itself, offense always is the best defense.

CHAPTER 5

The Six-Hundred-Ship Navy

After establishing the intellectual foundations of the new maritime strategy, we spent most of the year in 1981 translating that strategy into detailed policy plans and programs. Many of the policy and program issues had been settled during the transition but needed detailed implementing decisions. Others had to be faced for the first time, and existing programs brought into conformity with the new strategy.

Simultaneously, through much of the year the new Defense Resources Board (DRB) met almost daily. Secretary Weinberger had reconstituted the DRB as the executive committee for the Defense Department. Under Frank Carlucci's chairmanship the DRB became the center of decision-making for all the defense budget and policy issues for the department.

Weinberger had been true to his word and, in setting up the DRB, he included the service secretaries as principals, along with the under secretaries of defense, the defense comptroller, the director of PA&E (systems analysis), and assistant secretaries as the policy issues dictated. For the first year this group was extremely effective as a decision-making body. We began at once to prepare a major supplemental to the fiscal year 1981 budget then in force and an even larger revision of the fiscal year 1982 budget submitted by President Carter. We began also to prepare from scratch the first full Reagan budget, for fiscal 1983.

The DRB sessions were very substantive, meaty discussions about all of the services' programs and included some quite sporty debates. The presence of the service chiefs as advisers, and the service secretaries as full members, educated each of the service leaders in the problems and programs of their counterparts. This was a dramatic contrast to the Carter administration, when only the staff members of the secretary of defense were present at the DRB.

The year 1981, of course, was not a normal one, because we were really preparing not one but three budgets.* This made for a sometimes entertaining exchange, especially because more than half of the issues raised by OSD were targeted against the navy. The debating lessons of the Cambridge Union served me well in those arguments; normally eight or ten critics, front or back bench, spoke against us. My staff and I also had the great advantage of having developed the intellectual foundations for all the issues and programs in the preceding several years. We knew them cold.

The Reagan administration's leisurely personnel appointments procedure guaranteed that there were many faces around the table that first year who were holdovers from Harold Brown's staff, including the JCS chairman, David Jones. Most irksome was their reluctance to acknowledge that there had been an election, that there was a new president, and that he had expressed himself explicitly on important naval issues. There was strong opposition to the six-hundred-ship navy itself, maritime superiority, aircraft carriers, battleships, and so on. Frank Carlucci was very fair-minded. As a result, when there was some reasonable case to be made by the critics, which occasionally there was, he always let them have the floor. At first I resented the reopening of basic issues, but I even came to enjoy it as we won issue after issue. It got so that I took to bringing the Republican platform to the meetings when an issue taking on the navy was scheduled. As the OSD critics would state their case, I would pull it out and lay it on the table with a Cheshire cat grin. I would never refer to it,

---

* In a normal year, the budget process begins with "the fiscal guidance," a planning budget assigned to each department by the secretary of defense. Subsequently, the departments respond in what is called the program objective memorandum (POM). The POM, itself a product of hard bargaining, is then analyzed for several months by OSD's two thousand bureaucrats. Then the DRB meetings start, their subject the several hundred issues of OSD disagreement with the service submissions, ranging from the most fundamental—as in the permanent opposition of the OSD staff to more aircraft carriers—to the micromanagement of silly little issues. The DRB hears from the joint CINCs, the unified and specified commanders, and their critiques of the service budgets. At the end, the deputy secretary of defense makes program decisions that are issued in "PDMs," program decision memoranda. The service secretaries may then appeal directly to the deputy secretary decisions with which they disagree, and the final product then is used to "prepare" the budget. Budget preparation is a separate process with a separate bureaucracy that overlaps considerably with the programming process. Here the action switches to the OSD comptroller's staff of professional budget analysts, and there are no large meetings to deliberate. Nevertheless, very often as much policy change is made here as in the programming phase. If it sounds complicated, it is.

but would deal with each attack point by point. Finally, one day Dick DeLauer, the new director of defense, research and engineering, could stand it no longer. Dick and I were constantly jousting throughout his 4½ year tenure and, while it usually was in a good-natured and amused tone, he really didn't like anything we were doing with the navy. He liked to refer to the six-hundred-ship navy as "a target-rich environment." Really he just reflected the ingrained bias of his long-tenured career staff in OSD. Dick blurted out in exasperation, "Aw, cut that crap, don't give us that platform bullshit, everybody knows that you wrote it and you put in all that nonsense about the six-hundred-ship navy." Everyone in the room laughed. I replied, "Dick, I was but a humble scribe, a slender reed dutifully recording the sovereign will of the people in convention assembled. All good Republicans know that. But if you doubt me, I urge you to call Master Chief Petty Officer John Tower (USNR), who was overall chairman of the platform committee, or my brother Chris, special assistant to President Reagan.* They will both confirm to you the president's own fervent commitment to those simple and beautiful words in the platform." Much more laughter.

There has been criticism from some quarters in subsequent years that Cap simply threw money uncritically at everything on the military wish list. That is simply not the case. Those dozens and dozens of DRB meetings in 1981 gave the defense budget a more thorough scrub than had ever been done before. The plain fact was that after hearing the arguments, Weinberger believed, as did many of us around the table, that all of those programs were needed, and that so starved were all of the services for spare parts, ammunition, aircraft, tanks, guns, and pay that there just were not many bad candidates put forward for funding. But the debate was thorough and searching, and hugely beneficial to all the participants. When the year was over we were all experts on everyone else's programs.

After the first year, however, the effectiveness of the DRB declined. The reason was that more and more members of the OSD staff kept being added. And then all of the military chiefs were added as full members, and then all of the CINCs. It just got too big to work.

It was also clear by the end of the second year of the administration that the defense bureaucracy had reasserted its hold over the policy process to such

---

* Christopher Lehman, one of my younger brothers, had been legislation assistant to Senator Byrd, Senator Griffin, and Senator Warner in the 1970s and had been appointed to the National Security Council staff by Judge William Clark. Christopher is currently president of Commonwealth Consulting.

an extent that I could no longer get anything approved without going directly to Frank Carlucci or to Cap. But I rarely got to see Cap more than once or twice a week, and often he would sign off decisions on the navy prepared by the OSD staff without my having a say.

In any bureaucracy, access is power. And in both the State Department under George Shultz and the Pentagon under Cap Weinberger, the permanent bureaucracy soon established absolute control over access to the secretary. In State it is done by the Foreign Service through the State secretariat. In Defense it is done by the military through the "EA" (executive assistant) system that has been in place for decades. Directly outside the office of the secretary of defense sits an active-duty general or admiral. He heads a small military staff controlling administrative paper flow, scheduling, and appointments. Cap had four superb officers during his tenure,* and none of them abused their power. But the system is such that, unless they intend to retire, their future promotions and assignments will be made by the senior generals and admirals, especially the chairman of the JCS, and not by any civilians. The system, therefore, guarantees that the chairman of the joint chiefs has automatic and unimpeded access, while others do not, and his staff has a guaranteed avenue to get papers immediately before the secretary of defense, while others may be diverted for months into "further staffing."

Cap was very hard to turn around once the bureaucracy had obtained his signature. He did not share my cynicism about the separate agenda of the career bureaucracy. He viewed it as his very own staff.

By 1984 the DRB had grown so large it had to move out of the deputy secretary's conference room into a vast ceremonial reception room across the hall, so the table could seat all of its forty-odd members. Although Will Taft, who was by then Cap's deputy, did a masterful job in presiding over such a mob, it was no longer possible to have the kind of policy debates we had the first two years. It became more of a Kabuki theater. Everyone knew that what they said would be fully reported throughout the defense establishment, and if it was really neat, would leak immediately to the press, and so the character of the deliberations changed considerably. The action moved much more to ad hoc meetings in Taft's office, and his door always was open. Because he had no background in defense before becoming general counsel in 1981, his

---

* Major General Carl Smith of the air force; Major General Colin Powell of the army (he is currently national security adviser); Vice Admiral Don Jones of the navy; and Major General Gordon F. Fornell of the air force.

appointment as deputy secretary of defense was met with skepticism. His impressive intellect and his fairness, however, quickly established a firm leadership over the process. His avoidance of the media has hidden the fact that he has been one of the most effective incumbents ever in the job.

The important issues we thrashed through that process—first in the navy, and then in the DRB, and finally in the budget preparation—were those that made up what is now known as the six-hundred-ship navy. They were all debated and fought over during the first year, but by its end, we had won them all.

High-Tech Versus Cheaper-Simpler

Among the most important of these issues was the popular cry to cut the addition of the military to complicated high-tech weapons systems. In the 1960s and 1970s, as the integrated-circuit revolution arrived, there were many instances where systems were too complicated to operate and too difficult to maintain, compared to their worth. The military was slow also to build the infrastructure of maintenance and support and too slow in recruiting and training skilled operators and repairmen. Industry also went overboard in promising the moon and delivering green cheese. Very often systems were delivered that did not meet promised performance specifications, nor did the contractor provide the kind of technical support, training, and spare parts necessary for the systems to function.

In response to some of these well-publicized failures in the 1960s and the 1970s, a whole trendy school of military reform grew up in Congress around the ideas that complexity and technology were bad and that simplicity and cheapness were good. Senators Bob Taft and Gary Hart applied this simplistic idea to the navy and spent years preaching that smaller, simpler, cheaper, more lightly armed and armored ships were better than large, expensive ships.

Determined to apply the lessons learned from the mistakes made in the introduction of high-tech, I fundamentally disagreed with the argument that smaller-simpler-cheaper are better. The tremendous American edge in technology is an inherent advantage provided by our culture and our economic system. We must build to this advantage, not trade it away for cheaper, smaller, less capable ships and aircraft and weapons built in greater numbers, which is the forte of a totalitarian, centralized, Gosplan economy. For instance, just as Apple has made computers "user friendly," so the very technology itself can be directed at solving its own problems of complexity, by simplifying and making more maintainable and reliable both our new systems and our older systems. The rapid evolution of integrated-circuit technology makes possible new orders of magnitude in improved reliability and lower maintenance. As another example, we invested heavily in applying the latest technology in the F-18 and the Aegis cruiser to achieve mean times between failures 25 times higher than the Phantom and the Chicago class cruiser they replaced. The F-18 now achieves a maintenance-to-flight-hour ratio four times better than the Phantom. That has enabled us to reduce the manning of each squadron by 50 expensive, highly skilled maintenance technicians. In the case of the Aegis cruiser, we have a ship at least 20 times more capable than the ship it replaces and manned by only 350 officers and men, compared to 1,150 for the older cruiser. Thus today, thanks to high-tech and complexity, our latest fighters and ships are not only far more capable but actually much less expensive to own and operate.

A huge dividend, measurable not only in money but also in human lives, is the enormous increase in safety that the high-tech revolution has brought to military aircraft. Those in Congress who argue that we should go back to the good old days of simple day fighters like the F-86 SaberJet never had to attend the weekly funerals caused by the high accident rates of those unsophisticated day fighters. In those days a navy jet pilot had a 25 percent probability of being killed in a peacetime accident during a 20-year flying career. In one peacetime year in the 1950s, for instance, the Navy lost 2,250 airplanes and 1,700 aviators. Today, thanks to digital built-in test equipment, quadruple redundant controls, and other high-tech innovations, the current accident rate for our new high-tech aircraft, such as the F-18 and the A-6, is one-twentieth what it was in the good old days that reformers would like to return to.

It would be a great mistake for us to adopt a defense strategy at sea—any more than on land—that attempts to match totalitarian regimes in sheer numbers of cheap, reproducible items. Time and again the high-tech solution— tied together with common sense—has proved to be the wisest investment and by far the most advantageous one for the United States and its allies.

The naval actions of the recent past clearly indicate the benefits of high-technology forces. The three exercises that were held in 1986 in the vicinity of the Gulf of Sidra, and then the joint air strike with the air force against Libyan terrorist targets, were all conducted under the most demanding, restrictive, and difficult conditions of peacetime crisis management. Our successes testified to the wisdom of investing sensibly in high-tech. (See figure 4.)

In this particular policy debate, I had a strong ally in one part of the OSD staff, the Directorate of Defense, Research, and Engineering, headed by Dick DeLauer. That office always is a strong bureaucratic lobby for the higher-tech solutions. The low-mix advocacy is invariably provided by PA&E, the systems analysis office in OSD that has spawned most of the small-is-beautiful gurus in the reform movement.

Making Better Use of the Old

Interestingly, even the low-mix advocates were opposed to a corollary theme I was determined to pursue: the better utilization of older weapons systems. It had cost us $3 billion to develop the first F-18. The navy bureaucracy now wanted to start a brand-new interceptor to replace the F-14, and a new interdiction aircraft to replace the A-6. The two programs were estimated to cost $8 billion in research and development alone. We could never afford them and do all the other things needed to restore the navy. While high-tech had brought a true revolution, the laws of physics had not changed. There are many weapons systems in the inventory that can carry out their task as well now as they could twenty or forty years ago, and the navy had to capitalize on those assets. Rather than developing brand-new aircraft to replace the F-14 and the A-6, we began a plan to renovate them totally with the latest high-tech, for one fourth the cost.

With regard to ships, we had five modernized World War II Essex class aircraft carriers in mothballs. I liked Tom Hayward's idea of taking one of these, the *Oriskany*, to reactivate as an immediate force-builder. Since my days on the NSC, I was also convinced that we should reactivate the battleships, and perhaps the Salem class cruisers with their long-range automatic eight-inch guns, because they offered far more firepower on solid, survivable platforms than what it would cost us to build from scratch. Every one of these "old ways are the best ways" initiatives was universally opposed by the OSD staff because of their institutional antinaval bias. They knew well that the risks and costs of new construction, especially under the self-defeating procurement system we found in 1981, would weigh heavily against naval expansion.

Marine Corps

The marine corps has often been accused of having an institutional paranoia. But as Henry Kissinger once told me, "Even paranoids have some enemies." Since World War II, the corps has survived four decades of attempts to abolish or curtail it. The marines certainly enjoyed a distinguished list of adversaries: George Marshall, Harry Truman, and Dwight Eisenhower. But Kennedy, Johnson, Nixon, and Ford were, to use a marine expression, "friends of the corps." Jimmy Carter had no strong views, but his defense secretary, Harold

Brown, and most of his staff believed the basic marine mission of amphibious assault was completely obsolete; they viewed the marines instead as reserve divisions to be sent to Europe or Korea as reinforcements in event of war. All plans to modernize the amphibious force were canceled. The amphibious ship force levels in the navy were cut from two MAFs to one MAF (each marine amphibious force contains about 50,000 marines and sailors, their equipment ranging according to mission). Most of the initiatives to modernize their equipment were indefinitely postponed.

In 1968 we had 157 large, amphibious warships and many hundreds of the small assault landing craft that take the marines from ship to shore. By the end of the Carter administration, the fleet was down to 63 amphibs, and all plans to replace them had been canceled. Events, however, changed some minds. The development of the Carter Doctrine and the creation of the Rapid Deployment Force (RDF) used the marine corps as the primary force. The RDF consisted of aircraft and ships dedicated to delivering a MAB (marine amphibious brigade) of some 16,000 men, to the Persian Gulf, then mating the personnel with their supporting equipment and supplies to sustain initial combat operations. To this end, the Carter administration prepositioned 7 supply ships at our Diego Garcia island base in the Indian Ocean. The RDF was not capable of amphibious assault but required friendly ports at which to disembark.

Reagan and Weinberger were "friends of the corps." It was our firm belief that the capability to make opposed landings of MAF or MAB size anywhere in the world was an enormously valuable capability for every theater commander and that the capability must be rebuilt in the corps. We supported the Carter Doctrine and brought it to a vigorous life beyond Carter's own manpower plans. Instead of a single brigade of marines, we expanded it to include 3 full brigades with weeks' supplies of beans and bullets. We designed and built 13 combination roll-on, roll-off, and breakbulk ships to replace the 7 deployed in the Carter administration. In addition, we kept those 7 ships and added another 8 to carry for the air force and army for their role in the Persian Gulf. Thus to protect our allies' oil, we have now a vast investment in equipment stockpiled in the theater, and active forces in the United States ready to go there to man it.

With little dissension, the DRB adopted the plan that we put forward, which was essentially prepared by General Robert Barrow, the outstanding commandant of the marine corps. In size, the corps was already about the same size as the entire U.S. Army at the beginning of World War II: 188,100.

We planned an increase in manpower, primarily for the new Persian Gulf contingencies, to about 200,000.

Formally the corps is composed of 3 active divisions and a single reserve division. The actual operational units range from marine amphibious units (MAUs), each about 2,000, to MABs, amphibious brigades of some 16,000, to MAFs, amphibious forces of some 50,000. (See table 2.) In functional equivalents, the marine corps really is made up of about 5 active divisions and about a single reserve division. Instead of the force we inherited of amphibious ships sufficient to deliver only a single MAF, we planned to achieve the capability to deploy a single MAF in one theater and, independently, a single MAB in another. We included in the shipbuilding program the necessary new ships to achieve that.

TABLE 2. THE MARITIME STRATEGY
(NOTIONAL AMPHIBIOUS FORCE COMPOSITION)

COMBAT FORCES

	Troops	Tanks	Fixed Wt., G Aircraft	Helicopters	Artillery
MAF*	52,300	70	157	156	120
MAB**	15,700	17	79	100	36
MAU***	2,000	5	6	22	8

*Marine amphibious force (division/air wing)
**Marine amphibious brigade (regiment/air group)
***Marine amphibious unit (battalion/squadron)
Source: U.S. Department of Defense

We also funded what is called "sustainability"—the beans, bullets, parts, and consumables necessary to sustain the corps at combat consumption levels for months.

At the end of the Vietnam War, the corps had purchased 118 of the British Harrier Jumpjets. The theory behind this versatile aircraft was that it could be based right up with the ground combat commander, giving his own organic close air support, operating from unprepared forward locations without runways. While in practice the results, because of the equipment and logistics needed to support any tactical aircraft, were far less than the promise, it did provide a unique capability ideally suited for the integrated air-ground combat team of the marine corps. By 1980 the marines had crashed about half of the 118 aircraft (the early models were very difficult planes to fly) and were well along in designing, with McDonnell Douglas and British Aerospace, the replacement, Harrier II, a much safer and more capable jet. The marines and the contractors had made an alliance with the military reformers on the Hill and had successfully forced the money for the program into the defense budget, against Harold Brown's opposition. It is an interesting sidelight that in gratitude for Gary Hart's leadership in getting funding for the Harrier, several retired marines actively campaigned for him in his reelection campaign against a conservative Republican woman in 1980. In 1981 we included the Harrier II in the marine budget. We rejected, however, the adoption of this air-craft for the navy because of its very limited range and payload, compared to carrier jets.

We also included funding for a replacement for the medium helicopter fleet of the marine corps, the CH-46 Seaknight, which had been flying for some twenty years.

In the belief that years of underfunding had left the marine corps seriously behind in all forms of equipment, we funded virtually everything the com-mandant asked for, including a series of light-armored vehicles, suitable for airlifting ashore; the Mark-19 grenade launcher; the M-198 155mm howitzer; and a host of field equipment, including shelters, containers, motor transport, and materiel handling and service support equipment. What we did not fully understand at the time was that all of this new equipment had the effect of making the marine corps far heavier than it had been, requiring much more cube and tonnage of amphibious lift to get them to the fight, and more heavy-lift helicopters to carry things such as howitzers ashore. In retrospect, we went too far, and a serious review to "lighten up" the corps was in order and was begun after I left by the then-commandant, General Al Gray.

Naval Strategic Nuclear Forces

Ronald Reagan had played heavily in the campaign on the theme that the SALT process and the naïveté of the Carter administration had stopped us from modernizing our strategic nuclear forces and that we had lost parity to a major Soviet building program. We all believed this. A task force had been created during the transition to construct a strategic nuclear modernization program. The comprehensive program included for the navy an increase in the num-ber of Trident submarines, a large eighteen-thousand-ton replacement for the Poseidon submarine carrying twenty-four missiles that had begun in the Nixon administration. (See the introduction and chapter 6.) We included six new Tridents in the five-year plan for 1983 and projected building three every two years thereafter. The president decided to accelerate the introduction of the

Trident II missile to an initial operational capability in 1989. This so-called D-5 missile would extend the standoff range of the submarine to four thousand miles, would carry eight high-yield warheads, and would include an advanced stellar-inertial guidance system that has now proved to have accuracy so tight that even at full range it could target Soviet ICBM silos.

One of the most unsung but important elements of the Reagan strategic initiatives was the emphasis on secure and redundant command and control systems rather than more warheads and megatonnage. For the navy this meant funding a Boeing 707-based replacement for the EC-130 Tacamo aircraft. These aircraft fly as secure communications links between the president and the nuclear submarine.

We funded also the extremely-low-frequency (ELF) system for the north-central United States, which involved miles of buried antenna in northern Michigan, to provide additional redundant one-way communication links to the deployed submarine force. This unjammable frequency transmits through the Earth itself and the oceans, enabling communications to subs at any depth (the Soviets have this system also). We funded advanced research in communications by satellite through blue-green lasers that penetrate to great depths. This technology looks very promising indeed. As a consequence of all these communications improvements, the possibility of Soviet preemptive attack is now far more remote. By denying the Soviets any prospect for gaining any possible advantage by initiating the use of nuclear weapons, deterrence has been greatly stabilized.

Manpower and Personnel

The single most debilitating factor in the decline of the military forces during the 1970s was the steep drop in the morale and the quality of the men and women in the armed forces. That was brought about by the general post-Vietnam hangover and by low pay. After the all-volunteer force was instituted and substantial pay raises given in 1973, there followed seven straight years of a pay freeze while inflation climbed into double digits. The result was a precipitous decline in the standard of living for all the military. In the lower enlisted ranks, thousands of families lived below the poverty line and were eligible for public assistance. In my squadron at Oceana, Virginia, VA-35, the squadron actually organized buses to take the wives of enlisted personnel into downtown Norfolk to the food stamp office. The lack of funding for spare parts, training, and supplies further aggravated the morale problem, and our experienced people, particularly in the high-tech skills, left the navy and the marine corps in droves. During the late 1970s we experienced the lowest sustained retention in the history of the navy. Recruiting was so bad we almost had to resort to press-gangs. We were taking in sailors who were convicted felons, drug addicts, and illiterates. We actually had to open a school in Meridian, Mississippi, to teach recruits how to read. Still we could not attract sufficient numbers, and the fleet in 1979 was manned at only 91 percent. Four ships in that year could not sail on schedule because they did not have sufficient sailors to man them. Pilot retention had dropped to an all-time low of 28 percent, and because of that hemorrhage of experience, the accident rate was soaring. The retention of nuclear-trained personnel also dropped to record lows.

The Carter administration showed surprising insensitivity to this predicament. We really got very good political mileage from this issue during the campaign, as so many voters around the country had read human-interest horror stories and had relatives or friends in the military.

Senators Sam Nunn, John Warner, John Tower, and Fritz Hollings had taken the lead in passing legislation in 1980 that reversed the trend and enacted a large pay raise and a very effective system of sea pay and reenlistment bonuses. My brother Chris had been instrumental in the drafting, and Tom Hayward and Jim Watkins provided the push from the Pentagon.

In 1981 we got passage of a larger pay raise and a more complete filling out of the bonus and allowance packages. We were committed to restoring the standard of living of all the military families to what it had been after the initial raises of 1973. Pay, of course, was just one aspect. It was essential to restore human beings as the focus of our entire military buildup, rather than treating them as "human resources," as the bureaucracy does. Restoring quality and morale was really the highest priority of the naval restoration program. In the first year and all subsequent budget debates I took the position that if we had to take budget reductions, and they surely came in later years, then we would give up ships and aircraft rather than give up compensation and quality-of-life initiatives for the sailors and marines; and when the crunch came, that's what we did.

Readiness and Sustainability

Concurrent with the great decline of the size of the navy during the 1970s, there was an equally alarming decline in the readiness and sustainability accounts. These accounts are the nondramatic ones, with no political constituency and no sex appeal—spare parts, maintenance of real property, base operating support, overhauls, aircraft rework, depot repairables, war reserve materiel—not the stuff of television dramas. The navy was in terrible shape in all of these accounts. I was aghast to find in my first briefing that we had less than a week's supply of most major defensive missiles and torpedoes. Though the fleet had been cut in half since 1969, we could not even fill out the 479 ships' magazines even once, let alone refill them. In ship and aircraft spare parts we had a third of the minimum requirement. As a result, high-tech aircraft such as the S-3 antisubmarine aircraft were averaging only about 30 percent mission capability, which meant that on any given day only three of the ten aircraft in a squadron could perform their mission. Twenty-six ships were awaiting overhaul for lack of funding, and basic upkeep on the buildings on naval installations around the world was shockingly bad. One nice example was the gymnasium at Great Lakes Naval Training Center in Illinois; the gymnasium had had its maintenance deferred for so many years that it finally collapsed flat on the ground in 1981. In this account we faced no skepticism from the OSD staff or from Congress. Instead, they shoved and pumped money into every account to the choking point, and we trebled the money in most of those accounts in the 1981 supplemental and the revision of the Carter budget for 1982. We sustained a healthy level of funding in all those readiness accounts throughout the remaining six years.

During this process it was illuminating to discover the different standards of living that existed in the different military services. As a reserve aviator for the past twenty years, I have crisscrossed this country and abroad, staying overnight at many air force and navy bases. Virtually all enlisted barracks in the air force are nicer than the bachelor officers' quarters in the navy and the army. The air force funds the replacement of its buildings on a twenty-two-year cycle. By comparison, the navy cycle is fifty-five years and frequently goes well beyond that. In a classic demonstration of the effects of the four-to-one OSD staffing ratio against the navy, in 1986 navy funding for replacement of the hospital at Subic Bay was taken by OSD and given to the air force for funding of a new hospital at the Air Force Academy, because Subic Bay had not reached the navy standard of fifty-five years, while the Air Force Academy had reached the air force replacement term of twenty-two years. This is not a criticism of the air force because their standards are reasonable.

Tomahawk Cruise Missile

The Tomahawk cruise missile and its application to naval warfare was one of the first policy and programmatic issues that had to be settled. The jet-powered missile has three versions, the first an antishipping version with a range of eight hundred miles and with a large, conventional warhead. This model operates much like the Exocet missile, except that it can fly for hundreds of miles searching for each target before going into its sea-skimming attack. There is a conventional land-attack version with a range of eight hundred miles. This has two types of warheads for different targets. One is just a large bomb, and the other scatters small bomblets for attacking airfields and land forces. This version is called the TLAM-C; after launch from a ship, it can fly hundreds of miles very close to the ground, hiding in the nap of the Earth, following the terrain, and using mountains and valleys to avoid detection. It navigates by mapping the ground it flies over with a radar altimeter, matching it to a digitized map stored in its computer. After flying hundreds of miles it can come within feet of its target, or fly down the center line of a runway, dispensing munitions to make the runway unusable. The third version is equipped with a nuclear warhead for land attack and has a range of fifteen hundred miles. This missile was deployed briefly in Europe in a ground-launched version with the U.S. Air Force, until it was eliminated by the INF agreement signed in 1988.

All three of the sea-launched versions are interchangeably launched from torpedo tubes on submarines, and launchers on battleships, cruisers, and destroyers. The successful deployment of the Tomahawk has enormously broadened the capabilities of the U.S. Navy in striking targets with precision far inland from the sea. This has enabled the navy to bring an entirely new and stabilizing dimension to the theater nuclear balance by providing a thoroughly dispersed and mobile deployment of highly accurate nuclear weapons to NATO and in other theaters in the world. One could not help noting with irony that while at the very time NATO was paralyzed with debate over deployment of the ground-launched versions to England, the Netherlands, and Italy, the battleship *New Jersey* came right into the Mediterranean and stayed for many months, loaded with the very same missile, and received not a single comment. Today we have submarines cruising all over the world with the Tomahawk, creating absolutely no political problem. We have destroyers and cruisers deployed globally in their routine pattern with the Tomahawk aboard, again without any political fuss.

The history of this cost-effective new dimension to conventional and theater nuclear deterrence is an interesting one, and it illustrates well the interplays among military planning, defense politics, and arms control.

The idea for the Tomahawk came out of an Air Force concept for a cheap, armed decoy that would help B-52s penetrate defenses in the Soviet Union. There were two basic technologies whose successful development made the concept possible. One was a very cheap, disposable jet engine that could fly reliably for a long one-way trip and be very cheap to produce. The other was Tercom, a system for navigation enabling an on-board computer to record the terrain features under the missile flight path with a radar altimeter and match it with a stored digital map of the route to the target. Both of these technologies were proved achievable in the early 1970s. The common wisdom in Washington holds that the uniformed military is the great engine of new-weapon starts. The Tomahawk was different. Thanks to the foresight of Dr. John Foster, Mel Laird's deputy director, research and development, Dave Packard, the deputy secretary of defense, and Laird himself, the concept was developed further into the idea for an air-, sea-, and land-launched cruise missile with both nuclear and conventional capabilities.

The program received little high-level attention until the SALT I agreements were nearing completion in 1972. There was in the government at the time widespread skepticism about the deal that Henry Kissinger had constructed. Laird, Foster, and most of the service chiefs did not like the package. Opposition in Congress, led by Scoop Jackson, was very strong, and some of Kissinger's own advisers, including me, were telling him that he got a bad deal. The SALT I agreements essentially gave up a huge U.S. lead in antiballistic missile systems in return for a freeze on the very large numerical lead that the Soviet Union had achieved in offensive missile systems. The ABM treaty effectively killed the American ABM system, but the freeze on the offensive weapons was only an executive agreement for five years, and it legitimized a large advantage for the Soviets. The Soviets were allowed 1,618 ICBMs, and the United States was limited to 1,054. The Soviets were allowed 62 ballistic missile submarines and 740 SLBMs, while the United States was limited to 44 and 656, respectively.*

In a masterful performance of bureaucratic skill, Kissinger negotiated the acceptance of this bad deal, first with the JCS and Laird, and second but simultaneously with Scoop Jackson and the conservatives in Congress. He chose me to negotiate with Jackson, Tower, and the congressional skeptics because it was well known that I was very skeptical of the agreements and because my stock was very high with Jackson and the conservative Democrats and Republicans

---

* Kissinger justified SALT I on the ground that congressional opposition made any further increase of U.S. strategic arms or an ABM system highly unlikely. The United States would be getting limits on the Soviet arsenal that we otherwise would not match on our own. "The Soviets were giving up an additional offensive capability; we were not." (See Henry Kissinger, *White House Years* [Boston: Little, Brown, 1979]. pp. 546, 1245.)

who were coalescing into a strong anti-SALT block. He figured that if I was able to negotiate an agreement for their support of his SALT deal he could then step in and seal it with Jackson. If I was unable, then his hands were free to get President Nixon to commit his prestige to defeating the conservatives in the Hill battle.

In dealing with the Pentagon, Kissinger astutely fastened on two programs to buy their support. One was the Trident submarine and missile, then called the ULMS, and the other was the Tomahawk cruise missile. He became an enthusiastic booster of both systems and pledged his undying support to Tom Moorer and Mel Laird. While there were many other considerations that eventually brought the Pentagon around, these two were critical.*

Beginning in 1972, then, the Tomahawk program was funded by the Defense Department as a high priority. The program was taken out of the air force and the navy, and a joint cruise missile program office was set up under DDR&E.

By 1976 the Tomahawk was very far along, including specific plans for integration into submarines, destroyers, and cruisers. Henry Kissinger was equally far along in negotiating yet another SALT agreement, SALT II. At the time I was deputy director of the Arms Control and Disarmament Agency and very much involved in SALT policy. When in early 1976 Kissinger cabled back from Moscow the outlines of the new treaty, I was amazed to find that his enthusiasm for Tomahawks seemed suddenly to have disappeared. He had agreed to the banning of deployment of the Tomahawk on submarines and the limitation of its deployment on surface ships to only ten cruisers with ten Tomahawks each. While apparently keeping the Tomahawk alive, he well knew that Congress would never fund such a tiny number with so little military utility.

At the time, of course, Gerald Ford was running hard for reelection, facing a very strong challenge from Ronald Reagan and the conservatives, and an uphill battle against the Democrats in the post-Watergate election. President Ford was determined to have a SALT II agreement to run on in his reelection bid. Kissinger knew he must act fast, and he sent outlines of the agreement to Secretary of Defense Don Rumsfeld and General George Brown, the new chairman of the Joint Chiefs of Staff, who were attending a NATO ministerial

---

* Kissinger later claimed that the SALT posture (to go for an SLBM freeze) was determined by the Pentagon's decision to build Trident—the United States needed the breathing space of the five-year executive agreement to get Trident on its way to production. (See ibid., pp. 1130, 1232–33.)

meeting in Oslo, Norway. Based on what Kissinger sent them, both Rumsfeld and Brown approved the initialing. A hurried meeting was called by the National Security Council for the president to get everybody aboard. At the time Bill Clements was the acting secretary of defense, and Jim Holloway was the acting chairman of the JCS. Prior to the meeting I had several meetings with Holloway at the Pentagon, and Fred Iklé talked extensively with Bill Clements. We were concerned not only that Kissinger was giving up the Tomahawk, but also that he had caved in to the Russian insistence that the Backfire bomber be excluded. In addition, we feared that there probably were other things in the agreement we knew not of and that it would be far more prudent for the president to withhold approval until Kissinger returned and there was a chance to have a thorough debate over the concessions that had been made.

Holloway was under tremendous pressure to follow General Brown's lead and approve the agreement. He refused. He saw the advantages that Tomahawk held for the U.S. Navy, and he opposed giving it up for the sake of an agreement that allowed the Soviets higher missile numbers than they possessed. At that first NSC meeting Fred Iklé and Holloway were alone in opposing approval of the agreement. In the second meeting Clements joined them, and Ford was very upset. He could not afford to proceed with approval against the recommendation of the acting secretary of defense, the acting chairman of the joint chiefs, and the director of the Arms Control Disarmament Agency. Reluctantly, he withheld approval with the intention of knocking the dissidents into line when Kissinger returned. After Kissinger did return, he and the president with Brent Scowcroft, the national security adviser, and Scowcroft's deputy, Bud McFarlane, spent the rest of the spring trying to bludgeon Fred Iklé and the Pentagon into line to approve the deal. Instead, Holloway managed to convert General Brown to opposition, and Don Rumsfeld joined the opponents, too, after he studied the actual draft.

There was one final National Security Council meeting in which the president attempted to bring the Pentagon and the ACDA into line. As it happened, Fred Iklé was traveling in Europe and I was the ACDA's acting director, so on this occasion, I got to sit at the cabinet table rather than the back chairs lining the room. This was a wonderful opportunity to persuade the president with Iklé's irrefutable logic. The scales were sure to fall from his eyes. What I got instead was a most unpleasant tongue-lashing from President Ford. After the initial briefings to start the NSC meeting, the president went around the table and asked each member to state his agency's views on the draft agreement. Ford sat passively as each recited his position. When it came my turn, he frowned as I started to speak. I was seated across the table from him and two seats over. As I recited the concerns over the cruise missile limits and the exclusion of Backfire, the president's expression grew darker. When I finished, the president said in a most unfriendly manner: "What I'd like to know is why the *Arms Control and Disarmament Agency* is here supporting the Pentagon against an arms control agreement." Realizing I had failed utterly to impress the president with either my charm or my arguments, I figured I wouldn't soon be invited back, so I pressed on: "Mr. President, because a bad agreement is worse for arms control than no agreement, and giving up Tomahawk and leaving out Backfire is a bad deal." The president just glowered at me and moved on to the next person. And, indeed, I never was invited back. At the conclusion of the meeting it was clear that the president and Kissinger were losing rather than gaining ground. The issue was sent back to the interagency group and basically languished there in bickering through the election.

The Carter administration came to office determined to push through a SALT II agreement. On June 18, 1979, they achieved their wish, and it was worse than the deal Kissinger had approved. Tomahawk was once again effectively killed, though they kept the subterfuge that Tomahawk remained alive because it was banned in an interim protocol that would have expired on December 31, 1981, rather than being banned in the treaty. When the agreement was submitted to Congress for approval, there followed one of the great postwar debates, in which the value of Tomahawk played a prominent role. Both Republican candidates for the presidency, Ronald Reagan and George Bush, attacked the agreement as "fatally flawed." The final outcome was a sound defeat of the agreements in the Democratic-controlled Senate. Scoop Jackson, John Tower, and Fritz Hollings led the opposition, and their victory was a heavy blow to the Carter administration.

Throughout the Ford and Carter years the Tomahawk project office and the prime contractor, General Dynamics, were beavering away to complete development. Although developments repeatedly delayed the date for operational introduction of the Tomahawk, had it not been for his director of DDR&E, Bill Perry, and his commitment to the program, it never would have succeeded.

Thus when we sat down in 1981 to our first DRB meetings, we had a weapons system that had survived nearly a decade of political turmoil over its development, still had engineering problems, but was essentially ready for introduction to the fleet. There was no opposition around the table to the program. Yet the Tomahawk saga was not over. Within the navy itself, the weapon had no constituency!

Tomahawk had originally been assigned to a joint program office because the navy could not find a place for it. The professional submariners were uncomfortable because its primary means of deployment was to be on fleet fast attack submarines. Rightly, the professional focus of the submariner today is on Soviet submarines and not on surface ships, and certainly not on land battles. Therefore, the mission of the Tomahawk was a distraction from their primary responsibilities. Moreover, every Tomahawk aboard left them with one less torpedo to do their primary job, and if it was a nuclear Tomahawk they greatly feared that they would be tied to specific firing positions in the event of nuclear alert, frustrating their basic pelagic instincts.

The aviators certainly had no love of any system that did not carry a pilot and yet could do some things that carrier aircraft could do.

The destroyermen, the surface warfare officers, saw no great benefit from Tomahawk in helping their primary missions of antisubmarine warfare and anti-air warfare.

In 1981 the system was ready to be turned back to the services, and large expenditures would now be required for procurement. Tom Hayward and Jim Watkins had to force Tomahawk down the throats of the blue suit bureaucracy. The destroyermen, for instance, opposed using their scarce dollars to put vertical launchers on all our Spruance class destroyers. One of the huge benefits Tomahawk brings to the fleet is to turn every one of the 250 destroyers and cruisers into a serious threat to the Soviet Union in time of war. With every destroyer able to launch 90 Tomahawks, the Soviets are faced with an unsolvable targeting problem, compared to having to worry about only 15 aircraft carriers. In addition, the 100 attack submarines could fire Tomahawks from virtually any place around the periphery of the Soviet Union without warning.

Shipbuilding

In the 1940s we had several hundred shipyards operating and building and repairing ships in the United States. On the day of Pearl Harbor we were already geared up through Lend-Lease and were producing one ship a day. By 1942 we had doubled that production, and in one month alone, March 1943, we produced 145 merchant ships. During my tenure as secretary of the navy I visited most of the ports around this country that produced those prodigies for the arsenal of democracy. Those shipyards and that industrial base are gone forever. In ports such as Boston, New York, Philadelphia, and all up and down the West Coast and the Gulf Coast, where those building ways and graving docks used to be, now stand Marriott Hotels, parks, and low-cost housing. As of this writing instead of producing one ship a day, we are producing less than one merchant ship a year, and that only because of continuing subsidies. For several years preceding 1981, about five shipyards a year were going out of business. Commercial shipbuilding in the United States has disappeared because of foreign competition. A container ship can be built in Korea today for one fifth what it costs to build in the United States. It is not only lower wage rates that make Far Eastern and most European producers able to undersell American shipbuilders deeply, but also virtually all of them engage in grossly unfair trade practices, with open subsidies and a host of other subterfuges.

By 1981 the U.S. Navy had become the sole customer for American shipyards. The navy had aided and abetted the decline of productivity and competitiveness in the American yards by its own addiction to cost-plus contracting with sole-source shipyards. In 1981 a total of 85 percent of all navy shipbuilding contracts were noncompetitive. Obviously, if a shipyard has its profit established as a percentage of gross costs, it has absolutely no incentive to reduce those costs of labor, material, and overhead. When I took office, the cost of navy ships had been increasing nearly 20 percent a year for the same ship type. The Carter administration averaged only fourteen ships in the navy shipbuilding budget per year, and they were being built in only nine yards. A total of 75 percent of the construction was going to only three yards: Newport News; General Dynamics; and Litton, Pascagoula.

The entire navy shipbuilding program and the navy bureaucracy that managed it, the Naval Sea Systems Command (NAVSEA) had been bent to Admiral Rickover's will and his uncompromising attitude toward contracting. One could not custom-build ships the way Rickover demanded without cost-plus contracts. That contract form guaranteed massive overruns, and in the 1970s, as Rickover became more autocratic, his relations and the relations of the NAVSEA bureaucracy with the shipbuilders became bitter indeed. Because of the fondness for customizing and changing by the navy bureaucracy while ships were under construction, there were major claims for additional compensation against the navy from the shipbuilders for most of the post-World War II period. But in the 1970s they really got out of hand.

The Ford administration left Carter with a first-rate mess. The navy had accumulated a claims backlog of $2.7 billion, of which $2.3 billion were with the three major shipbuilders: the Electric Boat Division of General Dynamics, the Ingalls Division of Litton, and the Newport News Division of Tenneco. The atmosphere could not have been more poisonous, with Rickover accusing everyone of fraud and initiating criminal investigations of all the contractors. By late 1978, my predecessors as secretary of the navy, Ed Hidalgo and Graham Claytor, had negotiated settlements to all these claims. While they later became very controversial, I was immensely grateful to them that I was able to start with a clean slate with regard to claims. But poor management and other problems at the Electric Boat Division yard, which had been major causes of the claims that had been settled in 1978, were just as bad in 1981, and the twenty-one submarines then under construction at that yard were all in deep trouble. General Dynamics was again preparing to launch massive new claims against the navy. (See chapter 6.)

The most highly visible task for the six-hundred-ship navy on which President Reagan had campaigned and for which I had been hired was, of course, to build the ships. We immediately set an objective of doubling the number of ships from the Carter levels to about thirty a year, including combatants, support ships, and reactivations. To achieve that, we would have to straighten out the contracting mess and settle the Rickover problem. As I had no experience in the shipbuilding world, my top priority was to find some tough executives with a real track record in that industry. After a major search I was able to find two of the best men in the country.

Jim Goodrich had spent all his life as an engineer and executive in shipbuilding on all three coasts. Recently he had retired as chairman and CEO of Bath Ironworks, and I was able to persuade him to help me straighten out the General Dynamics problems on a temporary basis. While he was doing that I offered him the job of under secretary of the navy, to which, after some persuasion, he and his charming wife, Helen, agreed.

On my first week on the job, I created the position of assistant secretary for shipbuilding by redistributing some functions among other assistant secretaries. The navy and the nation were singularly lucky that George Sawyer was persuaded to take that job. He had been a very successful executive with Bechtel Corporation and was just entering the prime of his career as president of the No. 1 naval architect and engineering firm in the world, J. J. McMullen. George was a Yale NROTC graduate who had spent ten years as a nuclear submariner. He loved the navy and was excited by the prospect of rebuilding it in the Reagan administration. Unfortunately, his wife was terminally ill, and he had two teenage children. Moreover, it ended up costing him a huge amount of money in lost stock options and other compensation. Nevertheless, he took

the job because of his sense of duty. Without him we would not have succeeded in straightening out the shipbuilding mess.

Throughout 1981 the ambitious shipbuilding program that was put forward
to the DRB was highly contentious. There is nothing in the Pentagon that cuts
more across the grain than increasing the size of the navy, and the OSD
bureaucracy threw in every kind of argument. Cap and Frank Carlucci supported the navy, however, and we charged ahead.

Aircraft Carriers

The maritime strategy was the framework of reference for the types and numbers of ships included in the five-year shipbuilding plan. In that strategy the
size of the fleet is really set by geography, alliances, and the number of theaters
in which the national strategy requires naval power to be applied. It is a fact
of naval life that the navy must deploy in peacetime very much in the manner and to the same places as it must operate in wartime. For purposes of deterrence, crisis management, and diplomacy, the navy must be present in the
areas where they would have to fight if war broke out. Of course, the navy must
be able to deploy three times as many ships in wartime as in peacetime. Because
the navy is assigned to five widely separated theaters—Atlantic/Caribbean,
Mediterranean, Persian Gulf/Indian Ocean, western Pacific, and Pacific—
those requirements produced the need for a minimum of fifteen aircraft
carriers.

The Carter administration, in its infamous "PRM-10" strategy, had considered dropping to six carriers but finally settled on an objective of twelve. They
also bought the armchair argument that smaller, cheaper carriers were better, and they dropped the Nimitz class design and sent to Congress in 1978 a
proposal for a much smaller oil-burning carrier called the CVV class (fifty-five
thousand tons compared with the ninety-five-thousand ton Nimitz class). As
a kind of hobby, I spent a good deal of my time in 1978, 1979, and 1980 working *pro bono* with Senators Jackson and Tower, and lobbying all sorts of other
people in the House and Senate to kill the CVV and replace it with another
Nimitz class carrier. I wrote a book called *Aircraft Carriers: The Real Choices*[1]
in preparation for the debate. In 1978 we succeeded in getting money
approved by Congress for long-lead items, and in 1979 we managed to get this
into both the House and Senate bills, and it was included in the final defense
bill that was passed.

The Nimitz class carrier became a symbol of just what kind of foreign policy we were going to have. It enraged Carter's White House staff and other

Democratic McGovernites who saw in the carrier a dangerous increase in U.S. military power. In an unprecedented move, President Carter vetoed the entire defense bill to kill the aircraft carrier.

But the tides were turning in our favor. The veto of the aircraft carrier was added to the campaign litany of Ronald Reagan and George Bush. It played very well during the year, especially when Carter's primary response to the hostage crisis, then still going on in Teheran, was to place two aircraft carriers on station in the Gulf of Oman. By late spring 1980, the CVN-71 carrier was overwhelmingly approved and included in the bill that Carter signed.

Having spent hundreds of hours working to obtain authorization for that ship, it was most gratifying as secretary of the navy to name it after my hero Theodore Roosevelt and to choose another of my heroes—my wife, Barbara— to christen the ship. The *Theodore Roosevelt* has been part of my life ever since. I logged the first helicopter landing aboard the ship just before it was launched in 1984, and in an added twist of fate, after leaving the job of secretary of the navy my assignment flying in the ready reserve proved to be Attack Squadron 36, one of the squadrons aboard the *Theodore Roosevelt*.

Thus, with an objective of fifteen deployable carriers, in 1981 we inherited a navy with thirteen in commission, and one about to begin construction. Of the thirteen, two of them—the *Coral Sea* and the *Midway*—were approaching forty years of age and were scheduled for retirement. Seven others had been built at the rate of one a year during the Eisenhower and Kennedy years and were approaching the end of their thirty-year life span. The navy had begun a program called SLEP (service life extension program) to take them off the line for two and a half years and rebuild each one to extend their lives to forty-five years.

The plan put forward to the DRB in 1981 canceled the Carter plans to scrap the *Coral Sea* and instead funded an overhaul to extend her to 1991. It included money to reactivate the World War II carrier *Oriskany*, a strong recommendation of Tom Hayward's, and plans to begin one new Nimitz class carrier in 1982 and another in 1984. This scheme would have allowed us to go to fourteen carriers within two years by reactivating the *Oriskany*, and to fifteen by 1987 with the commissioning of the *Theodore Roosevelt*. We got initial approval of this plan from the secretary of defense, but we got nowhere in trying to sell the *Oriskany* to Congress. I found out why later in the year, while visiting Bremerton Naval Shipyard in Puget Sound, where four of the Essex class carriers are stored in mothballs. The *Oriskany* had been ridden hard and put away wet at the end of the Vietnam War, without an overhaul or proper preservation. It was a horror. The flight deck had buckled and actually had grass growing two feet high on parts of it.

My assistant secretary for shipbuilding, George Sawyer, having come aboard halfway through the year, had conceived an innovative new approach that involved negotiating one package for both of the Nimitz class carriers in the five-year plan, renegotiating the *Theodore Roosevelt* contract, and combining them in one package. This, he promised, would yield huge cost savings by contracting for three ship sets of equipment at once rather than one at a time. We would gain huge benefits also by stabilizing the work loading at Newport News, the one yard in the country that could build large aircraft carriers. The idea made great sense from a sound business standpoint but, like so many such ideas, it did not fit in the annual authorizing process, so I did not think we could get it approved. The blue suiters also were convinced we could never get political approval for two aircraft carriers in one fiscal year, as that had never been done since World War II. But Frank Carlucci became excited about the idea and came up with an imaginative approach to fitting it to our annual budget cycle. He proposed a deal to me whereby we would get a larger share of the 1983 budget for the navy to fund fully two Nimitz class aircraft carriers instead of one. In return we would pay back that share in the 1984 budget in exactly the same amount. We shook hands on the deal, and that is how we included two Nimitz class carriers in the 1983 budget.

Just as agreed upon, we accepted a reduction of an equal amount the following year in 1984. George Sawyer then went to work and negotiated one of the most successful and innovative ship contracts in history. While we were talking about fiscal year budgets of 1982, 1983, and 1984, all of this was going on during the calendar year 1981. By the end of that year we had a settled plan with full funding to SLEP all the older carriers, extend the *Coral Sea* to 1991, extend the *Midway* to the year 2000, and build three new Nimitz class carriers. This would enable us to grow to fourteen carriers with the *Theodore Roosevelt*'s commissioning in 1987, and fifteen with the delivery of the first of the two new carriers in 1989. The second of the new carriers would replace the *Coral Sea* when she retired in 1991. By 1986 the two-carrier deal had saved us more than $1 billion, so we repeated it in the 1988 budget to start carrier replacements for the *Midway* and the *Saratoga* in the late 1990s.

Large Versus Small Aircraft Carriers

It was very popular in the 1970s to debate constantly about ideal sizes for aircraft carriers. There is no longer any basis for a serious debate on the issue. All empirical studies that look at today's warfare environment at sea give over-whelming support to the large Nimitz class carrier. Maintaining air superiority is essential to modern warfare, and the smaller-size carrier is restricted in all capabilities. Compared to the large nuclear carrier, small carriers lack the speed and endurance of the big deck; the poor seakeeping qualities of smaller carriers curtail flight operations as much as 30 percent of the time; smaller deck areas limit the required aircraft in performance as well as in numbers; the reduced volume on smaller ships limits weapons mix and storage capability, which equates to reduced sustainability and increased requirements for under-way replenishment and, hence, the need for more replenishment ships. Since volume increases by the cube as surface increases by the square, bigger is better for carriers just as it is for supertankers. A ten-year review of carrier landing accidents showed the smaller decks with nearly double the accident rate of the Nimitz class; the large-deck carrier was able to sustain far greater combat damage and continue operating due to built-in redundancy as well as superior damage-limiting capabilities. Smallness of size does not diminish detectability. In today's world of satellite technology and sophisticated reconnaissance systems, a ten-thousand-ton or even five-thousand-ton vessel runs the same risk of detection as a ninety-thousand-ton carrier. But both are equally effective in utilizing tactical deception to evade targeting.

Some of the war-fighting features that make the Nimitz class the least vulnerable ship in any fleet include:

- high tensile strength steel armoring of flight and lower decks; magazine protection from high- and low-angle attack missiles and torpedoes; multiple provisions for torpedo protection from every aspect
- more than two thousand watertight, shock-resistant compartments
- counterflooding capability
- necessary power and pumps for dewatering flooded compartments
- protective fire-fighting and flooding systems for ordnance and fuel storage spaces
- extensive and redundant fire-fighting facilities throughout the ship
- chemical, biological, and radiation protection
- unlimited range at top speed

Vulnerability

The sophisticated technology of modern weapons and delivery systems makes everything vulnerable to a degree, through ships much less than immovable land targets. But large-deck carriers are the least vulnerable and most survivable ships we have, along with our recently refurbished battleships. Their speed and maneuverability make them far less vulnerable than a land base, which cannot move at thirty-one knots, and far less vulnerable than an army division, which moves at about four knots. It is one thing to hit a carrier with a missile; it is another to damage it sufficiently to prevent it from launching aircraft; and it is quite another order of magnitude to sink it.

Although smaller ships have far less to throw at incoming threats, and although a single hit by a cruise missile can put a smaller ship out of action, as we saw in 1987 with the *Stark* and in the Falkland Islands, the larger carrier can bring into play a far greater array of defenses to prevent itself from being hit. If it does get hit, its greater size, greater degree of watertight compartmentation, greater damage control resources, and other survivability features enable it to absorb several such hits under most circumstances and continue to carry out its mission. No ship currently in commission except the large carrier and battleship has the huge mass and structural strength to withstand repeated hits by modern Soviet cruise missiles. No ship but the large carrier can dominate the airspace within five hundred to eight hundred miles of the battle group, making an attack much more difficult and less likely to succeed. Thus, the vulnerability argument, when analyzed, becomes one of the strongest arguments we have for building large, powerful, survivable ships.

Nuclear Versus Conventional

For aircraft carriers the case for nuclear propulsion is overwhelming. The space needed in conventional carriers for fuel oil provides a nuclear carrier with three times the ammunition and four times the aircraft fuel storage. This provides greatly increased endurance in combat between replenishments and fewer replenishment ships. Its reactor fuel is good for twenty-five years, eliminating the oil tanker umbilical cord. The latter advantage is especially important when operating, for example, in the Indian Ocean. Also very important is the extra speed of the nuclear carrier. In a crisis in the eastern Mediterranean, for instance, a nuclear carrier can make a high-speed transit from Norfolk two days sooner than a conventional carrier. Pilots close-in on final approach, and corrosion control officers would add that it is good to get rid of stack gases and smoke. The initial investment of cost differential between conventional and nuclear-powered carriers is more than offset over the service life of the nuclear carrier.

Battleship Reactivation

The reactivation of the battleships met with some resistance largely because the opponents viewed these magnificent vessels as vulnerable and obsolete.

Neither was true. Outfitted with the latest communications and electronic warfare equipment, each battleship also was equipped with the Harpoon antiship missile and Tomahawk antiship and land-attack missiles. We equipped them with an extremely effective Israeli-designed drone called the Pioneer, which is launched from the battleship, circles over the target with a stabilized day and night video to spot and correct gunfire, and then is recovered by the battleship. Above all, the nine sixteen-inch guns on the ship are able to hurl twenty-seven-hundred-pound shells accurately up to twenty-three miles. In addition, they have twelve five-inch guns and the latest close-in defense system. So what we are getting are battleships as tough and survivable as the carriers, an unrefueled steaming range of fourteen thousand miles, and the ability to deliver eight hundred tons of accurate munitions on a target in thirty minutes—the equivalent fire power of twenty-seven destroyers. Each battleship offers this immense capability for about the cost of a new frigate.

The Aegis Cruisers and Destroyers

In simpler days of less congressional micromanagement it took the navy only four years to go from a blank sheet of paper to the first operational patrol of a Polaris submarine and its strategic missiles. In 1963 the navy started a research program to develop an air defense ship capable of dealing with the growing threat of Soviet cruise missiles and supersonic aircraft. The resulting Aegis cruiser was commissioned twenty years later, in January 1983. The Aegis system is based on the latest phased-array radar technology integrated with twenty of the highest-capacity computers available, and directing a defense of an entire ocean area with one hundred twenty surface-to-air missiles on each cruiser. The system automatically searches the air mass from the surface to space, two hundred miles in every direction. It tracks and identifies everything that moves in that airspace; prioritizes potential threats; and if cleared for firing, will automatically ripple-fire and direct missiles against several hundred targets. The first operational employment of these cruisers, during the Gulf of Sidra and Libyan operations in 1986, proved their effectiveness and their great reliability. In 1981 there were already four such cruisers under contract with Litton, and we put forward a program to build a total of twenty-seven. We also started a new destroyer program to employ this system on a combatant that was smaller and less expensive than the cruiser but with considerably more capability and firepower than the frigate. This new destroyer class was named after the man who had sponsored my commissioning in the navy, Admiral Arleigh Burke. We included

long lead money in the fiscal year 1984 budget for these ships to replace the old
DDG-2 and DDG-37 class destroyers on a one-for-one basis.

Attack Submarines

A perennial favorite of navy critics is that the navy should stop buying expensive nuclear submarines and buy instead diesel electric subs. Since *The Hunt
for Red October* has popularized the real nature of submarine warfare, that criticism has virtually disappeared. Diesel electric submarines cost a fraction of
the cost of nuclear boats and are very useful in coastal and choke point missions. When operating on battery they often are quieter than a nuclear boat,
but their great Achilles heel is that they must run their diesels regularly to
recharge their batteries. When they do this, they put so much noise into the
water that they can be pinpointed by every nuclear sub within hundreds of
miles. They are not cost-effective for U.S. Navy missions. This judgment rests,
however, on the assumption that we will continue to have committed in
wartime more than 140 modern diesel electric boats in the navies of our
friends and allies.

In 1981 we set an objective of growing from the sixty-eight nuclear attack
boats then in the inventory to grow to a stable force level of a hundred boats
as part of the six-hundred ship navy. Since these boats would have a maximum
life of thirty years, we planned to build three to four per year rather than the
one-per-year average of the Carter administration. We funded substantial
improvements to the SSN-688 Los Angeles class then under construction, and
we funded a major R&D program to develop the technologies to enable us to
begin construction of an entirely new fast attack submarine in 1989. During
the 1970s the Soviets deployed eight different classes of nuclear submarines
while we developed one. While we did not know of the Walker spy ring at the
time, we testified to Congress in 1981 that we were deeply concerned that the
Soviets seemed to be closing the technology gap much faster than predicted.

Mine Warfare

Because the navy had to pay for the enormously expensive Vietnam air operations out of its own hide for nearly ten years in the late 1960s and early 1970s,
naval modernization essentially ceased during that period. When authorization was finally received by President Nixon in 1972, the navy employed its
mining capabilities very effectively. The precision mining of the North
Vietnamese harbors in 1972 was one of the most important factors in bringing
the North Vietnamese to their knees by the end of that year. Had it been

employed eight years earlier, much bloodshed could have been saved. After the settlement, the navy then used its helicopter minesweeping capabilities to clear all the Vietnamese harbors, and a year later was called upon to do the same in the Suez Canal and the Gulf of Suez following the Yom Kippur War.

I was amazed to find in 1981, however, that while the chief of naval operations had been urging the start of a new minesweeper program, no minesweepers had been built since the 1950s, nor were any on the drawing board.

We therefore included in our six-hundred-ship program funding for an ambitious plan to design and build two new classes of minesweepers: a large, oceangoing mine countermeasures ship; and a smaller, coastal minehunter. Secretary Weinberger immediately approved the plan to build thirty-one of these ships. In the spring of 1981 I traveled to Europe and inspected the new British Hunt class minesweeper, and a new NATO Common minesweeper being built in the Netherlands. Both were excellent. I returned full of enthusiasm for those programs and proposed to the blue suiters that rather than reinventing the wheel we simply build those designs in the United States. Had we done so, we would now have at least a dozen operational in our fleet. Instead, I made a major mistake and succumbed to the blue suit arguments that they could build a brand-new ship better and cheaper than using a European design. It was a classic example of the not-invented-here (NIH) syndrome. The resulting two programs, the MCM and the MSH, were the only two disastrous programs in shipbuilding during my tenure. There was one botch and screwup after another until the program was overrun by $50 million and fell two years behind schedule. We finally got the first MCM, the Avenger, launched in 1986, but we had to give up on the MSH minehunter in 1986 and adopt a European design, which we should have done in 1981.

Amphibious Ships

With our new requirement for expanded marine amphibious assault capability, we had to include a substantial increase in new construction of amphibious ships. We drew up plans for modifying the design of the existing landing helicopter assault (LHA) ships of about forty thousand tons in size. Drawing on the experience in deploying Harrier jumpjets on the LHA, we designed a ship that could be converted from an amphibious ship to a VTOL carrier interchangeably. The result was the LHD (landing helicopter dock), for which I selected the name Wasp, after the famous World War II carrier, and more famous Revolutionary War warship. We increased the numbers of a new class of LSD, the LSD-41, which I named the Whidbey Island class, from the one ship in the last Carter five-year plan to eleven ships, which we subsequently increased by another four. In addition, we funded a previously designed hovercraft vehicle called the landing craft air cushion (LCAC), which would enable the amphibious assault ships to lie some fifty miles off the beach and send the landing force ashore at fifty knots, going right from the sea across the beach and across land.

Support Ships

Throughout the 1960s and 1970s funding of the supply ships to support the combatants had been eliminated either in the Pentagon or in Congress. As a result, we had a very aging and insufficient fleet. We had to include, therefore, a major new building program for support ships. We included a plan for twenty new civil service-manned fleet oilers (TAO) and included plans for new multiproduct ships for battle group support, AOEs and AEs. We included funding also for a variety of specialized repair and research ships.

Strategic Sealift

With the rapid disappearance of the American merchant fleet, we faced a major crisis in finding a way to implement our maritime strategy. Alfred Mahan wrote, "A nation's maritime commerce strength in peacetime is the most telling indication of its overall endurance during the war." A strong American flag merchant fleet had always been the backbone of our naval logistics support. Indeed, in our War of Independence our merchant privateers did far more to win the war than the much smaller American Navy. But since the 1970s the number of U.S.-flag dry cargo operators declined drastically, from 20 to only 7. The number of militarily useful U.S.–flag merchant ships has decreased from more than 600 to about 360. U.S. merchant ship construction contract awards dropped from 47 in 1972 to 0 in 1981. The plight of our merchant marine was a separate set of problems, which we would have to address elsewhere. In the meantime, we had to take measures to meet our minimum wartime requirements. One approach we hit on was to pick up dead men's shoes. George Sawyer pointed out that by the middle of 1981 there were 30 modern cargo ships on the market. Most of them, while not brand-new, would be extremely valuable in our ready reserve force. We therefore put funding in to begin a program to expand our ready reserve force from 36 ships to more than 100.

We included also full funding for a program conceived in the Carter administration to provide fast logistic ships for the very rapid deployment of a full mechanized army division. To save money we bought eight container ships capable of thirty knots from Sea-Land Corporation and converted them to Ro-Ro (roll-on–roll-off) military transports. For the Persian Gulf, we funded an upgrade to the prepositioned ships at Diego Garcia to a total strength of thirteen, including tankers, Ro-Ros, barge carriers (LASH), and breakbulk ships, as well as two tugboats. George Sawyer came up with an imaginative program to convert and charter the new TAKX prepositioning ships that had been designed to accommodate supplies and equipment for three marine amphibious brigades for the Persian Gulf. This innovative concept of chartering and converting existing ships instead of building them new enabled us to save the taxpayers about $4 billion and resulted in having the entire fleet for all three brigades fully deployed by fiscal year 1986 instead of fiscal year 1996, in carrying out our expensive Persian Gulf commitments.

Another aspect of the fleet that had been greatly neglected was combat medical support. There were two small hospital ships still in mothballs, but none in the active fleet. With the Carter Doctrine in place and the pledge to commit five army divisions and at least three marine brigades to combat in the Persian Gulf, we initiated an accelerated program to build two very large hospital ships to support that force. George Sawyer came up with another innovative approach, based on buying existing supertankers and converting them to thousand-bed hospital ships, each with twelve operating rooms. The first of these ships was the *Mercy*, launched in 1986. It did its shakedown cruise as a goodwill gesture of humanitarian aid to the Philippines in 1987. The Second, the *Comfort*, was commissioned in 1987.

Strategic Home-Porting

In the 1970s the navy budget was cut 22 percent, adjusted for inflation. The fleet shrank from 950 to 479 ships, and many naval bases were closed. Drastic shortages of funds forced a consolidation that brought military vulnerability. Today we have 129 ships based in the Norfolk, Virginia, area; 105 in San Diego; and 68 in Charleston, South Carolina. President Reagan's expansion adds 120 ships to our fleet, and it is necessary to home-port them in the least vulnerable, most affordable way.

A major initiative that was dictated by the adoption of our maritime strategy was included in our six-hundred-ship navy plan. It involved decreasing the vulnerability of our fleet and our vital merchant ports through an expanded strategic home-porting program. We planned and carried out four major home-porting initiatives: a battleship surface action group in Staten Island in

New York Harbor; a carrier battle group in Everett, Washington; a battleship surface action group, carrier battle group, and other vessels in Corpus Christi, Texas; Pascagoula, Mississippi; Lake Charles, Louisiana; New Orleans, Louisiana; Mobile, Alabama; and Pensacola, Florida; an expanded battleship surface-action group in San Francisco; Long Beach, California; and Pearl Harbor, Hawaii. We have done this through competition and working with the local communities to find the lowest-cost solutions.

A valuable dividend from those initiatives will be the salvation of the maritime business in those areas. The navy will save a lot of money by getting away from the monopolies in the overcrowded ports and tapping into a much broader competitive industrial base around the country.

Soviet capabilities in nuclear attack submarines, mine warfare, and conventional cruise missiles make an attack on our overcrowded naval home ports inevitable in wartime. Dispersal of forces to more ports and to less concentrated ports will make such attacks far less tempting. Home-porting in Puget Sound, Washington, and New York provides permanent naval capabilities in the northeastern and northwestern sea lanes and ports. Dispersed home ports in the gulf provide the same presence to the sea lanes through which must pass most of NATO's vital reinforcement shipping, now heavily targeted by the Soviet and Cuban navies. This new capability in the gulf will greatly enhance our responsiveness in Caribbean contingencies.

Naval Aircraft

With 70 percent of the Earth's surface covered by water, with only thirty-four U.S. air bases abroad, and with most of them politically unusable in a crisis, naval aviation provides the only capability to carry out sustained military air operations on most of the Earth's surface and in many of the critical land theaters. It cannot, of course, substitute for land-based air power essential to sustain military operations far from the seas. The nature of sea power requires different types of aircraft that can conduct integrated operations under the sea against submarines, on the surface of the sea against hostile surface craft, in the airspace over the seas, and against land targets and in the airspace over land. Because of all the different kinds of aircraft needed to do these integrated missions, land-based maritime patrol, land-based marine corps support, four-dimensional carrier air wings, and helicopter and VTOL aircraft dispersed through smaller surface ships, the navy must build, produce, and operate many different types of specialized aircraft. If that aircraft development and production is managed in a tough competitive manner, the existence of a large number of production lines can be a real benefit to the navy in bringing the costs down low through competition and optimizing for low-rate production. If it is managed on a sole-source basis, it is a formula for unilateral disarmament through the cost escalation brought about by lack of competition and inneconomies of scale from low-rate production lines. This is precisely what happened to the navy following the Vietnam war.

In each of the eight years preceding the Reagan administration, the Department of the Navy was not able to procure enough aircraft to replace those lost through peacetime attrition. During that period, sixteen different aircraft were in production.

To reverse the disarmament we had to double aircraft procurement. Having been in and around naval aviation for a good part of my life and having worked with the aerospace industry during my business career, I felt I had a pretty good grasp of our aviation problems. The navy needed a first-rate industrial executive from the aircraft industry who also had a good military background. I found the right man for the job in Melvyn Paisley. An air force fighter ace with nine Messerschmitt kills to his credit and an accomplished aeronautical engineer with Boeing, he was then serving as vice president for Boeing International. Despite the fact that it cost him a great deal of money to do so, he agreed to come aboard. The CNO, Tom Hayward, had a distinguished record as a carrier aviator, and his program planner, Vice Admiral Stacer Holcomb, was also a tailhooker. The four of us put together a comprehensive plan to submit to the DRB to achieve the restoration of naval aviation. It was based on the following principles:

- Totally restructuring and toughening up or contracting approach, to end the culture of constant design changes and engineering change orders (ECPs).
- Requiring the contractors to reorganize their production lines to optimize efficiency at lower production rates.
- Beginning to compete within naval aircraft different combinations of aircraft against other combinations of aircraft, to force all the contractors to compete every year.
- Reintegrating marine aviation with naval aviation, deploying more marine squadrons aboard carriers, and having more navy squadrons assigned ashore with marine air wings.
- Using to the maximum existing aircraft designs. At the time we had only one aircraft in production that was new, the F-18. All the other front-line aircraft were based on designs more than ten years old; some were more than twenty

years old, and a few were more than thirty years old. We wanted to capitalize on the investment in these aircraft because the F-18 had cost the Navy $3
billion before the first aircraft was produced. We intended now to emphasize
sticking with proven designs and making planned product improvement by
updating them with the latest high-technology.

- Dramatically improving aircraft safety. We were losing about ninety aircraft
per year in peacetime accidents.

Fighter/Attack Aircraft

The navy and the marine corps were operating six different tactical aircraft. Two
of these, the A-7 Corsair II and the venerable F-4 Phantom, are being replaced
by the new F-18 Hornet swing fighter. The famous A-4 Skyhawk had been a
front-line attack aircraft for thirty years. In the Carter program it was scheduled
to be replaced by the FA-18 rather than the advanced version of the AV-8
Harrier jumpjet. I approved General Barrow's recommendation to proceed with
the AV-8B as the replacement for the A-4. We planned to move rapidly from six
to four modern high-tech aircraft. The navy would then operate from its carrier
decks only the F-14 Tomcat, the finest air-superiority fighter in the world; the
A-6 Intruder, the best all-weather night attack aircraft in the world; and the flexible FA-18 Hornet, which can do both fighter and attack missions.

The U.S. Marine Corps would then operate the FA-18, the A-6, and the
Harrier.

Instead of funding replacements for the F-14 Tomcat and the A-6 Intruder,
we funded programs to update both aircraft completely, using the advanced
technology we had developed for the FA-18, along with new engines and
radars. This had a price tag of less than a third of what new aircraft would cost.
We put off funding replacements for these two aircraft until the latter part of
the decade.

The FA-18 strike fighter had an interesting history. The original design was
the loser in the air force competition for a "lightweight fighter." The PA&E
Office of Systems Analysis in OSD had long been the institutional home of
the "smaller and cheaper is better" school of reform. They had succeeded in
the 1970s in converting both Dave Packard and later Bill Clements, the deputy
secretaries of defense, to their cause, and the air force and the navy were
directed to cancel plans to upgrade the F-15 and the F-14 and instead fund a
"lightweight fighter." Neither the carrier aviation community in the navy nor
the Tactical Air Command in the air force wanted any part of lightweight

fighters. Instead they wanted to stick with the high-tech approach of the F-14 and F-15 and put the money into upgrading those aircraft. The air force proceeded reluctantly with their competition and picked the YF-16, and later the navy did a source selection and selected the YF-17.

By the time the honeyed promises of McDonnell Douglas and Northrop, the YF-17 (renamed F/A-18) contractors, were brought into conformity with reality and when the many naval offices involved in the development got finished gold-plating the aircraft, it cost three times its original estimate and in its first production run was even more expensive than the F-14. The navy took what was a small, lightweight fighter and increased it in size, making it both a fighter and a bomber. It did not have the range or the payload of the A-6 nor the air-to-air capabilities of the F-14, but it could do both missions quite well. Its greatest advantage, however, was the payoff from maintainability, saving fifty technicians per squadron compared to the Phantom.

To achieve competition among the F-18, the A-6, and the F-18, all of which were sole-source, we established a program to deploy different mixes of aircraft on different carriers. We put an air wing on the U.S.S. *John F. Kennedy* that was made up of all F-14 and A-6 tactical aircraft; an air wing on the *Coral Sea* and the *Midway* that was made up of F-18s and A-6s; some air wings with F-14s, A-7s, and A-6s; and others with F-14s, F-18s, and A-6s. We made it clear to the contractors that there was no single airplane we could not do without and that we would decide on the size of the buy each year according to which contractors brought their prices down the farthest.

Antisubmarine Warfare Aircraft

The navy land-based maritime patrol aircraft, the P-3, based on the old Lockheed Electra turboprop, was one naval aircraft for which there was no shortage. We would not need more new aircraft until 1992, when the older of the P-3Bs reached the end of their service life. Major investments had to be made, however, in modernizing the sensor technology to keep abreast of the much quieter Soviet submarines. The decision was made, therefore, to stop production of the P-3 airframe for five years, reopening the line in 1988 to begin replacement of the retiring airframes in the 1990s. The P-3 was built in Burbank, California, and because of the effectiveness in Lockheed mobilizing the Californian delegation in Congress, our proposal to cease production of the P-3 for five years was prohibited by the secretary of defense, and we ended up building, at a sole-source price, fifty airframes that we really didn't need.

The SH-60 Seahawk helicopter program had been started in the Nixon administration and finally was to enter production in 1983. This helicopter was to bring a whole new dimension of outer-zone antisubmarine warfare to the surface combatants. Based on cruisers and destroyers, it carried a full complement of sensors based on sonobuoys that would extend the effective range of those ships against submarines to more than a hundred miles. We fully funded this program, and under a tough new management approach, Sikorsky produced the entire program on budget.

The older helicopter that had done this mission was the SH-2 Sea Sprite, which had much less capability but cost about half the price of the SH-60. Since the SH-60 was too large to go on the older frigates, we decided to reopen the SH-2 production line, which had been closed for ten years. The reopened line turned out to be very successful, coming under budget and ahead of schedule for every helicopter, thanks to the designer of the airplane, Charlie Kaman, who also owned and ran the company.

The main carrier-based antisubmarine aircraft was the S-3 Viking. It had been out of production for years and needed considerable modernization. But more than that, it needed adequate funding for spare parts and maintenance, because it had averaged only 30 percent mission capability since it had been introduced to the fleet. We fully funded both initiatives.

The SH-3 helicopter was more than twenty years old in 1981 and provides the carrier-based inner layer of defense against subs. It attacks subs using an active sonar lowered into the water while hovering, and once it locates the sub, it drops a homing torpedo to kill it. They do double duty as plane-guard and search-and-rescue aircraft for the carrier airwing. We funded a replacement for these old helicopters based on a low-cost modification to the SH-60. We put a fixed price cap on the development costs of $50 million, and Sikorsky met it.

Medium-Lift Helicopters

In 1981 the marine corps was operating eight different helicopters of every description. We decided to reduce the inventory to five helicopter types. We approved the CH-53E, a new heavy-lift helicopter capable of lifting sixteen tons. The primary helicopter for the amphibious assault mission was the CH-46 Seaknight, which was nearly twenty years old. The marine corps staff recommended developing an entirely new tandem rotor helicopter, called the HXM. Instead the commandant and I decided to use the new technology proved in the XV-15 tilt-rotor prototype and develop a revolutionary new type of aircraft that could take off and land like a helicopter but fly as a conventional aircraft at turboprop speeds. I was able to get approval from Carlucci to require the army and the air force each to pay a third of the costs, since they needed it as badly as we did. In a fit of savvy bureaucratic gamemanship, once the secretaries of the army and air force saw that we were totally committed to the program, the following year they refused to fund their thirds. In the typical double standard applied by OSD, that ploy was approved in the DRB, and the navy was forced to fund the entire $1.7 billion development cost even though all the services would use the aircraft. Later, when another joint service program for the hypersonic aircraft was begun, I refused to fund the navy contribution, since it was to be an air force-only aircraft. The OSD, as usual, required the navy to pay for a third of the share for this air force aircraft.

Attack Helicopters

The marine corps operated two models of the Huey Cobra attack helicopter, the UH-1J and the UH-1T. The OSD was advocating that the marine corps procure the army's AH-64, which was then under development. We took a hard look at that helicopter but found that it was just too expensive for the navy budget. We elected instead to modernize the old Cobras and build some new ones with more powerful engines.

Research and Development

I believed that our ability to maintain effective deterrence with the Soviets over the long term at an affordable cost depended on our ability to use the richness of our high-tech industrial base and our technologically literate population to compensate for the massive numbers that any totalitarian regime could produce. Research and development, therefore, needed to be a primary focus of our attention. Not only the spending money but also spending it more effectively for advanced development, and shortening the cycle for deploying technology once developed. As mentioned above, it had taken the navy only four years from a blank sheet of paper to the first operational patrol of Polaris missiles and submarines. It took us twenty years to do the same thing with the new Aegis cruiser, a simpler challenge. The primary reasons for this was the explosive growth of the Pentagon bureaucracy, and legislative anarchy and micromanagement from Congress. Nevertheless, there was much that the navy could do to streamline its own R&D process.

In the early 1970s the R&D funding for the Department of the Navy was about the same as in the 1981 budget in constant dollars. Over that period, however, the navy had doubled the number of R&D programs. Thus too few dollars were spread over too many programs. I set an objective to reduce funded R&D programs from over six hundred to four hundred. We set up a much stiffer review process to enable us to stop "chasing rainbows" and to put the dollars saved into the most promising development programs, with a strong awareness that the best is the enemy of the good enough.

We set out to get sprawling baronies of navy laboratories and engineering centers around the country into conformity with our new priorities. It has proved to be a far tougher task than we originally thought. The navy possesses some of the finest government centers for research and engineering, and some of the most dedicated and underpaid R&D professionals and scientists in the world. A good example is Dr. Jerome Karle, chief scientist, Laboratory for the Structure of Matter, at the Naval Research Laboratory in Washington. He won the Nobel Prize in chemistry in 1985. But the navy also possesses many labs that are vestiges from past wars and eras that no longer serve a useful function. Strong congressional protection has kept them alive and they evolved on their own, in some cases with only a random coincidence of interest with the navy. It took Mel Paisley until 1986 before he was able to produce a really rigorous plan for rationalizing these labs, but he produced more than $200 million in savings in the first year of its implementation.

One of the first initiatives we approved in 1981 was the implementation of an experimental plan that had been authorized by the Carter administration's Civil Service Reform Act. This enabled us to install an entirely new personnel management system for the civil service personnel at our China Lake and Point Loma laboratories. Essentially it gave local supervisors far more discretion and authority to set compensation and bonuses. In 1986, after it had been operating for five years, it was so successful at both labs that we urged the Packard Commission to spread it throughout the government. The Office of Personnel Management under Connie Horner became quite enthused about it and put it in the president's legislative proposals for 1987. As of this writing, it is slowly gaining some support in Congress.

By the end of 1981, the secretary of defense and the president had approved the detailed program to build the six-hundred-ship navy and restore American naval superiority. The fact that, unprecedented among such government programs, our original program has not changed to the present day in any important detail is a tribute to the effort and the logic that we put into the strategy and the initial building of the program in 1981. Getting it all approved by Congress and implemented in the navy and the marine corps, however, was another matter entirely. Now the fun began.

During 1981 and 1982 I spent about 30 percent of my time selling and defending the program with Congress. It was an enjoyable process. There were many formal hearings before our oversight committees, the Armed Services committees in the Senate and House and the Defense Appropriations subcommittees. Generally these are well attended by members, who take a serious, continuing interest in the complexities of defense. Their staffs are, by and large, serious professionals with some military background. Although we often disagreed on details, the interaction was a healthy, productive one in retrospect.

With Scoop Jackson and John Tower in charge of the Senate Armed Services Committee and John Stennis and Ted Stevens in charge of the Senate Defense Appropriations Subcommittee, the nation was very well served indeed. There has never been a better combination. The defense consensus began a rapid disintegration when Scoop was sadly lost to a heart attack on September 1, 1983, and Tower, frustrated by the steady decline of the Senate, declined to run for reelection a year or so later. But while the oversight committees were a good influence, there was a very bad new dimension of legislative activity that began after Watergate. With the collapse of the seniority system in the House in 1975, the lower body has descended into chaos and licentiousness. Scores of new subcommittees were created by chairmen to buy support from committee members, so that now even a freshman sits on 4 or 5. Instead of the 4 oversight committees, I found the navy having to testify before 46 subcommittees, and all wrote legislation affecting the navy. Congressional staff exploded to 39,000, and since elected members attend fewer than 10 percent of their subcommittee meetings, most of the legislation is written by anonymous staffers and summer interns. By actual measurement in 1985, existing legislation and case law governing navy procurement alone had grown to 1,152 linear feet of shelf space in the library.

Much of my time was spent lunching, meeting, and telephoning members and especially staffers, explaining our strategy and how each ship and each sailor's reenlistment bonus fit into it. Much time also was spent meeting publicly and privately with the media. I followed a policy of being easily available to the working media and allocating much time to them. I gave them as much information as security allowed and helped them find answers when I didn't know them. The media professionals who cover defense are very good. The distortion and unfair treatment usually come from the left ideologues and the part-time stringers who just don't know their subject. I was guided in this effort by one of the best public affairs professionals in the country, Captain Jim Finkelstein, later promoted to rear admiral.

But the most serious challenge to the six-hundred-ship navy came not from Congress or the press but from within the Pentagon, when Frank Carlucci was replaced by Paul Thayer as deputy secretary of defense early in 1983. Most of us were surprised by the choice because Thayer had that very year criticized the Reagan defense buildup and publicly called for major cuts in the defense budget. He was a very colorful former navy pilot with a distinguished war record who had just retired as chairman of LTV Corporation. We had crossed swords when he tried a hostile takeover of Grumman in 1981, a move the navy strongly opposed. I feared for the worst when I got a call, shortly after his appointment, from a mutual friend who had been hunting with him. "John, you better batten down the hatches; Thayer was telling everybody last week that his first task is to cut you down to size. He said the navy is out of control and that we don't need six hundred ships and we already have too many carriers, and boy, did he dump on your idea of reactivating the battleships. He said he would cancel that his first week on the job."

Less than an hour after that call, another friend called. He was on the same shoot with Thayer. He said, "You know, you and Paul should get together — for some reason he really has it in for you. You know LTV is still bitter about losing the F-18 competition, and Thayer made a strategic decision to abandon navy business and make LTV the army's main missile supplier, and they have done very well at it. Thayer plays golf with 'Shy' Meyer [the chief of staff of the army] every week, and Thayer told me that he aims to move ten billion dollars a year from the navy to the army budget."

While I wasn't optimistic, I tried hard in the months preceding the 1983 DRB to make friends with Thayer and to try to brief him on our strategy. It was a waste of time. I found almost immediately that he was talking to senators and staffers opposing our carriers and the Grumman aircraft in our budget request. Then we had our first confrontation when I decided to open for competition the contract for the management of the Center for Naval Analysis, then held sole-source by the University of Rochester. When he called me to his office to tell me he was overruling me, I said well, I would take that up directly with Cap, because Cap had already told me he supported what I was doing. Thayer then said to me, "You will not take this up with Cap, my word is final." I replied, "Your word is not final, I work for the secretary of defense, and you will not interfere with my access to him."* With steam pouring out of his ears,

---

* The deputy secretary of defense becomes acting secretary in the absence of the secretary of defense. In those periods he has direct authority over the service secretaries. Otherwise, his authority depends on what the secretary of defense delegates to him.

he then made a statement that was later widely reported in the press, when he said, "Lehman, this building is not big enough for both of us!" I replied, "You may well be right," and went straight in to see Weinberger. Cap immediately deferred and set up a meeting for the three of us several days later, allowing a cooling-down period. When we had that meeting, Cap was as uncomfortable as I have ever seen him, as Thayer and I had it out in front of him. Thayer maintained that he could not carry out his position as deputy if people could appeal beyond him, and I cited the law saying that I worked for the secretary of defense and not for the deputy except when the deputy was acting for the secretary. If Cap ordered me not to see him or communicate with him, but to delegate this responsibility to Thayer, of course, I would be bound to comply. But I made it clear to Cap that that was unacceptable to me and should be unacceptable to him as well. Cap avoided making any definitive decision, but he later made it clear that his door remained open to me. I went ahead and carried out my action on CNA, but the stage was set for even more dramatic fireworks in the future.

Over Thayer's objections I retained my access to Cap—primarily by telephone—and I raised hell about Thayer's opposition to the navy. Cap said he would talk to Paul and said, "Let there be no doubt, the president and I are in total support of the six-hundred-ship navy and the fifteen carriers."

Thayer's opposition, however, continued unabated, and to the glee of our few opponents in Congress, notably Kennedy, Hart, and Biden. Then one day, out of the blue, I got a directive signed by Thayer ordering me to cancel one aircraft carrier and drop the goal from fifteen to fourteen. A call to Cap confirmed there was no change in policy and fifteen should still be the number. After discussions with friends at the White House I suggested that it would be useful if the president reaffirmed specifically the six hundred ships and fifteen carriers.

Infuriated by my resistance, Thayer stepped up his lobbying against the navy on the Hill, and directed OSD staff to prepare major navy budget cuts for the summer DRB. Now came the first DRB meetings, and they could have sold tickets at a thousand dollars apiece. Everyone could hardly wait for the shoot-out at the OK Corral. With few exceptions, the OSD bureaucrats looked forward joyfully to my immolation and the subsequent dismantling of the six-hundred-ship navy. During the first week there were preliminary thrusts and sallies, but the main event arrived the second week, on August 11, when the agenda got to the shipbuilding program. Prepared by PA&E, Thayer took on the program ship by ship. Our incomparable staff, led by Paul Miller and Ev

Pyatt, had gotten all of Thayer's questions in advance, and I had all of the answers and data and slam-dunked his every question. He was getting redder and redder, which I could see quite well because, to his great discomfort, I was seated right next to him. Finally he was reduced to his last resort, which was to claim that we had underpriced all the ships and would have to reduce ships sufficient to make a fund of $600 million to cover cost overruns. This was, of course, the same argument the Democrats were making on the Hill with the same numbers, because, of course, the systems analysts staffing Thayer were also giving the stuff to our opponents on the Hill. But I was really laying for him on this one and had a should-cost analysis and parametric regression studies and all that nonsense to back up every single price estimate. As I rattled them off in refutation, I finally overloaded his circuits. He could take no more. He shouted, "Shut up!" I felt sorry for him but I couldn't resist rubbing it in. In the stunned silence I just said, "Mercy!" in mock shock.

Later that afternoon, Cap called me to tell me that Thayer had threatened to resign if Cap didn't back him and so he was ordering me to reduce ships sufficient to fund a $450 million overrun line. While that was frustrating, in fact, it didn't make any real difference because we just agreed with the Hill committees to cut that $450 million as our share of that year's Congressional reduction, and away it went.

The biggest blow to Thayer, however, was delivered by the White House. My earlier discussions on the carrier issue bore fruit that same August day of the great DRB shootout. A press release from the president stated as follows:

> The President has approved Secretary of the Navy John Lehman's recommendation to name the Navy's two new carriers *Abraham Lincoln* (CVN-72) and *George Washington* (CVN-73).
>
> Recalling the enormous contributions the two former Presidents made to our nation's history during difficult periods of war, President Reagan said, "In naming our two carriers after Abraham Lincoln and George Washington we honor their memory, reflect upon their understanding of sea power, and dedicate ourselves to achieving the requisite naval superiority we need today, by building a 15-carrier, 600-ship navy."
>
> When completed, these ships will bring the Navy's deployable carrier strength to 15.[2]

Knowing I had solid White House support I decided to go public. In an interview on page one of *The Washington Post* on October 11, I blasted Thayer for sabotaging the president's navy program. It was great fun and really livened up a dull autumn. The next day Cap called me in and said, "Thayer is wrong, but we shouldn't be airing these disputes in the press."

Thayer resigned the following January and was replaced by Will Taft, Cap's longtime associate, and while we, too, had our disagreements from time to time, we got along very well for the remainder of my tenure. Nor was there any further overt challenge in the Pentagon to the six-hundred-ship navy.

ABOVE: Mrs. John F. Lehman, Sr. (Connie), with daughter, Patricia, age four, and son, John, Jr., age two, Christmas, 1944. *Lehman Family Collection*

RIGHT: Lieutenant John F. Lehman, Sr., on the bridge of his ship in the Western Pacific, 1944. *Lehman Family Collection*

Cambridge University, 1966: The First Team of Gonville and Caius College. John F. Lehman, Jr. (*shown seated, front row, center*) is Captain of Boats. *Stearns, Cambridge*

ABOVE: John F. Lehman, Jr. (holding megaphone), with other members of the Schuylkill Navy, in his freshman year at LaSalle College High School, Philadelphia, Pennsylvania, 1956. *Lehman Family Collection*

ABOVE RIGHT: The agony of defeat at the Henley Royal Regatta, 1966. *Lehman Family Collection*

The author's uncle George Kelly, actor, director, and playwright. *Lehman Family Collection*

Prince Rainier and Princess Stephanie of Monaco with John F. Lehman, Jr. (*right*), at a meeting of the Princess Grace Foundation in New York City, April, 1987. *Lehman Family Collection*

Grace Kelly attained a perfect balance between disciplined achievement and strength of character on one hand and caring, warmth, and compassion on the other. Princess Grace is shown here with John and Barbara Lehman at their wedding, May 24, 1975, in Philadelphia. *Lehman Family Collection*

Barbara Lehman, as wife of the secretary of the navy, christening the U.S.S. *Theodore Roosevelt*, Newport News, Virginia, October 22, 1984. *Harold J. Gerwein, U.S. Navy*

Barbara and John F. Lehman, Jr. disembarking from the U.S.S. *Missouri* at its recommissioning on April 19, 1986, in San Francisco. *Harold J. Gerwein, U.S. Navy*

Barbara Lehman assists the landing safety officer directing her husband's Intruder jet to an "OK three wire" landing on the U.S.S. *Kitty Hawk* in 1981. *Harold J. Gerwein, U.S. Navy*

John F. Lehman, Jr. a naval officer in the Ready Reserve: *Top:* On active duty at Firebase Charlie in 1970 in the Demilitarization Zone between North and South Vietnam; *Center:* "manning up" (*second from left*) an OV-10, on duty with VAL-4 in South Vietnam, July 1971; *Below:* on annual active duty in 1980 at Oceana Naval Air Station in Virginia. *Lehman Family Collection; John H. Sheally, II, The Virginia Pilot/The Ledger-Star*

"Learning the ropes": *Above:* John F. Lehman, Jr. shown sitting behind President Richard F. Nixon during a critical meeting on Vietnam between Nixon and congressional leaders, January 24, 1973; *Below:* three years later, at the big table (*sixth from left*) across from President Gerald Ford as acting director of the Arms Control Agency, at a full meeting of the National Security Council. *White House photographs*

John F. Lehman, Jr., with
Secretary of Defense
Caspar Weinberger at the
recommissioning of the
U.S.S. *Missouri* on April
19, 1986. *Harold J.
Gerwein, U.S. Navy*

A calm moment before the storm: President Ronald Reagan, Secretary of the Navy John
F. Lehman, Jr., and Admiral Hyman Rickover at the start of the meeting on January 8,
1982, in which the admiral was "piped over the side." *White House photograph*

The secretary of the navy with his civilian deputies in 1987: (*left to right*) Everett Pyatt, assistant secretary for shipbuilding; Chase Untermeyer, assistant secretary for manpower; Jim Goodrich, under secretary; John F. Lehman, Jr.; Mel Paisley, assistant secretary for research and engineering; Bob Conn, assistant secretary for financial management; Walter Skallerup, general counsel. *Harold J. Gerwein, U.S. Navy*

The 1984 Defense Resources Board, the instrument of decision-making for all budget and policy issues of the Department of Defense, which was reestablished by Caspar Weinberger in 1981. The author is seated up front, in the second row (*center*). *Helene Stikkel, Department of Defense*

Chapter 6

Electric Boat and the Reform of Shipbuilding

My experience in government had taught me one acute lesson: No matter how brilliant the scheme, no matter how clever the bureaucratic maneuvers, nothing would be done unless the system itself could be made to produce. To produce in the navy's case meant to build the ships and planes we needed, when we needed them, and at a cost we could afford. My enthusiasm, if not my determination, for quick results had already been dampened by the slow pace of change on strategic thinking. At the DRB, it was clear that the navy would not have an easy time of it. We could count on the president and Cap Weinberger and some of the most powerful congressional barons, but we had to watch every program every step of the way. None of this would matter, however, if we could not get the navy bureaucracy on the one hand, and the contractors on the other, each to do their part of the job. And that remained very much in doubt.

These were the thoughts that agitated me as I prepared for a crucial meeting on March 17, 1981, with David Lewis, chairman of the board and CEO of General Dynamics, whose Electric Boat Division was one of only two shipyards in the nation capable of building nuclear submarines and ships. A savvy aerospace executive of long experience, Lewis had previously headed McDonnell Douglas Corporation. The news I had for him was not pleasant. But the Electric Boat situation was so bad that all our plans for a naval renaissance hung on its resolution.

After gaining approval for a plan from Weinberger and Carlucci to clean up the EB mess, I had kept it close with a very few advisers. Lewis had no inkling of what I was going to tell him. He was very upset indeed when I informed him that there would be a public announcement that afternoon that the Navy was setting aside the competition for the four SSN-688 Los Angeles class submarines that Electric Boat had won for 1980 and 1981, and instead would begin negotiations with the other nuclear-capable shipyard, Newport News, to award three of the four to them and defer decision on the fourth indefinitely. I told him also that we would not go forward with the contract for the fiscal year 1981 Trident submarine, the ninth of the class, and that he could expect no further work from the navy until all of his problems were resolved. The navy had concluded that Electric Boat had been bidding low on submarine contracts, that the yard was out of control, and that very major management changes would have to be made. Navy procurement officials simply did not believe the claims of Takis Veliotis, EB's manager, about progress at the yard. I concluded by telling Lewis that our naval personnel on the scene were not allowed to have access to the most fundamental data and that, further, they believed that Lewis himself was being misled by Veliotis.

Lewis was not amused to hear this. In fact, he was thunderstruck and left my office tight-jawed.

One published account of these events[1] recounts that Lewis had hired my predecessor, Mr. Hidalgo, as a consultant, and that Hidalgo had advised him that I was of little consequence in the administration and would have no real say in the decision. If true, that probably explains Lewis's shock. But as the public official charged with responsibility in the matter of the navy's shipbuilding, I had suffered a shock of my own when I fully understood the disastrous state of affairs between General Dynamics and the navy.

Throughout 1980, especially during the transition, there had been many warnings that the serious problems of the General Dynamics Electric Boat Division had not been solved and were growing worse. Admiral Rickover fueled some of it; he was furious at the compromise agreement reached by the Carter administration in 1978, which was supposed to have settled the largest shipbuilding claims dispute in the nation's history.[2] But even those within the navy who had supported that settlement were warning of real trouble.

Disputes between the navy and its contractors were nothing new, of course. Contentious claims by shipbuilders against the navy go all the way back to the construction of the U.S.S. *Constitution*, which overran by 200 percent. Ships take a long time to build, and labor and materials costs and the vagaries of economic trends over four to seven years are difficult to predict. In addition to those facts of life, both the navy and the contractors have a strong temptation to be optimistic to keep the initial price as low as possible while selling it to Congress and to them-selves. There also is an enormous temptation on the part of naval officers super-vising the construction, just as a man supervising the building of his yacht, to make changes and adjustments in the design almost daily. Since World War II the navy had been dealing with contentious shipbuilding claims all the time.

The 85-804 claims, however, were of a magnitude never seen before, at $2.5 billion, and the largest of these was for General Dynamics for building nuclear submarines.

The problems associated with this settlement and General Dynamics ran to the heart of our plans. Two of the highest priorities we established in the six-hundred-ship navy program were the Trident SSBN nuclear strategic missile submarine, and the Los Angeles class 688 nuclear attack submarine programs. At the height of the Polaris/Poseidon submarine building program begun by the Eisenhower administration, the navy was building nuclear submarines in seven different yards, private and naval. By 1981, however, there were only two remaining shipyards equipped and manned to produce nuclear submarines: the Electric Boat Division of General Dynamics at Groton, Connecticut, and Quonset, Rhode Island; and the Newport News Shipbuilding and Drydock Division of Tenneco in Virginia.

The "nuke" portion of our six-hundred-ship navy program required build-ing at least one Trident per year and three or four SSN-688 attack subs per year, plus two new nuclear aircraft carriers. The two yards in theory had a capability to exceed that total number of nuclear-propelled ships and thus provide ade-quate competition for our sustaining submarine business. But if this were to happen, it was absolutely vital that the mess at Electric Boat be cleaned up.

That mess was the product of an unusual confluence of political, military, and commercial events, each of which aggravated the other. I had begun work-ing on the Trident program with Kissinger in 1970. Then known as the Un-derwater Launch Missile System (ULMS), it was only a concept drawn from a McNamara study on a longer-range replacement for the then brand-new Poseidon missile submarines. It was suddenly rushed into a real program by the SALT I negotiations, which were beginning to look like they would pro-duce a treaty. As recounted earlier, the JCS were very unhappy with the out-lines of the agreements as they began to emerge in 1970, and Kissinger's sup-port for building the Trident proved to be a powerful piece of persuasion in getting them to accept the deal. With Kissinger's commitment, the program raced forward. Secretary of Defense Mel Laird and his deputy, David Packard, accelerated the program to develop an interim missile of 4,000-mile range based on adding another stage to the Poseidon missile. As had been done in the past, this was given without competition, sole-source, cost-plus, to Lockheed. Another program was also begun to develop a brand-new 6,000-mile range missile, given also to Lockheed.

In December 1971 Laird added a huge $900 million request for ULMS to the defense budget for fiscal year 1972, then renamed it Project Trident, after the three-pronged spear of the ancient sea god Neptune.

The original concept was to build a fairly austere submarine of about 8,000 tons, roughly the size the British are now building for their Trident program. There was no real need for a new larger reactor, because the concept involved concentrating on keeping the submarine quiet and sacrificing speed. Admiral Rickover, however, would have none of any of this. He had then on the drawing boards a huge new 60,000-shaft-horsepower natural circulation reactor, and he simply ordered that no other design be contemplated. As we saw in the introduction, in a conservatively designed natural circulation reactor, the size of the reactor determines the minimum size of the submarine. The size of the 60,000-shaft-horsepower reactor decreed a submarine not of 8,000 tons but of 18,000 tons, almost two times the size of the Aegis class cruiser. To accommodate the reactor it required a diameter of more than 40 feet, and an optimum length-to-beam ratio decreed a submarine 5 feet longer than the Washington Monument. Such a leviathan could carry many more than the 16 missiles carried in the Polaris/Poseidon and even more than the 24 eventually assigned. In May 1972 the SALT I agreements were signed and the uphill battle for passage through Congress began. Kissinger made good on his pledge to the chiefs, and strongly supported the initial $908 million request for the Trident program. As his legislative strategist I was the point man in the Senate and the liaison among the Defense Department, the NSC, and the Congress. We had a battle royal on the Senate floor with Senator Bentsen of Texas leading the fight to knock out production money. We beat him, 47 to 39. The real battle, however, was the following year, in 1973, for the fiscal year 1974 budget request for Trident of $1.5 billion. This was a most exciting battle, which went on through September. Bud Zumwalt was the quarterback for the administration and did a magnificent job. As part of the maneuvering and deal-making, one of the many side deals was to give Admiral Rickover his fourth star (as recounted in the introduction). The antidefense forces were led this time by Senator Thomas J. McIntyre of New Hampshire, who offered an amendment to cut $1 billion out of the program. The outcome was in doubt right up until the last vote was tallied, when we finally won, 49 to 47.

Shortly after the very close vote on the authorization bill, I learned one of my many lessons that served me so well as secretary of the navy. Week after week, month after month during 1973 leading up to the September vote, we on the NSC repeatedly returned to the navy and the Pentagon to see if there was any fat that could be pared from the $1.5 billion Trident authorization. In each case Rickover's office provided detailed talking papers showing how the entire program would fail if $1 were cut from that total. Therefore we had pledged in blood to all of our supporters on the Hill that no compromises could be made, and that was one of the reasons why the victory was such a narrow one.

Having put the victory behind us, in mid-October the crisis began anew when Scoop Jackson called me to say that Senator John McClellan and Congressman George Mahon, the chairmen of the Senate and House Appropriations committees, respectively, had tentatively agreed to cut $240 million from the Trident program in the Appropriations committees. Our answer, approved by President Nixon and sent to McClellan, said in part,

> It has been proposed to cut $240 million from this program for fiscal year 1974, forcing a delay in operational deployment of the Trident system. Such a delay would affect our deterrent posture in the late 1970s and, of immediate concern, would have direct consequences for our negotiating position in the current SALT talks.
>
> I respectfully ask your committee, therefore, to reject such a substantial cut and to ensure that we preserve the option to continue Trident on its current projected deployment schedule.

At my insistence Kissinger himself called both McClellan and Mahon as the battle in the Appropriations committees swayed back and forth during November. In our naïveté we really believed the success of the program hung in the balance.

In reality, what Rickover had given us was what the Pentagon calls a WAG, a "wild-ass guess." In fact, the ship had not been designed, and contract negotiations had not even begun. On December 6, therefore, I felt Kissinger's full fury when I was called over to his office: "Look what those sons of bitches at the Pentagon have done to us," he said. He threw a Pentagon press release at me that read as follows:

> Deputy Secretary of Defense William P. Clements today communicated to Senator John L. McClellan, chairman of the Senate Appropriations Committee, an alternative to the $240 million reduction in the fiscal year 74 Trident

appropriation recommended by the House Appropriations Committee. Secretary Clements proposed, instead, a reduction of $198 million.

Secretary Clements pointed out that the proposed reduction would not impact upon the construction and initial operating date of the first ship . . . the lesser reduction of $198 million proposed by Secretary Clements would continue the capability to build the first ship on schedule and the option to build more than one submarine in fiscal 1975.

The cut was made in final appropriation without a ripple in the program.

In the debate the cost of the first Trident was firmly stated as $1.35 billion. This number was the roughest of estimates but it became sacred, and the contract request for proposal went out in may 1973 based on that number on a fixed-price basis. At this point there was no design for the ship, only a size, driven by the 60,000-shaft-horsepower reactor. It was utterly foolhardy to let a contract for a new class of ship without the ship having been designed, yet this was a practice the navy had resorted to many times in the past. The only practical way to contract for a ship that isn't designed is on a cost-plus contract, because there is no way to estimate time and materials.

Because of the political pressure and the urgent desire of the nuclear submariners to get on with the ship, the navy insisted on a fixed-price contract based on the WAG of $1.35 billion, which proved to be unrealistically low for a ship that had not yet been designed. Newport News told the navy that they would bid only on a cost-plus basis. After initially taking the same position, Electric Boat was jawboned by Rickover into submitting a fixed-price proposal. When they did so, they were chosen by the navy, and detailed negotiations ensued that lasted for another full year. The resulting contract was a subterfuge. It appeared to be a fixed-price contract with a contract price that was within the budget, but in reality it was a cost-plus contract with an agreed ceiling that was 150 percent of the amount in the budget.*

The Trident contract signed between General Dynamics and the navy on July 25, 1974, was the worst of all possible worlds—essentially in the form of a fixed-price, incentive-fee type, but with a share line such that the navy would bear 95 *percent* of the costs exceeding the contract target cost. It then included a ceiling price that was 152 percent of the target price. Thus, masquerading under the guise of a fixed-price-type contract, it was really a cost-plus contract,

---

*To understand completely how that works it is necessary to explain a few fundamentals of navy contracting. The interested reader can find this in the appendix.

virtually certain to exceed the contract "ceiling," with even that inflated figure driven still higher by design changes. It was certain also that because the ship was not designed when the contract was let, and because it was being designed under Admiral Rickover's control, his obsession with zero safety defects would mandate almost daily alterations. In the case of each such change, the builder has the right to alter the contract target price and schedule. This "equitable adjustment," as it is called, constantly moves up both target and ceiling prices under the contract.

This ill-conceived contract incorporated the worst features of the entire system. The navy was under tremendous pressure to keep the public price of the ship down for fear of losing its narrow margin of political support. So large a boat offered an entirely new construction challenge. To poison the devil's brew further, the navy was proceeding full speed with General Dynamics and Newport News on the brand-new attack submarine, the SSN-688 Los Angeles class. Its design had been only 5% completed when the initial construction contract was signed and was already beginning to run into serious difficulties.

The political environment dominated the proceedings and reinforced the worst tendencies of the navy bureaucracy. There was deep concern that the huge Soviet strategic building program must be met by an accelerated American response. Nixon and Kissinger were extremely anxious to gain support of Senator Jackson and his followers for the SALT agreements, and Trident was a major part of his entire price. The secretary of defense and the joint chiefs were anxious to make hay while the sun shone and get as much as possible approved while they had such strong support from the White House.

The navy was under pressure to wrap up the contract, and, of course, General Dynamics pressed its advantage to the maximum. Even so, the navy made some incredible concessions. The navy agreed, in addition to the hugely generous share line, to pay 100 percent of all additional costs attributable to "inflation" without defining just what that was. They then put no binding contract delivery date in, but only window dressing. Electric Boat agreed to make its "best efforts" for a contract delivery of December 1977, and then accepted a "binding" delivery date of April 1979, but without any penalty for failing to meet the date. The ship was named the U.S.S. *Ohio,* and its keel was laid April 10, 1976. It was not finally delivered to the navy until November 1981.

The navy also agreed to terms that gave General Dynamics in effect a long-term monopoly. To induce GD to make the necessary investments for the new facilities required both at Quonset Point and Groton to build the huge new boats, the navy agreed to include options for three more ships in the original contract, which had the effect of precluding Newport News from making a serious effort to compete in subsequent years.

This had to stop, and one of the objectives I set in 1982 was to achieve competition for the Trident missile and submarine by bringing in another missile builder to compete against Lockheed and persuading Newport News to compete against General Dynamics for the boat. Both initiatives were adamantly opposed by the nuclear submariners—with the exception of Jim Watkins—but we finally succeeded in 1986. Late in 1986 Martin Marietta agreed to bid against Lockheed's monopoly for the Trident missile, and Newport News committed to compete against General Dynamics for Trident submarines. Ultimately, as soon as I announced that I was resigning, the nuclear submariners moved immediately to end the initiative to compete on both, and they remain monopolies.

During my very first week on the job I began to get briefed on the overall shipbuilding program and the problems at Electric Boat. It was truly shocking. My predecessor, Ed Hidalgo, had every reason to believe that the 85-805 settlement he had negotiated with Electric Boat had ended the problems. In the latter months of the Carter administration, as new problems emerged, it became apparent that many of the fundamental problems that had brought about the great "omnibus" claims of the mid-1970s had not been solved. They were, in fact, made worse because of the deep bitterness that had developed between Admiral Rickover and his staff on the one hand and Takis Veliotis, the Electric Boat yard manager, and the rest of the General Dynamics management on the other. As my investigations and briefings unfolded during the first week, it revealed the following situation:

- Electric Boat had a total of twenty-five submarines under construction at its two yards, including a monopoly of all Tridents, and since 1977 they had won every SSN-688 contract made by substantially underbidding their rival, Newport News.
- The twenty-five submarines under construction at Electric Boat were at the same time a total of twenty-one years behind schedule, and the situation was getting worse. It was obvious the yard had taken in far more work than it could handle.
- The lead ship of the Trident class, SSBN-726, the U.S.S. *Ohio*, was more than two and a half years behind schedule. The huge new base for the

Trident submarines at Bangor, Washington (in Scoop Jackson's home state), had been built for more than $1 billion, to be ready to operate in 1978. It had been fully manned, and the delay of the first ship was causing tremendous disruption in personnel assignments and, of course, total waste of the facilities. Vice Admiral Earl Fowler, commander of Naval Sea Systems Command, told me that his best estimate was that Trident would slip still further and likely not be delivered until early 1982, nearly four years after its original delivery schedule.

- Fowler estimated that new delays and mismanagement were going to cost the navy a further $50 million beyond what was in the budget for those submarines, and all over and above what was agreed in the settlement of the 85-804 claims.

- The principal causes of these new delays were the shocking discoveries of major flaws found in many of the submarines under construction. Because of sloppy workmanship and negligent supervision, thousands of welds in many of the submarines then under construction at EB were discovered to have been done faultily or not at all. In addition, some of those subs were found to have steel that was not acceptable for use. Correction of these two serious errors required that many of the subs were having to have major work torn out and done all over again.

- To make matters even worse, the navy had badly managed some of the equipment suppliers that supplied components directly to the navy for installation in the ship by Electric Boat. Since the navy had the obligation to supply this government-furnished equipment (GFE) to Electric Boat to meet construction schedules and had failed to do so on time, this was causing more tumbling of the schedule dominoes. And, as discussed earlier, the standard terms and conditions of our submarine contracts were vague and sloppily written on the essential matter of handling engineering changes and modifications, virtually guaranteeing disputes and claims. (As an example, in 1980 alone the navy made three thousand design changes to the U.S.S. *Ohio*, under construction.) Finally the Carter administration had slashed the requests for SSN-688s, including only one per year in their budgets, and since 1977 all of these had been won by the low bids of Electric Boat. Therefore, Newport News was running out of work and was beginning to lay off skilled submarine building teams. If that process went any further, they would pass the point of no return in being able to compete effectively in the future against Electric Boat.

- The Rickover organization and the Naval Sea Systems Command, as well as the staff of the chief of naval operations, were constantly micromanaging the engineering and arbitrarily and capriciously making design and engineering changes that had to be incorporated in already written contracts.

Whatever the differences in the interpretation of the lessons of the 85-804 or omnibus claims of the mid-1970s, I was convinced that Electric Boat had "bought in" to the original contracts—that is, they had knowingly bid prices lower than they knew they could build ships for, confident that change orders would enable them to get well. Yet despite this obvious lesson, it was clear to me that Electric Boat had continued the practice even after the settlement and had won the competition for four more SSN-688s authorized in 1980 and 1981 by bidding well below what now was "hard data" (consisting of return cost information) on what the ships actually cost to produce.

Secretary Hidalgo, however, believed that the bids were valid and told me that the new automated welding facility that Electric Boat had built at Quonset and the new preoutfitting modular methods of construction being adopted at EB were going to bring new efficiencies that would show those bids to be realistic. He had intended to approve the award of those contracts plus the additional Trident authorized for 1981, but Admiral Rickover had put a hold on any processing of those contracts the day after the Carter administration lost the election. This, of course, is standard practice. Having participated in the Nixon, Ford, Carter, and Reagan transitions, I observed each time how the career military in all of the services switched their allegiance instantaneously to the newly elected administration. Thus all contracts with which the uniformed bureaucracy was unhappy were held up and dumped on my desk during the first week.

Plunging in at once to attempt to understand the problem, it was clear that I would need the judgment of real experts in ship and submarine construction. Secretary Hidalgo was very helpful, as was his undersecretary, Bob Murray, an outstanding public servant whom I asked to stay on for about six months until a new under secretary could be selected and taken through the confirmation process. He provided the senior institutional memory. The next step was to convene a blue ribbon panel of experts to study the situation in depth and advise on options for dealing with it. I asked Jim Goodrich, the retired chairman of the board of Bath Ironworks, who had been a shipbuilder all his professional life, to head the panel.

George Sawyer was another vital member of the management team. Among the foremost naval engineers in the country, he was confirmed in June 1981 to fill the new position of assistant secretary for shipbuilding, but informally he became part of our management team in April. The rest of the group, in addition to Admiral Hayward, included Admiral Jim Watkins, the vice chief of naval operations, whom I later selected as Hayward's successor; Admiral Al Whittle, the chief of naval materiel; Vice Admiral Earl Fowler, commander of the Naval Sea Systems Command; and Walter Skallerup, my selection for general counsel.

Soon we had a clear grasp of this extraordinary mess:

- Electric Boat had reached gridlock at its Groton shipyard, with twenty-one ships under construction and twenty-five thousand employees in a very cramped yard.

- Manning of certain specially skilled trades was insufficient to meet the contract schedules.

- Management at the yard was out of control. When our blue ribbon panel returned from the yard, they reported to me that they observed and were shown data by the local supervisor of shipbuilding showing continuing malingering, goofing off, and drinking in the yard instead of working.

- It was our opinion that Takis Veliotis, the manager of the yard, was not providing the navy or senior management at Electric Boat with accurate data on manning numbers and actual progress on each ship. Some of the panel members believed that some were cooking the books and loading the workers onto the earlier ships covered by the 85-804 settlement for which General Dynamic was bearing all the cost, and charging the labor to the newer ships, in effect rolling an even larger loss four or five years ahead into the future.

- The bitter hatred between Rickover and Veliotis had created the most poisonous possible atmosphere, making progress impossible. It was obvious that both men were spending more time conducting their personal ego duel, both in public and in private, than they were solving their mutual problems.

- Rickover's repeated charges of criminality and fraud against the shipbuilders meant that they would conduct no business without teams of corporate lawyers at every step (for which the navy paid, as corporate overhead expense). Even by 1981, the atmosphere remained poisonous between the navy and the "big three" shipbuilders (General Dynamics, Newport News Shipbuilding, and Litton), even in the conduct of normal everyday business. Suspicion and genuine personal animosity dominated essential dialogue at all levels between these contractors and the navy and continually impeded progress. In his later years Rickover's practice of charging criminality and instigating FBI investigations against some with whom he disagreed illustrated one of his most unattractive sides. (In recent years Admiral Rickover had instigated criminal charges against most of the shipbuilders with which he did business: Litton in 1976, General Dynamics in 1977, Newport News in 1977, and Lockheed Shipbuilding in 1974. Of these, only the Litton case resulted in an indictment.) Almost as soon as the Reagan administration took over, he instigated a criminal investigation of Secretary Hidalgo as an act of retaliation. Of course, it proved groundless.

By March 15 we had put together a draconian plan to clean up this disaster once and for all. A simple list of what we had to do was enough to illustrate the magnitude of the trouble.

1. Rickover must go, which I had been convinced of for years in any case.
2. Veliotis must go and a "hands-on" manager acceptable to the navy put in charge of Electric boat.
3. Full and open communications must be reestablished, including the provision of all data by Electric Boat to the navy. Electric Boat must increase its manning in selected skills to meet the requirements of the work in the yard.
4. A new schedule of realistic delivery dates must be established for all the ships under contract, and then it must be strictly adhered to.
5. Electric Boat would get no more work until we had solved all the problems. That meant that I would have to reject the 1980 and 1981 awards, which I was convinced were buy-ins.
6. Genuine annual competition must be reestablished between Electric Boat and Newport News, with a system of genuine incentives to hold out the opportunity of earning higher profits through improving schedules and lowering the overall price to the navy by reducing costs.
7. Competition must be brought into the Trident program to break Electric Boat's monopoly on that ship.
8. New and stricter accounting procedures must be established and closely monitored to prevent costs actually incurred on ships covered by the 85-804 settlement being charged to ships like the *Ohio* with essentially unlimited cost structures.
9. A basic change in the nature of our submarine contract form to a fifty-fifty share line above and below the target cost to force the contractor to share any overrun immediately at fifty cents on the dollar up to the ceiling, when he would pay 100 percent, and also provide the incentive seriously to

reduce the costs by being able to share any underruns at fifty cents on the dollar.

10. Complete revision of the standard terms and conditions of our submarine con-tracts, requiring negotiation and pricing of any modifications or change orders within six moths, and tightening up the vague language that led to so much dispute.

11. A complete revision of the then-standard insurance clause in all our ship-building contracts, to eliminate any potential for abuse.

12. Most important of all, the establishment of a review board at the highest level at the Department of the Navy whereby proposals for all design changes that would impact cost must first be carefully cost-estimated, budgeted, and sub-mitted for approval.

After brainstorming this strategy with my advisors we were convinced that it was the only way to go, though the tactics and timing of each of its elements would have to be modified as we went along.

During this period there was much grumbling and complaining by Rickover's organization and NAVSEA about the concessions that had been made to Electric Boat in the 85-804 settlement. But when I asked each of them and the other members of my group of advisers whether they would recom-mend that the navy reopen the ten-year old issues and the settlement itself, not one recommended it. There was such complexity in the issues, so much ambi-guity in the language of the contracts, and such a record of detailed negotia-tion and compromise that to start all over gain would have been impossible. The 85-804 settlement had been approved by President Carter and Congress, and we would not reopen it.

In early March I met with Frank Carlucci and Cap Weinberger to walk them through the details of the problem and our proposed solution. Both agreed. I warned them that as soon as Dave Lewis was hit with the first step, he would appeal at once to Weinberger to overrule me. Having watched how General Dynamics and many other contractors played both sides of the polit-ical street during the Nixon, Ford, and Carter years, it was also clear that Lewis would appeal to the White House staff if the Department of Defense failed to satisfy him.

And so it was. On March 17 came the meeting when Lewis learned of our plan, to his displeasure. In further conversations in April I told him that our negotiations would be based solely on performance from 1981 forward, with-out reference to the years of disputes and difficulties of the past. The navy's

addiction to design and engineering changes, the vastness of the navy bureaucracy, and the problem of Rickover did not excuse the current production difficulties, inadequate labor, and bad management. There would be no more
work going to Electric Boat until these problems were on their way to solution.
His response was ten minutes of vituperation against Rickover and then a
strong defense of Veliotis. Lewis tried to convince me that all of my people
were misleading me, that things were in great shape at Electric Boat, and, by
the way, that he was not going to take this lying down.

What Lewis meant by that threat soon became apparent. His strategy
involved four elements: first, a threat to slow down or stop work on existing
subs; second, a threat to file an entirely new set of legal claims for reimbursement of costs for the faulty steel and welding, which, if successful, would crack
through the capped prices of the 85-804 settlement; third; an end run around
me, first to Weinberger and then to the White House to have me overruled;
and fourth, a lobbying blitz in Congress.

On March 12, Admiral Fowler testified before the Sea Power Subcommittee
of the House Armed Service Committee and laid out what was essentially
Admiral Rickover's case against Electric Boat. It was a detailed account of the
history of the discovery of the missing, incomplete inspection records, the
faulty steel, and the improper and missing welds. It was a rounding attack on
Electric Boat and its management.[3]

The Electric Boat problem was much larger than just the ships and contracts involved. We had an enormous task to double the shipbuilding rate and
to restore the readiness of a larger navy within the 5 percent growth budget that
the president had projected for us. None of this could be achieved if the cost
of procuring navy ships continued to escalate at a steady 20 percent a year, as
they had averaged in previous decades, nor could we tolerate the enormous
delays involved in completing our ships. And none of it could be achieved if
we got bogged down from the very start in endless legal disputes with our principal shipbuilders. The problem of Electric Boat was *the* critical obstacle that
had to be removed if the six-hundred-ship navy was to succeed. We not only
had to resolve the existing disputes but also eliminate their root causes and
place our shipbuilding program on a credible baseline that would restore the
confidence of the president, the Congress, and the public in our ability to
manage the ambitious shipbuilding program to which we were committed.[4]

Veliotis's testimony on March 25 was the first move in the counterattack.
In it he admitted that there were serious problems when he took over the yard
in 1977 but that he had solved them all and that things were humming along

now. He dismissed the bad steel and welding problems as inconsequential, but he flashed a long stiletto with the new threat of starting major new claims against the navy through a novel interpretation of the construction contract insurance clause then in effect. He said:

> There has been a considerable amount of public comment in recent months to effect that Electric Boat is "setting up" the navy for huge omnibus claims, especially on the Trident program. I would like to clarify Electric Boat's position on this matter and lay to rest, once and for all, these unsubstantiated allegations. At this time Electric Boat has no claims being prepared or under consideration—as we all understand the term "claims." There are, however, "insurance reimbursement requests"; being prepared to recover, under the builders risk insurance provisions of our navy shipbuilding contracts, the cost consequences of faulty workmanship performed by Electric Boat employees.[5]

When I read this in Veliotis's testimony I called our lawyers in and had them explain to me what he was talking about. Since 1942, early in World War II, the navy has not carried insurance on risk on its ships while under construction. In effect, the navy self-insures such risks, and it does not allow a contractor to charge the costs of all-risk insurance coverage on its contracts—that is, any loss or damage to property in a shipyard resulting from accident, fire, explosion, water damage, or catastrophic equipment failure. The navy insures the contractor for all such risks and reimburses them for damage suffered. Here for the first time a contractor—with incomparable chutzpah—was asserting that the navy insurance also should cover the contractor's own negligence, faulty workmanship, and poor management in the bad steel and welding problems. My general counsel, Walter Skallerup, and his NAVSEA lawyers were not in total agreement as to whether a serious legal case could be made for such a ridiculous claim because of the vagueness of the contract language and precedents in commercial shipbuilding insurance.

Electric boat's next move followed a week later, when they announced that they were going to slow down and stretch out their submarine schedules to maintain their base of key trade personnel, and instead of increasing the manning, as we had demanded, they announced the intention to reduce manning to conserve the work they had.

On April 20, Jim Goodrich provided to me the report of this select committee. The committee had been charged to assess Electric Boat's problem; its current projections on delivery; whether they could meet the navy's schedule on Trident and SSN-688; and finally, develop a method for the navy to monitor all submarines under contract to the firm.

Goodrich's committee was directed not to dwell on past difficulties or to allocate blame, but to draw appropriate lessons from the problems of the past and to assess current work force and management capabilities.
The panel reached the following conclusions:

1. The necessary plant facilities and work force were in place at Electric Boat to build at least one and a half Tridents and two SSN-688s per year, and potentially more.
2. There were serious management and supervisory shortcomings at Electric Boat that called into question whether EB could be successful in realizing its potential.
3. A new and realistic schedule of delivery dates for each ship should be agreed upon and then strictly adhered to.
4. A weekly detailed progress report based on precise data, tracking daily progress on every ship, should be provided to the secretary of the navy.
5. The fourth remaining SSN-688, authorized in 1981 and held out of the award to Newport News, should be awarded to Electric Boat only if progress on all the ships becomes consistent with the new delivery dates.
6. The contract for the ninth Trident, authorized in 1981, should be completely redrawn to:

   - eliminate the overgenerous share line basing the target cost on the reality of what can be achieved in efficiency rather than the unachievable Veliotis promises on which the existing Trident contract is based;
   - clean up numerous areas of language ambiguity, particularly with regard to changes and claims;
   - most importantly, tighten up the scope of the navy insurance clause to avoid any possibility of future "imaginative constructions" such as that which GD had invented.

7. Award of the ninth Trident should not be made until achievement of the milestones outlined in the committee report are successfully achieved.
8. Achievement of a stable production base without risking the loss of skilled personnel will require a tenth Trident to be awarded within eight months of the ninth Trident award.

Based on the Goodrich report, we settled on a very straightforward and effective method to monitor actual performance in the shipyard so we could know without any uncertainty just what progress was being made. The system involved two elements: first, a manning graph for each of the twenty-five ships in the yard that plotted the daily manning level on every ship; and second, a major progress milestone/task bar graph for each ship. The first element required direct access to those actual figures and having our on-the-spot supervisors check every ship every day so that the data would be accurate. The second element required definitive agreement on what constituted the major milestones and the dates for their accomplishment. Together these elements would preclude the kind of shell game that our supervisors said Veliotis had been playing. I established a formal shipbuilding status review committee every Friday, one item of which was to review these graphs of EB performance so we would have constant and current attention to what was happening. It was amazing to find that for the past several years the navy had been unable to put together such charts because Veliotis had refused to give them access to even this most fundamental management information. There was no point in studying such graphs if they were not based on precise, current information.

In late April I met again with Dave Lewis and explained to him how we would use these data to track progress and decide when the yard had achieved sufficient production. I proposed to meet regularly with him to go over the data together so we were all working from the same base. Nothing could happen, however, until we started to get the accurate data; Electric Boat would get no work while I was secretary of the navy until the mess at Groton was straightened out. The proposed insurance claims were worth only a brief comment: They were ridiculous. Lewis still strongly supported Veliotis and said he did not believe that Veliotis was withholding data. He agreed, however, to get directly involved and ensure that the data would flow, and to meet with me regularly to review the data together. Lewis's attitude at this meeting was one of condescending sufferance. He did not yet understand the layout of power in the new Reagan administration, but he was clearly under the impression that the secretary of the navy was of little consequence in decision-making.

After the meeting Lewis told *Forbes* magazine (May 11, 1981), "When we had our very first meeting he handed me the letter saying he was going to award the contract to Newport News. We talked for quite a while and I told him in words of one syllable that he didn't know what he was doing. I've been in this damned business an awful long time and I've never known anyone to take such drastic action without making an effort to find out the whole story."

A few days later I got a call from Senator John Warner, saying, "General Dynamics has been spreading it around up here on the Hill that the reason you took those submarines away from Electric Boat and awarded them to Newport News was a political payoff to me. You and I know we never even talked about that award, but you ought to get them to cut that out. While it sure doesn't hurt me in Virginia, it doesn't help your credibility up here on the Hill." I fully agreed, but there was nothing I could do about it. It was the kind of chicanery that is typical procedure with the lobbying trade. Whenever I made a hard decision against the interests of one or another contractor, invariably there were newspaper stories planted by their lobbyists that I was running for the senate in Virginia or governor of Pennsylvania, or paying off some political debt or other.

Of course, I was not without my own ways of keeping the pressure on Electric Boat. In April I traveled to the Electric Boat's facilities at Quonset Point, Rhode Island, where the round frame and plate sections of the submarine hulls had been fabricated. While there I met with the press and told them how concerned we were with the problems at Groton and that we were not at all sure they would be solved. We were looking at options for building some submarines abroad with the British and the Canadians, and a trip had been scheduled to discuss this with the first lord of the admiralty.

This last point illustrates a great difference between sound business management in the Pentagon and in industry. I have often envied the orderly environment in which corporate CEOs operate. They have only a simple bottom line and their stockholders to answer to. In the Pentagon, however, not only do we have the exact same management challenges, as illustrated in our negotiations with Electric Boat, but also we have layers of micromanaging bureaucracy second-guessing us in OSD, powerful political forces in the White House capable of overruling specific action, and the many subcommittees and committees of oversight in Congress that ultimately dispose of our fate. In the case of the Trident we had to try to prevent the cold-blooded showdown we were having with GD from being used by the antidefense forces in Congress and the press to block our ambitious funding requests pending in Congress for the 1981 supplemental and the 1982 budget. "How can you appropriate two more Tridents while Lehman can't even conclude a contract for one that we appropriated a year go?" argued one key congressional staffer.

The heat soon turned up from the General Dynamics lobbying organization as they called in their chips with the Connecticut, Rhode Island, Missouri, and other delegations that had GD plants or major subcontractors. In meeting after meeting on the Hill I was beaten about the head and shoulders for holding up the submarine contract. In turn, I worked the corridors pretty hard myself, and I made repeated public statements that we were seriously considering reopening construction in naval shipyards and possibly building abroad. Later that month the first lord of admiralty, Keith Speed, came to visit and we discussed seriously the possibility of a cooperative venture on a new class of Trident submarine. The Thatcher government had decided to go forward with a new Trident submarine to replace their Polaris boats, but they planned a ship of about eight thousand tons to carry sixteen missiles rather than the eighteen-thousand-ton Ohio class. That ship is currently under construction in the Vickers yards in the United Kingdom, and is a very fine ship indeed. While intellectually it made a great deal of sense to me, politically it was not feasible. But it was fun to talk about it. As one General Dynamics lobbyist said on the Hill, "Who knows what that inexperienced young punk will do?"

In May 1981, over Admiral Rickover's objections, we selected Rear Admiral Ted Young as the new navy supervisor of shipbuilding at Electric Boat. A savvy engineer, shipbuilder, and manager, Ted was one of the few "EDs" (engineering duty officers) not under the thumb of Rickover. Ted had done a first-rate job commanding Portsmouth Naval Shipyard, and he turned out to be one of the major contributors to our eventual success. Paralleling Ted's appointment, we later selected an equally fine officer, Captain Mal McKinnon, as supervisor of shipbuilding of Newport News. The contribution made by both of these "hands-on," knowledgeable naval officers with the navy's two major nuclear shipyards were outstanding. Both men handled the navy/contractor relationship on the firing line, and both were largely responsible for the success of our subsequent nuclear shipbuilding efforts.

In mid-May, after learning for the first time that GD was able to book claims, however bogus, as an asset, Sawyer came up with the idea that gave Skallerup and O'Neill the clout we needed to resolve the issue on our terms. If contractors could create paper assets simply by filing claims, why couldn't we create paper liabilities to balance them by pursuing claims against them for our legitimate losses from their negligence? We set up a strike team of litigation lawyers under Skallerup to do just that. Working with NAVSEA, they documented a claim against GD for $300 million in consequent damages, including costs of the unused Bangor base, extending Polaris subs because of Trident delays and others. "Wow, wait 'till I lay that one on Dave Lewis." I could hardly wait.

Early in June Admiral Fowler gave me a full report based on the new flow data from GD, and in mid-June, Dave Lewis met with me to go over the data. He was genuinely surprised, realizing for the first time that things were not as he had been led to believe. He agreed that our meetings to go over these data were very worthwhile and that he would continue to make himself available.

Late in the meeting I told him casually that we intended to pursue damages against GD if they persisted in their insurance claims, and that they would be large indeed. He did not react, but I had gotten his attention.

The next report, on June 18, showed a little more progress:

"Despite the delay in some key events on their latest schedule, EB is manning to deliver the first Trident and SSN-688 class submarines this calendar year."

EB management, however, seemed up to its old tricks. Despite the fact that everyone believed that they were undermanned to meet the new schedules, they began laying off a thousand people, which I believed they did to create union and political pressure in Congress against us. They said that it had to he done "to even out the work load and maintain an industrial base for future work." Our supervisor on the scene reported, "Many work stations that could be worked are not manned. With a concerted effort on additional manning and improved productivity, the delivery dates of all submarines, with one exception, could be met or improved."

On Monday, June 28, I invited Lewis to a working lunch in my office. Lewis brought Ted LeFevre, his vice president for government relations; Jim Goodrich and George Sawyer were with me. Lewis's attitude in this meeting was totally changed. It was businesslike and conciliatory. He disavowed Veliotis's unilateral schedule delays and layoffs, leaving the impression that our development of key facts had shaken his confidence in his manager on the critical issues.

Most of the meeting, however, was spent discussing the insurance claims. On June 16, General Dynamics had submitted the first claim, for $18.9 million, for their negligence relating to the bad steel and welding on the U.S.S. *Bremerton*. They informed the navy that they were preparing claims on all the other ships involved and would deliver each claim as each ship was delivered. The total would be between $100 million and $200 million. Lewis repeated his case. He said that my predecessor, Ed Hidalgo, had agreed with General Dynamics that the claims had merit, that GD's corporate lawyers had advised them that their legal position was sound. Becoming more ardent, Lewis said that he had no other choice, that he could not possibly lose another $100 million on those ships. He then berated me for "stirring up the Congress on this issue."

I responded that, of course, his multitudes of lawyers (whom we had essentially been paying as part of his overhead) would advise him that they had a legal case because that is what they are paid to do, to litigate. But this issue was not simply a legal issue, it was a business determination of major proportion. As to our stirring up Congress, we were merely defending ourselves from the massive lobbying campaign he had launched. Further the Congress was fully aware of the unacceptable—indeed, disastrous—implication of this matter. My ardor now exceeded that of Lewis. This claim, after all, went to the very heart of the relationship between the government and industry; if we were to accept the precedent that the navy pays for the negligence and poor management of its contractors, it would destroy any vestige of discipline and accountability in all of this nation's defense procurement. I would have none of it, Cap would have none of it, and the president would have none of it. If he pressed these claims, we, the U.S. government, would fight back with all of the vigor and resources at our disposal. The protracted and bitter dispute that would ensue would make the omnibus claims fight look like a Sunday tea party and would likely spill over into all of General Dynamics' relations with the Pentagon, including their F-16s and their missiles—even their coal mining and cement business.

We were, moreover, very serious indeed about pressing claims of our own for the very substantial damages consequent to the late deliveries caused by the negligence of General Dynamics, covering all of the additional costs incurred by the government, such as additional crew training and rotations, the present worth capital carrying and operating costs for idle facilities, and so forth. I was so convinced of our case that I almost quoted Clint Eastwood and said "Go ahead, make my day," but I caught myself.

The meeting eventually returned to a calmer tone, and we summarized, with Lewis agreeing to accept the blue ribbon panel schedules, and that he would revise the milestone and manning plans at Groton to reflect those schedules. He pledged to continue the new flow of full information to the navy, and that we would continue to meet regularly to review the data together to monitor progress.

I, in turn, conceded that there was merit to his complaint that, in the case of the *Ohio* only, the navy may have contributed to some of the schedule slippage and overrun because of problems the navy experienced in developing and delivering some of the government-furnished equipment, and in directing arbitrarily more than three thousand design changes in the previous year. I pledged to see that the navy made a good-faith effort to price out those changes and late deliveries we were responsible for.

Our strategy seemed to be working, but the play was far from over. On July 2 Ted LeFevre met with George Sawyer to follow up on the agreements in our meeting. LeFevre told Sawyer that Lewis was disposed to recommend to the board that the claims be dropped, but that he must have some quid pro quo to get the board to buy it. He wanted to know what the navy could do in offering work in the future that Lewis could use to satisfy the board. He reiterated that Hidalgo had made a firm pledge that GD would get the four 1980–81 boats in return for dropping the claims.

LeFevre said that there was "active consideration" being given to management changes at EB and that Lewis was determined to restore a better corporate relationship with the navy. But Lewis must have something positive and tangible to give his board before he could justify accepting the $100 million write-off for the bad steel and welds.

Sawyer rejoined that the quid pro quo for GD dropping the $100 million claims would be that the navy would then consider dropping its $400 million claim for consequent damages. He widened the threat by saying that once such litigation begins, there would, of course, be no way to prevent it from being extended to all of General Dynamics' defense activities. "Nevertheless," he said, "the navy is in the shipbuilding business, not the litigation business; Lehman meant exactly what he told Lewis — get your act together, improve your performance, keep us well informed, and change your general corporate management demeanor toward your only client — and you will undoubtedly obtain your share of future SSN/SSBN business. Once your act is together and you start working the waterfront, you should find that you can make a profit in naval shipbuilding without having to resort to your customary procedure of low-balling the bids, slipping the jobs, and searching around for arcane legal mechanisms to pursue your claims."

George warmed to his peroration. "Continuance of the status quo in General Dynamics/navy relations is intolerable. Just how many SUPSHIPS [navy supervisors] or, for that matter, COMNAVSEAs [commander, naval sea systems] do we have before General Dynamics will be happy? The historic pattern of 'initial love/subsequent hate' in navy/EB personal relationships has been noted and filed in the navy's corporate memory. Any further changes in personnel from here on must be at General Dynamics."

The reaction was not long in coming to my stun bomb on counterclaims. Lewis and Veliotis went to work on the Hill raising alarms with their supporters and key armed services chairmen. They met twice with Charlie Bennett, the chairman of the Seapower Subcommittee, on July 23 and 27, and followed up with a letter stating their case. They sounded panicky. They pleaded with

Bennett to intervene to prevent the navy from suing them for consequent damages. They claimed that it was not "fair dealing" for the navy to hold up new contract awards just because General Dynamics was claiming millions from the navy for their negligence on previous contracts.

It was a rather pathetic last-ditch effort to try to get somebody somewhere to let them return to business as usual. When Charlie Bennett sent me a copy, I knew that they were done for.

By mid-August we had made much progress in renegotiating a fair and realistic but demanding adjustment of new contract delivery dates (see table 3), based on a fair acceptance by the navy of its share of delays caused by late delivery of GFE and of design changes, and an acceptance by GD of its responsibility.

TABLE 3. CONTRACT DELIVERY DATES — ORIGINAL AND NEW

SSBN	PRIOR CONTRACT DELIVERY DATE	REVISED CONTRACT DELIVERY DATE
726	February 1981	October 1981
727	November 1981	September 1982
728	July 1982	June 1983
729	March 1983	February 1984
730	November 1983	October 1984
731	July 1984	June 1985
732	March 1985	February 1986
733	May 1986	October 1986

By October 1986 we were able to inform Congress that General Dynamics, in fact, met or beat every single one of those delivery dates.

Throughout the summer congressmen and senators from the affected states hectored me without letup. Cajolery, lamentations, and vile threats were received every week. I told them that progress was being made but that the problems had not been solved. By mid-August threats were being made in retaliation against the entire navy budget. The flames were being fanned by the General Dynamics lobbyists and those of their subcontractors, and by the unions.

On August 13 I issued a press release announcing that we had concluded our sole-source negotiation with Newport News for the three SSN-688 submarines we had taken away from General Dynamics. The contract was a real breakthrough and was the first to embody the new, fairer, but much tougher terms and conditions I described previously. The release said: "This contract is particularly noteworthy in that the contractor has accepted an equal sharing of cost growth or savings. . . . The contract precludes payment by the Navy for insurance coverage for costs of corrective defective workmanship or materials. This contract provides a profit incentive to the contractor for delivering high-quality ships on or ahead of schedule and budgets."

It was the first award of a submarine to Newport News since September 1977.

Before I released the announcement I called Senator John Chafee of Rhode Island to give him a heads-up. Chafee, a good friend and a former secretary of the navy, had been under tremendous pressure but had always been extremely helpful. He agreed to call the Rhode Island press and give them a statement, and he did a great job. The headline in the *Providence Journal* said, "EB Told: Drop Claim to Get more Subs!" The article went on to say, "Navy Secretary John F. Lehman, Jr., yesterday said Electric Boat will not get any more submarine contracts from the navy unless the company withdraws an $18.9 million insurance claim for faulty workmanship on the submarine *Bremerton*, according to Senator John Chafee. Chafee, who spoke with Secretary Lehman on the telephone yesterday, said Lehman was 'very adamant' about not sending new work to EB while the claim was pending. And, to make matters worse for Electric Boat, the Navy announced yesterday that it had agreed with EB's only competition, Newport News, Virginia Shipbuilding and Drydock Company on not only a contract for three new 688s, but on an option for three additional 688s."

By now it was apparent that Lewis was making a strong effort to straighten out the problems at Electric Boat and essentially had accepted our view as to the causes of the problems. It was also apparent, however, that he had no intention of dropping the meritless insurance claims. His lobbyists on the Hill had let it be known that General Dynamics believed I was using it as a negotiating ploy and would eventually back down and throw the claims issue to the lawyers, as always had been done in the past. To disabuse them of this notion, the best move would be to take a very-high-profile position on the claim that would in effect burn the bridges and make it clear to everyone that there would be no backing down. Because of the closeness with which Wall Street follows Washington developments as they affect government contracts, the pressure on General Dynamics from a public flogging would be very helpful.

At the same time, the navy was in the midst of another dispute, with McDonnell Douglas, over their refusal to pay for an F-18 aircraft belonging to the navy that crashed while bailed to them for a marketing tour in Europe. Their reason? When aircraft had been lost in similar circumstances, the

Pentagon had never asked for compensation! This chutzpah and the attitude it reflected toward the taxpayer roused me to a luncheon speech at the National Press Club in Washington on August 19, when I denounced publicly and by name both McDonnell Douglas and General Dynamics. For those corporations to claim that their own faulty aircraft or their own shipyard negligence should be compensated by the taxpayer was simply preposterous.

The speech got wide coverage on radio, television, and the press, and the effect on both General Dynamics and McDonnell Douglas was immediate. Within weeks McDonnell Douglas agreed to build us a new replacement F-18 free, and Dave Lewis called to resume negotiations.

As usual, these moves were accompanied by fresh counterpressures. On August 24 the president of the Metal Trades Council, one of EB's unions, delivered to the White House a petition with fifteen thousand signatures on it urging that contracts be awarded to Electric boat. On August 25 Governor J. Joseph Garrahy of Rhode Island delivered a letter to Vice President George Bush urging the same.

My next meeting with Lewis, on August 25, started us toward a final solution. Lewis brought Ted LeFevre into the meeting, and I had George Sawyer. The meeting began with Lewis orating that he was not going to be intimidated by my use of the media to attack Electric Boat, that he had found my speech insulting, and that he didn't need any lectures from me on ethical conduct, that he had been working with the navy for forty years, which was before I was born. It was good theater, and I enjoyed it. I couldn't help grinning. Lewis continued his histrionics at a higher decibel level, saying that he wasn't kidding, that those claims were worth something, and that I'd offered him nothing in return for dropping the claims, that all I wanted was for him to appear in a picture groveling before me.

It was now my turn for histrionics, and I bestrode the carpet accordingly. I told him that I had written the Press Club speech myself and had given it as high a profile as I could so he could understand that I had meant what I said and after such a public airing could not and would not back down. The claims were preposterous, and we would not pay a nickel of the taxpayers' money directly or indirectly to have them dropped. I reminded him that he now knew for himself what the real data showed, that the problems had not been solved as Veliotis had been telling him, and that we would not put any more work into that yard until they were solved and manning was matched to the contract dates. I would far rather accept a delay of several years while we followed Rickover's urging and started to build submarines in naval shipyards again than to continue on the current basis. That would be far better in the long run than the endless cost overruns, which really amounted to massive unilateral disarmament.

Our task was to build a six-hundred-ship navy, and to do it on a limited budget. Electric Boat had the capacity if it was well run to bring the costs down and the efficiency up, and that was my objective. The picture I wanted to see in the newspaper, I told Lewis, was not of him prostrate before the navy but of General Dynamics and the navy together announcing that they had resolved the problem and were getting on with building submarines. That could not happen, however, until our terms were met.

It was clear that my speech had stung Lewis and also clear that the moment had arrived to strike a deal. I asked the others to leave so that we could speak alone. Sawyer had drawn up plain sheets of paper with our final terms, eight points in all, which I gave to Lewis.

The first point required reaching agreement on settling change orders, new delivery schedule, and labor manning on the Trident subs and dropping all claims on them.

The second point required that EB must achieve the manning on all subs required by our agreed schedule plan.

The third point committed the navy and EB to stop the public "pissing contest" (Lewis's words).

The fourth point was contingent on the first two. When those were met, I would approve the award of the withheld Trident and issue a "request for proposal" (but not award) for the withheld SSN-688 sub.

The fifth and sixth points would be done simultaneously: EB would drop all claims for all SSN-688s, and I would approve the award of the withheld SSN-688 to EB.

The seventh point required the replacement of Veliotis as manager of the Groton yard with someone who could work with navy shipbuilders.

The eighth point committed the navy to speed up the competition for the three newly authorized SSN-688s by the end of the year.

These terms had been discussed with Lewis by Sawyer in the weeks prior to the meeting, so Lewis was not shocked. After some discussion we reached an agreement with a handshake. He seemed most reluctant, however, about removing Veliotis and about finding a replacement.

It was not the navy's business, of course, to dictate Veliotis's replacement, but we would definitely insist that the replacement be a known and proven person who had the confidence of the navy. Electric Boat was not barren of good managers. The contrast during these difficulties between performance and attitudes at the Groton yard, where the ships were finally assembled, and at the Quonset, Rhode Island, hull fabricating facility was quite dramatic. The reason for this contrast was Fritz Tovar, a very tough, smart industrial manager who had a reputation for bluntness and integrity. I strongly recommended to Lewis that he replace Veliotis with Tovar. Lewis was at first reluctant; he had another candidate in mind.

While Lewis and I had reached an agreement, he still had his work cut out. He had to sell the settlement to his board and find a graceful way to get Veliotis out by November 15. We had to keep some of the details secret from our own troops lest stories appear about GD caving in to us and putting Lewis in an untenable position. GD had to be given room to save face. This was to take the form of a joint press conference when we had concluded the deal.

In late August Lewis delivered on the first two points, and I delivered on the third and fourth in early September.

On September 22 I held a full-scale press conference in the Pentagon press auditorium with all the networks and Pentagon reporters. Dave Lewis was with me on the podium. I included Senator John Chafee, because his forbearance and service as an intermediary had been very helpful. The purpose was to project to the world (including Congress) that we were on the road to solving all the problems at Electric Boat and were getting on with building the six-hundred-ship navy. I threw bouquets to Chafee and Lewis, and both were very pleased with the results. I was very pleased indeed because I now had Lewis's commitment to drop the claims without compensation and to make the labor and management changes necessary to bring the cost of future submarines down, and the navy had paid nothing directly or indirectly to achieve it.

On October 18, 1981, EB dropped all claims on the SSN-688, and four days later I approved the award to EB of the withheld SSN-688 from fiscal year 1981 (on the same tough new terms we had negotiated with Newport News), and I issued the RPFs for the three SSN-688s from fiscal year 1982. Only the seventh and eighth points remained to be fulfilled.

In November Lewis delivered on his commitment and promoted Veliotis upstairs as executive vice president, marine and international. Fritz Tovar was named as his replacement to manage Electric Boat. Soon after we completed negotiations on the Trident and awarded the contract based on much tougher terms and conditions and a fifty-fifty share line.

In December we conducted the competition for the three fiscal year 1982 boats on a fixed-price basis with the same terms and conditions. EB won two submarines with the lowest price, and NNS got one submarine at a slightly higher price.

On May 12, 1982, Veliotis resigned and then in September he was indicted for accepting kickbacks from suppliers to both Electric Boat and the General Dynamics' Quincy yard. He immediately fled to Greece to escape prosecution where the lack of an extradition treaty gave him safe haven.

With Veliotis gone, Tovar asserted an increasingly strong and effective management. On the navy's side the replacement of Admiral Rickover by the equally intelligent and far more personable Admiral Kinnaird McKee reestablished a solid and honest flow of communications between the navy and all of its nuclear contractors and shipyards. The steady application of the lessons learned and the new business culture we applied navywide has brought about six years of steadily improving performance and productivity with Electric Boat. The schedules that were recommended as achievable by the blue ribbon panel in April 1981 have all been achieved or exceeded. So effective has Tovar's management been that the navy is now very hard-pressed in keeping up with him in providing the government-furnished equipment to meet his schedules. The prices of the ships themselves have come steadily down each year as both EB and NNS continue to compete effectively with their brains and hands instead of with the relative merits of their legal briefs. It is a great success story. As important, it also provided the laboratory in which our new management team developed the contracting and business approaches that we applied then to the rest of navy shipbuilding, which has brought about the unprecedented management success and made possible the six-hundred-ship navy.

Chapter 7

The Hornet and the Reform of the Navy Department

The settlement with General Dynamics announced on October 22, 1981, placed our submarine shipbuilding program on a sound basis. Groton's excellent performance in improving quality and bringing the costs down over the next six years was the result. Moreover, it had given our navy management team the tools to straighten out the rest of our shipbuilding contractor relations, and to address the larger issues of reform that had been raised.

Being heaved into the General Dynamics problems within a week of my swearing in turned out to be the most fortunate of developments. It rid me of naïve complacency about the basic soundness of the "system." My primary interest in seeking the job and my experience in government to that point had been focused on strategy and policy, not on engineering and facilities management, aircraft development, ship design, and contract law. I smile at the recollection of my first meeting with the CNO, Tom Hayward, when I confidently announced that my focus would be to rebuild strategy, to articulate and sell the navy's mission and the six-hundred-ship navy program in the media and on the Hill. Twelve years of dealing with the Pentagon still had not disabused me of the belief that while the Defense Department, of course, has the inefficiencies of all bureaucracies, it still is basically a humming machine that only needs tending.

Within days of that meeting, Electric Boat changed all that. Every day was consumed by the complexities of the procurement process and the multilayered, randomly organized system of Pentagon bureaucracy for managing it. As the weeks chased the weeks, it soon dawned on me that the Electric Boat mess was not an anomaly but just a larger and longer mess than many others spawned of the same causes in lesser Pentagon programs. As we tackled others, such as the F-18 Hornet fighter plane and the Tomahawk cruise missile, we saw the same common threads, and eventually we saw the same root causes. "The system" was a catastrophe. Nor was the Navy Department by any means the worst such system in the Pentagon. Indeed, in many ways it was the best.

What worried me most was that the "blue suiters," the friendly term that navy civilians use for the uniformed navy ("green suiters" in the army) on whom I was counting for saving the day had a total, almost childlike confidence in "the system." Such unquestioning devotion to the organizational status quo is, of course, bred into them at the Naval Academy, where midshipmen are conditioned never to question the wisdom of "the system."

By nature, reorganizing as a solution or blaming problems on the organization chart leaves me cold. I am a firm believer that quality people can make any system work. But here was a different phenomenon. Military discipline and hierarchical procedures added to a huge, layered bureaucracy that regularly defeated common sense.

By midsummer 1981 my cynicism with regard to the system had become complete. As great as my cynicism had grown, so also had my admiration for the tremendous quality of the navy and marine career officers and civilians. In mid-July Tom Hayward shook his head after I complained about a report I had just gotten from NAVSEA. "You have just got to have more faith in the system," he said. "You never give it a chance." "You have got to be kidding!" I replied. By then it was clear that we would never achieve a six-hundred-ship navy with the Department of the Navy as it was.

Ending Unilateral Disarmament Through Price Escalation: The FA-18 Hornet

Whatever residual faith I had in the system disappeared with the FA-18 Hornet episode and the whole issue of aircraft costs, which were driving us to unilateral disarmament. The price of navy aircraft had been escalating between 10 and 20 percent higher than the rate of inflation since 1950. Cuts in the navy's budget amounting to 22 percent in constant dollars during the 1970s resulted in massive loss of capability. As the prices went up and the dollars went down, by 1980 the navy was able to buy only half the number of aircraft it lost each year in peacetime attrition. The six-hundred-ship navy, with its fifteen carriers and four marine air wings, required doubling the procurement rate of tactical aircraft that had prevailed during the late 1970s. Because we were projecting only a 5 percent annual increase in funding during the Reagan years, it was obvious we had to break the back of the steady cost of escalation of those aircraft.

The issue was brought to a head by the negotiations with McDonnell Douglas over the Hornet in 1982. The 1981 purchase of this new navy swing fighter was for sixty aircraft, and the flyaway price to the navy was $22.5 million. We had to be careful about what these figures really meant. It is very difficult for the layman and even the expert to ascertain what a modern high-tech aircraft actually costs. The reason is that the programming and budgeting system uses several different prices. The one most commonly used is the most misleading and meaningless—that is, program unit cost (PUC). The PUC is the number resulting from taking the total buy of thirteen hundred aircraft, adding all the nonrecurring research and development costs, all of the costs for each of the aircraft, estimating long into the future what the inflation rates are likely to be, all the spare parts and support materiel, all the test equipment and simulators and ground support equipment, adding it all up, and dividing by 1,300. This gives the number that defense critics always like to use, because they can say that, for instance, the F-18 is a $50 million airplane. It would be equivalent to your taking the purchase cost of your Chevrolet, estimating the cost of all the spare parts and equipment it is likely to use throughout its life, and adding in a portion of the cost of your garage and driveway. That would give you the program unit cost of your Chevrolet.

The only meaningful way to track the price of a modern aircraft is the flyaway cost—literally, the cost of the aircraft as it flies away from the factory and is ready to go to war. By this measure each F-18 priced out at $22.5 million. In 1982 the prime contractor, McDonnell Douglas, raised the price to $26 million per aircraft. Even more disturbing to me than the huge increase in the price was the way the navy system dealt with that proposal by the contractor. When presented with the increase, they did what the Pentagon system dictates: They had the auditors check the validity of the contractors' accounting, check the overhead rates, and then negotiate a little bit on the profit rate but still allow them to base it as a percentage of the increased costs.

The price increase was presented to me in a pitch by the deputy chief of naval operations for air warfare, the commander of the Naval Air Systems Command, and the vice chief of naval operations. A briefing with the usual charts and exhibits reviewed the elements of the cost increase point by point, ending with the recommendation that while the increase was regrettable, it was based on "fact of life" cost escalation and was not out of line with those of prior years. It was embarrassing to remind them that the navy had testified for the past five years that this was to be a low-cost fighter originally projected to cost $7 million apiece and that even with inflation, the learning curve was supposed to bring the price down by 15 percent a year.

Refusing to approve negotiations based on the McDonnell Douglas proposal, I asked instead for a more detailed breakdown of what the "fact of life" increases really were. The breakdown illustrated perfectly how the cost-based pricing system of PPBS in the Pentagon guarantees annual escalation. What was called "fact of life" because it had been audited, was an average 250 percent increase in the prices of the top thirteen subcontractors, and a projected increase in wage escalation of some 20 percent a year. When we really dug into the details of each of the price increases from the thirteen subcontractors, what we found was obvious. The subcontractors knew that the "should cost" studies done by the OSD staff had required the navy to add 20 percent for possible escalation when the 1982 budget was prepared. They also knew that the program, after years of controversy in Congress, now had solid support and was on its way. They had simply raised their prices to the maximum they thought the market would bear.

Now, in private industry, that simply would have been the opening step, with the customer immediately responding, "The hell you say," and the prices would have been negotiated back to a sound economic level. The system the Pentagon had evolved with their parametric "should cost" study already said in preparing the budget that such escalation would happen, and so the system simply accepted it without further negotiation. It was a classic self-fulfilling prophecy built into Pentagon procurement by the cult of system analysis. With regard to the projected labor costs, a contractor was simply accepting what he knew would be the opening wage demands of his unions in the coming several years. In both cases the prime contractor knew that his profit would be calculated as a percentage of the costs, so obviously it would have been idiotic for him to have tried to negotiate hard with his unions for more reasonable wage demands or with his suppliers for competitive price proposals, because in both cases he would be cutting his own profits in so doing.

It was obvious that we had to make our stand on the Hornet if we were to solve the problem of unilateral disarmament in aviation, just as we were doing with General Dynamics, in shipbuilding. There was a difference, however, in that General Dynamics was our most troublesome ship contractor, with deeply ingrained management problems, whereas McDonnell Douglas was one of our best-run and least-troublesome aerospace contractors. They were simply operating according to the system that had evolved in the Pentagon.

Tom Hayward had a distinguished record as a carrier aviator, and we had no disagreements on aviation issues while he was CNO. His four-year term was coming to an end, however, in the spring of 1982, and the vice chief of naval operations (VCNO), Admiral Bill Small, also an aviator, assumed day-to-day responsibility for procurement matters in the weeks prior to Hayward's retirement. Small was the unhappy recipient of my decision not to approve negotiating a contract with McDonnell Douglas for the Hornet that was one dollar over $22.5 million per copy. The alternative was to cancel the program. We simply could not afford a "low-cost fighter" that cost $26 million. They gave a not-so-cheery aye, aye and instructed the chief of NAVAIR to negotiate accordingly. At that time, in accordance with the Gosplan culture of the Pentagon, all procurement organizations in the Department of the Navy had been centralized under the chief of naval operations. As one of the lessons from these early years, we later changed the reporting chain for each of the procurement commands to report directly to the secretary of the navy and concurrently to the chief of naval operations.

Mel Paisley, my assistant secretary for R&D, was point man on these negotiations, and we set up a little working group of Paisley; George Sawyer; and Sawyer's deputy, Ev Pyatt. As Sawyer was our principal ship man, so Paisley was our airplane and aerospace man. Paisley was an air force fighter ace in the Second World War and had spent thirty years in the aerospace industry. He is one of the most effective troubleshooters I have ever worked with, and in dealing with air force and navy aviators, he spoke with an authority that was rare among Pentagon civilians. There was, of course, no serving admiral or general who had nine enemy kills to his credit. Paisley took over day-to-day oversight of the negotiations with McDonnell Douglas.

For several weeks there was no progress at all, with McDonnell Douglas refusing to budge except in the most marginal way. Calls started coming from some of the top management at McDonnell and the principal subcontractor, Northrop. They gave the usual pitches, insisting that they were doing everything humanly possible to lower the cost but that $26 million really was the fair price. In the meantime, their lobbyists on the Hill began to stir up some of the members from their constituencies.

After three weeks had gone by with no progress, the VCNO made another pitch to me that we should reexamine our position, that it really was not reasonable to ask such a large reduction in their price. I told him he was beginning to sound like the way the State Department negotiates with the Russians. We put a position on the table, they don't budge, then we say, well, it's nonnegotiable, we need a new compromise.

It soon became obvious that there was rampant blue-suit defection from our hard-line position, and congressmen began calling to the effect that, "Well, we've been talking to some people in NAVAIR who tell us that you're all wet on the Hornet and you are just trying to kill the program." A senior member of the Senate Armed Services Committee staff told me that a senior admiral had just told him that I really wanted to kill the F-18 because I was part of a different aviation community flying A-6s.

Then came the systems analysts who argued that the F-18 was superior to both the F-14 and the A-6 and therefore was worth the price of $26 million, even if the F-14 and A-6 had to be canceled to pay for it. This was done simply by assigning high numerical values to what the F-18 Hornet did well and low numerical values to what the F-14 Tomcat and the A-6 Intruder did well. Supporters of the F-18 Hornet in Congress and elsewhere received this study, too.

Luckily, I had better systems analysts on the navy secretary's staff, and borrowing some help from the Rand Corporation, we did a more thorough "Gold Team analysis" that gave a much more empirically valid conclusion, showing that the F-18 was excellent but that the combination of A-6s and F-14s would be a very viable alternative if we decided to kill the F-18. This analysis was made available also to the congressional committees and the OSD staff.

Soon a few things came to light that explained some of the opposition. A tremendous advantage for the secretary of the navy since Forrestal's time is that the comptroller of the navy, the chief financial officer, has always worked directly for the secretary rather than the uniformed chief, as was the case in the army and the air force (the latter services are now changed to the navy system by legislation). My very able comptroller, the assistant secretary of the navy for financial management, was Robert Conn, whom I recruited from Arthur Andersen. In delving into the financial management of the Hornet program with Mel Paisley, they discovered that the project officer was covering up a $22 million cost overrun in the development of the infrared targeting pods for the F-18 and had actually released funds for production without approval. They also discovered that part of the $26 million flyaway cost was $1.5 million for another twenty sets. This, of course, was mission equipment and not part of the flyaway cost of the airplane but had been artfully hidden therein.

When I heard this, I was furious. I called in the VCNO and ripped him up and down. "How the hell can we run the navy with this kind of dishonesty and chicanery going on?" He promised to get to the bottom of it. After this I really began to suspect that the undermining of our position from the blue suiters was being sanctioned at a very high level. By this time, our new chief of naval operations, Jim Watkins, was getting up to speed and was enthusiastically supporting the program. When I told him of my fear, he said I was being paranoid.

Some days later, my paranoia was confirmed. A good friend who was a prominent defense journalist in Washington called me to say, "Journalistic ethics prevent me from naming names, but I was just called in by a very senior admiral in NAVAIR and given a detailed background briefing on the F-18. The condition of the interview was that I must not reveal the source and the thrust of the story was that you and Paisley did not know what you were doing, that $26 million was a fair price for the airplane, and that you were out to kill the program. He said further that the entire navy was against you and your amateur assistants."

An hour later another good friend in the Pentagon press corps called me with the same story. That reporter told me the name of the senior admiral. I knew that there was no way that the admiral would have done such a thing unless he had approval from a very high level. I was angry not so much at being subverted, because it was obvious for weeks what was going on, but more because of the clumsiness and amateurism of the way they did it. They really must have thought I was a bumpkin.

When I conveyed this information to Jim Watkins, he was shocked, and while he gave a feeble defense of the admirals involved, two of them submitted their resignations within a year, and the vice chief of naval operations was reassigned to a unified command.[1]

As in every one of our management initiatives, our efforts on the F-18 were relentlessly opposed by the OSD staff. To the extent that firm line management was strengthened in the services, the matrix whiz kid system that McNamara had built was weakened. Moreover, the F-18, like the F-16 for the air force, was the pet project of the systems analysis cultists in OSD and had been imposed on the navy. The OSD staff therefore believed that I was out to kill off the F-18, so they actively took the side of the contractor. Happily, as in most such disputes, Weinberger and Carlucci backed me.

With the revelation of the press backgrounding, the CNO whipped the blue-suiter community into line, and Mel Paisley took direct control of negotiations with McDonnell. McDonnell Douglas now realized that they had to deal with us and they, in turn, went with a jawbone to their unions and subcontractors.

Within a month we had almost reached agreement. Paisley and I met with Bob Little from McDonnell Douglas and Kent Kresa from Northrop to negotiate the final outlines of a contract settlement.

We finally sealed the deal in a meeting with Sandy McDonnell, the CEO. He agreed to the $22.5-million-per-year price, to the learning curve that would bring the price down every year, and to a settlement of the F-18 that they had crashed at the Farnborough Air Show. When they had initially refused to reimburse the navy for the loss of that aircraft while it was bailed to them, I had responded by deducting $40 million from their progress payments on another of their programs, the Harpoon missile. I agreed to release the $40 million in exchange for their commitment to add an extra two-seat airplane to the 1982 buy at no cost to the navy. That aircraft is now flying at LeMoore Naval Air Station in California and is the only existing military aircraft that was never authorized or appropriated by Congress. It was a replacement for the lost development aircraft.

On the navy side we committed to protect him from the arbitrary and capricious change orders from the navy that had become such a plague to all contractors, and I explained to him the new system that we were imposing to prevent that gold-plating called the PMP (Program Management Proposal) system. We were also committed to support forcefully the need for the aircraft with Congress, and to maintain a strong program of F-18 production in future budgets, though there was no commitment to any exact numbers.

Having settled the Hornet contract, we immediately turned on Grumman, which had simultaneously presented us with proposals for substantial price increases on all their aircraft. Using the analysis that the OPNAV staff had cooked up in support of the F-18, we took the position with Grumman management that we could do without the F-14 and the A-6 by improving the F-18 to do both missions. We told them that we could not afford $40 million and $50 million fighter planes, as they were projecting, and that we would cancel those programs that did not fit the navy budget. Having seen how close we actually came to canceling the F-18, they believed us.

Ev Pyatt was assigned to work with Grumman to help them bring about some production changes to optimize their plant for the five different aircraft they were producing. Since the earliest days of aviation, Grumman had had the closest conceivable relationship with the navy and was in reality a kind of custom shop for naval aviation.

The nature of a carrier air wing with its ten different types of aircraft to deal with the four dimensions of naval warfare will always dictate that the navy must have numerous specialized aircraft types that must be produced at low rates of production. It is not true, as so many defense experts would have it, that higher production rates always bring lower prices. If a production line is optimized for low rate production, and if the work force is trained for cross-crafting of skill—that is, one man able to do several tasks on the production line—then efficiencies very close to high-rate production lines can be achieved. After six months of major management efforts supported from the top by Grumman's CEO, Jack Bierworth, and Grumman Aircraft's president, George Skurla, Grumman was able to achieve that optimization by integrating its A-6 and EA-6 production lines and combining the rework of A-6s on the same line; combining the C-2 carrier on-board delivery aircraft production with the E-2C radar early-warning aircraft, which had many common components; and making a major capital investment in new plant tooling. As a result, Grumman dropped their proposal for major price increases and they, too, began a decline of prices even as the aircraft were being improved.

We applied the same technique to our helicopters program. The new SH-60 Seahawk antisubmarine warfare helicopter was just entering production at Sikorsky. It was to replace the SH-2 Seasprite helicopter and would bring double the range and considerably more on-board computing capacity. Both of these helicopters are designed to operate from cruisers, destroyers, and frigates. They are directed to hostile submarine targets by the ship on which they are based, and they prosecute the submarine with sonobuoys and torpedoes. They also have excellent surface search radars for over-the-horizon targeting of Harpoon and Tomahawk missiles and can carry antishipping missiles themselves.

The Seahawk was running into real cost and schedule problems, and it was evident that Sikorsky did not have the production line well in hand at their Connecticut plant. The navy had wisely preserved the tooling for the SH-2, which had been out of production for ten years. Tom Hayward recommended that we put the SH-2 back in production for the Knox class frigates. I had approved it on that basis. But it had the added benefit of giving us real competitive pressure against Sikorsky. The SH-2 had only about half the capability of the SH-60. It only cost half the price. It was under a firm-fixed-price contract with one of the most well-run small aircraft companies in the world, Kaman, whose founder, chief engineer, and chief executive, Charlie Kaman, is one of the last genuine aviation pioneers. The SH-2 has the added benefit of being able to operate from any ship with a helicopter pad.

Thus armed with a real competitive threat, we began to work with Sikorsky to straighten out the problems with the SH-60. Here again we were juggling congressional and OSD pressures to kill the program based on issues having nothing to do with cost. United Technologies, the parent company of Sikorsky, put their best managers, Bob Daniell and his deputy, Bill Paul, in charge of straightening out the plant, and they did an excellent job. By the end of 1982 we had gotten the airplane on a firm-fixed-price with a good learning curve to bring the price down each year. Since that time we have been able to compete the two aircraft lines, keeping both in production, and both aircraft have underrun their budgeted price each year.

Reforming the Navy: The Boston Meetings

More than half of all my time during 1981 was spent immersed in procurement and management issues, being educated by the first-rate management team that had come aboard and the many navy military and civilians who really wanted to do something about the system. After the Electric Boat and the Hornet episodes, we evolved a coherent management philosophy that was drawn from our experience rather than from textbooks. We started at once to implement our approach through concrete changes in people and organization. The new management philosophy placed the focus on individual human beings and their performance rather than organization charts. We wanted to decentralize decision-making and delegate authority to the lowest appropriate level, but then to hold people accountable by name. No organization chart will ever solve one's problems, but an overbureaucratized organization chart creates enormous obstacles to good men and women performing well.

Success depends on taking a firm grip on policy, but decentralizing and delegating authority to strong, proven executives. I had to find men and women up to the task. There were some few to be found among the blue suiters, but the most able and ambitious were of little use in management because they had to chase after all the assignments necessary to make flag promotion. To succeed in the traditional career path, a naval officer rarely stays in one job more than eighteen months. One of the best, Jim Watkins, moved his household thirty times during his career.

Some few also were in the civil service. The United States, has, of course, one of the most egalitarian civil services in the world. Everyone at the management level makes nearly the same salary, and that is very low, because Congress links it with congressional salaries. Although many first-rate people are found in the civil service, it is very hard to hold the best. But happily some of the best, because of patriotism (and a working spouse or private wealth), do stay, and I searched for them.

From each of these sources we had the good fortune to recruit superstars. From the blue suiters, in addition to some, like Admirals Al Whittle and Earl Fowler, who were in place, I grabbed some of the best operational leaders from the fleet, such as Ace Lyons and Frank Kelso, and younger standouts such as Paul Miller, Tom Lynch, Dan Murphy, Ted Gordon, Stu Platt, Mac Williams, and Jim Finkelstein.

From the civil service we recruited Ev Pyatt, Charlie Nemfakos, Harvey Wilcox, Bill Lindahl, and Frank Swofford to the team.

The toughest job was seducing from industry the top business talent we needed to build from scratch a new management culture in the navy. Using the excitement of a new administration with a new conservative vision and the glamour of the six-hundred-ship navy challenge, we put together, in my judgment, the best management team ever assembled in the navy, or in any other department: Jim Goodrich, under secretary, former chairman and CEO of Bath Iron Works; Mel Paisley, assistant secretary for R&D, vice president of Boeing, and former Air Force fighter ace; George Sawyer, assistant secretary for shipbuilding, president of J. J. McMullen; Bob Conn, assistant secretary for financial management, senior partner with Arthur Andersen; John Herrington, assistant secretary for manpower and reserve affairs, prominent San Francisco lawyer; Walter Skallerup, general counsel, a distinguished Washington lawyer; and Hugh O'Neill, principal deputy, prominent Philadelphia lawyer. Later Chapman Cox succeeded Herrington (who is now secretary of energy) and he in turn was succeeded by Chase Untermeyer.

To paraphrase Churchill, it was these people who had the heart of the lion, I merely had the good fortune to make the roar. The success of the six-hundred-ship navy was really the success of this team. Nearly all of them stayed with me the whole six years. The reason we all stayed together was not only the satisfaction of daring greatly and winning, but also, as one of the team quaintly put it, "We just had more goddamn fun than anybody in town." We had tremendous team loyalty and were blessed with a great collective sense of humor. I normally had a full staff meeting in my office two mornings a week, and invariably people down the hall were startled by two or three explosions of laughter each meeting. One morning we had left the door open to the E Ring corridor, through which guided tours were progressing. During a lull in our conversation we suddenly heard the following exchange between a tourist and a young sailor tour guide:

SAILOR: "And this is the office of the secretary of the navy, the Honorable John Lehman."
TOURIST: "Why is this corridor filled with all these old portraits?"
SAILOR: "'Cause the navy likes it like that."

We all cracked up. But the phrase became a standard among us for the next six years every time we couldn't get a straight answer from the blue suiters. I would ask the meeting, "Why did Admiral so-and-so tell the OSD such-and-such when we decided the opposite?" Someone would invariably pipe up from the back of the room, "'Cause the navy likes it like that." Another favorite was drawn from Inspector Clouseau. In one of the *Pink Panther* movies Peter Sellers enters a hotel lobby and sees a man with a dog. He asks, "Does your dog bite, *monsieur?*" The man replies, "No." Sellers then pets the dog, and it bites him. A furious Sellers exclaims, "But you said your dog did not bite!" The man replies, "But, *monsieur,* zis is not my dog." We used it often. Whenever the navy or marine bureaucracy wanted to keep us out of an issue, they simply would never volunteer anything. Questions would be answered to the absolute minimum. One of many examples: After pleas from the medical community, I ordered that twelve graduates of the Naval Academy be allowed to go to medical school each year to provide a steady input of doctors fully motivated as career officers. When I asked three years later how it was going, the system responded, "The secretary's program is fully implemented." When I asked how many officers had actually gone into med school, the system responded, "We have not yet found any with just the right qualifications"— "But, *monsieur,* zis is not my dog."

Since I knew we had a long haul if we were to succeed, I wanted no Stakhanovites or workaholics. I saw too many good people in my NSC days lose the fun and burn themselves out in a year or two by working twelve hours a day and weekends. In any military organization the work hours are set by the example of the boss. If he is in the office weekends, so is everyone else. If he stays till 9:00 P.M., so does everyone else. My normal schedule began at 8:30 A.M. and ended at about 6:30 P.M. In the six years I came to the office on a Saturday only twice (during Beirut) and never on Sunday. Lots of paperwork came home, and often I had to travel on weekends, but the pace was civilized, and everyone appreciated it. As a result, the enthusiasm remained high through the whole six years, and we wore down the opponents instead of the reverse.

As lessons and experiences rolled in, Mel Paisley suggested that we borrow a concept from private industry called a "management retreat." The idea is to take the decision-makers and put them together with a minimum of staff at a secluded location so they can grapple directly with the problems. In August 1983 we held the first Navy Strategy Board meetings at conference facilities of the American Security Council in Boston, Virginia. These "retreats," which included the key players, were convened annually and proved crucial to our reforms of the navy. A major side benefit was the breaking down of the institutional barrier between the uniformed navy and marine corps and between them and the civilian leadership. We ended each retreat with dinner at the nearby Inn at Little Washington, arguably the best restaurant in America.

As I look back on these meetings, I realize how valuable they were in getting our priorities and programs in line, isolated from the ever-present telephone and schedules, the details and the staffs, the flood of ten-minute problems that fill up a day but leave one too distracted to concentrate on the bigger picture. A steady flow of innovations emerged from these meetings: the elimination of the cumbersome and counterproductive Navy Materiel Command; creation of the first "competition advocate general" to break the sole-source pattern of procurement; the Ship Characteristics Improvement Board to control gold-plating; the creation of a new group of navy acquisition specialists—materiel professionals—up to the job of their counterparts in private industry; organizational changes to strengthen accountability; the Program Management Proposals (PMP) system to extend gold-plating controls throughout the navy. The ideas for all of these were hatched, and the consensus for carrying them out formed, in the long brainstorming sessions at Boston, Virginia.

DECENTRALIZATION: ABOLISHING THE NAVY MATERIEL COMMAND

The Navy Department has assets with a book value equal to the first seven companies in the Fortune 500 list combined. It has 1.2 million employees in every conceivable skill and occupation. It has a budget twice the size of IBM, about $100 billion a year. It runs, equips, and trains a force of two hundred thousand marines, two air contingents totaling seven thousand aircraft, a fleet of combatants totaling five hundred and eighty ships, and more than two hundred merchant ships, and it manages social services cradle to grave to half a million families. Imagine the absurdity of attempting to manage such an operation through a centralized bureaucracy in which all authority was held by anonymous matrix staffs in Washington in which the average officer stayed less than eighteen months in any job.

A single centralized procurement bureaucracy called the Navy Materiel Command reported to the chief of naval operations through his staff. In theory the system funneled every bit of information up and down through the single person of the chief of naval operations. As secretary of the navy my staff and I were in theory perched precariously on top of that system, like a Christmas tree star. In practice, of course, it never worked quite that way. Within each of the major systems commands—NAVSEA for ships, NAVAIR for aircraft and their weapons systems, and NAVELEX for electronic command and control systems—each was organized in the same way. Rather than vertical line authority and accountability, there were horizontal "whiz kid" staffs. This was called "matrix management." The propulsion staff, for instance, worked on all the propulsion systems for all the different ships rather than each project having a single team. Project managers were simply paper handlers who coordinated what all the matrix staffs were doing. As a result, as we found in the Electric Boat situation, when there was a horrendous screwup, as with the *Ohio*, there never was anyone to hold accountable. Matrix organizations shared responsibility, so no one ever could be blamed, and no lessons were ever learned. The same mistakes kept being made over and over again.

Another problem of the overcentralization was that all the procurement and business organizations were under the total domination of the headquarters staff of the chief of naval operations, the OPNAV staff. That staff is oriented entirely to meet the operational requirements of the fleet. Their perspective is, as it should be, to write requirements to put the best ships, aircraft, and weapons into the hands of the fleet and not worry about the cost. Thus a huge imbalance was built into the system. If the requirements writer stipulated that a plane must go faster, then NAVAIR must produce a faster airplane regardless of the cost. If the OPNAV staff, responding to complaints from the fleet, rewrote a particular specification or characteristic for a ship or airplane, then the systems command must change the contract regardless of the cost. Although it took us five full years to implement real organizational change, it brought about the most fundamental restructuring in modern naval history.

We abolished the entire Navy Materiel Command of six hundred uniformed and civilian billets. One hundred fifty of these were moved to the systems commands, and the rest were eliminated. None of the human beings involved was fired. More than 10 percent took voluntary early retirement, and the rest were reassigned to vacancies in other commands. Overall, during the five years we eliminated twenty-four hundred headquarters billets in the Department of the Navy in the Washington, D.C., area alone. Within each of the activities we abolished the horizontal matrix staffs, except in areas such as contract service and other functional services where they were appropriate, and instead reestablished a clear vertical line authority. In NAVSEA, for instance, the SSN-688 submarine project manager reported directly to the deputy for all submarine programs, who reported to the commander of the Naval Sea Systems Command and his deputy.

When we abolished the Navy Materiel Command we changed the reporting authority to have the commander of each of the systems commands report directly to the secretary of the navy and, on a parallel line, to the chief of naval operations for informational purposes. I had direct lines put on my telephone to each of the systems commanders, and we talked back and forth almost daily.

TRUE COMPETITION

The philosophy that developed in the Pentagon in the postwar period was quite hostile to competition. McNamara's management approach had been based on a new confidence in empirical methods of operations and systems analysis, statistical-based policy and computer-aided decision-making. The two-thousand person staff in the Office of the Secretary of Defense, including its Systems Analysis Office, had developed an approach called planning, programming, budgeting system (PPBS), which brought an orderly system for preparing a Pentagon budget, but with it came an inherent heresy that budget and programming would determine execution. It was at its worst in trying to deal with business and industrial matters. The system worked as follows: Parametric measures of labor, materials, and overhead were used to project empirically what a new weapons system "should cost." Other parametrically derived values for performance were then assigned and a computer model built to analyze the projected cost versus projected performance, the classic "cost-effectiveness analysis" that McNamara was so famous for. The computer then picked an optimum point in performance and cost for a weapons system, which was then put into the budget, and a program was established to build the system. In theory it is elegant. In practice it is nonsensical.

Thus, if the computer had parametrically established what the "should cost" of, say, a new fighter plane was to be, then, of course, there was no point in having competition. A second competitor would only increase the cost because of the duplication of effort and tooling required. Classic economic determinism.

The PPBS bureaucracy has always opposed and to this day still opposes second-sourcing and competition because to the extent that they produce savings they are a standing refutation of the accuracy of the "should cost" paramet-rics of the systems analyst.

The second fallacy of the system is the assumption that budgeting will deter-mine what actually gets carried out. In fact, planning and budgeting have almost no effect on how programs actually get executed. But 85 percent of the Navy Department staff in the Pentagon was oriented to the annual PPBS process, and only about 15 percent to executing the budgets approved in prior years. So money put in the budget for, say, buying minesweeping equipment, under a carefully worked plan, probably will be spent for something else when it is finally disbursed two years later. Bud Zumwalt used to say he felt like one of his little children in the 1950s sitting in one of those car seats with a little steering wheel, thinking he is actually steering but in fact the wheel is not con-nected to anything.

The Navy Department had gotten into the illogical organization that existed in 1981 because it had been driven and molded into that position by the "reforms" of the prior thirty years. Thus in decentralizing as we did we were going against the entire organizational grain of the rest of the Pentagon and the trendy centralizing orthodoxy of the congressional reformers on the Hill.

We sought to achieve true competition rather than the mere appearance of competition, which had been the case in prior years. Most often what was called competition was merely holding a beauty contest among competing designs and selecting a favorite for a fighter or a missile or whatever, and then awarding a monopoly to one company for decades of production. Instead we pursued doggedly a policy of establishing second sources in every appropri-ate program. We ended up raising the percentage of competition from about 15 percent overall in navy procurement in 1980 to 74 percent overall in 1987. As mentioned in the chapter on shipbuilding, we achieved 92 percent com-petition in shipbuilding, which produced an audited savings of $6.8 billion in cost underruns as of 1987—the first period in the history of the Department of the Navy. In fiscal year 1986, competitive awards for aviation spare parts pro-curement were more than four times the percentage awarded competitively in fiscal year 1983. Contracts for shipboard parts procured in 1986 were 10.5 percent lower on average than the previous year procurements, marking the third successive year in which we achieved a major decrease in average price through competition.

In 1983 I established a flag-rank job called the competition advocate gen-eral, the first such position within the Defense Department, and appointed to it a dynamic young Supply Corps admiral, Stu Platt. The office now has a network of more than 250 competition advocates throughout the navy's acquisition commands. Defense contractors feel the heat of competition and are making the productivity improvements to lower their costs so they can effectively compete. Dual-source acquisition strategies are producing remarkable results as contractors strive to undercut their opponents' price to win a greater share of navy business. Innovative teaming arrangements are being made by industrial firms, who join forces to form more competitive teams. The navy is reaping the benefits of these arrangements: We are getting the best expertise available in the marketplace at the most competitive price.

GOLD-PLATING CONTROL

Without question, competition and fixed-price contracts are the formulas for reducing costs in major procurement. But they also can be formulas for disaster, litigation, and claims if a military service does not discipline its tendency to increase capabilities and change requirements during contract execution— known in the trade as "gold-plating." We realized in 1981 that we absolutely had to find an effective way to control the gold-plating lust if our cost controls were to work. George Sawyer and his deputy, Everett Pyatt, who later succeeded him as assistant secretary, conceived the idea of a Ships Characteristics Improvement Board chaired by the assistant secretary; its membership would include the chief naval barons and lords in the Pentagon. This board would control design, engineering, and equipment changes for all new ships and upgrades of existing ships. This board started to operate in 1982 and had an immediate effect. It worked so well that we extended the concept to NAVAIR and created the Air Characteristics Improvement Board (ACIB). These boards operated effectively in most cases, but we soon found that on issues that had a very strong "blue suit" push behind them, the assistant secretary's authority was insufficient to rule the issue. The blue suiters simply would not recognize any authority but the chief of naval operations. Thus in 1983 we added a new procedure called the Program Management Proposal (PMP) system. We applied the PMP system to the top 112 programs in the navy. The program works as follows:

Under our reorganization, maximum authority was delegated to the project-manager level. The project manager for a program such as the SH-60 helicopter had complete authority for the management of his program in dealing with the contractor once the program had been approved by the secretary of the navy and the secretary of defense. This approval involved the detailed specifications that the new helicopter must meet, a schedule of milestone dates that had to be met, and an approved budget to carry it out. We instituted a reporting system requiring a three-page progress report, including simple graphs showing progress in achieving the three parameters of specifications, schedule, and budget. As long as he did not bust any of these, he was free to make trade-offs and manage with his own authority. We made every effort to protect him from micromanagement from the different barons within the navy and, most difficult of all, from the dabblers elsewhere in the defense establishment.

By and large, it worked well. If he or any other authority in the navy wished to make any design, engineering, or equipment change to the helicopter, he had to submit a proposal to the ACIB. If the ACIB recommended approval, then a PMP was drawn up. This three-page proposal had to include the additional cost for development, the additional cost impact on production unit costs, and the benefits that such a change would bring to make it worth the cost. The PMP was then sent to the chief of naval operations, or the commandant of the marine corps (if a marine program), for his approval and forwarding to the secretary of the navy for final decision.

Once we got it operating, the PMP system was a huge success. It was a minimum of bureaucratic paperwork, but it screened out all but the most cost-effective commonsense changes. By 1985 the number of change orders navy-wide had dropped to less than 5 percent of what they had been in 1981.

Along with this change we instituted a new "block upgrade" policy. Under this policy, necessary changes in modernization or design after approval by the secretary of the navy in the PMP process are made only with new annual contracts and are priced and negotiated at that time rather than piecemeal in the middle of production runs. Before we made this change, new engineering changes to a program could be ordered by many offices and were then incorporated into the production line. As a result, some aircraft, such as the F-14, had almost no two exactly alike. It was impossible to maintain a strict contract discipline on a firm fixed-price basis under such a system. Every new change order would require a different pricing, with the customer having absolutely no leverage over the contractor. With our block upgrade policy and the 95 percent reduction in changes we were able to move every one of our aircraft programs to a firm fixed-price contract.

PROGRAM STABILITY

The history of postwar procurement in all the military departments is a history of feast and famine, of ambitious goals constantly revised, of production runs that go up and down. As a result, the typical defense program is planned and the contractor tooled up for very large runs that are never achieved. Small production runs are then done in plants that are equipped for very large production runs with attendant inefficiencies. Moreover, ships, airplanes, and missiles are the most beloved playthings of congressional committees, and each year they make trades among them as if they were playing with children's toys. Because of such uncertainties, very often prime contractors would not take advantage of long-term contracts for components and materials, preferring instead to wait until they saw what each year's buy would be before ordering. Since most of the contracts were not fixed-price, they could pass the additional cost on to Uncle Sugar.

We set out to take advantage of the firmness of the president's commitment to the six-hundred-ship navy and our certainty about which ships and weapons programs were needed to achieve it, to plan a stable five-year program that would enable us to contract with a new discipline. As a result, even though Congress cut out nearly $70 billion during the first five-year plan, we were able to keep most of our aircraft programs at the steady long-term production rates we had originally projected. In those programs wherein we were unable to achieve competition among companies, as in the C2-B carrier on-board delivery aircraft and the CH-53E heavy-lift helicopter, we were able to achieve $180 million additional savings by taking advantage of the stability of production through multiyear procurement. Multiyear procurement is very popular in the defense bureaucracy because it lends itself to bureaucratic regularity. It yields far less in savings than annual competition, but for programs where you are stuck with a sole source, it definitely yields savings. Unfortunately, when we introduced this reform, Congress soon realized that by agreeing to multiyear procurement they reduced the ability of the members to play poker with defense programs by trading off and making deals such as "You give me twenty more fighters built in my district and I'll give you twenty more helicopters built in your district, and we'll make the navy pay for it out of the spare parts account." Congress now opposes multiyear procurement.

CONTRACT DISCIPLINE, ACCOUNTABILITY, AND QUALITY ASSURANCE

After the first year we moved very quickly from a policy of treating cost-plus contracts as normal to treating them as being acceptable only as an absolute last resort for very high-risk programs. Navy contract policy now requires more equitable risk-sharing between the government and its contractors, providing increased incentive for excellent performance and immediate contractor penalties for poor performance. We put all navy aircraft procurement programs on FFP contracts and all ships on FPIF contracts with a fifty-fifty share line above and below the contract price. We renegotiated the contracts inherited from prior years to eliminate the more lenient terms on programs such as CVN-71, Tomahawk, Trident, and SSN-688. The navy now provides contractors with the opportunity to make more profit than heretofore allowable by achieving performance that nets the taxpayer a substantially lower price. A corollary is that the navy now requires a contractor to bear immediately the cost of poor performance. Industry responded at first with reluctance, but those that prospered through their better efficiency are enthusiastic supporters.

PROFIT POLICY AND CONTRACTOR INVESTMENT

Under the central planning Gosplan management philosophy that evolved in the Pentagon in the 1960s and 1970s, state ownership of the tools of production became established policy. Contractors were no longer asked to risk their own capital in paying for production tooling. Some of this, particularly in the aircraft industry, was simply a pragmatic continuation of the wartime mobilization of World War II, where nearly all war production was done in government plants. But in the 1960s this practice was carried further and legitimized in theory. The navy was therefore required by OSD policy to put money into its budget for contractors' plant and tooling in nearly all its programs. This drove huge unnecessary extra costs into all navy programs for two reasons. First, except in shipbuilding, we were paying our contractors good profit margins for no risk and no investment. Second, we had to fund tooling and other capital investment according to the "should cost" parametrics of "whiz kid" analysts, which invariably ended up costing several times more than they would if contractors had to extract the investment from responsible boards of directors.

As an example, when we pushed through our initiative to get Bath Ironworks qualified as a second source to build Aegis cruisers, breaking Litton's monopoly, we were strongly opposed by the OSD bureaucracy. Their "should cost" studies indicated it would take a minimum of $250 million of new tooling at Bath Ironworks to enable them to build an Aegis cruiser, and their studies showed the extra cost could never be recovered because by splitting the production, the two yards could never be as efficient as the one Litton yard could be with all the ships. As in every other case of our establishing the second-source competitions, while we were opposed by the OSD staff, we were supported by Cap Weinberger and Will Taft. While Cap approved our initiative, the OSD staff, nevertheless, forced the navy to budget an extra $250 million of navy money for funding the capital investment at Bath Ironworks. With encouragement from us, Congress eliminated the $250 million (using it as the navy share of the overall defense cuts that year). Since Bath Ironworks could get no navy money, they were able fully to tool up with an investment of less than $20 million of their own money. They then were able to undercut Litton's best price by more than $20 million on their very first ship.

The "socialist" approach to the tools of production by the Defense Department leads to a great deal of confusion. On the one hand, some demagogues in Congress point to excessive profits made by some defense contractors. As measured as a percentage of assets, these numbers often look grossly out of line. For instance, General Dynamics has averaged more than 54 percent a year as a percentage of assets on the F-16 program, but only about 13 percent a year as a percent of sales. The difference is that GD builds its jets using government assets, in a government plant. The closest model in economic theory for current defense policy is found in the socialist Gosplan system rather than in free-market economies. The nearest American analogous relationship is found between commissions regulating utilities and private utilities companies.

In 1984, Ev Pyatt commissioned an independent study of the profitability of the top ten navy contractors.* We then had the results reviewed and validated by Peat, Marwick, Mitchell & Co. They were startling. Return on assets for the ten averaged 30 percent per year on Pentagon contracts and 7 percent on commercial business—more than four times the profit rate. Return on sales averaged 9.5 percent on Pentagon contracts and 6.6 percent on commercial business.

Starting in 1983, we began a major change in navy policy to shift more facility and tooling start-up costs from the navy to industry. Under the new policy finally formalized in a secretary of the navy instruction, once production has been approved, contractors are expected to provide all production tooling and test equipment and the required facilities. Recovery of these investment costs will be through standard business practice—depreciation and profit—as negotiated between the navy and the contractor.

Here again one of the most important tenets of our new acquisition policy is its emphasis on program managers being given authority to be flexible and being held accountable for the results. They are encouraged to exercise

---

*The ten are Boeing, General Dynamics, Lockheed, McDonnell Douglas, Rockwell, Litton, Tenneco, RCA, Texas Instruments, and FMC.

creativity in structuring acquisition strategies to meet the particular needs of their programs and the unique capabilities of the contractors with whom they deal. A good example was found in the teaming arrangement we had for a revolutionary new tilt-rotor aircraft, the V-22. One member of the team, Boeing, had plenty of cash to invest; the other, Bell Textron, had none to invest. Therefore we worked a compromise that committed the navy to buy initial production tooling amounting to the first third of capital investment required. After that, both Bell and Boeing could support their required investment from cash flow, and each build their own production line to compete head to head for each year's production.

The next effect of these reforms on the contractors was well summarized in *The Wall Street Journal*:

> United Technologies Corp. is reducing its supervisory staff by 10%, shortening delivery time and greatly reducing scrapped parts and waste. . . . Boeing slashed overhead costs to 25%. . . . Lockheed . . . is combining three separate operating subsidiaries into one, and General Dynamics Corp. hopes to chop a whopping 40% off its costs. . . . Martin Marietta recently announced a new wave of cost cutting that eliminated an entire level of corporate management. . . . "With a firm fixed price contract, buying in is just too dangerous nowadays," says Kenneth Russell, a Boeing executive . . . etc., etc., etc.[2]

PEOPLE

The underlying philosophy for every management change we made in navy acquisition policy was to bring human beings back into control, give them the authority, and then hold them accountable. To carry out these policies, of course, the navy had to have experienced and highly skilled people performing program management and contracting functions to implement our acquisition strategy and cost-reduction initiatives.

Historically, navy acquisition and procurement management has been plagued by rapid turnover of personnel and inadequate experience and qualification in those assigned. To correct those shortcomings, we designed the most far-reaching reform of naval officer career patterns undertaken in this century. In 1985 we established the "materiel professional" career path. There are now over nine hundred officers, from commander to admiral, so designated. The career path of the materiel professional integrates sea tours with acquisition tours for an officer's entire career. Once an aviator, submariner, destroyerman, or other individual is selected to be a materiel professional, the warfare specialty is relegated to a secondary role. Acquisition tours are now for a minimum of four years each. A manager now knows he will have a job long enough to make a difference and to be judged accordingly. Before, tours averaged less than two years. Approximately one third of our flag officer billets have been set aside for materiel professionals. Now, pursuing a career in procurement and acquisition provides a path to promotion all the way to four stars that is as attractive as a line career.

Establishment of the materiel professional's career path provides the education, experience, and, most importantly, the career incentives required to make our acquisition managers capable, skilled business professionals with the warfare background necessary to manage weapons systems properly. No procurement or acquisition billet may now be filled by other than a materiel professional without a personal waiver from the secretary of the navy. The program has been a great success.

One of the most pleasant surprises in my first year was to discover how many truly first-rate people we had among our navy civil servants. There are a remarkable number of people who could easily make top executive salaries in industry who get hooked on the importance and, quite frankly, the patriotism of what they do in the Navy Department, and accept having to live on a small fraction of what they could make in the private sector.

One of the most successful reforms of our civil service ever attempted was carried out by the Carter administration with their Civil Service Reform Act. It enabled managers finally to get some carrots and sticks for the senior civil service. It brought much more flexibility to move, reward, and punish through a system of bonuses and increased management authority. We attempted to take maximum advantage of the Carter legislation and the Senior Executive Service (SES) it created by integrating them into our reforms. Many have responsibilities equal to or greater than those of chief executive officers and vice presidents of Fortune 500 industries. To give our SES members a better range of experience and to help them understand a wide variety of navy programs and areas, we have mandated a five-year rotation plan. That plan is based on the private-industry philosophy that, as an executive advances, he or she needs to understand—hands on—wider aspects of a company's business.

We have established a system to allocate fairly the available bonuses based on real management performance rather than simply serving time in grade. Because of the frustrations of bureaucracy and the low pay, the attrition rate in navy SES personnel in 1981 and 1982 was about 25 percent a year. Since our reforms, that number has been cut nearly in half.

Another excellent innovation of the Carter administration was allowing government agencies to carry out some experimental new approaches to managing their civilian work force. In the navy we used the new Carter authority to begin in 1981 a plan at two of our labs, in China Lake and Point Loma, California, described in the last chapter.

RESEARCH AND DEVELOPMENT (R&D REFORM)

A corollary to the tendency to gold-plate within each of the military departments is the tendency to chase R&D rainbows. In a major effort to put our scarce R&D dollars where the maximum payoff was and to shorten substantially the time from conception to delivery of a weapons system we made fundamental changes in the management of navy R&D. In 1981 the navy had nearly 600 R&D programs. By the fiscal year 1988 submission we had reduced that number to 387. We have moved away from cost-plus contracts for full-scale engineering development and now require the contractor to participate in prudent risk-sharing.

IMPROVING INDUSTRIAL ACTIVITY OPERATIONS

The Navy Department is unique in the U.S. government in the huge size of its industrial facilities. It has six separate industrial organizations that would each rank in the Fortune 500, led by the shipyards, which alone would rank ninety-second. To put the industrial house in order, we spent three years of developing a series of reforms to streamline industrial operations and place them under management emulating the best-run private industries. We identified and achieved annual savings of approximately $1.1 billion from those reforms based on deep reductions in the costs in shipyards, air rework facilities, public work centers, and weapons/ordinance activities. Shipyards' and air rework facilities' civilian manning was reduced by 5,500, while still a far cry from private enterprise, it was progress.

As part of the obsession with centralized management, all authority in the yards had been drawn to the Washington bureaucracy. As a result, costs for the same work escalated 20 percent per year through the 1960s and 1970s. The yards were under the absolute authority of the fleet operators, who absolutized schedules ("I must have that frigate repaired in three weeks!"), and the "nukes," who absolutized engineering ("Tear it out and do it again until you get it right!"). Shipyard superintendents were promoted only with regard to how well they met the schedule and quality requirements of the nukes and fleet commanders without regard to cost. So far had this process been taken that actual cost accounting was abolished and a system called "stabilized industrial rate budgeting" established during the McNamara era. Under that centralized system all costs for the year for all yards were aggregated, making individual cost performance per project invisible. This made the budgets in the Pentagon easy to prepare, but the yards immune to cost control. We had to start from scratch to establish basic cost accounting in each of the facilities. This in turn required analyzing for the first time the sources of costs among direct labor and materials, indirect overhead, and mobilization base expenses. The immediate result of that effort brought about a 10 to 12 percent cost reduction in each yard. The navy has now institutionalized that process throughout all the industrial facilities.

The system for managing these industrialized facilities that we found in 1981 was, like the rest of the Pentagon, totally centralized in Washington. Yard and facilities commanders had virtually no discretion to make decisions themselves. Decisions were made by whiz-kid matrix staffs in Washington. As an indicator, we found that 90 percent of navy SES management personnel were located inside the Washington beltway, and there was not one SES in any of the eight shipyards.

We hired Coopers & Lybrand to assist us in this three-year massive effort, and they did a first-rate job. One of the things that they exposed, to my amazement, was that though the navy operated six Fortune 500-size industrial companies, it did not have one human being who was an industrial manager. The shipyard commanders were chosen for their engineering, not their industrial management experience, nor were there any civilians there with such experience or skills. Coopers & Lybrand recommended and ran for us a talent search around the country, advertising in *The Wall Street Journal* and other trade journals for industrial managers to put in charge of production at each of the shipyards. Sadly, the results of this nationwide search resulted in not one successful hire. The reason, of course, was that any industrial manager worth his salt can command two to four times the maximum pay he can make under a government salary. We therefore accepted the fact that the navy would have to begin to grow its own, a process that will take years.

We proved that the same management techniques found in successful private companies, where emphasis is on efficiency and accountability, work just as well in navy industrial facilities. For example, we redefined the process of ship overhaul management; we improved procedures for forecasting, providing and managing needed materials and repair parts; we instituted for the first time modern management information systems (MIS) and refocused procurement of materials and services in support of industrial operations to minimize on-hand inventories. Above all, we delegated authority and held people accountable, using our Washington headquarters to try to protect the operators and managers from the incessant interference and micromanagement by the thousands upon thousands of bureaucrats in the Pentagon and in Congress.

The tremendous success of the reform of navy industrial facilities, spearheaded by Under Secretary Jim Goodrich, could not have succeeded so dramatically had it not been for the driving force of Chief of Naval Operations Jim Watkins, who helped initiate it and who instinctively understood the importance of the specific management changes, many of which he helped to conceive.

ACQUISITION STREAMLINING

Because of the vastness of the Pentagon bureaucracy, a huge driver of waste and unnecessary cost in all the military departments has come to be overspecification of everything. The specifications for one solicitation for cookies, for instance, ran to sixteen pages. We found that the average request for proposal in 1981 carried so many detailed specifications that the document literally could not be carried by one person. Like barnacles, these specifications grow constantly as a result of micromanaging and special-interest legislation on the Hill, by the hundreds of bureaucratic offices within the Pentagon, and because we have learned from hard experience that if you don't have a rigid specification for cookies, some contractors will cut the price and make them with sawdust.

Much of the overspecification, however, can be eliminated and can bring huge cost savings. In 1985 we established the specification control advocate general's position at the SES level, the first such dedicated position within the Defense Department. He and his staff must now review every RFP, looking for ways to reduce specifications and to stipulate off-the-shelf commercial items instead of "milspec" custom-made items where this is appropriate.

We have also included in our contracts incentives for the contractor to propose value engineering changes to our specifications that make common sense in reducing costs. During 1986 alone the results of this streamlining initiative produced savings of over $1 billion in reducing budgeted costs. Here again we placed the emphasis on letting the project manager apply his common sense, giving him the authority to do away with unnecessary detailed military specifications and to use commercial standards and substitutes where he believes it makes sense; and then holding him accountable for the results.

Taking a lead from the air force, which long ago decentralized authority over its installations to its base commanders, we set about in 1985 to bring the air force system to the navy. Like everything else, the control over the management of navy bases all over the world had been pulled into the Washington bureaucracy. We decentralized that authority back out to the base commanders, giving them direct line authority over budget and over personnel for everything but the fleet operational activities that were tenants on their bases. Here we were greatly aided by Will Taft's overall defensewide effort in the same lines called the Model Installation Program, which enabled us to expedite the delegation of authority and initiative. We got great assistance also from Connie Horner of the Office of Personnel Management, who allowed us to make the commonsense breakthrough to have our installations manage to payroll rather than to specific personnel end strengths, as any business does. These changes have paid huge dividends, enabling base commanders to make sensible capital investments and reduce personnel costs, as well as increasing the number of personnel from some functions where that can bring about overall cost reduction.

SHRINKING THE PAPERWORK

In a phenomenon related to centralization, I found during my active-duty training with the fleet a growing crescendo of complaint about the burden of administrative paperwork. It got to such a level by 1985 that we had to do something. I appointed a blue-ribbon panel to travel around the fleet and document exactly the nature of the problem. In operational squadrons, aviators were forced to spend an average of two thirds of their time on nonmission-related paperwork. One officer per squadron, for instance, spent nearly two thirds of his time all year long just managing the Combined Federal Campaign. Jim Watkins, P. X. Kelley (commandant of the U.S. Marine Corps), and I immediately ordered the abolition of some eight hundred different reports that were required of operational units by navy and marine corps headquarters staffs. There were another three hundred required by the Office of the Secretary of Defense staff; I unilaterally ordered these reports suspended until Cap told me specifically which ones *he* really wanted. At first Cap agreed with me, but after being beset by his own bureaucrats he ordered me to reinstate every one. Nevertheless, the result was a very substantial net reduction of silly make-work in the operational units. Once again the price of maintaining the vast defense bureaucracy burdens every level of our defense effort.

An interesting sidelight was the contrast that the blue-ribbon panel found between navy and air force squadrons. They found that air force squadrons are far more oriented to training and war fighting than to administrative work. The reason is because the air force has a four-and-one-half-to-one enlisted-to-officer ratio, while the Navy has a seven-to-one ratio. Air force squadrons are relieved of the burdens of administrative paperwork and of the burdens of maintenance and logistics administrative work load. The Air force has it right. Their war fighters are oriented to train for their mission, and the navy needs to increase its officer end strength to achieve the same level of efficiency.

BOSS AND THE $700 TOILET SEAT

Fiscal year 1988 was the fifth consecutive year for Project BOSS (Buy Our Spares Smart), our initiative to correct problems in the procurement of spare parts. The whole philosophy on reforming the spare-parts mess was to base it on the common sense of the sailors and civil servants at the working level. Overwhelmingly the sailors, marines, and civil servants will take the initiative when they see a gross overcharging for spare parts, but the problem we inherited was enormous. The navy had more than 1.2 million different inventory stock items for spares, and the bureaucratic system for buying these spares was so vast that it was just too frustrating to try to do anything about it. The centralization mania in the Pentagon had taken away 65 percent of navy spare parts and put it into the Defense Logistics Agency, a vast, 60,000-person bureaucracy of civil servants. While they overwhelmingly are hardworking people wanting to do the right thing, they are embedded in an impossible bureaucracy. The result was that, to our horror, we found that 94 percent of our spare parts were being bought sole-source on the equivalent of cost-plus open-ordering agreements. When we began to dig into the problem we began to uncover huge overcharges and ridiculous prices that had been paid for years and years because of the total absence of competition and discipline.

But as always in Washington, the press and Congress shot the messenger. As we dug out example after example of abuse and began to do something about it, we were pilloried, as if these were abuses we started. For a while I carried around in my wallet the 10-cent part called a diode, which we had discovered was costing the Navy $100. Then there was the $700 toilet seat cover, which the cartoonists unjustly fixed forever around Cap Weinberger's head. Obviously, only an acquisition system of 60,000 billets unaccountable to anyone can tolerate prices that a normal human being would reject out of hand.

The most fundamental change we brought about through Project BOSS was one of attitude. Competition and buying parts directly from the manufacturer were instituted to replace the traditional reliance on prime contractor monopolies for spares. Buyers and spare-parts consumers alike were given the responsibility down to the lowest level to challenge prices that failed the commonsense test. To enable people to make the commonsense test, we instituted a system to require suppliers to put the actual price we were paying on each package so that a clerk could look at a bolt and if the price on it was $500 he would see the absurdity. We then set up teams by region with telephone numbers so that each clerk or sailor could immediately take the package, pick up the phone, call the 800 number, and turn the matter over to these "price fighter" teams. It was then their responsibility to go after the manufacturer. It brought about immediate and truly staggering returns in cost savings that we used to buy more parts.

The combined results of BOSS brought about savings over $900 million since 1983, with $381 million in 1986 alone. This is a nearly five-to-one return on the $188 million investment to set up this system over the first three years.

DEPOT LEVEL REPAIRABLE COMPONENTS (DLRs)

In a major innovation in the management of maintenance funding, we instituted decentralization of the repair of expensive components for expensive ships and aircraft (called DLRs) to the ship and the air-station level. The purpose of these initiatives was to establish a commonsense buyer-seller relationship between the stock fund and its customers within the fleet, who are then held accountable for their expenditures. The commonsense result was as expected and immediate, a much more frugal approach to ordering and repairing these critical and valuable spare parts, with huge cost savings.

HORIZONTAL INTEGRATION OF THE NAVAL RESERVE

Our Founding Fathers had a justifiable fear of standing armies and professional soldiers. The military coup in England of Cromwell's armies was referred to often in the constitutional debates. That is one reason why the language in the Constitution speaks of maintaining militias but "raising" armies when the need arises. Navies had never posed a threat to civil authority, as had armies through history, and were less of a concern to our Founding Fathers. The Constitution calls for "maintaining" a permanent navy. But the traditions of our navy were founded nevertheless in the privateers and by merchant sailors such as Barry, Jones, and Barney. For a democracy this is a very sound view, as it should be the basis for the maintenance of our defense structure. During periods when we directly face a hostile foe with a large standing armed force, this sound principle must be compromised. The forty years since World War II is the first such sustained period wherein we have maintained large standing military forces in peacetime.

Unfortunately, during this long period the emphasis on the career forces has gone too far. In World War II itself, the ratio of career naval officers to reserve "citizen sailors" or "ninety-day wonders" was one to seventy. It is time to move steadily back toward a more reserve-based defense force in all the military services.

Convinced of this necessity, in 1981 I proposed a set of initiatives I called "horizontal integration." Since World War II the navy had steadily reduced its reserve components and organized them into separate, vertical compartments. These reported not to the fleets but to a separate reserve command in New Orleans. They were given obsolete equipment cast off from the active forces. Except for some exceptions, such as the P-3 antisubmarine warfare reserves, which for years have carried a third of the peacetime ASW patrol requirements, the reserve naval forces in 1981 could not go to war. The surface reserve was training on old World War II destroyers that could not interoperate with the modern fleet, the aviators were flying 1950s-generation aircraft that could no longer be supported on fleet aircraft carriers.

With horizontal integration we set out to convert the reserves into a percentage layer across the top of all the different warfare units in the navy, training them and equipping them with equipment just as good as what the fleet was operating. The purpose was not only to enable reservists to mobilize immediately, fully capable of operating modern fleet equipment, but also to begin to carry more of the burden of peacetime deterrence on a day-to-day basis short of the president declaring a national emergency. In the force structure we eliminated two active-duty carrier air wings and replaced them in the long-range plan with the existing two reserve carrier air wings and initiated at once a program to equip those air wings with modern fleet aircraft.

While Tom Hayward did not disagree with the theory of what I proposed to do, he shared the general skeptical attitude of most "ring knockers" toward reservists. He cooperated fully, however, and indeed came up with the initial idea of moving immediately to put new Knox class and Perry class frigates into the naval reserve. When Jim Watkins replaced him as CNO, however, he brought a real enthusiasm for the idea and produced quite a number of innovative ideas of his own to implement it.

Reorganization to a horizontal integration got under way in 1982, and by 1987 it had the desired effect of shifting a portion of our force structure manning to the ready reserve. Increased reliance on the ready reserve has enabled us greatly to reduce our original estimates of required active-duty end strength for the six-hundred-ship navy.

By 1989 a total of forty-eight of the six hundred ships will be manned by selected reserves, in addition to the augmentation of all naval units by selected reserves upon mobilization.

The fifteenth active carrier air wing has been deleted from the program, and the fifteenth carrier will carry a reserve air wing.

Seventeen modern Perry class and Knox class frigates have now been transferred to the naval reserve, with a total program of twenty-six frigates planned by 1990.

By the mid-1990s a total of twenty-four new minesweepers will be assigned to the naval reserve. All the naval reserve ships are now manned 50 percent by active-duty sailors so they can be immediately deployed in time of crisis, with augmentations of personnel from the active fleet and from reserve volunteers, as was done during the Persian Gulf crisis in 1987 with the reserve MSO minesweepers.

The first reserve squadron completed transition to the F-18 in 1987 and the second in 1988. Four reserve squadrons have now transitioned to the F-14A, and modern A-7E, E-2C, and SH-2F Sea Sprite aircraft have been transferred to reserve units, with complete modernization of the two reserve air wings to be completed by fiscal year 1990.

Copying the very successful air force reserve program, squadron augmentation flying units were established and are operating successfully with each active-duty air wing, providing current trained aviators and maintenance personnel for immediate augmentation to active-duty squadrons. When I left the job as secretary of the navy I was assigned to the squadron augmentation unit for Attack Squadron 36 aboard the *Theodore Roosevelt*, the carrier we got through Congress over President Carter's veto and that my wife, Barbara, christened. I have been flying with them ever since.

The naval reserve now contains several components that exist only in the reserve: 100 percent of the Navy's United States-based logistic support squadrons; 100 percent of light attack helicopter squadrons; 100 percent of our combat helicopter search and rescue capability; 100 percent of naval mobile inshore undersea warfare units—"the brown-water navy"—structured for combat on inland waterways. Upon mobilization, the naval reserve will provide 99 percent of naval control of shipping organization manning for merchant ship mobilization and convoy formation for overseas operations; 86 percent of our oceangoing minesweepers; 86 percent of the cargo handling battalions vital to port management and loading operations in combat theaters; 85 percent of military sealift command military personnel; 68 percent of special boat forces; 35 percent of maritime antisubmarine warfare patrol aircraft squadrons; 34 percent of naval intelligence personnel; 21 percent of ASW helicopter squadrons needed for fleet and convoy maintenance defense efforts; and 14 percent of our tactical sea-based aviation capabilities.

The marine corps relies heavily on a fully trained and capable reserve component to provide up to 33 percent of marine corps wartime manpower requirements. The reserves provide 40 percent of marine tanks; 33 percent of the heavy artillery; 30 percent of the light attack aircraft; and 33 percent of the antiaircraft missile capability. We equipped marine artillery battalions with the latest M0198 howitzer, infantry units with the latest TOW antitank missile systems, and we began equipping marine reserve flying units with the AH-1 Cobra attack helicopter, new KC-130 tankers, and F-18s. In addition, we stood up a reserve marine squadron of Israeli Kfir fighters to train active duty forces as aggressor aircraft simulating potential adversary fighter types.

Results for Naval Shipbuilding

The application of these different programs have produced dramatic results in navy shipbuilding. The disputes, litigation claims, cost overruns, and schedule delays that characterized naval shipbuilding in the 1960s and 1970s were largely eliminated. During calendar years 1982–86, a total of 114 ships were delivered to the navy, of which 40 were ahead of schedule, 50 on schedule, and only 24 behind schedule. The net of all five years was 33 months ahead of schedule for all ships. After years of bitterness and massive cost overruns and claims in the submarine programs, all submarines were delivered at or under budget through 1986.

- *Aircraft carrier savings.* The acquisition strategy for nuclear aircraft carriers has been very effective in reducing the cost of achieving air power at sea and in accelerating the growth to a fifteen-carrier battle-group force level. Originally a split buy of two new aircraft carriers in separate annual procurements for the *Abraham Lincoln* (CVN-72) and the *George Washington* (CVN-73) was estimated to cost $8.024 billion. Our multiple-ship-award strategy in fiscal year 1983, one of the first and largest "multiyear" procurement programs in the Reagan defense acquisition budget, brought these costs down to $5.996 billion for the two CVNs, and each will be delivered twenty-two months earlier than with a traditional approach.

- *Aegis cruisers.* Bath Ironworks was selected in 1982 as a second source to compete with Litton for construction of Aegis cruisers. Contracts were signed in December 1983 for the first three cruisers, to be awarded competitively: two to Litton and one to Bath. In November 1984 the second year of competition resulted in Bath winning two fiscal year 1985 ships and Litton one. In December 1985, the third year of competition resulted again in Bath winning two ships and Litton one, for fiscal year 1986. Contract savings from this new competitive approach in shipbuilding have been enormous. In the fiscal year 1982 five-year defense plan submitted in March 1981, nine cruisers in fiscal years 1984, 1985, and 1986 (of the twelve cruisers then proposed) were each estimated to cost more than an average of $1.2 billion. After second sourcing in the fiscal year 1987 budget, the estimated cost is now less than an average of $890 million for each of these nine Aegis cruisers. This second source initiative has therefore contributed to about $3 billion in cost reductions for those nine ships.
- *Battleships.* One of the first demonstrated successes in our new shipbuilding program, the *New Jersey*, was recommissioned in December 1982, ahead of schedule. The second battleship, the *Iowa*, was delivered well ahead of schedule and under budget in April 1984. The third, the *Missouri*, which was in large part funded from contract savings, also was reactivated ahead of schedule, at Long Beach, and was recommissioned in San Francisco in 1986. The *Wisconsin* (BB-64) was reactivated, like the *Iowa*, at Litton's Ingalls shipyard, on schedule, in October 1988.
- *Amphibious ships.* The competitive acquisition strategy for the LHD program has achieved significant cost savings by introducing competition into this previously sole-source program. The estimated end cost for three ships is now $2.5063 billion, for a total savings of almost $1 billion.
- *Build/convert and charter programs.* All thirteen maritime prepositioning ships (MPS) and five T-5 tankers have been delivered. These ships provide a dramatic new capability to preposition the equipment and supplies to support three marine amphibious brigades in areas of potential crisis around the world. The innovative contracting approach used in this program was the first in recent memory to apply one of the principal recommendations of the Packard Report (made five years later), to encourage use of commercial standards and methods wherever possible in defense procurement. Our total commercial approach resulted in a six-year span from program conception to full implementation—saving at least two years over the customary navy design and military specification (MILSPEC) approach. The

first six of the MPS ships were completed two moths ahead of original schedule and under budget. The first of two U.S. Navy hospital ships converted from tankers, the U.S.N.S. *Mercy* (T-AH19), was delivered in December 1986; the second, the U.S.N.S. *Comfort* (T-AH20), was delivered in August 1987. The primary mission of these ninety-thousand-ton ships is to provide full medical support to the Defense Department's rapid deployment task force in the Persian Gulf. Their secondary role is to provide full hospital service to other government agencies involved in disaster relief. The *Mercy* and the *Comfort* will be part of the Military Sealift Command's strategic sealift force. Both ships will be manned and operated by MSC civilian mariners and will also have a naval medical detachment on board. The *Mercy* deployed on her shakedown cruise on a humanitarian mission to the Philippines in early 1987, calling on various Philippine ports to provide medical care. They performed hundreds of major surgical procedures and saw thousands of patients during that cruise.

- *Shipbuilding competition.* Navy contracts in the shipbuilding industry include new construction of ships, ship overhaul and repair, major ship marine systems, and materials applied in the operation and life-cycle support of ships and ship systems.
- During fiscal year 1986 a total of 83.1 percent of navy new-ship construction dollars placed under contract were awarded competitively. Savings in shipbuilding amounted to $1.144 billion in fiscal year 1986 and included $282 million in the CG-47 class Aegis cruiser program, $255 million in the SSN-688 class attack submarine program, and $280 million for the lead ship in the LHD class. As in previous years, all small-craft construction was awarded competitively.
- *Overhaul competition.* In fiscal year 1986 all private-sector surface ship overhauls were solicited and awarded competitively. Confronted with unrealistically high bids for private-yard overhaul of SSBNs, we took similar action in the submarine overhaul program. The results have been impressive, as contract prices have spiraled down instead of up in response to competitive pressure. During fiscal year 1986 each of the formerly sole-source ballistic missile submarine overhauls was competed for.

Results

1. From the 479 battle-force ships in the fleet when President Reagan took office, the fleet has grown to 584 ships by mid-1988 and will reach 600 by the end of 1989 unless ships are prematurely retired.

2. The third maritime prepositioning ship (MPS) squadron became operational in the Pacific Ocean in 1987, completing deployment of these vital store ships and bringing to 13 the number of MPS ships constructed and deployed in the Reagan years. The MPS program progressed from conception to completion in just five years and provides a force deployment capability equal to about 4,500 C-141 aircraft sorties, enabling us to deploy 13 Marine brigades with weeks of fighting sustainability worldwide.
3. From 1980 to 1986 we procured and converted 8 commercial SL-7 cargo ships to fast sealift ships. These 8 highly versatile ships can transport an entire heavy mechanized army division to Europe at 30 knots.
4. After the settlement with Electric Boat, the modernization of our sea-based leg of the strategic deterrent has been proceeding very well. We have added 10 Ohio class Trident SSBNs to the fleet since that settlement, with 6 others authorized. The U.S.S. *Tennessee* (SSBN-734), commissioned in January 1989, is the first ship that can carry the Trident 2 (D-5) missile.
5. The first 8 Ohio class Trident SSBNs are outfitted with the Trident 1 (C-4) missile, joining 12 Poseidon SSBNs currently equipped with the Trident 1. Over the past 6 years the development of the Trident 2 (D-5) has progressed well, and the missile will be operational in 1989.

There are currently 80 naval ships under construction, conversion, or reactivation at 17 different yards throughout the United States. A substantial benefit to the economy and to deficit reduction of our shipbuilding conversion and overhaul programs has been the immediate creation of very substantial numbers of jobs in the declining shipbuilding and repair industry. Navy shipbuilding and repair programs now account for over 90 percent of all employment in that industry in the national shipyard mobilization base. On the larger impact of navy shipbuilding, it has been estimated that every billion dollars in the navy shipbuilding program creates 26,000 jobs directly and 12,000 jobs secondarily.

Results for Navy Aircraft Procurement

Navy aircraft procurement also shows a dramatic reversal after the application of our reforms. In constant-year 1980 dollars, the average recurring unit price of fiscal 1986 combat aircraft dropped 33 percent from the average price paid in fiscal year 1982. In fiscal year 1986 alone, that had resulted in savings relative to the budget submitted to Congress of approximately 11.3 percent. (See figure 5.)

The year 1986 was the fifth straight year when all naval aircraft procurement programs were on a firm fixed-price contract basis, precluding the possibility of production cost overruns. Because the price came down on all but one naval aircraft, the navy was able to meet the production numbers needed for a fifteen-carrier battle-group force.

In addition to procuring nearly twice as many aircraft per year, the navy was able to build the force significantly by a dramatic turnaround in the accident rate. Because of the tremendously increased retention of experienced naval aviators and experienced maintenance personnel and because of the trebled expenditures on maintenance and spare-parts funding that the Reagan increases brought about, the accident rate for naval aviation began to plummet in 1982 and continued to decline each year. Because of the military pay freeze that lasted essentially throughout the late 1970s, and because of the tremendous increase in naval commitments and forward deployments, the combination of low pay, long family separation, and insufficient funding to fly the required number of training hours per month led to a mass exodus of experienced aviators.

In implementing our policy to husband scarce development money, we decided against developing a new trainer, and we deferred development of new fighter and attack aircraft. With regard to the trainer, we ran a competition in which we selected the existing British Hawk trainer design because it was about a third of the cost of brand-new development aircraft. We ended up signing a firm fixed-price development contract with McDonnell Douglas, which was teamed with British Aerospace to produce the T-45 GosHawk to train naval aviators with a carrier-capable, safe, high-performance jet. The first of these development aircraft was delivered in 1987 ahead of schedule and under the $438 million budget.

Summary

By the time I departed as secretary of the navy, the Reagan rearmament program had run out of steam. Congressional budget-cutting, fueled by relentless publicity on defense waste, had plunged us once again into the cycle of the 1970s. These cycles were bred not only by swings in public mood but also by a system that could barely produce the right things when it was bloated with money and always produced the wrong things when it was not. The experience of the Reagan years teaches, however, that this is not inevitable. We proved that the navy could break with escalating costs and overruns; that we could have *underruns*; that ships and planes could be delivered on budget, on schedule, and built right; that high-tech was not a synonym for low reliability; and that our contractors could do their job right, to their profit and ours.

Responding to a public furor fueled by procurement scandals the Pentagon itself had uncovered, a commission headed by former secretary of defense David Packard suggested a series of reforms. It was gratifying to me and to our dedicated team that many of these reforms, especially in the acquisition, accountability, and "gold-plating" control, replicated what the navy had already undertaken.

Predictably, adoption of many of these reforms throughout the Defense Department would have disestablished the systems analysts, held many officials to an unaccustomed accounting, and required too many contractors to perform. And then, of course, there is Congress itself, with its Washington Monument—1,152 linear feet of statutory and regulatory law governing procurement alone.

At the end of the day, however, all of this pettifoggery should not be allowed to obscure the obvious. The management reforms we brought to the Department of the Navy were not based on esoteric theories. They were an attempt simply to apply logic and common sense to the problems and were based on a philosophy that individual human beings, not organizational charts, are the key to success. We sought to find the really good people who were willing to accept the challenge and responsibility of authority and then tried to clear away as many of the bureaucratic obstacles in their path as we could. In reorganizing we were not trying to fashion an elegant chart but trying instead to eliminate bureaucratic layering and matrix dabbling. We were trying to shorten and streamline chains of command and lines of authority and to put accountability back into the system. If a program succeeds with cost savings and quality performance, then the man or woman in charge should be rewarded. If a program gets in trouble through ill management or inattention, the program manager should be sacked.

We sought to delegate authority and decentralize to the maximum extent practical, but to hold accountable those to whom authority had been delegated.

We sought also to integrate the uniformed staff of the chief of naval operations and the commandant of the marine corps with the staff of the secretary of the navy. The Navy Department we inherited had three totally separate staffs that dealt with problems in series or parallel, but never together. The system we attempted to fashion was to deal with the issues simultaneously and as one.

The results that were achieved through this philosophy speak for themselves. Whether they will last depends entirely on the individuals who succeeded to the positions of responsibility. But this should be certain: The system can be changed. It can be reformed. Defense costs can be brought under control.

Afterword

The naval strategy that we put in place to implement President Reagan's national security strategy was a success. It was integrated with the other services and the theater commanders and made a significant contribution to cold war victory. It was simple, logical and based on the Mahanian principle of offensive defense. Since this book was written, it has now been revealed that the strategy was also based on very detailed intelligence of Soviet planning gathered by certain U.S. submarine "special operations." This was a huge advantage.

The end of the cold war brought about the need for a major redirection of naval strategy. That process was made extremely difficult during the Clinton administration since, unlike previous administrations, there was no comprehensive national security strategy from which to derive the naval strategy. Nevertheless the navy has done a good job of formulating a strategy directed towards projecting power ashore. The navy has also adapted to a greatly increased emphasis on joint operations. In the past naval strategy tended to emphasize independent operations with self-contained task forces, the pendulum has now swung far toward an overemphasis on joint operations with all services participating in all operations.

The national security strategy established in the administration of George W. Bush can be expected to establish the framework for a more balanced approach.

The process described in this book of constantly challenging, re-evaluating, and renewing naval strategy through the interaction of war-gaming, strategic thinking and fleet exercises remains active in the Department of the navy today.

Naval strategy for the post-cold war era does not require 600 ships. The size of the fleet is determined by commitments assigned to the navy and the mix of ships required to carry them out. During the Clinton years the fleet was reduced from just under 600 ships to just over 300 ships. At the same time deployments to crisis areas were doubled compared to the 1980s. The size of the fleet should be determined by strategic requirements. Peacetime deployment, however, should be determined by the need to maintain readiness and morale. Regular deployments to all the areas of our vital interests are an important part of maintaining the stability of our global security interests. Nevertheless it is all too easy to allow the desires of diplomats to generate long deployments beyond what the fleet can support over the long term. Such has been the case for the last eight years. Either the size of the fleet must be significantly increased to cover these peacetime deployments or the deployments must be significantly reduced. Indications are that the national security strategy of the Bush administration will not be as profligate in making overseas commitments and deployments as its predecessor. Nevertheless a fleet of only 300 ships is not big enough to meet our minimum global commitments. A number on the order of 400 is likely to be optimum. With an average life of about thirty years, we will need to build ships at the rate of twelve to fifteen per year. For the last decade we have been averaging between three and six per year.

Unfortunately the new ship development programs currently being pursued do not seem likely to be able to achieve these kinds of numbers.

To maintain a 400-ship navy, the navy will have to return to the pursuit of the high-low mix that has been the traditional compromise between quality and quantity. As it has often been said quantity has its own quality. The navy needs a true lower-cost nuclear attack submarine and it needs a replacement for the FFG-7 affordable and expendable surface combatant. The attack on the U.S.S. *Cole* has once again reminded us that surface combatants—unless they are of the size and armor of an aircraft carrier or a battleship—are vulnerable and therefore must be expendable. At more than $1 billion a copy today's *Aegis* cruisers and destroyers are already on the edge of being irreplaceable.

The lengthy recounting of our difficulties with Electric Boat contained in chapter 6 was included because the issue was much larger than the ships and contracts involved. Achieving the president's goal of a 600-ship navy utterly depended on solutions to that mess. In successfully solving the EB problem, we applied a number of basic management precepts that have since proven to be essential for the success of major acquisition projects and remain as relevant in today's Pentagon as they were then.

1. Competition really works and should be applied wherever and whenever feasible. There are of course programs where it is not feasible to conduct full and open competitions as it turned out not to be with *Trident* submarines or with nuclear aircraft carriers. Where it is not possible to have such competition then there should be de facto competition maintained between those programs and alternate ways of achieving the mission. For instance if nuclear carriers were to become too costly we could return to convential carriers, which could be built by more than one contractor. But the navy should never allow

nuclear capability to become the monopoly of one shipbuilder. The threat of having real options to move to alternatives keeps a competitive pressure on the monopoly supplier. We were able, for instance, to maintain strong competitive pressures on McDonnell Douglas in the F-18 program by having a very viable alternative in a mix of F-14s and A-6s.

2. The lead ship of any new class of warship is basically a research and development undertaking, with all the attendant budgetary and technical risk involved. Thus a cost incentive type contract should always be employed for the lead ship of a class, or where two shipyards will be involved in production, a cost-plus contract for each yard. After the delivery of the lead ships, subsequent awards should be made on a fixed-price basis.

For less complex auxiliary and non-combatant vessels, commercial acquisition fixed price contracts should be used and wherever possible consideration should be given to the build (or convert) and charter approach that was such a success in the maritime pre-positioning ships built in the Reagan years that made Desert Storm possible.

The success of naval aircraft procurement during the Reagan years was the result of the firm application of two principles: competition and control of gold-plating. The most important initiative that brought the most success was the discipline of the PMP program described in chapter 7 whereby new bells and whistles and new design changes to aircraft could not be made without being fully budgeted and then approved for block upgrades at the highest level of the Navy Department. The second most important element was the fact that we had alternatives to virtually all navy aircraft and their manufacturers knew it. We were not stuck in any monopoly situations. If the F-18 costs got out of control, we had in hand the modernized F-14 and the modernized A-6. Or if either of those programs got out of hand we had the F-18. Thus the different kinds of aircraft were kept in competition with one another and costs were kept very firmly under control. Sadly this is not the case today.

Shortly after I left, OSD killed the F-14D, the A-6F, and the A-12, and then retired early the entire A-6E force, eliminating the deep-strike capability of the carriers. In retrospect, many naval aviators have told me that I should have killed the short range F-18 when I had the chance. That was not feasible.

A very high profile initiative which was very successful was the effort to dual-source the F-404 fighter engine. By getting United Technologies into production on a GE engine we were able to bring the price of that excellent engine down by about fifty percent. Just as it got into full production, however, the cold war ended and the numbers of aircraft required by the navy using those engines were cut in half, severely undermining the rationale for maintaining two separate contractors building the same engine. Nevertheless the savings from GE were enormous and would never have been achieved without the viable alternative of the United Technologies production. At the reduced production numbers after the cold war the decision was taken to stop the United Technologies production and return to General Electric sole source.

A major reform initiative that did not have such success was our attempt to apply fixed-price disciplines into full scale engineering development. The concept was simple and logical, that new technologies should be kept in a cost plus contracting environment until the contractors felt that the risk had been reduced sufficiently to accept a fixed price contract. At that point the navy could accurately budget whether the new airplane or system was worth the cost and could fit in the budget. Some of these initiatives were very successful, like the F-14D and the A-6F. The T-45 was a success for the navy but not for the contractor, who had to pay the costs of fixing an unforeseen weight problem. But the largest of these, the A-12 stealth program, was a disaster. In retrospect, the approach for such revolutionary programs does not work for two reasons. First, the contractors do not know what they do not know, and they proved to be willing to sign up to the risks of fixed price contracting when in fact the programs were not nearly far enough along to warrant the risk. The navy procurement system lacked the internal controls to prevent the creeping in of frequent requirements changes which invalidated the cost estimates underlying the fixed price. In retrospect the approach was logical and elegant, but did not fully take into account the complexity of the procurement system. More complex development programs should not be done on a fixed price basis. The corollary is that there should never be a de facto commitment to production until the production costs are able to be accurately estimated and the contractors are willing to sign up to a fixed price contract. Otherwise it would be impossible to budget responsibly for weapons systems.

It was unfortunate that the A-12 program and the air force's F-22 program were started simultaneously and budgeted at the same cost level. The navy attempted to keep costs under control by fixed pricing, and the effort was only partially successful with the projection that it would overrun to a cost of almost $6 billion. As a result of those estimates the program was canceled. The air force, however, made no such attempt and kept the entire program on a cost plus basis while still maintaining highly optimistic estimates of development costs. As of this writing, the F-22 is still on a cost plus basis seventeen years later, and the costs so far are four times the projected end cost of the A-12. The lesson to the bureaucracy has not been lost.

September 1, 2001

PART III

The Navy in Action

Chapter 8

The Falklands War

On March 31, 1982, at 6:30 P.M. Washington time, President Reagan called the president of Argentina, General Galtieri, to warn him against the seizure of a nearby British crown colony, the Falkland Islands. After a two-hour delay, Galtieri replied with a fifty-minute diatribe. He declined the offer of American good offices and insisted instead that the Falklands were the Malvinas, an Argentine territory usurped by British colonization. When the president asked for an assurance that there would be no imminent attack, Galtieri answered by silence.[1]

The invasion had already been launched. Within two days, Argentine Marines overwhelmed the few Royal Marines defending the colony, suffering several dead but, under orders, harming none of the British. As rejoicing broke out in Buenos Aires, an outraged Prime Minister Margaret Thatcher in London brushed aside the hesitations of her ministers and ordered the Royal Navy to recapture the Falklands Islands forthwith.

Since the great Pacific naval war forty-three years ago, U.S. naval forces have been engaged in crisis and combat more than two hundred times. Overwhelming air superiority kept the U.S. Navy immune from enemy interference through most events. The Falklands War was the first real naval conflict since 1945 to pit a modern Western navy against really determined resistance. There were important lessons for the U.S. Navy to be learned from this struggle, though our critics were quick to misinterpret them—particularly the vulnerability of surface warships. But this peculiar war also illustrated what we often forget. Sometimes nations fight for principles, not just for interests. For Argentina, that principle was sovereignty over an area she had claimed for one hundred fifty years. For Britain it was the principles of self-determination and international law. Thus two civilized societies made war over this remote, cold, and boggy territory so near the Antarctic Circle and home to only twelve hundred Britons and six hundred thousand sheep.

The year 1982 had marked a century and a half of British rule over the Falklands, based on a claim of discovery in 1592 and continuous British settlement since 1832. The Argentines argued, however, that the Malvinas, as they called them, had been part of the Spanish patrimony passed to Argentina with her independence in 1816. After years of fruitless bilateral negotiations that preoccupied several generations of diplomats, the dispute had in 1967 been turned over to that haven of lost causes, the United Nations. Seven years later, it was not nearer to solution.

To determine the future of the Falklands, Britain now added a new element: a poll of colonists. Predictably, the British population preferred the queen's dominion to the misrule of the Argentine military junta, then presiding over a deepening economic and political crisis—an endemic state of affairs for the Argentines.

No doubt these troubles led the junta to the usual recourse of failing dictatorships, an adventure abroad. But that does not entirely explain the enthusiasm kindled in Argentina by the seizure of the Falklands. The truth is that the Argentines *did* feel aggrieved at what they believed to be a history of British perfidy, which fit well into a national ethos at once admiring and deeply resentful of John Bull. It does not seem to have occurred to them that London's decisions would be based on principles other than simply material calculations.

Once decided that the Argentine action challenged Britain's fundamental beliefs, Mrs. Thatcher's only material calculations seem to have been the assurance by her first sea lord that the Royal Navy could indeed retake the Falklands. In the event, of course, it proved to be, as the duke of Wellington said of Waterloo, "a near-run thing."

In Washington, I watched the unfolding drama with a mixed sense of professional curiosity and sheer astonishment. Along with most naval observers, I had watched with disappointment the steady decline of the Royal Navy since World War II. Britain's economy, smothering under Fabian socialism, her commitment to a large standing army and air force, and the costs of nuclear deterrence had lead a succession of governments to reduce the navy to second-rate status. In 1965 a Labor government had decreed the end of full-size aircraft carriers. At the time I was an undergraduate at Cambridge and was amazed at the silly arguments used against the carriers. (The arguments were just as silly when critics used them fourteen years later to get President Carter to veto a nuclear carrier.) Both the Labor minister for the navy, Christopher Mayhew, and the first sea lord, Admiral Sir David Luce, had resigned rather than carry out this decision, a remarkable display of principle rarely seen in our own military.

In 1981 Mrs. Thatcher's Conservative government announced its commitment to the Trident missile and submarine strategic deterrent, and a consequent major reduction and deemphasis of conventional naval forces, including elimination of the Royal marines, a 20 percent reduction of surface combatants, and the selling off of the new Invincible class VTOL cruisers.* Shorn of all aircraft, the Royal Navy was to become a coast guard.

In a politically courageous act, the Conservative minister for the navy, Keith Speed, spoke out against these cuts. He was promptly fired by Mrs. Thatcher, who then abolished the historic office itself to ensure no repetition of naval apostasy. As the only worldly counterpart of the U.S. secretary of the navy, Keith and I had become good friends. I greatly admired his willingness to speak out, knowing it would end his promising ministerial career for the remainder of Mrs. Thatcher's long tenure. While all the peacetime admirals cheered him privately, not one would jeopardize his career by a similar stand on principle.

Fortunately for Britain, when the Falklands were seized, the order to sell and scrap the ships had not yet been carried out. Even more fortunately, the Royal Navy had retained its high level of professionalism. And unlike the American merchant marine, London could call upon extensive private maritime assets. Fifty-eight ships were pressed into service, including the luxury liner *Queen Elizabeth II*, in a program called STUFT (ships taken up from trade). Only three weeks after Mrs. Thatcher's order was given, the British war fleet, a hundred strong and carrying twenty-eight thousand men, assembled near the Falklands.

Meanwhile, it was hard to believe that a war would actually take place. The United States had offered to mediate because the clash seemed both senseless and self-defeating. We could not desert the British on principle; we did not want to lose the Thatcher government. On the other hand, the Reagan administration was well launched in the difficult task of reviving badly strained relations with Argentina, which offered not only influence in Latin America but also a chance to shape the political evolution of an important country.

---

*These twenty-thousand-ton ships were designed to operate antisubmarine helicopters but were adapted also to operate the Vertical Takeoff and Landing (VTOL) Harrier jet fighters.

Moreover, Argentina had become the leader among Latin American nations in taking active, concerted measures to confront Soviet, Cuban, and Nicaraguan subversion in Central America. Any perception that the United States was tilting toward the United Kingdom would undermine this dimension of our Central American policy.

On April 3, after the invasion, the U.N. Security Council adopted Resolution 502, calling for a cease-fire, Argentine withdrawal, and a negotiated settlement. With this in hand, Secretary of State Haig was dispatched by the president on an exhausting series of shuttles between London and Buenos Aires to head off the war. He carried a proposal that would place an international peace-keeping force on the island in place of the Argentines, while renewing negotiations before British and Argentine forces clashed. In London, Haig found a determined Mrs. Thatcher rapping the very table at which Chamberlain had decided to appease Hitler in 1938. Some of her other ministers still expressed doubt, yet it was clear that an unequivocal restoration of British authority was Mrs. Thatcher's minimum.

Haig's trip to Argentina was of a different sort. The shuttle took eighteen hours, with three refueling stops and a passage from spring to autumn. In Buenos Aires, vast crowds shouting patriotic slogans greeted the secretary. At the Casa Rosada, the presidential palace, a brilliant display of uniforms suggested determination. But the reality was that the army, navy, and air force were deeply divided. The navy, most ardent for the war, in the end played the least role. The army, bearing the brunt of defense on the islands, had not even been informed of the invasion. And the air force, which took the highest-percentage losses and did most of the fighting, had been opposed.

Hours of exhausting negotiations finally produced an Argentine agreement: Troops would leave, the British authority would be restored, but an Argentine administrative presence would remain. On Easter Sunday, after prayer, Haig flew off to London. The negotiations there were undercut by signs, public and private, of an Argentine double-cross.

Haig decided to rely on the pressure of the impending arrival of the British fleet and European sanctions voted against Argentina to bring the junta to its senses. In the meantime, he negotiated a further agreement with Mrs. Thatcher. The Argentines were to withdraw; the fleet would be halted; a U.S.-U.K.-Argentine joint interim administration would govern the islands; and negotiation, free of sanctions, would be completed about the future of the Falklands by the end of 1982.

Once more Haig returned to Buenos Aires, to find the Argentines in a state of flux. The full junta had assembled to impress him, and howling crowds accompanied his motorcade. But this had the opposite effect, leading the secretary to conclude that neither Galtieri nor his colleagues could actually deliver anything. A further series of advances and retreats reinforced this conclusion. On April 19, Haig returned to Washington. Another week of proposals passed back and forth. Meanwhile, as we had come to expect, bureaucratic warfare broke out. This time it was Haig and the "Europeanists" arguing for full support of Britain, versus U.N. ambassador Jeane Kirkpatrick and the "Americanists," who advocated a tilt toward Argentina. The Europeanists won. On April 30 the United States declared its own sanctions against Argentina, who then immediately informed us of their cancellation of active support of our policy in Central America.

There had, in fact, been a massive de facto tilt toward Britain from the very first day in the Pentagon itself. It was not the result of any bias one way or the other, nor was it really the result of any specific political decision. It was the inescapable result of the naval manifestation of the "special relationship." On the merits of the issue, none of the senior officials in the Pentagon felt strongly one way or the other. There was strong sympathy for the active role that Argentina had lately played in leading the beginning of a concerted policy to confront the Sandinistas and Cubans and Russians in subversion of the hemisphere. Moreover, in the Navy Department there were bonds among naval aviators with their counterparts in Argentina, one of the very few navies in the world that operated a conventional aircraft carrier. Most of the pilots in the Argentine Navy were trained at Pensacola and at Kingsville, Texas. I had flown with several at Kingsville, and they were all of very high quality and were warmly regarded.

Nevertheless, the depth and breadth of cultural, social, and historic ties between the establishments of the United States and the United Kingdom were an overwhelming reality. The special relationship between the Royal Navy and the U.S. Navy is one of the strongest in the web.

While the origins of the U.S. Navy owe as much to the French Navy as to the Royal Navy, the intertwining of naval professionalism and tradition between the Royal Navy and the U.S. Navy is very deep indeed. The highly skilled masters and mariners of the Yankee colonies were actively sought in the preindependence Royal Navy, and, indeed, George Washington's first military appointment was as a midshipman in the Royal Navy at age sixteen (though he never actually served). Mount Vernon is named for Admiral Vernon of the Royal Navy.

The continuation of the practice of pressing Americans into Royal Navy service was one of the principal causes of the War of 1812. There were three hundred Americans aboard the crew of Nelson's flagship H.M.S. *Victory* at the Battle of Trafalgar in 1805. The common language and literature developed a common dialogue in naval practice, theory, and strategy. The young Teddy Roosevelt's classic *History of the War of 1812*, for instance, was adopted as the official history by the Royal Navy. Roosevelt's theorist Captain Alfred Thayer Mahan had at first considerably more influence on the Royal Navy than on the U.S. Navy. His writings became the basis for the historic rebuilding of the Royal Navy prior to World War I, led by Mahan's disciple Sir John Fisher. Mahan was given honorary degrees by both Oxford and Cambridge. The great naval historian and later admiral Samuel Eliot Morison was alternately a professor at Harvard and at Oxford.

In World War I, the close cooperation in the transatlantic naval conflict exemplified by U.S. naval destroyer operations out of Queenstown, Ireland, continued actively during the interwar period. The destroyers-for-bases deal, and FDR's ordering the U.S. Navy into active antisubmarine warfare against German U-boats prior to our entry into World War II cemented the relationship that led to fully integrated naval operations throughout the war.

The creation of the Joint NATO Supreme Allied Command Atlantic in the postwar period added a new dimension of common command and full integration of wartime planning, doctrine, and logistics. Through this framework, the two navies developed a substantial integration of doctrine, weaponry, operations, and logistics. Perhaps even more important, it provided a system of very active exchange of personnel between the two navies, building bonds of friendship and familiarity.

This common framework proved to be decisive in the Falklands War. Because there was a system in place for sharing communications and intelligence, the web of liaison offices routinely set up to handle the sale, loan, and other transfer of weapons and equipment, there was nothing to be set up and no hard decisions to be made in the first days of the crisis. At least once every year a major exercise took place involving the U.S. and Royal navies as part of the normal SACLANT-NATO maneuvers. Already U.S. liaison personnel were in place at Royal Navy headquarters at Northwood outside London; the five-hundred-person U.S. Navy headquarters staff in London; large numbers of Royal Navy personnel in the SACLANT staff at Norfolk; and the naval staff headed by Rear Admiral John Hervey at the British embassy.

Requests through these channels began to flow from the first days of the crisis in April. At first, before the task force arrived at the Falklands, the requests were handled routinely, without reference to higher authority. As the requests began to involve more substantial logistical assistance, communications equipment, and intelligence, we kept the secretary of defense informed, and he then required us to submit a daily report to his deputy, Frank Carlucci. As a well-known Anglophile (he was given an honorary knighthood by the queen in 1988), there was little doubt where Weinberger's sympathies lay, but because of the deep divisions within the administration, we did not want to raise the level of consideration of increasing the flow of assistance to the Royal Navy. We made sure that Cap knew at every step what we were proposing to provide. Because of the special relationship there was no need to take any special action, but rather it would have been necessary to step in and interfere with the broadening flow of assistance. It is highly unlikely that Jeane Kirkpatrick or anyone at the State Department or the White House understood at first the extent of the assistance we were providing, especially in communications and intelligence.

Shortly after I became secretary of the navy, the British Defense Ministry invited me to make an official visit to the United Kingdom. The date was set long in advance for May 3, 1982, and my itinerary included the usual official meetings and visits to Royal Navy ships and facilities. On May 2, however, the war got off to a highly dramatic start when a British submarine, H.M.S. *Conqueror,* sank the Argentine heavy cruiser *General Belgrano* using fifty-five-year-old Mark 8 torpedoes. Although the Argentines had an aircraft carrier, the sinking of the *General Belgrano* and the loss of 308 sailors of her 1,000 man crew shocked the Argentine Navy into passivity. They played no significant role for the remainder of the three-week campaign.

The bloody inauguration of the war at sea put a different cast on my reception. On my first day of discussions at Whitehall with ministry and Royal Navy officials I was perplexed to find that many of the civilian members of the ministry seemed to be resentful of what they perceived as reluctance by the U.S. government to give full support and assistance to the United Kingdom. Jeane Kirkpatrick and, surprisingly, Al Haig came in for some considerable criticism in those discussions. The Royal Navy, by contrast, could not have been more grateful and appreciative. I later concluded that the Royal Navy had not fully shared with their ministers everything that was in fact going on between the two navies.

In the historic paneled rooms of the Admiralty Board in Whitehall we had one of our most vigorous discussions of what was happening in the Falklands and what the United States ought to be doing about it. It was hard to keep one's mind on the subject at hand as I looked around the room at the large half-moon cutout of the table at the end, done to accommodate the vast potbelly of one very rotund first lord of the admiralty. Around this table Sir Francis Drake gave his report on the routing of the Spanish Armada in 1588; Nelson gave his report to the Admiralty Board on the total defeat of the French Navy at the Battle of the Nile; and his survivors, the reports of the glorious victory at Trafalgar. It was there that the first lord of the admiralty, Winston Churchill, planned the ill-fated Dardanelles campaign and where, to an admiral's protest that he violated naval tradition, he retorted, "Naval tradition? Bah! Rum, sodomy, and the lash—that is naval tradition." Still operating on the wall looking down on the Admiralty Board is the famous wind-driven compass showing the wind relative to the coast of France. This was essential for tactical planning in the days when the threat was from France and success required gaining the windward position.

That afternoon of May 4, we received word that the Argentines had exacted their revenge for the *General Belgrano* by sinking H.M.S. *Sheffield*, a destroyer. It had been hit by a French Exocet antiship cruise missile fired from a French-built Super Étendard. The missile had failed to explode, but the unexpended fuel ignited fires that went out of control and eventually destroyed the ship. The *Sheffield* was in fact one of Britain's most modern surface ships, built not of aluminum, as so many in the press reported, but with a steel superstructure. It sank with considerable loss of life because, among other reasons, it had been caught by surprise and its crew was not at general quarters. The British were now face-to-face with the limitations of their fleet and the consequences of their antinaval budget-cutting over the past fifteen years. The Royal Navy had deployed a large surface task force eight thousand miles from home without effective protection against air attack. Listening to false prophets, they had retired their large aircraft carriers as obsolete, depriving the fleet of airborne early warning and supersonic interceptors. To save money they had not funded the installation of existing cruise missile defenses nor made the investment in three-dimensional air defense radars for their ships. Now they began to pay a mounting price in blood and treasure.

That evening the government hosted an official dinner in my honor at Lancaster House. It was a very emotional evening as news of the dead arrived during dinner. In my toast I expressed the deep commitment of sympathy and support of the U.S. Navy for the Royal Navy, but of course I could not speak publicly of the actual extent of what we were doing. Across from me sat one of the most senior officials in the defense ministry. It was obvious from his attitude and conversation that he did not know the full extent of what was being done, and his remarks reflected a bitterness toward what he clearly believed to be an American ally deserting Britain in its time of need. In fact, he was rude. Weeks later, when he learned the truth, he resumed his cordiality. Because of events in Washington I had to cut short my visit and go straight to my P-3 after dinner and fly through the night back to Washington.

The war now moved into its crucial phase. The admiralty had calculated that the fleet would be in more danger from the Argentine air force than from the navy. If the Port Stanley airfield in the islands were lengthened to accommodate the regular Argentine Skyhawks and other effective, if dated, aircraft in the Argentine inventory, then the whole operation would be endangered.

Fearing the worst, the British had attempted to put the airfield out of action. A squadron of Vulcans, an obsolete strategic bomber, flew from England to Ascension Island on April 28. Then, on May 1, one of the Vulcans, fueled en route by ten tankers, dropped twenty-one one-thousand-pound bombs on target. It was the longest-range bombing raid in history. The airfield was damaged but not disabled, so later that day, all twenty Sea Harriers based on the VTOL cruisers *Invincible* and *Hermes* raided the site again, despite heavy antiaircraft fire. The airfield still was not destroyed. Luckily for the Royal Navy, however, the Argentines never did lengthen the runway to take jets. So the fleet faced the single sorties of fuel-short daredevil Argentine pilots flying at maximum range from the mainland rather than from the islands. The Argentines performed brilliantly and inflicted great damage, but they paid a heavy price.

Ninety-one Argentine planes were lost to gunfire and to the Harrier jump-jets. But six major British ships were lost, and ten others were damaged. All told, it was estimated that if all the bombs dropped by the Argentine pilots, some flying as low as twenty feet above the waves, had actually exploded, a quarter to a third of the British fleet would have found the bottom.

On May 21 the British landed on the main islands. They met variable resistance. Bad weather, air attacks, and a helicopter shortage impeded their advance. Nonetheless, three and a half weeks later, as the Argentine defense dissolved into chaos, the Royal Marines took Port Stanley. All told, on both sides, a thousand men had died and over seventeen hundred were wounded.

Amid these scenes, the United States tried once more to end the war. Once the British landed, various formulas were put forward, encouraged by the U.S. mission at the United Nations, that would have eased Argentina's defeat though not prevented it. Haig, preparing for the president's visit to Europe for the Versailles economic summit, generally opposed these actions as "misleading signals." In the end, however, he suggested "magnanimity" to Mrs. Thatcher for the sake of further relations with Argentina. "Magnanimous," she replied, "is not a word I use in connection with a battle on the Falklands."[2] Despite the risk of offending London, as the war neared its end, the presidential party already at Versailles instructed Mrs. Kirkpatrick to abstain on a U.N. cease-fire resolution that Britain vetoed. The instructions reached her too late. She cast a veto, then reversed it. Luckily for Washington, this final burst of diplomatic confusion had little impact on either British or Argentine sentiment.

A political reckoning in Argentina was not long in coming. On June 17, General Galtieri and the junta resigned, mystified to the end why the United States had not stopped the British. They were arrested later as Argentina lurched into a more democratic phase of its history. In London, Prime Minister Thatcher accepted the accolades of a triumphant Britain. A grateful Parliament voted large sums to improve conditions in the Falklands. The prewar Thatcher naval reduction that precipitated Keith Speed's demise was quietly withdrawn and the three VTOL cruisers taken off the auction block.

Unlike the Lebanon War or the Vietnam War, with their extraordinary press coverage, London took no chances with the media. Deception was used freely as a tool of war to fool the Argentines about the extent of British losses and even the timing of its invasion. In fact, the defense ministry convinced more than one analyst and pundit that there would *not* be an invasion — just a blockade. The Argentines, for their part, fell to believing their own propaganda, including the oft-repeated story that Prince Andrew, the queen's second son, had been killed. Truth as reported by the press during the Falklands was undoubtedly a casualty, but the complaints of the journalists were silenced by the roar of victory.

For a brief period following the war, it appeared that another truth might also be a casualty: the real naval lessons of the conflict. Armchair strategists in Washington who for years advocated small, lightly armed ships now declared that because small, lightly armed ships could be sunk by one Exocet, therefore large, armored ships, such as carriers, were a waste of money. In fact, the opposite was true.

We did not want to chance losing any lessons from this first truly naval war since the 1940s, and before it was over we assembled a team of our best experts to assemble the facts and find the useful lessons for the U.S. Navy.

Lessons Learned

I. PERSONNEL

By far the most important elements of military capability are the quality, training, and motivation of the troops themselves. The Falklands War was a perfect illustration. Except for Argentina's air force and navy pilots and the marines, their forces were primarily conscripts with minimal training and virtually no experience. The British armed forces, like their U.S. counterparts, were entirely volunteer and were made up of highly trained and experienced people. Their extensive training and exercising prepared for combat against the formidable Soviet armed forces. In the actual land fighting, the quality difference was overwhelming and decisive.

By contrast to the army conscripts, Argentina's air force and navy pilots performed extremely effectively, demonstrating a high degree of dedication and courage. The thousand Argentine Marines who took part in the conflict had also had a considerably higher level of experience and morale than their conscript counterparts.

2. INTELLIGENCE

Next to the quality of personnel, the most important determinant of the war was intelligence. Because of the quality and timeliness of intelligence available to the Royal Navy from the United States, the U.K. forces had available to them far better information about the location, training, and intentions of the Argentine forces than the Argentines had about the British; in fact the Argentines were frequently in the dark about the British. Some of the most senior British officials have gone so far as to say that without that substantial intelligence assistance, the British would have been defeated. I agree. The lesson for U.S. forces is not only the essential inputs from technical and human intelligence sources but also the proper training of operational personnel in the fusing and interpretation of intelligence.

3. DEFENSE IN DEPTH

The repeated successes of Argentine aircraft in penetrating British defenses in daylight, and attacking forces afloat and ashore, reveal the complete lack of Royal Navy fleet air defense in depth, especially the airborne early-warning and long-range air-defense fighters. Virtually none of the aircraft that hit the British ships from mainland bases in Argentina could have reached their targets had a carrier air wing been part of the British force. The last British aircraft carrier, the *Ark Royal*, had been retired in 1980. It carried Gannet airborne early-warning aircraft and supersonic Phantom interceptors.

I remembered so well the arguments of the Labour government not to replace the carriers. They said that such carriers were vulnerable and required destroyers to protect them. Now here were the destroyers in battle being sunk because they had no carrier to protect them! Defense of surface ships, whether merchant or combatant, clearly requires a well-rounded complement that includes aerial surveillance aircraft, interceptors, antisubmarine aircraft, and all-weather attack bombers. All must operate with effective antiair command and control. The weapons on the surface ships need modern 3-D radars, sophisticated target identification systems, data management systems, and electronic warfare equipment.

The Royal Navy had not a single 3-D air defense radar in its Falklands fleet, and its only air cover consisted of the twenty-eight Sea Harriers on the two VTOL cruisers, H.M.S. *Hermes* and H.M.S. *Invincible*. These Harriers were used in outer air defense, usually consisting of four Sea Harriers, each with a short-range intercept radar, carrying only two visual-range Sidewinder heat-seeking missiles each. Due to the range of these patrol stations from the carriers, the Harriers were able to maintain station for only about twenty minutes each. Moreover, they had to depend entirely on their own short-range radar and visual acquisition, because the Argentines flew low, close to the surface, out of range of the surveillance radars on the British ships. Most of the attackers were able to penetrate this thin outer air defense.

In the inner zone, the attackers faced the British surface-to-air missile systems Sera Dart and Sea Wolf. These systems were always saturated by the numbers, but did succeed in knocking down thirteen attackers. But because none of the British ships carried close-in weapons systems other than guns aimed by sight, a great many of the attackers reached their targets. Two destroyers, two frigates—all equipped with missiles and guns—a landing ship, and a merchant ship were lost. Another ten ships were hit by bombs that did not explode. This high ratio of duds mocked the courage of the Argentines, who pressed their attack low and close in to evade the Harriers and who were let down by the failure of their ground crews to adjust the bomb fuses. Seven anti-ship missiles were launched: five from aircraft and two from shore launchers. Three ships were hit by these missiles, and two of those were lost, but to fire, not to the explosions of the missiles.

As a result of this obvious lesson, Watkins and I reviewed the numbers of our own combat ships equipped with the latest close-in defense systems and were appalled to find that only 5 percent were so equipped, even though the system had been in production for nearly ten years. We ordered an immediate reallocation of funding to accelerate immediately the installation of these systems aboard all our combatants. These systems were the Sea Sparrow system; the Vulcan Phalanx Gatling gun, which fires a curtain of spent uranium bullets (spent uranium, with no radioactivity, is much heavier than lead and does greater damage to a target) at a rate of four thousand per minute under radar and computer control; and a variety of electronic warfare measures.

Altogether in acting on this and many other lessons from our study, we reallocated $855 million in R&D and $2.7 billion in procurement of weapons, damage control, personnel equipment, fire-resistant uniforms, etc., in the fiscal years 1985–89 Five-Year Plan.

Nevertheless, in comparing the Royal Navy in the Falklands to an American formation, we concluded that the percentage of aircraft or Exocets that could have gotten through the interceptors, the Aegis air defense system, and its Standard missiles into the inner zone would have been very small indeed. Those that did would face today a far thicker and more capable range of close-in defenses. The most effective defense that the Royal Navy had in the Falklands against cruise missiles was the use of chaff to confuse radars on aircraft and missiles. Based on what we learned from the Royal Navy, we substantially increased the per-ship allocations and the sophistication of chaff systems on all our ships.

4. LARGE WARSHIPS VERSUS SMALL WARSHIPS

One of the clearest lessons of the Falklands is that smaller, cheaper, less well-armed combatants can be a very false economy because of their much higher vulnerability, as demonstrated by the loss of the five Royal Navy combatants. If any of the twenty-three successful attacks against British ships had instead hit the battleship *New Jersey*, it could not have done sufficient damage to prevent continuing operations of the ship. The Exocet missile that sank the *Sheffield* would not have been able to penetrate the armor anywhere on a battleship. Unlike many of its critics, the navy retains its institutional memory of World War II, when it lost a destroyer a day at Okinawa because of their lack of armor and air defenses. By contrast, except for three carriers, no large ships were lost after Pearl Harbor, but in many battles there were examples like the battleship *South Dakota* sustaining forty-five hits from fourteen-inch naval guns while still continuing full operations, or when the Japanese battleship *Musashi* absorbed fourteen torpedoes and twenty-two large bombs and continued to operate. None of the attacks sustained by British ships would have penetrated a vital space of one of our aircraft carriers or done it sufficient damage to force it to cease operations. We never lost an aircraft carrier of over thirty thousand tons in World War II. The small through-deck VTOL cruisers in the Royal Navy, by contrast, are vulnerable to complete loss from torpedo or missile or bomb attacks because they lack the multiple hulls, armor plate, and redundant damage control systems that are inherent to the design of large U.S. carriers.

The small British VTOL cruisers, though well designed and professionally manned, are incapable of accommodating modern high-performance aircraft. Despite high reliability and effectiveness of the small VTOL Harriers and the heroic performance of their pilots, the British never established anything approaching control of the skies above the Falklands. Even Argentine resupply craft from the mainland were able to land at Stanley right up until the night before the surrender. Fortunately for the British, Argentine air attacks were confined to daylight hours only, which limited the air threat to about eight hours of every twenty-four. A U.S. carrier could have maintained a vastly more capable air superiority twenty-four hours a day over the battle force.

Under peacetime conditions the British cruisers accommodate only five Sea Harriers and nine to twelve Sea King antisubmarine helicopters each. Combined, the *Invincible* and the *Hermes* displaced about the same tonnage as our Midway class carrier. The Midway class carrier carries some seventy of the highest-performance aircraft, of eight different types. The equivalent of two British ships could carry only a combined total of twenty-eight much less capable Harriers and a dozen helicopters.

The small VTOL cruisers are far less sustainable than a large carrier. They have only a fraction of the endurance without refueling, and they have very limited space for onboard stowage for bombs and ammunition. In the Falklands both ships accepted very great danger by stacking bombs, missiles, and fuel tanks unprotected on deck to sustain the necessary high tempo of operations. The volume of U.S. carriers enables the storage of weeks of ammunition not only belowdecks but also below the waterline, immune from attack. In addition, the large volume of our carriers enables far more extensive repair and maintenance to keep the air wing operating week after week at full mission capability.

5. AIRCRAFT PERFORMANCE

Small vertical-takeoff-and-landing Harriers, both Royal Navy and RAF versions, were surprisingly reliable and versatile during the battle. The twenty-eight Sea Harriers deployed to the South Atlantic flew more than twelve hundred sorties in forty-four days. Their availability was exceptionally high—90 percent. Fewer than 1 percent of planned missions were scrubbed because of aircraft unserviceability. The radar and attack weapons-control system in the Sea Harrier proved to be reliable and versatile but limited in range and capability.

In air-to-air combat, Sea Harriers destroyed at least twenty Argentine aircraft, sixteen of them with United States–produced Sidewinder missiles. Many of these missiles had to be transferred to the Royal Navy by the U.S. Navy during the campaign to prevent them from running out. In many engagements the Harriers were attacking aircraft that were operating at the extreme limits of their range and could not afford to maneuver if they were to return home safely. Similarly, the Harriers had limited time on station and limited air-to-air ordnance loads. They were placed at great disadvantage by lack of adequate radar-controlled cueing and vectoring for intercepts. The Argentine aircraft, however, attempted to attack the Sea Harriers on the first day of the air battle only.

The performance of both types of Harriers in air-to-ground action was much less impressive. Together they delivered fewer than two hundred general-purpose bombs during the land battle.

Four Sea Harriers and one RAF Harrier were lost in operational accidents, and two Sea Harriers and four RAF Harriers were lost to enemy action, one in air-to-air combat.

Helicopters were an invaluable part of the British force. They were used successfully as antiship missile platforms; for at-sea replenishment and logistics support; for troop lift and equipment lift to the battlefield; and for command and control, commando raids, and many utility functions. Most of the heavy-lift helicopters were lost when the ship carrying them, the *Atlantic Conveyor*, was destroyed by an Exocet. As one lesson learned by the United Kingdom, it has modified Sea King helicopters with an early-warning radar and now operates them routinely from their VTOL cruisers.

Flying from Ascension Island, the RAF flew five strike missions by using Vulcan strategic jet bombers against the Falklands. Three Vulcans, each carrying twenty-one one-thousand-pound bombs, attacked Port Stanley Airfield, but only one actually reached the target. Two single-plane sorties with antiradar missiles attacked Argentine radar installations. Each of these sorties required multiple in-flight refuelings and had virtually no impact on either the Argentine surveillance radars or on Port Stanley Airfield. Both the airfield and the radar installation remained operating until the last day of the war.

The venerable C-130 Hercules provided the backbone of airborne logistics for both the United Kingdom and Argentina during the conflict. The British operated theirs as aerial refuelers and used them to air-drop critical supplies at sea and ashore. Right up to the final day of the war, Argentine C-130s flew critical resupply missions from the mainland, usually under threat of Harrier attack. Argentine bombers were aerially refueled by Hercules tankers to extend their operating range.

Argentina's navy and air force operated about sixty-four A-4 Sky Hawk light attack aircraft with considerable effect, inflicting most of the damage on the British fleet.

Argentina's navy operated five Super Étendard French-built fighter-bombers. They were very effective as the firing platform for Exocet missiles, with their attack radar and inertial navigation system permitting them very low-level ingress, with a pop-up to fire, and then a rapid egress. The Argentines did not hazard these aircraft in iron-bomb attacks over the target.

6. LOGISTICS

The old aphorism that amateurs talk about strategy while professionals talk about logistics was validated again in the Falklands. The outcome of the battle may be seen to be a failure of Argentine logistics and a major success of British logistics. While a huge cache of supplies was built up after the initial Argentine invasion, the Argentine command in the Falklands was never able effectively to distribute the supplies and ammunition, and troops in the field were usually critically short of important items that were languishing close by in supply dumps.

The battle was relatively brief. The British forces required enormous quantities of munitions, provisions, fuel, and other supplies. Logistics operations were severely hampered by the seven-thousand-mile distance from the United Kingdom, by an initial shortage of shipping, and by limited stocks of certain supplies. Fifty merchant vessels were used in supporting British operations. They included a variety of merchant, container, roll-on, roll-off, and passenger ships, tankers, and several special-purpose ships. Most of the merchant ships were modified rapidly for at-sea refueling and given maritime communications satellite terminals. Nineteen ships were additionally fitted to operate helicopters. A small number of merchant ships were also fitted with 20mm or 40mm antiaircraft guns or light machine guns.

Although the U.S. Navy has developed plans in conjunction with the Maritime Administration to use merchant ships from trade and the ready reserve force, the Falklands are a reminder of the magnitude of the problem we face by the decline of the American merchant marine. It required 50 merchant ships for the British to carry out the three-week Falklands campaign, and currently we have only about 250 American-flag merchant vessels. Although we instituted in 1982 a major program to buy up modern merchant ships from bankrupt operators and have increased our ready reserve force from only 29 ships at the beginning of the Reagan administration to a current 121, it is only a very partial answer to the larger problem. It underlines further the truth that we will be very hard-pressed without any interference from the Soviets to find sufficient merchant vessels in wartime. If we allow Soviet submarines and land-based bombers to inflict attrition similar to that in World War II, we will lose any such war very promptly. Allied naval forces can only defend a strategic sealift by ensuring a forward offensive posture against Soviet submarines, and maintaining air superiority over shipping of allies through a combination of land-based aircraft near shore and carrier aircraft far at sea.

7. SUBMARINE OPERATIONS

Argentina's navy began the conflict with two of their four submarines operational: one relatively new West German-built diesel electric submarine, and one older U.S. Guppy-type submarine. The latter was destroyed by a British helicopter firing a Sea-Skua antiship missile off south Georgia on April 25.

The West German-built *San Luis*, built in 1974, made a patrol of an estimated thirty-six days during the conflict. It located and operated against the main British task force for several days. She was, however, unable to make a successful attack despite repeated attempts, because of serious materiel problems, reportedly the work of British sabotage.

The British force was aware the sub was in the area and prosecuted more than a hundred suspected submarine contacts without success. Some fifty anti-submarine torpedoes were actually fired, probably at whales or schooling fish.

The ability of a modern diesel electric submarine to engage a naval task force that is essentially stationary while operating in a specific area is not surprising. These submarines are extremely quiet when operated at low speeds, and for this reason a variety of active helicopter and subsurface antisubmarine warfare defenses are required whenever a naval task force is constrained to a limited area. While effective in such constrained areas and choke points, diesel subs do not make sense for the U.S. Navy, which must operate at speed all over the world. We would, however, have to procure substantial numbers of them if it were not for the fact that there are more than 140 modern diesel electric submarines in the navies of our allies.

As the crisis escalated in the South Atlantic in late March, three British nuclear attack submarines were directed to the Falklands area. Their ability to transit such a long distance at high speed permitted the United Kingdom to establish an exclusion zone 200 nautical miles in radius around the Falklands before the task force arrived. The SSNs began at once to enforce this exclusion area to prevent any further reinforcement of the Argentine contingent. They were completely successful, forcing the Argentines to rely solely on C-130s. On May 7 the British government warned that any Argentine warships sighted more than two miles from the Argentine coast would be regarded as hostile and subject to attack. Ultimately five U.K. SSNs and one diesel electric submarine were sent to the Falklands. One of the SSNs, H.M.S. *Conqueror*, successfully intercepted and sank the Argentine cruiser *General Belgrano*, an old World War II single-skinned cruiser, using fifty-five-year-old design steam torpedoes.

8. SHIP SURVIVABILITY

No defense in depth, however effective, can be relied on as impenetrable. Thus, no matter how good, naval ships must be built to take substantial hits and keep fighting. The Falklands War is rich in such lessons to be relearned.

The *General Belgrano*, a forty-four-year-old cruiser in very poor material condition, had very limited damage control equipment and training and as a result suffered uncontrolled flooding and eventual loss of the ship.

The British lost one destroyer to a fire started by the residual fuel from an unexploded Exocet missile, one destroyer to bombs and strafing, two frigates to bombs, one landing ship to bombs, and one container ship to a fire caused by one or two Exocet missiles that did not detonate. In addition, two British destroyers, fourteen frigates, and one landing ship were damaged during the conflict, all by Argentine air attacks with bombs, rockets, or strafing, except for the destroyer *Glamorgan*, which was damaged by a shore-launched Exocet missile. Despite much erroneous press commentary, there is no evidence that the use of aluminum in the construction of British ships contributed to the loss of any of the combatants.

In summary, the Falklands experience demonstrates that modern surface ships can be defended against modern weapons like cruise missiles but must have defense in depth and must be able to sustain hits, absorb damage, limit it, and keep fighting. On the one hand, the crew of the *Sheffield* was not at general quarters, was unready to sustain damage, and was ultimately lost, even though the missile did not detonate. By contrast, the *Glamorgan* was struck by an Exocet missile that did detonate, and while a major fire and shrapnel casualties killing thirteen men resulted, the ship was able to continue operations with armament and weapons systems intact because she was ready.

The Exocet attack on the U.S. frigate *Stark* in 1987 underlined those very same lessons. The *Stark* had the defenses to defeat the Exocet but they were not turned on in part because of confusion over rules of engagement. After the two Exocets hit with at least one exploding, the training and equipment of the crew enabled them to contain the damage and save the ship.

But I was infuriated to learn that the vast defense logistics bureaucracy had defeated one life-saving lesson from the Falklands. Following our study we ordered the replacement of polyester uniforms, adopted in the 1970s for shipboard use, by cotton for fire resistance. Polyester melts to the skin and burns at low temperatures. Five years after the order, it had not been carried out by the vast consolidated Defense Logistics Agency, and many *Stark* sailors were burned in polyester uniforms.

9. COMMAND AND CONTROL

A new lesson to be learned from the Falklands War, in contrast to earlier wars, is that the modern era of computer and satellite communications brings an entirely new challenge to efficient command control and rules of engagement. First, modern communications are now able to provide a veritable Niagara of communications to every level of operator in a conflict. The British commander in the Falklands was at times overwhelmed by the volume of information coming to his flagship. Much greater attention must be given to disciplining and limiting communications in future conflicts. An American warship today gets an average of seventeen hundred written messages daily in its communications center.

A side effect of such modern real-time communications has been for commanders back in the bureaucracy to be tempted to micromanage operations in the field. This does not seem to have been a problem for the British force commander because he had been given a broad delegation of authority, and he ignored much of the micromanaging from higher authority. As we shall see in Chapter 10, this certainly was not the case with our forces in Lebanon. It was, however, successfully employed in the delegation of authority and the proper rules of engagement to the Sixth Fleet commander in the Libyan operations. This is of the utmost importance in crises short of war, as in war itself, because as Admiral Gorshkov has put it so well, there is an enormous premium on "the struggle for the first salvo."

10. AMMUNITION SUSTAINABILITY

The Falklands conflict reminded us yet again that in every war the rates of consumption of high-technology weapons always exceed even generous estimates by planners. There was no allocation in British planning for shooting high-tech torpedoes at whales, yet it was done often. The systems analysis culture of the Pentagon has used analytical techniques to assign specific numbers of U.S. weapons like torpedoes to specific numbers of potential Soviet targets. Thus U.S. submarines have essentially been limited by the OSD to only a magazine and a half of old torpedoes for the entire war. Moreover, the U.S. Navy always has had a policy of getting rid of older weapons, lest they be used by Congress and the OSD to argue against the procurement of new ones. Thus there are no older-but-effective torpedoes (such as sank the *General Belgrano*) left in the American inventory, and it is a fact still that an American SSN has no torpedo that could be wasted on a low-value surface ship. As a result of the Falklands War, I instituted a program to purchase an off-the-shelf European torpedo to be used against surface ships in time of war. All of the candidates cost one fifth the price of the Mark 48 torpedo we equip our submarines with. The program was effectively killed by our own submariners as soon as I departed because they feared that it would undermine arguments for a more expensive and sophisticated successor to the Mark 48.

11. AMPHIBIOUS OPERATIONS

The British landing forces, consisting of Royal Marines and British Army soldiers, were carried to the Falklands in a small number of LSL- and LSD-type specialized amphibious ships as well as several passenger-carrying merchant ships.

Through careful planning, deception, and luck, the main landings at San Carlos were carried out without initial opposition. This illustrated an often overlooked advantage of amphibious assault. While it is difficult in an era of modern communications and intelligence to achieve strategic surprise, it still is quite possible to achieve tactical surprise and to land "where they ain't." For instance, a marine amphibious brigade off the coast of the Virginia capes at dusk can land troops ashore between the eastern tip of Long Island and Cape Hatteras before dawn.

The British amphibious assault suffered considerable damage from air attack because of their lack of air superiority. Our own marines often forget that they are utterly dependent on the total air superiority provided by aircraft carriers whenever an amphibious assault is employed. That is a major reason why General P. X. Kelley and I instituted a major program to assign marine squadrons back aboard U.S. carriers, a traditional role that had fallen into disuse during the 1970s.

12. NAVAL GUNFIRE SUPPORT

The Falklands again illustrated the essential value of naval gunfire support. During the battle 14 British destroyers and frigates mounted a total of 18 naval guns, and fired 7,900 rounds in support of the landings and subsequent campaign. This fire supported friendly troops, suppressed enemy fire, destroyed enemy supplies and aircraft on the ground, and seriously hurt the morale of the defenders. The British had only small 4.5-inch-caliber guns.

A dramatic increase in U.S. naval gunfire support was brought about by the reactivation of the battleships. Each battleship can deliver 803 tons of 16-inch and 5-inch ammunition in only 30 minutes. That is the equivalent of four times the total naval gunfire support of the entire British force in the Falklands.

Conclusion

The effect of the Falklands War was far greater than simply the retaking of the islands. It greatly improved the credibility of NATO's deterrence in demonstrating the willingness of a Western democracy to fight for principle, and its skill in doing so. It granted the Royal Navy a stay of execution in the planned substantial downgrading.

Politically the war destroyed the Argentine junta, leaving a new democracy as the alternative by default, to wrestle with Argentina's accumulated problems. But the casualties were not limited to Argentina. Lord Carrington, Mrs. Thatcher's promising foreign secretary, resigned. The Falklands War and the infighting it aroused no doubt hastened the departure of Al Haig as secretary of state. The success of the operation, however, gave new impetus to Mrs. Thatcher, virtually assuring her reelection. It added luster to the "Iron Lady," who has led Britain longer than any other prime minister in this century and who contributed so much to making Britain's the most productive and growing economy in Western Europe.

These results notwithstanding, Washington would have preferred that the Falklands War never happened. It forced an unwelcome distraction and aggravated conflicts within the administration. There can be no doubt, too, that it aroused anti-Yankee passions in Latin America. Argentina and others in Latin America would no longer be counted in the ranks as those who rallied to our Central American policy.

Chapter 9

Grenada: What Price Jointness?

When President Reagan was awakened on October 23, 1983, to be told of the marine disaster in Beirut, he had already had a bad weekend. Together with Secretary of State Shultz, the president's plan for a short golfing holiday in Augusta, Georgia, was interrupted when a would-be assassin crashed the club grounds.

Something else was on his mind as well. A few days earlier, the president had ordered the diversion of a marine amphibious group and the U.S.S. *Independence* carrier battle group from its mission to relieve the forces standing off Beirut. Instead, the force headed for the southeastern Caribbean island of Grenada. A thousand Americans, most of them medical students, were caught up in the bloody self-destruction of the island's Marxist government. It was soon to become a theater for the successful exercise of American military power, a cathartic post-Vietnam intervention that featured cheering students, a thankful population, and sharp reversal of Cuban and Soviet fortunes. But this "famous victory" also provided yet another example of the "Jointness obsession," the Washington ideology that demands that every element of the U.S. military must participate jointly in every combat action.[1]

Grenada was an odd place for these events. Discovered by Columbus in 1498 and settled initially by the French, it ceased to interest statesmen after the British finally took it permanently in 1783. Only a hundred miles from Venezuela, this southernmost of the eastern Caribbean islands eventually became the placid residence of some 110,000 mostly literate, devout farmers of small plots who exported cacao, nutmeg, and spices for a modest living. In 1967 the British had set Grenada on the road to independence within the

Commonwealth, and by 1974 that had been achieved under the leadership of Sir Eric Gairy.

Sir Eric, an eccentric figure with a profound interest in astrology, soon tired of parliamentary democracy. In March 1979 Gairy traveled to New York, his purpose to instruct the U.N. General Assembly on the relationship between voodoo and UFOs. When Maurice Bishop, leader of the New Jewel Movement, and his associates seized the government in a bloodless coup, Grenadians were happy to be rid of Gairy.

The new leader had been schooled in Britain. Those who knew him described Bishop as a charismatic speaker, an ambitious politician, and an idealist who dreamed of a new society. Given Grenada's limited resources and growing population, common problems for the island, the obvious course was economic development. In fact, Grenada's natural beauty had begun to attract tourists. It also was the location of a large American-run medical school, with eight hundred students. But Bishop and his associates were bent on a more radical course.

Gairy was deposed on March 13, 1979; on April 9, the United States recognized Bishop's government. On that same day, however, the new prime minister announced that he would seek arms and economic assistance from Cuba. The Carter administration, confused by the Nicaraguan revolution and perplexed by Castro's aggressive policies in the Caribbean and elsewhere, cautioned Grenada, but to no avail.

Among the Communist revolutions of our time, the myth has grown that Castro's Cuba and Ortega's Nicaragua could have been put on a different course if only the United States had been wiser and more generous. After all, we had allowed Batista and Somoza free reign. Their tyrannies had set the stage for the revolutions.

It is one thing, however, to acknowledge that we had been negligent in the past and quite another to assume that we were dealing with would-be democrats. Castro and Comandante Ortega were and are devoted Marxist-Leninists, period. American economic aid could subsidize their consolidation of communism, but it could not divert them from it. This was true of Maurice Bishop and his closest comrades, General Hudson Austin and Bernard and Phyllis Coard. We know this because U.S. forces captured a vast archive of the Grenadan government's plans, diplomatic exchanges, and secret military agreements with Cuba, the U.S.S.R., North Korea, and East Germany.

Over a four-year period, as Grenada sank into economic distress and increasing indoctrination, Bishop obtained over $33 million in aid from Cuba alone. Arms sufficient to equip a ten-thousand-man force were piled onto the island. At Point Salinas, an airport was begun by an armed six-hundred-man Cuban construction brigade. Ostensibly to improve tourist access to Grenada, the airfield, if finished, was designed for servicing Cuban and Soviet warplanes, reconnaissance craft, and supply operations.

Bishop took the world stage to proclaim his support for the Soviet invasion of Afghanistan. Huge pictures of the triumvirate of Castro, Ortega, and Bishop began to decorate Grenadan public buildings. On the island itself, the familiar apparatus of a Communist police state was erected, complete to an East German–designed personal security system—manned by Cuban bodyguards. In 1983 Bishop had an audience with Soviet foreign minister Andrei Gromyko, during which Bishop volunteered Grenada's help in keeping the "cauldron boiling," as Gromyko described Soviet policy toward the Caribbean.

During the Carter years many of us had marveled at his administration's obtuseness in ignoring the growing soviet threat to our interests in the Caribbean and Central America. The young left-wing intellectuals on the National Security Council staff, the central-front fundamentalists at the Pentagon, and the NATO-only leadership at the State Department had ignored totally the geopolitical shift of power against us in the Caribbean region. The open sympathy with the Sandinistas and refusal to recognize the existence of a genuine Communist insurgency in El Salvador were the handiwork of the NSC ideologues. The failure to perceive the tremendous shift that had taken place had grown tremendously in our oil trade, wherein the Caribbean and Central American oil imports, was a manifestation of the myopia of the State Department. But the dumbest omission of all was the failure of the "continentalists" at the Pentagon even to perceive what the Soviets were doing in the Caribbean and the impact of Soviet efforts upon our ability to carry out NATO defense. Fully 85 percent of army tonnage to Europe or the Middle East must be shipped from ports on the Gulf of Mexico. It must transit through either of only two exits into the Atlantic: the sixty-mile wide Straits of Florida, or the ninety-mile-wide Yucatán Channel.

While Congress noted the strategically meaningless Soviet "brigade" in Cuba, the Carter administration took no notice of the steady building by the Soviet Union of a naval force based in Cuba to attack our commerce and NATO resupply, and our growing oil dependence in the Caribbean. And there could be no doubt that the Soviets had built in Cuba an effective naval interdiction force of some five hundred tactical aircraft, more than a hundred missile and torpedo patrol boats, three frigates, and three modern diesel electric submarines. Moreover, they built the infrastructure to operate Soviet combatants and submarines in time of war. They began at once following the Sandinista victory in Nicaragua to build the same infrastructure to the same purpose in Nicaragua. The Soviets were building a military airfield and support infrastructure in Grenada, too, though on a smaller scale and at a more cautious pace, as befitted the circumstances.

Our geopolitical concern about these developments in the Caribbean area had been an important element in the formulation of the initial Reagan foreign and defense policy in 1981. As secretary of the navy I was particularly pleased that the president and all of his national security advisers shared our naval concern with the steady success of Soviet Caribbean policy.

Indeed, as early as March 1980, Reagan declaimed in a major campaign address the "totalitarian Marxist takeover of Grenada, where Cuban advisers are now training guerrillas. . . . Must we let Grenada, Nicaragua, and El Salvador all become additional Cubas, new outposts for Soviet combat brigades?"

While I wish it could be said that the global Reagan strategy gave rise to decisive action in Grenada, the Communists probably would still be there were it not for their own ineptitude. Over the opposition of Frank Carlucci, then deputy director of the CIA, the Carter administration had ended its last intelligence efforts in Grenada as part of its shriveling of the CIA. The fact is, we did not really have any on-scene intelligence sources on the island but had to depend solely on overhead pictures and other technical intelligence. That enabled the inveterate pollyannas in the CIA and the State Department, always hoping for the best, to argue against interpreting developments in Grenada as hostile to us. The British Foreign Office was even worse in this regard. Up to the very day of the invasion, its area "experts" had adamantly maintained to Prime Minister Margaret Thatcher that there was nothing on the island that justified intervention.

Ultimately, the Grenada crisis did not arise from American grand strategy or efforts to undo Bishop but from the inherent instability of the would-be Leninists on the island. When a government is ruled by conspirators who justify their actions according to an exacting creed, personal ambitions can take the guise of ideological disputation. In the end, the Grenadian Communists consumed themselves.

Bishop's ambitious plans ran afoul of both economic incompetence and the increasing reluctance of his Cuban and Soviet patrons to foot the ever-larger bills. In the spring of 1983 he was advised to mend relations with

Washington, which had excluded Grenada from its Caribbean Basin Initiative and blocked loans from the International Monetary Fund.

Nothing better illustrated this course of action than Bishop's sudden public announcements in early April of his plans for a new Constitution and free elections, even while he was completing a secret military pact with North Korea. The Black Caucus of the U.S. Congress was prevailed upon to invite him to the United States where, upon the advice of sympathetic congressional staff members, he depicted himself as a democratic social reformer. By all accounts, however, Bishop's meetings, including those with Judge Clark, the President's national security adviser, did not get him very far. The track record had worked against him. After four years of going Marxist alone, it was a little late to try to pose as a democrat who could be brought out of the closet with a little American money.

There are Grenadans and others who believe to this day that the populist Bishop had begun to rethink his political creed. Perhaps his colleagues suspected him of it, too. Whatever the case, when he returned to Grenada, a faction led by Coard and supported by Hudson Austin accused Bishop of insufficient zeal and demanded a shared leadership, to which Bishop very reluctantly agreed on September 23. But on October 10, after a brief trip to Eastern Europe, and to Cuba, where he received high respect from Fidel Castro, Bishop demanded a "review" of the agreement on joint leadership with Coard. Three days later, following tension-filled marathon meetings of the New Jewel's Political Bureau, he was arrested.

At this point the documents show that neither the Cubans nor the Soviets protested. However, events soon got out of control. After a week of growing tension on the island, Bishop was freed by a mob of three thousand, who then marched on the main military barracks at Fort Rupert. A massacre ensued, and on October 19 Bishop was killed. Austin seized control, issued orders to shoot opponents on sight, and broke communications links with the outside world. Two days later, on October 21, the Cuban government denounced the murder and demanded normalization of conditions in Grenada.

In mid-October the 22nd Marine Amphibious Unit (MAU) completed loading aboard amphibious ships and set sail to rendezvous with a carrier battle group led by the U.S.S. *Independence*, both bound for Lebanon. Since the early 1950's the United States has met a NATO commitment to keep a MAU and two carrier battle groups permanently operating on station in the Mediterranean. Each MAU and each battle group stays on station forward-deployed for about six months. Normally, they spend about six months building their capabilities in training off the U.S. East Coast before they deploy.

Normally a MAU consists of a completely self-sustaining force of up to two thousand combat marines, with tanks and armored personnel carriers, assault helicopters, attack helicopters, field artillery and self-propelled artillery pieces, and associated support equipment. With weeks of supplies and ammunition they are combat-loaded aboard one large helicopter carrier, either an LHA or an LPH, and a combination of amphibious assault ships, LSDs, LPDs, and LSTs. It was one of these normally deployed MAUs, the 32nd, that had been put ashore in Beirut originally. It had been replaced by the 24th, and now the 22nd MAU was to be the third to rotate ashore in Beirut.

On October 21, as a contingency, the president ordered the diversion of the MAU and the *Independence* battle group from their course to the Mediterranean to go instead to the Caribbean. The final decision on their use had not yet been made. The diversion of the Beirut-bound U.S. fleet toward Grenada, however, apparently convinced Castro that Cuba would not interfere, while dispatching a highly trained military expert, Colonel Pedro Tortolo Comas, onetime head of the Cuban military mission to Grenada and chief of staff of the army of the center in Cuba, to organize the resistance. Apprised of the danger, Austin promised a return to civilian rule. But it was too late.

Shocked by the violence and convinced that Grenada had become a threat to the neighborhood, four of the seven eastern Caribbean states appealed for British and American help. Based on the ostrich view of the Foreign Office, the British declined. On October 23, in the midst of his grief for the killed marines in Beirut, the president approved Operation Urgent Fury to rescue the thousand Americans on Grenada; to restore order; and, in coordination with the other Caribbean states, to bring democracy back to Grenada.

Once again the three service secretaries found themselves back at "Camp Swampy." This was the way our staffs described our position during every military crisis, like the cartoon general in the comic strip Beetle Bailey, who sits at his desk at Camp Swampy waiting for someone in the Pentagon to call. By law the Armed Forces Policy Council (AFPC) is the senior policy-making and crisis-management board for the secretary of defense. Unlike the JCS, it includes in addition to their membership the service secretaries and the under secretaries of defense, adding a civilian perspective to the views of the uniformed military during the conduct of hostilities or during crises.

Not once during my tenure was the AFPC used for that purpose. Whenever a crisis was at hand and the armed forces were about to be employed, or were being employed, the senior civilian authorities for each military department were institutionally excluded from the policy process. During the decision-making leading up to Grenada, and during the conduct of operations itself, the service secretaries depended on corridor gossip and the press to find out what was going on. The commandant of the marine corps and the chief of naval operations were formally involved and consulted, and they shared their thoughts and information with me after a fashion, but they, too, often were excluded from the final decision-making. This process worked in Grenada the way it worked in every one of the crises during my tenure. Once the president made the decision to launch Operation Urgent Fury, it was properly turned over to Cap to carry out. Cap, in turn, turned it over to the chairman of the JCS, General Jack Vessey, a highly experienced, able, commonsense army general. He in turn consulted with the chiefs and with the two unified commanders concerned, General Paul F. Gorman, commanding general, Southern Command, CINCSOUTH, located in Panama; and Admiral Wes McDonald, commander, Atlantic Command, CINCLANT. On the recommendation of CINCLANT, Vice Admiral Joseph Metcalf, commander of the Second Fleet, was designated the task force commander.

Military logic dictated the classic textbook marine amphibious and air assault of the island, supported by the *Independence* air wing and surface combatants, as the preferred option. Grenada was an almost perfect target for such an operation, and everything needed for rapid success was aboard the ships of the amphibious group and the carrier battle group.

In the event, however, two factors prevented such an operation from taking place. The first, understandably, was a near total lack of intelligence. Urgent Fury had to operate "in the dark" because there had not been enough time to work up detailed geographical data, and human agent intelligence—the most valuable kind—was totally absent. This bred caution.

The second, less understandably, was Pentagon ideology. No one on the 1,700-man joint staff dared to point out that, however much defense reformers may not have liked it, the fact was that the carrier battle group, with its air wing of 85 aircraft of 10 different types, and the MAU, were completely self-contained and sufficient for the task at hand. There was no need for the army and the air force; yet, under the prevailing doctrine of "It must be joint, it must be unified," the army rangers, the 82nd Airborne Division, air force C-130s to carry them, and the special operations Delta Force were included. The airport at Barbados was transformed overnight into a huge American supply depot to accommodate these forces.

The result was to array a force of some 15,000 U.S. troops, plus a contingent of 300 soldiers and police from 6 neighboring countries against the Grenadan

People's Revolutionary Army of 1,000 men, several thousand ill-trained Grenadan militia—and the Cubans. There were over 700 Cubans on the island, the largest number (636) in a construction crew finishing Point Salinas Airport, and all of whom had had militia training. Forty Cuban instructors assigned to the Grenadan Army, 43 regular soldiers, 44 women, and 18 diplomats rounded out the Cuban presence. There was also, of course, Colonel Pedro Tortolo Comas, sent by Castro to organize and control the Cuban resistance.

In retrospect, it was not a formidable opposition, but the size of the Cuban force, their training, and the Grenadans' will to fight were not known with certainty. Then there was the additional hazard of rescuing the American students while avoiding civilian bloodshed or a hostage situation. Finally, the only recognized legal authority on the island, the queen's governor, General Sir Paul Scoone, had to be released from house arrest.

So instead of a classically simple *coup de main*, which would have isolated the main Cuban force at Salinas and landed overwhelming numbers of America troops at every other key point, including the nearby capital of St. George's, the concocted "joint" plan called for small elite units from each of the services to attack separate critical points, while the marines were sent to the lightly defended Pearls Airfield at the far northern end of the island. The main army airborne force was assigned to the southern periphery, including Salinas. These tactics brought mixed results, perhaps the most important being that it allowed the Grenadans and the Cubans to hold off small U.S. forces before the main weight of the invasion could be brought to bear.

The lack of intelligence told at every point. One navy Seal team, paradropped offshore the night before, was never heard from again. Their fate remains a mystery. Another Seal team quickly located and captured the building in St. George's where Scoone was held and freed him, only to be pinned down by opposing forces until the marines captured the city the next day. Again, without proper intelligence information, another Seal team was assigned to capture Radio Grenada but attacked the wrong building.

We did know, however, the location of the two medical school campuses and the dormitories. In a perfectly executed move, the army rangers located and rescued some of the American medical students on the first day. Comic relief and American patriotism then combined when the students arrived back in the United States aboard air force transports. The TV networks covered it live; already some were openly contemptuous of the administration's action, which had been justified in part as a rescue of the students. As the first plane came to the ramp, the comments were "Now we'll get the *real* story." The first student

rushed down the steps as one commentator said, "Oh! He seems to have fallen—
why, no, he is actually kissing the ground!" The students supported the president's decision to use military force in Grenada with great and visible
enthusiasm—and they corroborated how dire the situation had become—to the
great and visible chagrin of the TV commentators and other nay-sayers.

The marines had little difficulty in securing Pearls against light opposition
on the first day.

The joint Delta commandos were assigned to capture Richmond Hill
Prison, but their daylight assault was repelled, with the loss of a helicopter. The
prison was secured after a bombing raid damaged the building, killing several
of the guards and frightening the rest away.

Most of the drama, however, involved some of the rangers and the 82nd
Airborne, assigned to take Salinas. They ran into the bulk of the Cuban force,
which put up fierce opposition under the command of Colonel Tortolo Comas.
Taking great care to avoid civilian casualties and not knowing the size of the
opposing force, the Americans proceeded very slowly. On the second day, the
twenty-sixth, Metcalf redeployed two companies of marines to help the 82nd.

The usual claque in Washington were quick to criticize the slow advance,
but the U.S. forces were under strict admonition to limit civilian casualties,
and the size of the opposing forces still was not known.

In any event, the drama did not last long. By the third day most of the
Cubans had been captured, and Richmond Hill Prison had been seized. On
the twenty-eighth the marines linked up with the main army units, and St.
George's was secured. Late that Wednesday afternoon the bulk of the American
students were secured as U.S. forces took control of the Grand Anse campus
of the medical school. U.S. forces also surrounded the Cuban embassy.
Colonel Tortolo Comas evaded capture, reaching safety in the Soviet embassy
with a speedy sprint that made him the butt of jokes when he was repatriated
to Cuba.[2] The Coards were captured in a coastal village. And large caches of
Soviet army equipment were discovered on the Mirabeau estate.

By November 3, after further mopping-up operations, Urgent Fury was
brought to a successful conclusion. Eighteen American servicemen lost their
lives, and 116 were wounded. Twenty-four Cubans had been killed, and 59
were wounded. Forty-five Grenadans died, and 337 were wounded.

Lessons Learned

Although the principal object of the operation was to rescue the American students and to show that we and our friends in the Caribbean could act in

defense of our own interests, there were important lessons to be learned from the military operation itself, some of which have been obscured by heresy and misinformation during and after the event.

The first lesson has to do with intelligence. Despite the fact that we as a nation have publicly congratulated ourselves for the past twenty years on the brilliance of our satellite and electronic intelligence, Grenada pointed out that we have the worst human intelligence network of any major power. We simply had no one on the scene in Grenada, even after several years of visible Communist penetration. Right up to the invasion itself we had to depend on intelligence, such as it was, shared from other nations; newspaper accounts; and most valuable of all, reports from returning tourists.

The second and most important lesson was that the current defense ideology of "jointness" hobbles our military effectiveness and, in the event of a major war with the Soviet Union, could well have grave consequences. In Grenada it made little if any difference in the outcome, but the confusion it imposed on the operation brought joy to our enemies and new grist for the cottage industry of defense reform.

Integrated joint operations in a large war often are precisely what is appropriate for a military operation. But the test should be pragmatism and common sense, not ideology. With a longer time to prepare, the army and the air force could undoubtedly have secured the island with an airborne assault, securing Point Salinas Airport, followed by C-5s bringing in the appropriate heavy armor and artillery. But the fact was that we happened to have a fully worked up MAU and carrier battle group ready to go. There was no need for additional forces. While in all things military more usually is better, in this case it brought the problems of lack of interoperability between land forces and sea forces. The task force commander on his flagship had difficulty communicating with the army and air force elements. Army forces on the ground had difficulty directing naval gunfire. There was the apocryphal story of the army major who supposedly used his credit card to call back to the United States to communicate with ships offshore, a story that was never confirmed. The most serious problem was the difficulty of communications between the army forces on the ground and the A-7s from the *Independence* providing close air support.

The lesson here, however, is not that the navy A-7s should be completely interoperable with U.S. Army forces. Only so much equipment can be crammed into a fighter plane, or carried by a combat soldier. That equipment and the radio types and frequencies should be optimized for the environment in which those forces normally will be employed. Naval carrier aircraft carry radios and train constantly in interoperating with U.S. Marine forces on the ground, and vice versa. Their radios are optimized for the marine environment at sea, and for the U.S. Marine Corps ashore. U.S. Army and U.S. Air Force equipment and frequencies and procedures are optimized for interoperability with the other fourteen NATO armed forces in Central Europe, and for the land environment, not the sea environment. That is as it should be. Why should a soldier whose operational contingencies require him to operate in places such as Central Europe, Korea, and the Middle East, possibly hundreds of miles from the nearest shore, be expected to have radios to be fully trained in the complex procedures of directing naval gunfire from ships lying offshore? The marines had no such problems in calling in naval gunfire, because they train in those procedures and have spotting teams with every unit.

Where land and sea forces interact there are established procedures and equipment for operating together, with the exceptions noted, and interoperating, as we do in NATO exercises every year. These special procedures and equipment, however, need some advance planning and time to be put in place. This was not available in Grenada. The lesson is that separate armed forces exist because separate geographical environments exist, and each service is optimized as it should be to operate in that environment. When planning a joint operation, the problems of interoperability should be realistically addressed and not ideologically ignored.

In point of fact, all four of the armed forces involved performed well, but faulty intelligence, planning haste, and the undue complications of jointness made the operation more difficult than it had to be. Eventually and in most cases, interoperability worked. With no preplanning, the marine helicopters moved smoothly and effectively to support the army forces in the South, after the marines had secured their positions. It was the army who ran into the more determined resistance from the Cubans; and the marine Cobra gunships flew many sorties, giving direct fire support to the army. The Marine CH-46 trooplift helicopters were similarly used for direct support of the army forces.

A firsthand account of some of the operations was given to me by Captain Timothy Howard, who had been wounded while providing close air support to the army forces in the South. He and his copilot, Captain Jeb Seagle, had returned repeatedly to the helicopter carrier to rearm and refuel, and on their fifth sortie of the day, as they were preparing to roll in for a strafing run, Howard felt an explosion. He looked down to find that a 23mm Cuban antiaircraft round had shattered his right leg and severed his right arm below the elbow. Another round had knocked Seagle unconscious in the front seat, and still another had disabled the engines. Having qualified in the Cobra, I can attest to how difficult a procedure it is to autorotate that helicopter in a power-out situation, with everything else under control. It is practiced constantly and requires perfect coordination of stick, collective, rudder pedals, and instrument scan. Now suddenly Howard found himself with an unconscious copilot, his right leg shattered, his right arm severed, and a complete loss of power. Incredibly, he managed to execute a successful autorotation. The Cobra hit the ground hard and rolled over. Howard was unable to extricate himself from the cockpit, but Seagle now regained consciousness and managed to pull him free. Howard ordered Seagle to go immediately to find help. Unfortunately, he was almost immediately killed by Cuban soldiers who arrived on the scene. In a disgusting breach of journalistic ethics, *Time* magazine published a full picture of his bullet-riddled body the following week.

After being pulled from the wreckage by Seagle, Howard was sitting on the ground when he suddenly noticed puffs of dirt exploding around him and between his feet. He quickly dragged himself to cover behind a tree, and the Cubans started to close in on him. At this point, as in a Western movie, a Marine CH-46 helicopter appeared on the scene, having spotted the Cobra on the ground. The Cubans started firing at the helicopter, but it had a door gunner with a fifty-caliber machine gun. He sprayed the Cubans soldiers, who immediately fled. The 'copter crew picked up Howard, stopped the bleeding, and flew him immediately out to the helicopter carrier, where he was put straight on the operating table.

Some weeks after I flew down to Camp Lejeune to visit with the wounded survivors from the Beirut disaster, and I paid a visit on the one patient from the Grenada operation, Captain Tim Howard. As I walked into his hospital room, he was lying on his back doing one-handed pull-ups on the frame over his bed. After introduction and small talk, Captain Howard said, "Mr. Secretary, please don't take this personally, but I'm going to be suing you." I said, "Oh?" He said, "Yes, the doctors have told me that under current navy regulations, I cannot stay in the marine corps, but must be retired on a medical disability. I won't accept that, and they told me that my only recourse is to sue the secretary of the navy." I told him that I didn't think that would prove to be necessary, but that I would await the findings of a medical board and personally review his case and talk to him directly. When he was released from the hospital months later, the medical board recommended immediate retirement on a complete disability. He was right-handed, and his right arm was gone from just below

the elbow, and the Cuban shell had shattered his thigh-bone and left a stub-
born long-term infection that necessitated keeping the wound open and drain-
ing. He was, however, utterly determined to stay in the corps and was making
steady progress. He had a strong wife and little girl, and they were all determined to stay a part of the marine corps. After talking with P. X. Kelley, we
both agreed that Howard had shown that he was capable of doing with one
arm what most people are not even able to do with two and that there certainly
would be a place for him in the corps. As a result, I ordered that he be kept
on active duty and assigned to Navy Department headquarters. He served
there for a year and a half, undergoing constant therapy at Bethesda Naval
Hospital, but putting in a full day very productively in the Pentagon. In an
unprecedented move, the marine corps then assigned him to a field command of the first operational remotely piloted vehicle unit, in Twenty-nine
Palms, California.

Helicopter losses overall were very high in the operation. Of the one hundred helicopters that took part, 30 percent were hit by enemy fire, and nine
were destroyed. There were no SA-7s or other sophisticated antiaircraft missiles or radar-guided guns. All the damage was done by visually aimed 57mm
and 23mm antiaircraft guns, and by hand-held rifles. In Vietnam we lost five
thousand helicopters over ten years. In Afghanistan the Stinger hand-held,
heat-seeking missile used by the Mujaheddin was devastating to Soviet helicopters. In my judgment we will see similar helicopter attrition rates in any
future conflicts.

One of the more controversial decisions of the Grenada operation was that
of the task force commander, Vice Admiral Joe Metcalf, to exclude all media
from the operation until the island had been secured. It was his strong belief
that without a system of censorship such as existed in World War II, the presence of TV and press media reporting in real time to the United States would
compromise operational security and help the enemy. He believed that it was
hard enough as task force commander to keep a clear picture of what was
going on and that hundreds of media would greatly complicate his operation. He believed, moreover, that providing transportation and security for
the media would needlessly burden his forces to an unacceptable level.
Once it was secured, some four hundred media representatives descended
on the island.

The media never forgave Joe Metcalf for his decision. They pounced on
the first opportunity to attack and discredit him. When returning from
Grenada in a navy transport, he had his staff bring back some captured

AK-47s, which they had liberated for souvenirs. I have never met or heard of a victorious commander, back to Alexander the Great, who did not do something of the same sort. Nevertheless, this was a violation of Defense Department regulations, and the media pilloried him for weeks on the seven o'clock news and in newspapers throughout the land. That will teach him to mess with the fourth estate's rights.

There was an interesting footnote to the operation concerning the disposal of the Cuban prisoners of war. The State Department and the JCS were extremely anxious not to treat the Cuban soldiers and other Soviet bloc "advisers" as prisoners of war but to return them to Castro and their other commanders without delay. Whether they feared that retaining these characters in our custody would needlessly distress our relations with those nations or that turning them over to the Grenadans might have grisly results, I do not know.

I do know this: In 1979 Castro had expelled hundreds of hard-core felons, murderers, and assorted undesirables to the United States in the Mariel Boatlift. He bragged that he had "flushed his toilet on the United States," and so he had. After sorting out the noncriminal elements, the remainder had been put in detention by the federal government. The navy recommended to Cap that the criminals be returned on the same planes with the Cuban POWs that Castro wanted back so badly. Cap liked the idea, but the State Department and the joint chiefs were horrified. They threw up so many bureaucratic obstacles that we finally gave up. Five years later and many millions of dollars of U.S. taxpayers' money later, they were still in detention, and the State Department finally got around to negotiating an agreement for their return to Castro. This led to the riots in their place of detention in Atlanta, Georgia, in November 1987, and as of this writing, their fate has yet to be decided.

There was also some unhappy diplomatic fallout between the United States and Britain over the Grenada operation. Unlike in the Falklands, we and the Brits did not work together at any level. The Foreign Office had persuaded Mrs. Thatcher that no serious interest was at stake in Grenada; that no British citizens were in real danger following the Bishop murder; and that, in any event, only a British ship should be made available to evacuate those who wished to leave. Grenada's neighbors did not share this view, and they sought American rather than British help.

That was insulting, no doubt. To compound it, neither Mrs. Thatcher nor the queen, whose governor, Sir Paul Scoone, was the legal authority on the island, were informed of the impending operation. (The prime minister was reportedly dining with the U.S. ambassador when she was informed of the U.S.

move.) Sir Geoffrey Howe, the British foreign secretary, told the House of Commons the day before the assault that no such action was to be expected. These were embarrassing and unnecessary lapses for two countries so close to one another—to say the least.

The most important lesson of the Grenada operation, however, was that it was a success. It set out with a proclaimed objective to rescue the American citizens, and the unproclaimed and equally important objective of ending the Communist takeover. Both were achieved with what in the world of military operations was minimal loss of life. There were mistakes made by some units, and a dismal failure to provide the task force with adequate intelligence. The unnecessary "jointness" imposed without adequate time to plan caused many inefficiencies. But every American was saved, the Cuban and other Communist soldiers and advisers there were ejected, and a democratic regime was returned to the island. We had decided to do something, and we had done it. Small-scale though it might have been, it sent a message of resolve to friends and adversaries around the world

John F. Lehman, Jr., introducing Ronald Reagan at the 1984 commencement of the U.S. Naval Academy in Annapolis, Maryland. *Harold J. Gerwein, U.S. Navy*

Breakfast with Vice President George Bush, April 4, 1987. *White House photograph*

The U.S.S. *Iowa* firing its Mark 7 16-inch 50-caliber guns off the starboard side on August 15, 1984, in the Caribbean. *Jeff Hilton, U.S. Navy*

The only navy aircraft that was never paid for. This two-seat F/A-18 was built for the U.S. Navy free of charge in 1982 to replace the one that crashed at the Farnborough Air Show. *Harold J. Gerwein, U.S. Navy*

Secretary of the Navy John F. Lehman, Jr., with Chinese Minister of Defense Zhang Ai Ping during a visit to China, August 1984. *Harold J. Gerwein, U.S. Navy*

John F. Lehman, Jr. (*at left*), negotiating with Israeli Defense Minister Yitzak Rabin (*fourth from right.*) *Harold J. Gerwein, U.S. Navy*

At the South Pole November 1986: (*left to right*) Brigadier General Mike McQueen, U.S. Marine Corps; Captain Jack Jensen, U.S. Navy; Captain Joe Prueher, U.S. Navy; Secretary of the Navy John F. Lehman, Jr.; Lieutenant Commander Rick Hess, U.S. Navy; Roger Duter; and Captain Mac Williams, U.S. Navy. *Harold J. Gerwein, U.S. Navy*

Near the North Pole, April 1986: Secretary of the Navy John F. Lehman, Jr.; Lieutenant General Ben LeBailly, U.S. Air Force; Captain Joe Prueher, U.S. Navy; and an unidentified polar bear sentry. The sail and diving planes of their submarine are showing through the ice. *Harold J. Gerwein, U.S. Navy*

Naval exercises during which the author did his annual reserve flying: *Above:* Aboard the U.S.S. *America* flying strikes from deep within the Norwegian fjords, Exercise Northern Wedding 1985; *At Right, Above:* flying an A-6 past the pyramids of Egypt in Exercise Bright Star, 1984; *At Right, Below:* debriefing a flight in a Russian MIG 21, with Egyptian Air Force, 1980. *U. S. Navy and Curt Winsor, Jr.*

John F. Lehman, Jr., aboard the U.S.S. *John F. Kennedy* in New York Harbor during Liberty Weekend, July 4, 1986. *Harold J. Gerwein, U.S. Navy*

Dr. Robert Ballard and the secretary of the navy testing the waters at the opening of "The Living Sea Pavilion" at Walt Disney World's EPCOT Center in 1986, Orlando, Florida, while son John F. Lehman III watches from the dry safety of the observation room. *Photograph courtesy of Walt Disney Productions, 1986*

Awarding Dr. Robert Ballard the honorary title of "Bottom Gun" upon his return from the navy-sponsored, successful exploration of S.S. *Titanic* in 1986. *Harold J. Gerwein, U.S. Navy*

With actor Tom Cruise in May 1986, at the premier of Top Gun, whose accurate depiction of naval aviation, with the help of the U.S. Navy, greatly contributed to its box-office success. *Photograph courtesy of Greg F. Mathieson*

Farewell dinner, April 1987, hosted by General P. X. Kelley (*second from left*), commandant of the U.S. Marine Corps. *Photograph courtesy of U.S. Marine Corps*

The Lehman family, Liberty Weekend, July 4, 1986: Barbara and John with Alexandra, nine, John III, seven, and Grace, three. *Harold J. Gerwein, U.S. Navy*

Chapter 10

Operations in and over Lebanon

The Setting

On a sunny afternoon in early May 1983, Dr. Harvey Sicherman, a consultant and close friend, offered me a truly alarming analysis of recent events in Lebanon. He had just returned from a trip to the Middle East, convinced that Israel was going to withdraw its troops from the mountains overlooking Beirut. When that happened, he argued, the Syrians and their local allies would attempt to overthrow the pro-American government of President Amin Gemayel. We both knew that between Gemayel and the Syrians stood only the Lebanese Army (unhappily called the "LAF") . . . and eighteen hundred U.S. Marines.

Sicherman's analysis was correct. It meant that our marines would now become a major target, fulfilling the doleful prediction that the commandant of the marine corps and I had made when they were put ashore the year before. The marines were assigned to a peacekeeping mission, a "presence," as part of an American, British, French, and Italian multinational force put in Beirut after the 1982 Lebanon War. What would we do now if the marines were attacked?

As secretary of the navy, I had had little to do with making our foreign policy, and even less to do with our specific purposes in Lebanon. The ferocious struggles for turf during the Reagan administration among the State Department, the Defense Department, and the NSC had already made Kissinger's Byzantine plots of the 1970s charmingly innocent by comparison.

Now here I was face-to-face with the most disagreeably frustrating aspect of what is otherwise the best job in Washington, secretary of the navy and the marine corps. For the entire six years I was in the Pentagon, Weinberger never formally discussed operational decisions with the service secretaries. He did, however, discuss them with the four service chiefs and the chairman of the JCS at least once a week. The most important part of the decision-making process is in fact the daily meeting between the chairman of the JCS and the secretary of defense. This vital daily access of the chairman has been zealously guarded for many years by the office of the military assistant to the secretary. That person, always an outstanding officer of two- or three-star rank, has charge of the secretary of defense's schedule. His most important, but unwritten, duty is to guard the access of the chairman of the JCS to the secretary of defense. Because Congress has given the chairman now dominant power in the assignment and promotions of senior general offices, the civilian secretary's military assistant can surely not risk the disfavor of the chairman.

Civilian secretaries of defense come and go, but the military system is forever. Thus, while Congress and the American people tend to hold the service secretaries accountable for what happens when their services are employed, they rarely have any real influence on decisions to employ them.

Having been in office little more than two years in the spring of 1983, I assumed that even though the service secretaries were not in the know about what we were doing in Beirut, there must be a brilliantly conceived—and of necessity, very secret—set of contingency plans for the ominous clouds gathering around our marines ashore. In fact, there was no strategy and there were no contingency plans for this rapidly developing "worst case." As unfortunately happens all too often with our bloated, layered bureaucracy in Washington, we had fallen behind events and were merely improvising reactions. Therein lay a tale that, when it was finished, wrecked the president's entire Middle East policy and cost the lives of 241 young Americans. Our military's most basic structure, the chain of command, was proved hopelessly ineffective in a scathing inquiry that laid the blame where it belonged. Because of the inconvenience of these findings, the inquiry was ignored and quickly buried and forgotten, and the stage set for a repetition of failure, which came inevitably just months later.

Lebanon is one of those curious, half-misbegotten countries formed in equal parts from imperial ambition, ethnic rivalry, and religious strife. Historically an appendage of French imperialism in the Levant, Lebanon gained its independence in 1943 but remained heavily influenced by French politics and culture. From the beginning, Lebanon lived a risky life. Its more powerful neighbor Syria, which as a province of the Ottoman Empire had included Lebanon, never recognized it as a sovereign state. In Lebanon itself, a bizarre national pact assigned the central government posts according to creed and ethnicity. On the basis of the 1936 census, which found Christians in the majority, the Christians dominated the state.

For a brief, golden period, Lebanon prospered because it was too weak to endanger its neighbors and because it was assumed that Lebanese independence would be upheld against external threats by France or some other power. That other power turned out to be the United States. In 1958 when, in the aftermath of the Suez fiasco, Nasser's anti-Western forces threatened to undo Lebanon, President Eisenhower landed twelve thousand marines to steady the Lebanese regime. It worked.

What could not work, however, was the undoing of the internal balance through Muslim population growth and the appearance of the PLO. In 1970, while at the NSC, I had lived through the dramatic events that drove the PLO from Jordan and defeated a Syrian invasion. U.S.-Israeli cooperation, which between them mustered the region's best air force and the striking power provided by four U.S. carriers sent to the Mediterranean by Nixon and Kissinger, offered crucial support for King Hussein. Evicted from Jordan, Arafat had regrouped his forces in the refugee camps that dotted southern Lebanon and the shantytowns around Beirut that sheltered Palestinian refugees from Israel's war of independence two decades earlier. Helped by Syrian ruler Hafiz Al-Assad and the Soviet Union, the PLO soon outgunned the modest Lebanese Army. Within five years, Beirut's authority had ceased to exist in the South as the PLO and Israel exchanged blows across the border. Even more ominously, Arafat had begun to aid those Lebanese factions that wished to undo the national pact of 1943.

When the Lebanese Civil War erupted in 1975, the PLO and its Druze and Shiite allies soon acquired the upper hand. Again the appeal went out for U.S. help. But in 1975, Washington could not help. The best we were able to do, with Israeli agreement, was to acquiesce when Syria intervened on behalf of the Christians. Tacit rules with Israel called "red lines" regulated Syria's penetration south and its level of arms. In this way, the PLO was checked.

By 1981, however, these arrangements, too, were breaking down. The Syrians, isolated and fearful after the Camp David accords secured peace between Egypt and Israel, made common cause with the PLO. Israel's government, under Prime Minister Menachem Begin, had conducted extensive armed sweeps into Lebanon while solidifying an alliance with the Maronite Catholics, especially Bashir Gemayel, the commander of the strongest Christian militia, the Phalange. Both border incidents and internal tension rose. Finally, in May 1981, when the Syrians and the Phalange clashed, Israel planes shot down Syrian helicopters. The Syrians promptly moved SAM batteries into the Bekaa Valley, threatening Israel's air reconnaissance over Lebanon.

As Americans, we were sympathetic to Lebanese independence. Through private groups, notably the American University of Beirut, we had nurtured generations of well-educated Lebanese and other Arabs, many of them at the forefront of their professions. But we did not want a war that wrecked Lebanon, that risked engaging the U.S.S.R. on Syria's part, or that damaged the delicate peace we had brokered between Israel and Egypt only a few years earlier. We were also engaged in the tricky business of rebuilding our prestige and power in the region after the disastrous revolution that had toppled our friend the shah, putting in his place the fanatic Ayatollah Khomeini.

Between the missile crisis of May 1981 and the Israeli invasion of Lebanon in June 1982, Washington tried in vain to delay the inevitable. Ambassador Philip Habib, President Reagan's special negotiator, bore most of the diplomatic burden during this period, under the policy direction of my old NSC boss Al Haig.

When Haig had been proposed for secretary of state, he was opposed by some because of his hard-line views, and by others because of his close ties to Kissinger, but the president picked Haig anyway. Haig proved his skill as a diplomat by securing a cease-fire on the border while trying at the United Nations and through local governments to defuse the buildup of forces. Time and again Haig dissuaded Begin and his defense minister, Ariel Sharon, from a full-scale attack on the PLO in response to provocation. But diplomacy was ultimately of no avail in the face of brutal logic. Assad wanted to dominate Lebanon and to harass Israel; Arafat wanted to harass Israel and needed to dominate Lebanon to do it; and Israel wanted to crush the PLO, which meant somehow lifting both Arafat's and Assad's domination of Lebanon in the process.

Israeli tanks rolled on June 6, 1982, following the attempted assassination of the Israeli ambassador to the United Kingdom, and an exchange of air and artillery blows with the PLO. From the sidelines, I watched two dramas unfold: Israel's expansion of the war to bloody the Syrians and besiege Beirut; and Al Haig's battle to preserve a coherent policy while pitted against elements in the

State Department, the White House, and the Defense Department, who were outraged by the Israeli attack and wished to redirect U.S. policy to punish her.

Israel's military success had clearly dealt a heavy defeat to American enemies, among them the PLO, Syria, and by implication, the U.S.S.R. The Israeli Air Force's successful application of American technology to destroy the SAMs and over a hundred Syrian MiGs without loss held important lessons for our own military tactics. But the diplomatic outcome hinged on the removal of the PLO from Beirut, the withdrawal of all foreign forces, and the reestablishment of an authoritative Lebanese government. For a brief moment this seemed possible. On June 25, 1982, however, the embattled Haig resigned as the administration thoroughly undercut him by offering mixed signals about its intentions. The PLO stalled for time, and in the ensuing Israeli bombardments, the fragile Lebanese political coalition pulled together by Haig and Habib collapsed. There was now no force in Beirut that stood for Lebanon.

Into this void the United States, supported by London, Paris, and Rome, proposed to put a multinational force. As originally conceived, it was to be one element in a far-reaching agreement that provided for the withdrawal of *all* foreign forces—PLO, Israeli, and Syrian. But with Haig's departure, its scope was narrowed. The president's announcement on July 6, which I first read in the newspapers, that the United States would participate in such a force was pitched to a temporary supervision of PLO withdrawal. Neither Assad nor Brezhnev in Moscow believed, however, that the Western military presence would be temporary. Though strongly at odds over each other's performance during the crisis, the Syrians and the Soviets now saw a common threat. They resolved their quarrel, and their newfound harmony took the form six months later of an even more formidable Soviet-supplied air defense for the Syrians.

In the third week of August, when Ambassador Habib finally achieved agreement to the PLO's departure, eight hundred U.S. Marines, along with eight hundred French troopers, four hundred Italians, and a two-hundred-man British logistics unit, landed in Beirut to supervise Arafat's withdrawal. This multinational force was supposed to stay in Beirut for one month, until after the inauguration of Bashir Gemayal, who had been elected the new president of Lebanon. But on September 10, at the urging of Cap Weinberger, the marines were withdrawn. Four days later, Bashir was blown up by a bomb universally believed to have been planted by the Syrians. Despite its earlier pledge not to do so, the Israeli Army entered West Beirut, in the name of "restoring order." Instead, the Phalange militia revenged themselves on the Palestinians in what became known as the Sabra and Shatilla massacres, on September

16–18. This led the United States, France, and Italy to return their contingents, and on September 29, the 32nd Marine Amphibious Unit, twelve hundred strong, landed in Beirut, to take up positions near Beirut International Airport between the Israeli forces and West Beirut. Then, in early November, the 24th MAU replaced the 32nd. Later that month, marine mobile training teams began to instruct the Lebanese Army in the hopes of making it a true fighting force.

The Mission

What was the mission of our marines? The JCS on September 23 ordered General Rogers, who as Commander in Chief, Europe (CINCEUR) was also the theater commander for the Lebanese operation, as follows: "To establish an environment which will permit the Lebanese armed forces to carry out their responsibilities in the Beirut area."[1] The airport was chosen for the marines' deployment apparently not only because of its international significance but also as a buffer line against the Israelis. From the military point of view, however, the position depended upon friendly control of the mountains overlooking the airport and, of course, a friendly attitude by the civilian population — people already experienced in seven years of the most brutal civil war, and many of whom opposed the Maronites and had access to significant arms. The marines were instructed to be a "presence" — to show themselves, to be helpful, and to react only in self-defense. Eventually this was codified in "rules of engagement" that Colonel Timothy Geraghty, the marine commander at the airport, interpreted to prohibit our men even from keeping rounds in their rifle chambers.

The time allowed for the marine mission was supposed to be sixty days but later became indefinite. Meanwhile, a fatal diplomatic blunder was in the making. Washington struggled exclusively to gain a Lebanese-Israeli agreement providing for the withdrawal of Israeli forces, but the Syrians, who had no intentions of withdrawing, were free of U.S. pressure during the period of their greatest military weakness. Assad was given a critical breathing space to rearm with Soviet help during the fall and winter of 1982 while Washington remained supremely confident that Damascus appreciated our "good offices" and our good intentions. But it was not 1958, when twelve thousand marines with a combat mission overawed sundry irregulars and when more skillful Lebanese leaders, unlike Amin Gemayel, Bashir's older brother, who was elected president in his stead, knew how to reweave the delicate threads of the national pact. It was 1982–83, when war-hardened guerrilla forces were still at large, when Syria was regaining its military balance with a new Soviet air-defense system.

Even worse, we and our ally Israel were engaged in a dangerous quarrel. It was painful to hear of incidents between the marines and the Israelis; a new low was reached when on February 2, 1983, Captain Charles B. Johnson had to draw his pistol at three Israeli tanks that refused to stop at his company checkpoint. There was an unseemly quarrel, too, over exchanges of data and military lessons from the war. This atmosphere began to affect plans for U.S.-Israel strategic cooperation, in which the U.S. Navy and the IDF both had a considerable stake.

Finally, in May 1983, Israel and Lebanon reached an agreement, cobbled together by Secretary of State Shultz himself. Not surprisingly, the Syrians denounced it. Astonishingly, the United States had failed to secure Israel's pledge to remain in the Shouf Mountains overlooking Beirut; there was no plan for an orderly turnover of Israel's positions to the Lebanese Army, which could not come to grips even with the problems of security in the capital. Washington's desire to see a rapid Israeli withdrawal now led to the helter-skelter return of the mountains to Druze and Syrian control, which threatened to put our marines in the airport below in an impossible military situation. It was an incredible malfeasance. The JCS and the State Department/Department of Defense bureaucracy had become fixated on the Israelis as the immediate opponents and ignored the question of who would replace them.

An even more ominous event had occurred on April 18, 1983, when a bomb carried by a pickup truck destroyed the U.S. embassy in Beirut, with heavy loss of life. This was a new factor. The bomb itself, a gas-enhanced explosive, bore the marks of very professional preparation. We were now faced by a deadly coalition: the Syrians, the Iranians, and Lebanese Shiites.

The Shiites, the most downtrodden of the Lebanese religious groups, were clustered in the poorest areas of South Beirut. Some of them were inspired by Khomeini's propaganda. A thousand Iranian revolutionary guards had been allowed by the Syrians to garrison the ancient town of Baalbek in the Bekaa during the Lebanon War. Money and munitions now flowed from the Iranian embassy in Beirut through Baalbek to the Shiite Hezbollah or "Party of God" in Beirut. The bombing had all the earmarks of an Iranian suicide attack facilitated by the Syrians.

At this juncture we made the mistake that doomed our entire policy. Since ancient times the eastern Mediterranean has been an area of constant shifting, intrigue, strife, and civil war. The only powers to maintain stability for any length of time had done so with *force majeure* and armed might. In modern times the Israelis have survived against the constant attacks of terrorism by a brutal policy of *lex talionis*, an eye for an eye. The Reagan administration prided itself on the realism and toughness of its national security policy and knew well the perils of stepping ashore in Beirut. Now the inevitable had happened and the very American embassy itself was destroyed, along with seventeen Americans and fifty other persons. If we were to maintain a serious role, then we had to retaliate against those who did it. We did not. We shrank from it and dithered and had study groups and interdepartmental meetings for days and weeks until finally the bureaucracy pushed and squeezed it down the "memory hole." Down with it went Ronald Reagan's and America's credibility in the Middle East.

We in the navy assumed that some great retaliatory plans had to be in the works. But as days stretched into weeks, it became clear there would be no response. That meant to me, at least, that we would soon be facing the "worst case": The marines would be put in the line of fire between emboldened radical factions who had lost any fear of retaliation from the United States.

The environment around the airport deteriorated steadily after the embassy bombing. During the summer, artillery and small-arms fire started falling on the compound.

In August I traveled out to the task force to do some active duty for training, flying with VA-65 aboard the *Eisenhower*. The *Eisenhower* had temporarily detached from the flotilla off Beirut to take part in Operation Bright Star, an extensive joint exercise with Egyptian forces. While the JCS bureaucracy tended to view Israel as a hostile power, they held no such prejudice against Arab states and had done a superb job in setting up what was one of the best military training exercises of this decade. Day after day throughout the month of August our air force and navy crews were able to fly realistic missions against Egyptian MiGs, F-16s, and Phantoms, and were able to attack training targets all over Egypt. On one of these I flew a particularly interesting training flight. The *Eisenhower*'s wing commander CAG, Commander Joe Prueher, a squadronmate of mine from the olden days (later to become CINPAC, and then ambassador to China), and I launched off the *Eisenhower* with a load of four Mark 83 thousand-pound bombs. We flew for one hundred fifty miles to our coast-in point, dropping down to two hundred feet as we streaked across Aboukir Bay, east of Alexandria, the site of Nelson's great victory over Napoleon's navy in 1798. High overhead several flights of Egyptian F-16s, under the direction of a U.S. Air Force AWACS radar plane, were trying to intercept us. As we hugged the deck, we could see them pass overhead, missing us completely, as the sheep and goats scattered in every direction on the Nile Delta farms below. We streaked across half a dozen branches of the Nile and suddenly were over the desert. In a short time the Suez Canal was off the port wing, and I could see the exact spot just south of Ismailia where I stood in December 1973 watching the Israeli tanks drive back across the pontoon bridge across the canal after their defeat of the Egyptian Third Army. I had returned to that spot a second time in February 1980, this time as a guest of the Egyptian Army. It was remarkable to me how similar the Egyptian accounts of the battle were to those I had heard from the Israelis. In both accounts the Egyptian Army had acquitted themselves very well indeed.

And here I was again, in the same spot for the third time. What strange coincidences there are in this business.

Heading due south, we flew over the Gulf of Suez, staying just fifty feet over the water to avoid radar detection. Turning west again, we crossed the desert bluffs and flew nap-of-the-earth across the most desolate, mountainous desert southeast of Cairo. Suddenly we hit the narrow green ribbon of agriculture on both sides of the Nile just east of Fayoum, and we headed due north. Soon, off the starboard wing, was the famous stepped pyramid of Cheops. And then we were at Giza, and we whizzed past the pyramids at five hundred feet. We then banked west and streaked off into the desert for our target, Wadi Natrun, an Egyptian air base destroyed by the Israelis in the 1967 war and that now was used as a live ordnance bombing target. I had flown through this very airspace in February 1980 in my first and only flight in a two-seat MiG-21, courtesy of the Egyptian Air Force. I was amazed to see, during our flight out across the western desert, ancient ruins of whole towns and small cities. How could anyone have ever survived in this barren desert?

By this time the sun had just set and, while the sky was still light, the desert floor was in darkness. I quickly set for a radar bombing run with the final hand-off to our forward-looking infrared targeting system. We cranked up the speed to five hundred knots. The cross hairs were smack on the buildings in the aircraft parking area along the runway, and on command of the computer we did a smooth 3G (three times the force of gravity) climb. On the way up, the A-6 lurched as the four bombs were released by computer one after the other. We completed the wingover and then did a sharp turn back to watch the explosion. It was too dark to see the target, but suddenly we saw *wham, wham, wham, wham*, four big orange fireballs in a row.

Back aboard the *Eisenhower* I flew by helicopter to each of the ships in the task force off Beirut. Without exception every one of the captains of the ships

I visited expressed deep concern that their current operating procedures left them extremely vulnerable to potential terrorist attack. To provide support to the marines ashore, the destroyers and amphibious ships remained very close in, from three to five miles offshore. We had intelligence reports that the Iranian-supported factions had acquired fast-speed boats and planned suicide attacks against the ships. There were also reports that the Syrians were training revolutionary guards to fly light planes on suicide missions. I was surprised to learn that very few of the ships had any defenses against such potential attacks. Because of the lack of funds throughout the 1970s, fewer than 10 percent of our ships had had close-in defense weapons installed. As outlined in chapter 8, when we first learned this during our Falklands lessons-learned exercise, the CNO and I immediately ordered a major acceleration of the installation of these systems, but because of the time lags involved there still was no visible effect on the ships I visited. The captains of the amphibs were particularly concerned because their procedures required them to anchor at night, making them sitting ducks for potential attackers. They all said they had expressed their concerns up the chain of command but had never seen any results. When I talked to Vice Admiral Ed Martin, our Sixth Fleet commander, he said he had shared these concerns and had asked for action up the chain of command but had never gotten any responses. I promised them all I would take this up and get action as soon as I got back to Washington.

On August 20 I took a helicopter into Beirut International Airport. We picked up the marine commander, Colonel Timothy Geraghty, and took off again to do an airborne tour of the area to look at the geography. We could see the Israeli tanks in their positions on the road heading south, and Colonel Geraghty expressed some satisfaction that there were rumors the Israelis finally would be withdrawing. He was concerned, however, that no arrangements had been made for an orderly turnover of the Israeli positions in the high terrain overlooking the airport. As we circled overhead he pointed out to me how vulnerable they would be if those commanding heights fell into the hands of a force hostile to our marines. We then landed and toured the marine positions at the airport, although I did not see the BLT headquarters building, where most of the marines were housed. Colonel Geraghty and his staff were concerned about the danger to our men from sniper fire and artillery attack.

There was no reason to question the specific security arrangements at the marine compound, and Colonel Geraghty had expressed to me his satisfaction with the rules of engagement he had to operate under, given the "peace-keeping" nature of his mission.

On the theory that the lack of a preplanned schedule was our best security, we got into a couple of unmarked cars and drove into town to visit the ambassador's residence and the downtown area. We went first to the site of the embassy that had been bombed in April. It was an incredible sight to see such a huge, multistory, concrete building totally collapsed by one bomb. The waterfront area looked like the old newsreels of Berlin after years of bombing and then street fighting at the end of the war. There were skirmishes going on in various parts of the city almost daily between one faction and another. And yet, life was bustling all around. How people could continue to pursue their day-to-day lives in such a place astounds me still. Whatever their reasons for being there, I could see none for the United States continuing its presence there.

I returned to Washington with my views unchanged, that it was a mistake to put the marines in there in the first place, and a compounding mistake to leave them there in such a situation. That did not change the fact that we had, however, to deal with the problem of the security of our ships. Watkins agreed to have orders issued through the operational chain of command to do the following:

1. Stop the practice of anchoring ships. Instead, keep them moving at all times.
2. Increase surveillance and vigilance against the small-boat threat.
3. Take measures to assign as combatant ships only those equipped with cruise missile defenses, which must include the Phalanx Gatling gun system.
4. Withdraw the unarmed amphibious ships over the horizon at night when not required for operations.

We further agreed that we should send the battleship *New Jersey*, currently engaged on its shakedown cruise in the Pacific, immediately to join the task force off Beirut. The *New Jersey*'s sixteen-inch and five-inch guns, able to deliver eight hundred tons of accurate fire in thirty minutes, were exactly what was needed to deter attack on our marine positions if hostile forces gained control of the Shouf Mountains. The nineteen thousand tons or armor of the *New Jersey* would enable her to stand close in to shore despite the dangers of land-based cruise missiles, suicide boats, and artillery.

The CNO reported back to me the next day that the orders had been sent and changes would be carried out immediately. He reported, however, that the European Command strongly opposed bringing the *New Jersey* into the theater and that the other members of the JCS also were skeptical.

The next day I took up the matter with Cap Weinberger, and he completely agreed with me. He said, however, that this was a matter for the chairman,

General Jack Vessey, to handle. Cap usually deferred to the chairman of the JCS and the collective JCS view on any matters involving military operations.

In the case of the measure that Watkins had directed be done to correct the vulnerability of the ships, they got lost in staffing in the European Command bureaucracy. Ironically, three days after the bombing in Beirut, the response to his initiative came back from the European headquarters. Watkins and I were infuriated. The message essentially said that things were in just fine shape, and not a single corrective action was needed!

With regard to sending the *New Jersey*, the opposition was particularly exasperating. Neither Jim Watkins nor I were ever given a military explanation for the opposition to sending the *New Jersey*, which stemmed from the European Command. We simply could not credit the rumors that SACEUR's dislike of the maritime strategy and antagonism to the battleship program weighed more heavily than the security of the marines. Yet by early September Watkin's and my recommendation had simply been dismissed out of hand, without even a chance to discuss the merits.

In frustration I appealed to Weinberger. I told him that the marines wanted the battleship support and that everybody in the navy chain of command felt it would dramatically increase the security of the force and reduce its vulnerability. Moreover, sending such a high-visibility capital ship certainly would underline the seriousness of intent of the president if that's what was desired. In addition to her ability to give direct support to the marines, I argued strongly that if we ever stopped dithering and decided to retaliate against the Syrians for the destruction of our embassy, the *New Jersey* was the perfect vehicle for retaliation. Given the formidable Syrian air defenses and the need to limit collateral damage, the likelihood of losing aircraft, men, and POWs in air strikes was very high. There were no such limitations to the battleship, and with proper air spotting, the *New Jersey*'s sixteen-inch guns could cover virtually all of the Syrian targets of interest with accuracy as good as or better than that of our precision bombers.

Cap agreed, and after discussing it with Judge Clark recommended it to the president. Several days later the president ordered that the *New Jersey*, then in Central American waters as part of her shakedown cruise, be sent immediately to Beirut. The battleship drew near to the battle-torn Lebanese capital on September 24, at a crucial moment.

The Attacks

In July Bud McFarlane, while serving as assistant national security adviser, had been abruptly appointed to replace Phil Habib. When McFarlane came to Lebanon in September, our forces at the airport had already been fired upon by rockets, artillery, and mortars. Two marines were killed on August 29, and on August 31, marine patrols were stopped. Two more of our men were then killed on September 6. Meanwhile, the Lebanese Army was fighting for its life in the small hill town of Suk Al Gharb, on the edge of the Shouf.

Bud himself came under heavy fire on September 16, while at the ambassador's residence. Finally, our ships were instructed to retaliate. Effective naval gunfire plus the arrival of the *New Jersey* on September 25 gave pause to the escalation. Intense negotiations then produced a cease-fire, which went into effect two days later.

There were those who claimed that these actions cost us the protection of our neutral status, ranging the United States conclusively on the side of the Christians so that the marines were seen by all factions as combatants—and therefore fair game. But that perception was in fact well developed long before September, everywhere except in the White House and the State Department. Between August 28 and September 6, four marines had been killed and twenty-eight wounded in action. Thus the marines were *already under attack* well before we returned fire.[2] As for the policy of neutrality, it was difficult to understand what our mission could be, if it was not to support the legal Lebanese government, however hopeless.

Congressional pressure also played a part in this clinging to the illusion of neutrality. At one point, in a burst of clarity, the White House issued a statement saying that the forces were there "to take what steps are necessary in support of the duly constituted government of Lebanon." After opponents in Congress then pointed out that this was in violation of the War Powers Act, the administration hastily revised its position and said that the forces were there solely "in support of the multinational force and protection of U.S. lives." I was unable to keep up with the changing line, and at a breakfast meeting with reporters I described what was in fact the case, that "we will be providing supporting fire to Lebanese forces and it isn't linked to incoming fire to the marines." The next day the White House issued a statement contradicting me, saying that "the secretary's assertions were incorrect," that "whatever we do is in support of the marines." I was ordered by Weinberger to issue a recantation in a formal statement, which I promptly did. The administration was now trapped by its own verbal acrobatics. Though everyone knew that the marines were never neutral, in attempting to pretend that this was so to avoid congressional strictures in the War Powers Act and to satisfy the diplomatists at the

State Department, the military chain of command institutionally *forgot* the reality of the marines' combatant status. The formal delusion that they were not combatants and rules of engagement to go with that delusion were left in place. Catastrophe was sure to result.

It came on Sunday, October 23, when a yellow nineteen-ton Mercedes truck loaded with the estimated equivalent of six to nine tons of TNT crashed through the perimeter of the Marine Battalion Landing Team headquarters building, a seemingly safe four-story concrete-reinforced structure in the marine compound at the airport. It passed through the guard posts and penetrated into the building, where it detonated. The force of the explosion lifted the entire building off its foundations and then collapsed it on the sleeping marines, killing 241 and wounding 100 others. The sentries, faithful to command guidance premised on the official delusion of neutrality, did not have their guns chambered and ready.

The Long Commission

Quite justifiably, there was outrage and consternation throughout the country and in Congress. How could this possibly happen? Both the House and the Senate immediately set an inquiry, and members tumbled over each other to make junkets to the scene. As the fire storm mounted and new investigations were being launched almost by the hour on the Hill, Cap announced on October 29 that at the recommendation of the marine corps commandant, P. X. Kelley, a blue-ribbon commission would be convened to make a thorough investigation and report to the president. Admiral Bob Long, a submariner who had just retired as the Pacific commander in chief, was asked to serve as its chairman. In addition to Long, the membership was made up of Bob Murray, from the faculty at Harvard University, and an under secretary of the navy in the Carter administration; Lieutenant General Joseph Palastra of the U.S. Army; Lieutenant General Lawrence Snowden, a retired marine; and Lieutenant General Eugene F. Tighe, the recently retired chief of air force intelligence and director of the defense intelligence agency.

The commission began work on November 7 and spent an exhaustive effort on the scene in Beirut, in the various commands in the chain of command in Europe and the United States, and back in Washington. They submitted their report to Secretary Weinberger on December 20, 1983, and it was indeed a blockbuster.

The major findings and recommendations of the commission were devastating indictments of the several causes of the disaster.

Cause 1. The Commission documented the fuzziness and contradictory policies pursued by the administration at the highest levels that put the marines into a "presence" mission and then kept them there for more than a year as the situation deteriorated and wholly changed in nature and objectives.

The Commission recommended that the National Security Council find some other way of achieving U.S. objectives in Lebanon than keeping the marines there.

Cause 2. The second finding documented the terrible trail of the evolving rules of engagement that the Marines in Beirut were forced to operate under. The original rules of engagement were issued by General Rogers as U.S. CINCEUR, on September 24, 1982, and were derived from the standard "peacetime rules of engagement." Under these rules of engagement force could be used only when required for immediate self-defense. They directed the marine forces to "seek guidance from higher authority prior to using armed force for self-defense unless an emergency existed." The amphibious task force commander out at sea was designated as the only authority able to declare a force hostile. The term "hostile threat" was not defined. The marine force was authorized to use force on its own initiative only if an intruder "committed a hostile act."

As the situation deteriorated seriously during 1983, attempts were made to modify the rules of engagement, particularly after the embassy bombing in April. But the myth of neutrality persisted. Two sets of rules of engagement (ROE) were issued, the "blue" card for embassy duty and the "white" card for all others.

The white card read as follows:

The mission of the multinational force is to keep the peace. The following rules of engagement will be read and fully understood by all members of the U.S. contingent of the MNF:

• When on post, mobile or foot patrol, keep a loaded magazine in the weapon, weapons will be on safe, with no rounds in the chamber.

• Do not chamber a round unless instructed to do so by a commissioned officer unless you must act in immediate self-defense where deadly force is authorized.

• Keep ammunition for crew-served weapons readily available but not loaded in the weapon. Weapons will be on safe at all time.

• Call local forces to assist in all self-defense efforts. Notify next senior command immediately.

• Use only the minimum degree of force necessary to accomplish the mission.

• Stop the use of force when it is no longer required.

• If effective fire is received, direct return fire at a distinct target only. If possible, use friendly sniper fire.

• Respect civilian property; do not attack it unless absolutely necessary to protect friendly forces.

The commission found that Colonel Geraghty did not believe that these rules of engagement included authority forcibly to halt vehicles attempting unauthorized entry into the marine compound.[3]

At the White House there had been a further attempt to instruct the marines when the battle for Suq Al Gharb commenced in early September. Explicit permission was given to the marines to support the Lebanese armed forces as part of the self-defense provision of the rules of engagement. This was based on the simple idea that loss of Suq Al Gharb would endanger the marine positions. USCINCEUR passed the new order through CINCUSNAVEUR to Colonel Geraghty ashore on September 12. Later that day, however, USCINCEUR reminded the marines that even if the support were directed to help the Lebanese Army, "Nothing in this message shall be construed as changing the mission or ROE for the U.S. Multinational Force."[4] The colonel was being told to assist the Lebanese—to take sides—but to retain his neutral, peaceful presence, which included the severely restrictive rules of the white card, at the same time!

Thus on the morning of October 23 there were no automatic or heavy weapons in the sentry posts, and the sentries did not have their M-16s loaded. (See figure 6.)

The commission report describes what happened:

Five eyewitnesses described a large, yellow Mercedes-Benz stake bed truck traveling at a speed reportedly in excess of 35 mph, moving from the public parking lot south of the BLT Headquarters building through the barbed wire and concertina fence, into the main entrance of the building, where it detonated at approximately 0622 Beirut time. . . . [The truck] was observed by the sentry on Post 6 accelerating westward and parallel to the wire barricade. The truck then abruptly turned north, ran over the wire barricade, and accelerated northward between Posts 6 and 7.

The sentry on Post 7 heard the truck as it ran over the wire, then observed it and immediately suspected it was a vehicle bomb. *He inserted a magazine in his M-16 rifle* [italics added], chambered a round, shouldered the weapon, and took aim but did not fire because by that time the truck had already penetrated the building.

Both sentries realized the truck was, in fact, a "car bomb" and therefore took cover within their respective bunkers. One sentry hid in the corner of his bunker and did not observe the detonation. The other sentry partially observed the detonation from behind the blast wall to the rear of the bunker. He saw the top of the building explode vertically in a V shape. He then took cover inside his bunker for protection from the falling debris.

The sentry on Post 5 also spotted the truck as it accelerated northward into the building. The truck passed so quickly that he could not react in any way, although he understood the truck's purpose. He was unable to take cover in his bunker and was knocked to the ground by the blast; however, he escaped uninjured. . . .[5]

Cause 3. The commission put the blame for the disaster squarely on the multilayered uniformed chain of command.

The commission meticulously traced the documented trail of rules of engagement, and other policy and decision-making between the president in Washington and his National Security Council, and the marine contingent ashore in Beirut. It exposed the enormous peacetime bureaucracy that our military chain of command has become, particularly in the European theater in the postwar period.

As noted earlier, for example, the September 12 directive that the marines should consider help for the Lebanese armed forces in the battle for Suq Al Gharb as "self-defense"—a very significant indication of increased danger for the marines—went from the president to the secretary of defense; from the secretary of defense through the JCS and their seventeen-hundred-man staff, to CINCLANT and CINCLANTFLT and Fleet Marine Force Atlantic in Norfolk for coordination; from the JCS organization thence to the European theater commander, General Bernard Rogers, in Belgium; from Belgium to the Deputy European Command headquarters in Stuttgart; from Stuttgart to the commander of U.S. naval forces, Europe, in Naples; from Naples to the deputy NAVEUR headquarters in London; from London to the U.S. Sixth Fleet command headquarters in Gaeta, Italy; from Gaeta back to the U.S. commander, Task Force 60, in Naples; from Naples to the U.S. commander, Task Force 61, off Beirut; and from CTF-61 ashore to CTF-62, Colonel Geraghty, in command of the marines. The commission documented how in whispering-down-the-lane fashion the chain of command simply neutralized the impact of the September 12 message by reminding the marines later that the mission and the ROE had not changed.

The conclusions of the commission with regard to the chain of command were as follows:

(a) The Commission is fully aware that the entire chain of command was heavily involved in the planning for, and support of, the U.S. MNF. The Commission concludes, however, that U.S. CINCEUR, CINCUS-NAVEUR, COMSIXTHFLT, and CTF-61 did not initiate actions to ensure the security of the U.S. MNF in light of the deteriorating polit-ical-military situation in Lebanon. The Commission found a lack of effective command supervision of the U.S. MNF security posture prior to 23 October 1983.

(b) The Commission concludes that the failure of the operational chain of command to correct or amend the defensive posture of the U.S. MNF constituted tacit approval of the security measures and procedures in force at the BLT Headquarters building on 23 October 1983.

(c) The Commission further concludes that although it finds the USCINCEUR operational chain of command at fault, it also finds that there was a series of circumstances beyond the control of these com-mands that influenced their judgment and their actions relating to the security of the U.S. MNF.

(2) Recommendation:

(a) The Commission recommends that the Secretary of Defense take what-ever administrative or disciplinary action he deems appropriate, citing the failure of the USCINCEUR operational chain of command to monitor and supervise effectively the security measures and procedures employed by the U.S. MNF on 23 October 1983.

Cause 4. The Commission found fault with the U.S. intelligence commu-nity, particularly the Carter administration decision greatly to diminish human intelligence, and made recommendations for improvement. (Our experience in Grenada rammed this point home once more.)

Cause 5. The commission focused on the command responsibility and the marine units themselves:

Every Marine interviewed expressed concern over the restrictions against insert-ing magazines in weapons while on interior posts during alert conditions II, III, and IV. The most outspoken were the sentries on Posts 6 and 7, where the penetration of the compound occurred on 23 October 1983. The MAU commander explained that he had made a conscious decision not to permit insertion of magazines in weapons on interior posts to preclude accidental discharge and possible injury to innocent civilians. This is indicative of the emphasis of prevention of harm to civilians, notwithstanding some degradation of security.

(d) The Commission further concludes that although it finds the BLT and MAU commanders to be at fault, it also finds that there was a series of circumstances beyond their control that influenced their judgment and their actions relating to the security of the U.S. MNF.

(2) Recommendation:
(a) The Commission recommends the Secretary of Defense take whatever administrative or disciplinary action he deems appropriate, citing the failure of the BLT and MAU commanders to take the security measures necessary to preclude the catastrophic loss of life in the attack on 23 October 1983.[6]

On December 27 the president issued a statement saying, "I do not believe that the local commanders on the ground, men who have suffered quite enough, should be punished for not fully comprehending the nature of today's terrorist threat. . . . If there is to be blame, it properly rests here in this office and with this president."

After the commission made its report to the secretary of defense, the service secretaries were given the report and asked for recommendations. Each of us was strictly enjoined to address ourselves only to the implications for each of our respective services. These were my recommendations to Cap:

1. Our entire military chain of command was bloated and paralyzed. We should use the lesson so clearly documented in the Long Commission report to reduce the uniformed bureaucracy, eliminate layers in the chain of command, and try to reverse the terrible trend that Congress had inflicted on the Pentagon of ever more centralized unified military bureaucracy.
2. Specifically with regard to the navy bloat, I recommended the elimination of the five-hundred-person staff in London, the deputy NAVEUR headquarters, and the combining of it with the NAVEUR command in Naples, eliminating one layer.
3. The Sixth Fleet commander and his headquarters should go back to sea in a warship, so he would no longer be a land-based layer in the bureaucracy but

would be wherever the action was. As a cost-saving measure during the Carter administration, the Sixth Fleet flagship, the cruiser *Albany*, was retired and the Sixth Fleet commander and his staff were put aboard a repair ship that stayed in port.

4. CTF-60 headquarters in Naples should be entirely eliminated.

5. Appropriate action (which must remain confidential) should be taken with respect to individuals.

A president has many more considerations to balance than a cabinet officer, and the secretary of defense has many more than a service secretary. For whatever reasons, the president and the secretary of defense decided that, as the saying goes, "Everyone has suffered enough." So the commission's recommendations for accountability were set aside.

With regard to the commission's finding regarding another method for Middle East diplomacy than keeping marines in Beirut, the public impact of the report demolished support for the mission. On February 7, 1984, the president announced "redeployment" of the marines from the airport to ships offshore. Amid heavy fighting, including bombardments of Syrian and Druze positions by the *New Jersey*, the marines gathered up their equipment, and their wounded memories of the "Root." The last of the 22nd MAU boarded ship on February 26, 1984.

The tragic Beirut peacekeeping mission was over, but not the repercussions.

Weinberger rejected my recommendations to reduce the number of layers in the chain of command and to streamline it. Because of General Rogers' opposition he rejected my strong recommendations to consolidate the Naples and London naval headquarters, but he did not object to my abolishing the CTF-60 headquarters.

With regard to the commission's recommendation that disciplinary action be taken against the marine commander, Weinberger directed that no punitive action be taken but that nonpunitive administrative letters of caution be sent to Colonel Geraghty and Lieutenant Colonel Gerlach.

By the end of the year, everything had been swept neatly into the memory hole, and the Beirut disaster and the inconvenient findings of the Long Commission on the chain of command were a closed chapter.

What President Reagan and Secretary Weinberger did was not unusual — in fact it has become the normal practice of presidents after a military fiasco. Jack Kennedy took "sole responsibility" for the Bay of Pigs fiasco and disciplined no one. President Carter took full responsibility for the

Desert I fiasco and gave medals to those Pentagon planners responsible for the debacle.

In each case the president's popularity improved by doing what was put forward as the "manly" thing. But in fact, it was a terrible practice. As Charles Krauthammer aptly put it, "Responsibility must carry with it some consequences. For reasons not of vengeance, but of justice—and as one of our few deterrents against fatal negligence. Responsibility that has no consequences is not just an exercise in cover-up. It is an invitation to the debacles of the future."

The same evasion of accountability and bureaucratization of policy were applied by the administration to the culprits themselves. Cap stated publicly on November 22 that the attack had been carried out by Iranians with the "sponsorship, knowledge, and authority of the Syrian government."[7] An argument broke out whether to attack the suspected culprits or those who supported them (the Iranians in the Bekaa). The marines, whose shattered battalion was still very much at risk, argued against retaliation until they had established their own security.

Retaliation

It was the hope and expectation of many of us that the president would order retaliation with a terrible, swift sword. This was in fact the president's immediate reaction. The navy had recommended strongly that action be taken using the Tomahawks aboard the battleship or a night bombing strike against the terrorist training center at Baalbek. Cap, as always, listened politely but gave me no indication of his own feelings. He was, in fact, with Vessey, opposed to any retaliation. Nevertheless, while everyone dithered Vessey approved sending the Baalbek strike plan, prepared by Ace Lyons, out to the task force by secret courier, with info copies to General Rogers.

But as the days passed and October became November, the administration still dithered and did nothing. Fears that a bombing raid might kill Lebanese civilians accidentally no doubt played a major role in staying the president's hand. But that risk had to be weighed against the increased risk to our forces from doing nothing. And the moral concerns about civilians had its counterpoint in this question: Why was nothing to be done about the massacre of 241 marines on a peaceful mission, all of whom had their own parents, wives, and children? The French, having suffered their own casualties, got tired of our indecision and bombed Baalbek on November 16.

At dawn on December 3 the Israeli Air Force carried out a large bombing raid east of Beirut. Later in the day, the U.S. carrier *Kennedy* launched an

F-14 photo reconnaissance flight on its daily reconnaissance over Lebanon. These daily flights had been ordered since the marine barracks disaster. While they didn't really provide much intelligence that wasn't known from other sources, they at least gave the chain of command the feeling that they were doing something. In their daily run the F-14s normally traveled very fast, at more than six hundred knots, and at about thirty-five hundred feet. They were nearly always fired at with antiaircraft guns. On this particular day, however, the aviators saw coming up at them a number of the telltale smoke corkscrews that were the signatures of the Russian SA-7 heat-seeking antiaircraft missiles. The pilots were in constant communication with the command center aboard the carrier and reported the missiles immediately. That information was passed up the chain of command and soon reached the president's desk. The president asked for the Pentagon's recommendations on a retaliatory response.

At the Pentagon, those who had strongly opposed and those who had recommended retaliation for the marine deaths all had thought it was a dead issue. Secretary Weinberger was in Paris on NATO business, leaving Paul Thayer in charge. I was visiting our marines on Tiger Island in Honduras. Paul Thayer and Jack Vessey, chairman of the JCS, went along to Camp David to meet with the president on whether to retaliate. Compared to the deaths of 241 marines, of course, a few hand-held missiles were hardly things to retaliate about, but it soon became clear that the president still was thinking of the marine barracks bombing. As I heard the story, Thayer and Vessey recommended that if a retaliation were to be ordered, it should be an air strike against Syrian targets and launched from the carriers off Beirut. The president asked why the sixteen-inch guns of the *New Jersey* could not be used. They responded that the *New Jersey* did not have the range or the accuracy to do the job—a misinformed answer, if ever there was one. Only the low-value targets on the eastern slopes were inappropriate to naval gunfire. Those could have easily been dropped from the lists. As for the important targets, the *New Jersey*'s sixteen-inch guns could easily have reached every one being considered. (See figure 7.)

The president ordered a retaliatory air strike. He did not specify any time, nor did he dictate any of the specifics. He just said to do it. Thayer and Vessey returned to the Pentagon and issued the orders through the same incredibly layered chain of command that had produced the marine tragedy. It quite predictably produced another fiasco.

For his book *Supercarrier*, George Wilson did an admirable job interviewing all the participants in the chain of command to try to chronicle exactly what happened in the twenty-four hours following the president's order to retaliate. No one in the chain of command had the same story, and each contradicted parts of the accounts of the others.

Several weeks after the retaliatory air strike, I traveled to the battle group and spent three days talking with the aviators who flew the mission and the men who planned and carried it out, as well as the flag officers up the chain of command. There is no definitive documentary record of these events because nearly all communication that took place during the twenty-four hours from Washington up and down the chain of command to the battle group was telephonic or by radio. This is what I believe happened:

Prior to December 3 the European Command had rejected the Baalbek target package prepared by Lyons (not invented here) and, exactly as in Vietnam, prepared instead a lot of valueless target packages composed of scattered suspected antiaircraft sites for potential retaliation, if ordered. During the afternoon of December 3, the task force commander, Admiral Jerry Tuttle negotiated by telephone with Stuttgart over which targets should be used for a strike. Stuttgart had picked essentially four sets of targets. Three of them were Syrian artillery and antiaircraft positions, and one of them was a radar site. Tuttle rejected one set of antiaircraft targets as being too heavily defended but accepted the other three. He told me, however, that he didn't think any of them was worth a damn as a military target. The radar site could easily have been handled by the *New Jersey*'s guns, but the other target sets were small antiaircraft gun emplacements and possible missile emplacements whose precise coordinates were not finally known. Many of them were on the eastward-facing slopes of the hills, which would have meant that the sixteen-inch guns would have had to use area saturation rather than precise targeting. Because the targets were so inconsequential and small, they could not be engaged by precision radar- or laser-guided munitions but would require visual identification by the aviators.

The F-14 reconnaissance missions (called TARPS, for tactical airborne reconnaissance pod systems) themselves were a case study in military bureaucracy. Having reviewed a lot of the product from those missions, I know there was very little added to the overall intelligence picture that was not available from other sources, and nothing that was critical to the on-scene commander. Nevertheless, to mount just one of these missions was very expensive and was, of course, asking for trouble each time they flew. For each mission the carrier had to launch fighter cap (combat air patrol), with refueling tankers and an airborne radar controller aircraft. In addition, armed bombers were kept on alert to retaliate if necessary, and search-and-rescue helicopters were kept on alert in case an aircraft was shot down. Just as in Vietnam, the men who were flying the missions began to realize it was all an enormous waste of time, but once the chain-of-command bureaucracy was set in motion, it stayed in motion. They flew TARPS missions continuously until the marines were withdrawn, with one exception.

An obvious question hovered over all these proceedings: Because the president was clearly retaliating not just for use of a couple of hand-held missiles but also for the marine deaths, why wasn't the raid launched against the terrorist training sites, which also happened to be targets far more safely hit by aircraft? The reason was that the military bureaucracy was still steeped in its Vietnam traditions. As one member of the JCS told George Wilson, "Those reconnaissance planes were shot at. There was a feeling at the time that a response in kind was a legitimate thing. In other words, if you're shot at, you shoot back. A tit-for-tat kind of thing."

It is ironic that the uniformed military always blames McNamara for what is in fact a hallmark of its own peacetime bureaucratic mind-set. If there were piddling, hand-held missiles shot at one airplane, then we must retaliate against idling, inconsequential targets. Thus no battleship and no juicy targets. The marine barracks must remain in the memory hole. The president, of course, was not privileged to hear any such discussion. He thought, in the words of one of his advisers, that "the Pentagon would kick the shit out of the Syrians."

Admiral Tuttle and his strike planners were warned during the afternoon of the third that there may very well be a retaliatory strike at "targets associated with firings at U.S. aircraft on December 3." Tit for tat. Admiral Tuttle planned for a time-over-target of eleven o'clock the next morning and ordered his two air wing commanders, Commander John Mazach of the *Kennedy* air wing, and Commander Ed Andrews of the *Independence* air wing, to plan their strikes and load their aircraft accordingly.

The *Kennedy* was preparing to leave "Bagel Station" (as duty off Beirut was called) and transit the Suez Canal for duty off the Strait of Hormuz. As a consequence, most of her aircraft were not loaded with weapons. The air wing began feverish efforts to prepare and load the ordnance in time for the eleven-o'clock strike. On the *Independence*, the loaded bombers had ordnance for the Sucap mission—ammunition useful against potential suicide boats and for possible close air support for the marines ashore. The nature of the targets assigned by the European Command included scattered antiaircraft sites and dictated use of cluster bombs rather than high-explosive bombs. The

Independence aircraft had to be de-armed laboriously and unloaded and then the cluster bombs built up, armed, and loaded back onto the aircraft.

Admiral Tuttle and both air wings worked through the night in the belief that they would just barely be able to make the 11:00 A.M. launch for an 11:30 A.M. time over the targets. At about 5:30 A.M., Admiral Tuttle was awakened and informed that the execute order had been issued with a hard launch time of 6:30 A.M. Tuttle immediately demanded more time but was given only an hour's delay. There followed a mad flail. Normally the strike crews must begin briefing at least two hours before launch time in order to be prepared properly. Now, neither air wing had sufficient numbers of aircraft loaded nor crews assigned, let alone briefed. Air crews scrambled to take whichever aircraft were available, and without any time to brief, launched on schedule.

Both wing commanders did an outstanding job in marshaling their strike force over carriers. However, it was unfortunately necessary in doing so to break just about every rule in the book. Twenty-eight aircraft had been launched, but none of them had the proper load-out of weapons. Some took off with only two bombs, and others with the wrong types more suitable to bombing targets in the Baalbek, a mission to which the wing commanders had expected to be assigned. There was no time for the normal cover and deception, so the Soviet "tattletales" (ships assigned to follow U.S. carriers closely to report all activities) were watching the entire evolution from several hundred yards away and radioing warnings to the Syrians. The Syrian early-warning radars were able to watch for half an hour as a swarm of increasing size circled above the carriers at twelve thousand feet. They could track exactly when they started in toward the targets, and if there was any doubt because of the confusion, radio discipline was impossible, so the Syrians had the benefit of listening in to radio communications.

The *Independence* air wing under Commander Andrews got eighteen A-6s and A-7s in the air and were scheduled to hit the target first, flying across the beach south of Beirut and turning up north into the target area. After hitting the target they were to head northwest out over the coast and back to the carriers.

The *Kennedy* air wing under Commander Mazach got ten A-6s launched. Their plan called for crossing the beach north of Beirut and turning southeast into the target area to arrive a few minutes after the *Independence* air wing departed.

It was a classic twenty-year old Vietnam "aluminum cloud" daylight alpha strike. No surprise, no deception, no countermeasures by the aircraft. Just fly in at medium altitude, between ten thousand and fifteen thousand feet, dive in, drop your bombs, and fly out at medium altitude. Due to the haste with which the plan had to be put together, both commanders had to use routes over the one target area, a ridgeline just northeast of the city, which Tuttle had rejected because it was too heavily armed with SAMs.

The *Independence* bombers arriving in the target area found that the sun was directly in their eyes and the targets in the shadows of the hills, requiring them to dive to very low release altitudes to acquire the target visually. From the time the air wing crossed the beach, the air over the target area filled with antiaircraft bursts and SA-7 and SA-9 missiles. It was a massive barrage. In the target area the aircraft were ejecting flares and chaff, and these effectively defeated the SAMs. Such bombs as they had aboard were put very effectively on the targets, but, of course, the targets were of little consequence. As soon as the strike planes were clear of the target they climbed northwest, heading for the coast. The route took them straight over the SAM-infested ridge. Wilson's book includes the following transcript of the radio transmissions of what happened next:

"SAMs! SAMs! SAMs . . ."

"SAM-7!"

"Left! Keep it coming. Keep it coming."

"I'm hit. . . . I'm hit"

"CAG, where are you at?"

"Mayday! Mayday! This is 305. I am proceeding out over the water now. I want you to join up with me. I got 250 knots."

"I'm looking for you."

"I'm back behind you."

"Right."

"They're shooting at us."

"How are we doing back there?"

"I'm fine. Almost clear right now."

"[CAG] Out of here." (Andrews' message that he had ejected from his burning A-7 light bomber).

"Good chute."[8]

Two of the *Independence* A-7s were hit going over that ridgeline. CAG Andrews ejected and was safely recovered and returned to the ship within an hour. The other A-7 made it back aboard the *Independence*.

As the *Independence* air wing was clearing out of the target area, the *Kennedy* air wing was heading into the target over almost the same route by the which the *Independence* air wing was exiting.

One of the last A-6s in the *Kennedy* formation was loaded with six 1,000-pound bombs. It was flown by Lieutenant Mark Lange, a twenty-six-year-old Naval Academy graduate who was separated and raising a one-year-old daughter; and Lieutenant Bobby Goodman, a twenty-seven-year-old black graduate of the Naval Academy, married with two children. As the formation started their descent into the target area over the same ridgeline from which had come the SAMs that bagged *Independence* A-7s, Bobby Goodman scanned the instrument panel. They were not yet in the target area, so they were not ejecting defensive flares. Suddenly Goodman saw a flash and felt a heavy jolt. The A-6 went into an immediate spiraling nosedive, trailing a plume of flame. Goodman ejected and the next thing he remembered was riding in a Syrian truck with his hands tightly bound and his eyes blindfolded. Lange was not so lucky. Apparently he ejected too late and did not get separation from his seat. Pictures taken at the scene that were distributed to the press showed Lange still sitting in his seat, alive. His leg, however, was severed in the landing, and he bled to death.

Although Goodman was roughed up during interrogation in Damascus, he was generally well treated during a month's captivity. He might have languished for some time longer if our latest special negotiator in Lebanon, former Secretary of Defense Donald Rumsfeld, who replaced Bud McFarlane, had not made clear to Assad that Goodman's release was not subject to bargaining. The Syrians, seeing in Goodman a wasting asset, then decided to intervene to their advantage in U.S. politics. In a very high-profile visit, the Reverend Jesse Jackson came to Damascus, and Goodman was released. I later suggested that we should modify all naval aviators' survival vests to include a packet of quarters and Jesse Jackson's telephone number.

Having lost Lange and Goodman, the *Kennedy* airstrike continued into the target area and found the same difficult environment as the *Independence* group. Flak from the antiaircraft guns was everywhere, and there was a blizzard of heat-seeking SAM missiles. They pressed their attack to about four-thousand-foot release altitudes because of difficulty seeing the targets. They put such bombs as they had effectively on the targets and, using their countermeasures, succeeded in avoiding all the SAMs. The flak were all exploding below their release altitude and caused no damage. The group departed the target area to the southwest, returned to the coast, and recovered aboard the *Kennedy* without further event.

While all of this was going on, I found myself very far from Washington. After being told that retaliation for the marine bombing had been ruled out, I accepted a long-standing invitation from our two dynamic ambassadors in Honduras and

Costa Rica, John Negroponte and Curt Winsor, to visit those two countries and El Salvador and observe some of the large exercises—"Big Pine"—that our navy and marine forces along with the army and air force were carrying out with our Central American friends. We left Washington on November 30 and flew directly to San Salvador. As I sat being briefed by the country team, I couldn't believe the similarities between what I was hearing and the visits I made to Vietnam in the early 1970s. The Soviets through Cuba and Nicaragua were supplying textbook Soviet insurgency. In classic form there were two parallel recruiting efforts going on to build the insurgency. The local foot soldiers were recruited from the countryside from the uneducated and the poor. These were trained primarily in Nicaragua or El Salvador itself. There was also a major effort at recruiting more educated young men and women, and these were sent first to Cuba for basic military training, then on to the Soviet Union for several years of more sophisticated training and indoctrination. Cadres for the leadership of future Central American satellites were being built.

Traveling to Honduras, we visited a U.S. Marine unit that had occupied a high island in the Gulf of Fonseca, where they had placed an air-control radar for the several months' exercise. Because of the unique location of this thousand-foot island, the air-control radar was able to see for several hundred miles into El Salvador, Honduras, and Nicaragua. In talking with the young marines who had been operating the radar for more than a month, I was interested to hear from them that virtually every day they watched supply aircraft take off from Nicaragua, flying low over the water into various landing fields in El Salvador. This was a principal method for the Sandinistas to convey the Soviet arms to the Salvadoran insurgency. The Sandinistas' apologists in the U.S. Congress, however, steadfastly maintained that this was not the case. We found also that the heavier-tonnage equipment was coming in steadily by boat from Nicaragua to various points along the Salvadoran coast, with the tiny Salvadoran navy having little capability to intercept.

When Ambassador Negroponte, his military staff, and I returned to Tegucigalpa, one of the embassy staff members was awaiting us with a flash newspaper account of the American air strike in Lebanon. I couldn't believe my ears. Two aircraft lost, a POW—it could not be possible.

Flying back to Washington aboard a P-3, we got the full navy account transmitted to us. When I read it I was so furious I was in danger of stamping my feet through the deck, like Rumpelstiltskin. Mark Lange dead, Bobby Goodman a prisoner, two planes lost, and another damaged. A twenty-year-old daylight alpha strike against absolutely useless targets! As if Vietnam had never happened! How *could* we have done such a thing? It was bitter gall. Before we landed in Washington we had begun planning an immediate visit out to the fleet off Beirut.

There was more gall to come. On December 14 the daily F-14 mission was again fired on from Syrian-controlled positions. This time the proper response was chosen and the *New Jersey* fired eleven of her sixteen-inch shells and destroyed six antiaircraft sites. A request for a TARPS mission the following day to assess the effectiveness of the fire was denied from Stuttgart.

Later, on February 8, 1984, after the marines were ordered to withdraw, Syrian artillery batteries began firing into the Christian-held areas of West Beirut, creating serious civilian casualties. They fired more than 5,000 rounds before the decision was made to answer the fire by responding with the *New Jersey*'s sixteen-inch guns. The army provided the *New Jersey* with grid coordinates based on their R-TAB radar, which tracked the shells and calculated the position of the firing guns. The *New Jersey* fired 270 rounds and totally silenced all Syrian batteries. In subsequent weeks it was confirmed that eight Syrian batteries disappeared completely from their orders of battle, having been totally destroyed. Admiral Tuttle requested a TARPS mission to get detailed battle damage. For reasons never explained, EUCOM headquarters suspended all TARPS missions for two weeks. Thus the only confirmation of the effectiveness of the *New Jersey*'s guns came from a CBS News interview of a Syrian spokesman who said that the *New Jersey* had killed only innocent civilians and goats.

Meanwhile, back in Washington, it was like pulling teeth to try to find out how the decision had been made to reject Lyon's Baalbek target in favor of EUCOM's useless targets and then compounding the mistake by using A-6s instead of the *New Jersey* in the first place. No one seemed to know, and those who did were behaving very oddly indeed. Cap refused to let me go to the fleet. Nobody in EUCOM wanted to see me over there, and Rogers strongly opposed my visiting naval forces in his command. In this case, however, I was determined to go and kept after Cap week after week until finally he said okay, but with the stipulation, in deference to Vessey and Rogers, that I not set foot ashore. On January 10, 1984, we left Washington and with only refueling stops flew directly to Naples. There I met separately with Bill Small, commander of European Naval Forces; Ed Martin, the Sixty Fleet commander; and Jerry Tuttle, the CTF-60 commander, who was the on-scene task force commander for the raid. From there we flew to Akrotiri, Cyprus, where we went by helicopter to the *Kennedy*. The attitude among the chain of command to my visit was perhaps best described by George Wilson in his book:

> The *Kennedy* drew distinguished visitors from the world, including members of Congress, admirals, and generals. Usually these visits were bothersome but not worrisome for the officers on the carrier who had to prepare briefings, find suitable living quarters on the crowded ship, and plan dinners and tours for VIPs. But the upcoming visit of navy secretary John F. Lehman, Jr., was, in contrast, indeed worrisome. He was bound to ask right after he arrived on January 11, 1984, how the hell the bombing raid of December 4 got so screwed up.
>
> "Answer his questions, but don't volunteer anything" became the unofficial guidance from the top of the admirals' club, perhaps the world's most effective protective society.[9]

Attempts to apply the classic Pentagon "mushroom strategy," which is "Keep 'em in the dark and feed 'em a little bullshit once in a while" were by this time only too familiar. When it was applied to me so obviously by the senior admiral aboard the *Kennedy*, I could not keep from grinning. It was disappointing that such a senior person would be so naïve. He actually gave me the Rotary Club version of how the strike had been perfectly planned and executed. Martin and Tuttle had been totally honest and forthcoming in explaining all of the screwups, but here on the carrier someone had given the order to clam up. Silly them. I thanked him politely and then went down to the squadron ready rooms to begin finding out what really happened in detail. The next three days were spent flying with several of the squadrons and talking with dozens of old friends and acquaintances throughout the ship and the rest of the task force. Using a borrowed Huey, I visited each of the ships in the task force and spent time with each of those who had played a role in the strike.

On one of these hops, I flew a fighter cap mission with one of the pilots who had flown in the controversial TARPs mission. After intercepting a fast mover that turned out to be a Lebanese Mystère trainer, we orbited at twenty thousand feet over the battle group on the normal air defense station. It was an incredibly clear day, and in one sweep we could see Cyprus and the long, curving coast of Syria all the way to the Turkish border to the north. You could see the ancient ports of Latakia, Tyre, and Sidon. Each had been sieged and destroyed by Alexander the Great as he advanced down the coast. Nevertheless, these people had been a constant source of harassment to his rear area after he had moved on. Looking south, we could see the great

Crusader fortresses at Acre and Caesarea, jutting out from the Israeli coast. Things had not changed in many ways, but at least Alexander and the Caesars, Richard the Lion-Hearted and Saladin, Suleiman the Magnificent, Napoleon, and General Allenby knew clearly what they were doing and how to do it. Neither did they shrink from putting their enemies to the sword. Since the United States was now prepared to do neither of these, we had no business staying here.

By the third day, a picture had emerged of what had happened—to the extent that it was knowable. After staying overnight aboard the *New Jersey*, Admiral Martin joined me at 4:00 A.M. for a last summing-up breakfast. He totally agreed with the validity of the picture I had put together, and we talked about the urgent need now to put together a program to correct the deep flaws it had revealed. Before taking off, we went up to the bridge and looked at the bright lights of the Beirut skyline and watched the tracers periodically floating back and forth across the Shouf Mountains above the city— a dramatic scene.

We manned up the helicopter and took off just as the sky was lightening along the mountaintops east of Beirut. I circled once around the *New Jersey*, which looked unusually awesome with a slight orange dawn glow against the still-black sea.

Returning to Cyprus, we boarded the P-3 and headed back to Washington. We flew over France, with George Wilson hitching a ride aboard, and one of our four engines malfunctioned and had to be shut down, requiring us to find a place to land immediately. We headed for London or Shannon, but the weather was below landing minimums. The only field ahead of us that was reporting landing minimums was RAF Mildenhall, just outside of Cambridge. We landed there and after examining the problem we were told it would take about five hours to repair. Since it was approaching dinnertime, we borrowed a small bus from the base commander and took my staff, along with George Wilson, into Cambridge to see some of my old college haunts. It was by luck the first day back from Christmas vacation, and we went to my old college, Gonville and Caius. There in the college buttery we found the captain of the boats and the rowing team, and they were drinking a preprandial beer. After several pints, we had the bus driver take us to one of the most charming pubs in England, the Tickell Arms, long the headquarters of Cambridge rowing. The eccentric and charming publican Kim Tickell welcomed us with the warmth appropriate to the relative fortune I had spent in this establishment in years gone by. After a superb meal we were driven back to Mildenhall just as the P-3 was fixed, and off we went to Washington.

Conclusion

Just before I left the *Kennedy*, the executive officer Captain John Peino summed up the implications of the raid by saying to me, "The aviators are going to be licking their balls for a long time over this one." Indeed they were. There was no doubt in my mind what went wrong.

There were three distinct sets of causes. First, the bloated uniformed chain of command had proved once again that it is not suitable for conducting any combat operations efficiently. Once sifted through its many layers and lack of accountability, the target sets became ridiculous. After deciding to retaliate, the president did not micromanage but left it to the good judgment of the military leadership. The chain of command then promptly turned it into a classic Vietnam "measured response" against useless targets. The president had declined to set a firm time, thinking that this gave the military flexibility; once the chain of command took over, however, flexibility was turned into a hard, unreasonable, and counterproductive seven-thirty time over target the next morning and against which there was no appeal. To this day, no one, from the chairman of the joint chiefs down to the carrier air wing, will acknowledge playing any role in picking that time. The urgent requests for extension on military grounds by Admiral Tuttle disappeared somewhere up the chain, and back down came an anonymous grace of only one hour.

The second cause was the very nature and confusion of our objectives in Lebanon. Sending daily photoreconnaissance flights served no real purpose and was a needless risk and provocation. They had all been fired on, and ordering a retaliatory strike simply because a heat-seeking missile was added to the shooting was totally out of proportion. The Pentagon's dithering divorced the timing of the retaliation from the real event that justified it—the massacre of the marines.

The third set of causes was inherent in the navy itself and in naval aviation. What I found in my three-day visit was that even if the chain of command had functioned efficiently, even if instead it had been cut out and the naval task force commander and his air wing commanders been allowed to do anything they wanted for retaliation, the result still would have been a twenty-year-old classic Vietnam daylight alpha strike. Left on its own, the task force still would not have used the *New Jersey* and still would not have done the kind of precision night strike that was done three years later in Libya. Left to their desires, the task force simply would have added more aircraft and loaded more bombs and gone later in the day, with possibly greater losses. To their credit, however, they undoubtedly would have picked better targets.

What to do About It

The raid added another indictment of the chain-of-command bureaucracy to the already devastating indictment contained in the Long Commission report. Once again the recommendation was made to clean up the chain of command and get rid of as many layers as possible. Vessey and Rogers disagreed and dissuaded Cap from doing anything. From that perspective, the lessons from the December 4 raid were swept into the same memory hole as the Long Commission report and disappeared without a trace.

With regard to the second cause, our confused purposes in Lebanon, by the end of January the president had lost all support for his Lebanese policy in Congress and, indeed, within the administration. His cabinet and his advisers had served him poorly on the issue from start to finish. The finish was at hand. By mid-February 1984 the last of the marines were withdrawn from Beirut and the Lebanese government moved immediately under the influence of Syria. That situation has prevailed for nearly five years while Washington has done its best to forget the entire disaster.

As secretary of the navy, there was nothing I could do but grind down my teeth as my recommendations for correcting the chain of command were ignored. A great deal, however, could be done to change the problems in the navy that had come to light through the episode. That was quite enough to keep busy for the next four years. A major reform of naval aviation was begun at once.

Chapter II

Naval Aviation

There is no sound in the world quite like the deep, guttural throb of a large radial aircraft engine. They are entirely gone from our skies today, but in the 1950s they were ever-present over suburban Philadelphia. As a boy living under the approach path of Willow Grove Naval Air Station, I heard them emanating from gull-wing Corsairs, Hellcats, and Skyraiders, the romantic gladiators of all the *Late Show* war movies. Many were the days that I bicycled the five miles with my pals to sit for hours outside the fence, watching them in the bounce pattern. Once in a while my father would take me to lunch at the Officers' Club, filled with pilots in leather jackets, and I felt I was in the holy of holies. There was never any doubt in my mind that this was the zenith of all human accomplishment, and I was determined one day to become one of them.

I will never forget years later, when I was in pilot training at Kingsville, Texas. As soon as I had my logbook signed off "safe for solo," my instructor and I took my first training cross-country to Willow Grove Naval Air Station. As I flew the A-4 jet low over the same fence on final, there were three or four young kids staring up, with their bicycles, and there also was my dad's car. My eyes suddenly misted up and I nearly blew the landing.

Naval aviation always has been part of my life, and I always have felt more at home with naval aviators than with any other peer group. As secretary of the navy this had advantages and disadvantages. Seventeen years of reserve experience had given me a great many contacts at every level in the fleet. Maintaining my professional skills as an aviator had kept me part of the deck-plate navy, a valuable antidote to the effects of the Washington bureaucracy. There was another priceless advantage: a broad network of friends from "JG" to admiral who knew me well enough to tell me what they really thought about what I was doing and what was going on in the Navy.

The disadvantage, however, was that my perspective was perhaps overly influenced by the ready-room view of an aviator. And more importantly, the other warfare communities, particularly the submariners, viewed me as an aviator and were ever watchful for signs of favoritism toward the aviation community. But the aviator admirals viewed me as a junior aviator, and a reserve at that.

Some people bend way over backward to be seen not to be favoring the group or community from which they have come, and very often discriminate against them as a consequence. I was aware of my biases, but I saw no reason to hide my special interest in aviation matters. Those who would be tempted to believe that aviators were favored will find no support in the facts. Statistically, submariners benefited disproportionately in promotions throughout my entire tenure, including those selections to three- and four-star rank that I recommended personally. And much of my special interest in aviation did not stem from satisfaction from with the way things were.

My experiences prior to 1981 as a participant in naval aviation, and as an observer of its use from the White House, had left me with a concern that it was not what it should be. The United States needs air power at sea for two purposes: to deter hostile action and to engage in military operations—two sides of the same coin. Sea-based air provides a capability to take forceful action of many varieties in most areas of the world, and in parts of certain theaters inaccessible to any other military capability. The navy exists to prevent those sea areas from being used as a medium for hostile attack against American interests and those of America's allies, and to ensure the unimpeded use of the seas in peace and in war. In war this mission requires active denial to the enemy of use of the seas, harbors, and adjacent air space. To do it, the navy has to be able to project power under the sea, on the surface, in the air above, and over land. The large aircraft carrier carries aircraft capable of all four missions.

A further mission for sea-based air is to augment or substitute for land-based forces against nonmaritime objectives, such as in the marine landings at Inchon, or Yankee Station operations in Vietnam. While this is definitely a secondary mission for carrier air wings, ironically it is the one most often spoken of by naval critics.

A further distortion of the understanding of the requirements for sea-based air is a hangover from the 1950s, when the navy itself tried to justify aircraft carriers on the basis of their strategic nuclear strike role. Although modern carrier aircraft can deliver nuclear weapons, they are not included in strategic strike planning.

By far the most actively employed role that sea-based air power has had since the Second World War has been in the more than 240 instances of successful deterrence of hostilities through peacetime deployments in crises.

The simplest and still the best explanation of the value of sea-based air is that of Admiral Chester Nimitz:

> The net result is that naval forces are, without resorting to diplomatic channels, to establish offshore, anywhere in the world, airfields completely equipped with machine shops, ammunition dumps, tank farms, warehouses, together with quarters and all types of accommodations for personnel. Such task forces are virtually as complete as any air base ever established. They constitute the only air base that can be made available near enemy territory without assault and conquest, and furthermore, they are mobile offensive bases that can be employed with the unique attribute of secrecy and surprise, which contributes equally to their defensive as well as offensive effectiveness.[1]

Although many of the tasks of sea-based air can be accomplished by land-based air in that third of the globe where land bases exist, land-based air carries with it enormous complications on the political level. In 95 percent of the crises since World War II, land-based air could not be used because of unwillingness of friends and allies to provide landing-base and support-base rights. In fact, the land-based air wing of today's modern aircraft costs slightly more to procure and operate per year, including related facilities, training, etc., than a carrier air wing able to provide the same number of sorties with the same kinds of aircraft, including costs of the carrier, training, ashore facilities, etc.

In a study conducted in the OSD during the Vietnam conflict, it was estimated that approximately five land-based tactical fighter squadrons and twenty KC-135 tankers would be required to produce the monthly sortie rate of one attack carrier. To construct the basing for each carrier equivalent, the cost was estimated to be $1 billion, and the time one to one and a half years. In the recent Libyan raid described in chapter 12, two complete tactical fighter wing bases for the F-111s and three additional bases for the thirty tankers were needed to provide exactly the same striking power on Tripoli that were provided by two aircraft carriers. The annual costs and amortization of capital of the five air force bases and their air wing are several times the costs of the full carrier and carrier air wings involved in the navy strike. It did not pass notice that the two air force bases in Spain, for which we have paid exorbitant rent since World War II, were once again unavailable, as in nearly every crisis over the past forty years. The Spanish government denied us permission to use it. Based on the Symington study of 1971, the cost today of the Spanish bases in rent alone could have bought eight full aircraft carriers, from which we would be in no danger of being evicted.

The greatest problem, however, of land-based air is its vulnerability to attack. Land bases do not move like a carrier at thirty-one knots, their geographic coordinates are in every targeting computer of every adversary, and we can expect them to be disabled by ballistic and cruise missile attack in the earliest days of any conflict with the Soviet Union. Nearly five hundred operating U.S. air bases were completely lost during the course of World War II. In Korea all air bases were captured by the North Koreans in the first five days. In Southeast Asia, of the dozens of major air bases constructed by the United States in the 1960s at the equivalent in today's dollars of $1 billion apiece, not one remains in U.S. hands. Two of the best, at Cam Ranh Bay and Danang, are now major Soviet operating bases, complete with bowling alleys. By the end of the Vietnam War, the United States had lost to enemy action more than five hundred aircraft destroyed on the ground and on land bases and more than four thousand damaged.

By contrast, in World War II, the United States lost only five small aircraft carriers and no large ones. Since World War II, no carrier has been lost, and no carrier aircraft aboard has been damaged or destroyed by enemy action. There are no U.S. aircraft carriers currently in the hands of potential adversaries. In 1957 we had 105 operational air bases overseas. That number now is fewer than 40 and is shrinking steadily. In time of crisis almost none of them is available for military action. In the 1986 Libyan operations, except for the full cooperation of the United Kingdom, none of our European allies would allow even overflight of their airspace. During the 1973 Arab-Israel war, in order to resupply Israel with A-4 aircraft, the Navy had to line up four aircraft carriers across the Atlantic and into the Mediterranean to hopscotch them across, since not a single nation would allow landing rights.

All of these advantages pay off, of course, only if we know how to employ naval aviation effectively. The Beirut raid had laid bare in the clearest and most inescapable way some very deep problems that many of our aviators had seen and worried about in the years during and since Vietnam. Naval aircraft had been fully engaged in Vietnam from the Gulf of Tonkin incident in 1964 until the settlement of 1973. A sideshow at first, by 1965 the war had come to dominate totally the tactics, training, equipment, and careers of the entire naval aviation community. Because the wide range of combat capabilities of the carrier air wing and land-based patrol aircraft was subordinated to the single purpose of "strategic" bombing and "measured responses," the Vietnam experience gradually institutionalized some deep distortions in the overall balance of carrier aviation. Around the Vietnam mission an entire aviation community, the light-attack community, was formed. The small A-4 Skyhawk, designed in the late 1940s to carry one nuclear weapon on a one-way strategic mission, became the principal workhorse for the bombing campaign in the North and the South. Along with the propeller-driven A-1 Skyraider, these single-seat, expendable, low-cost aircraft were the main batteries for air strikes into North and South Vietnam. At the beginning of the war the A-4 cost less than $500,000, and attrition rates in combat of 6 or 7 percent were affordable and acceptable. Some targets, like the infamous Thanh Hoa Bridge, were so well defended but deemed so interesting to staffs in the chain of command that constant losses were suffered in attacking them, with little effect throughout the war. At Thanh Hoa more than three hundred aircraft were lost in the ten years of war, with no noticeable effect. These horrendous costs in carrying out the "game theory" approach to warfare were inconvenient to the administration leaders, the whiz kids, and staff officers whose policy it was, and to the navy itself. They were never pulled together in one place.

To carry such a tremendous burden of attrition, the navy created more and more light-attack squadrons, training more and more naval aviation cadets to fly them.

Because of the specialized nature of the different types of carrier aircraft, it is normal and necessary that once a pilot is assigned out of flight school to an aircraft type, be it fighter, attack, early-warning, etc., he stays with that aircraft or its replacement throughout his entire career. Each aircraft type therefore has with it a cradle-to-grave fraternity. While each carrier wing is made up of ten different aircraft types, each type comes to the carrier from its own base in the United States. There all the squadrons of the same type of aircraft can live together, train together, and return again and again throughout their careers. Each community has the special bonds of sharing joys and griefs and lifelong friendships, and a passionate commitment to the mission of their community.

At the end of the Vietnam War, when the number of carriers was reduced from twenty-four to twelve, most of the light-attack squadrons needed for that far larger force were not decommissioned. The reasoning was that the JCS had continued to recommend a return to twenty-four aircraft carriers, and the light attack capabilities would be needed for future contingencies even though there were many more squadrons than could fit on the reduced twelve aircraft carriers. The real reason was that the navy had so many light-attack aircraft bought for the Vietnam War, and continued in production by the strong California and Texas lobbies, and had so many light-attack pilots on active duty that it was just too hard to bring the community down to size commensurate with the other aircraft-type communities. This last was not a frivolous concern. The light-attack aviators overwhelmingly bore the brunt of the air war for the navy. Most of the casualties, MIAs and POWs, were light attack, and there was a moral obligation to retain them. But they were the largest source of real combat experience also for the postwar navy, and it would have been foolish to allow them to leave.

Indeed, I myself did not discover that we had so many extra light-attack squadrons until the reform efforts in the aftermath of the Beirut raid. There were in 1984 more than twice the number of such squadrons compared to each of the other aircraft types.

This bulge also creates some career distortion in that all other aircraft types in the carrier air wing have more than one-man crews. That is very significant because the promotion system depends on fitness reports ranking an aviator with his peers in the squadron. Through those rankings, selections are made for those promoted to command squadrons. All the other aircraft types have double or more the number of aviators competing for the opportunity to command a squadron, which is a prerequisite for promotion to captain. Thus in the light-attack community there are nearly twice as many squadrons to command and half the number of people competing for them. As a result, light-attack aviators statistically have twice the likelihood of being promoted to command, and almost twice the probability of being promoted to captain.

Since the Vietnam War the light-attack community has come to dominate numerically the senior ranks of the naval aviation community. This had the effect of maintaining a strong light-attack orientation in tactics, training, and equipment for the whole carrier aviation force.

Nearly half of all air wing commanders and more than half of those staff officers in charge of fleet aviation training were drawn from the light-attack community. Consequently, the tactics developed and the training carried out in preparing air wings for deployment came to be centered around the large daylight dive bombing raids that had been the mainstay of the Vietnam War.

Up to and including the raid in December 1983, the final exam of each carrier worked up before deployment, the operational readiness evaluation

(ORE), consisted of a large massed daylight alpha strike against one of the training ranges off Southern California or Puerto Rico.

While there was a requirement maintained for night operations, it was in fact given very little attention in the actual air wing training. Under my persistent inquiry, both CAGs from the *Kennedy* and the *Independence* reluctantly admitted to me that they did not have one air crew in any of their attack squadrons who were qualified for a night mission at the time of the Beirut raid. They simply had not trained for it since they left the United States.

The long and short of it was that when the flag went up and the navy was asked to produce a major retaliatory strike, when the button was pushed, out came a twenty-year-old obsolete daylight alpha strike. The navy had trained and built that into its system, and that is what came out.

Admiral Watkins and his deputy chiefs of naval operations were not overly pleased with my conclusions, and still less with my determination to make fundamental changes. But Watkins and I had many long discussions of the issues, and he and his staff evaluated every one of my concerns. By the end of February he agreed with me, and he was indeed growing more and more concerned by the plans that were being submitted for contingency operations from the battle group strike planners themselves up through the JCS chain of command.

Shortly after returning from the Middle East, I had drawn up a plan of major changes for our air wing tactics training, personnel policy, and career paths. In early April 1984 I took this plan to the air board meeting at Nellis Air Force Base in Nevada. The air board is the unofficial board of the dozen or so most senior admirals and generals in the navy and marine aviation community. There are never any nonaviators or civilians. I made a three-hour presentation to the air board, complete with maps and detailed plans of the strike, going through it minute-by-minute and then laying out before them my conclusions. Some were quite reluctant to accept what I had to say, but a great deal of discussion seemed to produce a consensus that major changes had to be made.

After a full day of discussion and disputation I returned to Washington and finalized a plan of major changes, working with the deputy chief of naval operations for air warfare, the deputy chief of staff of the marine corps for air, and a selection of very able young tactical aviators. The plan was as follows:

Tactics

Over the years, flying with many air wings of the marines and the navy and from many different carriers had given me a unique perspective across the fleet and the fleet marine force. No two air wings had exactly the same tactics for the same mission, such as attacking an enemy ship or a precision deep strike, etc. It was very different, however, in the fighter community. Early in the Vietnam War, the navy fighter community realized it was not doing as well against the North Vietnamese MiGs as it had in previous wars. The ratio was only about two-to-one favorable. A school that has now become famous in the movie and named for it, *Top Gun*, was created to bring together all of the best wisdom and experience to test out, develop, and teach air-to-air tactics navy-wide. Once this school got functioning, the kill ratio rose to fifteen to one. After the war the air force adopted this approach and created the fighter weapons school at Nellis Air Force Base to do the same thing.

In the submarine world, one submarine squadron, in New London, is a designated developer and evaluator of antisubmarine tactics and doctrine. It has full responsibility for developing and then publishing the training doctrine for tactics. It is first class.

Since becoming secretary of the navy I had done a week's active duty every year flying with the 2nd Marine Air Wing on the West Coast, and I had attended each year a part of the training class at the Marine Air Warfare Training School (MAWTS) in Yuma, Arizona. MAWTS was way ahead of the navy in evaluating intelligence and experience from combat all over the world and developing tactics to deal with the growing threat from SAMs, electronic warfare, and guns. Marine tactics using the same aircraft as the navy were far better and far more effective than the navy's tactics. The marines had built a computerized radar range adapted from the navy's air combat maneuvering range used for dog fighting and had added the capability to track ground-to-air and air-to-ground tactics. This system enables crews to fly missions on the range against real-threat radars and computer-generated missiles and guns, all of which are recorded from three radar sites and fused in a computer. When the crews return from the training mission, they sit in a theater and have the entire engagement played back on three-dimensional screens that show whether they were shot down and whether they put the bombs on target. The marines found that when they tried many of the tactics commonly used in the navy air wings they always were shot down. The plain fact was that the twenty-year-old Vietnam tactics simply were inadequate to deal with the modern generation of heat-seeking and radar-homing missiles, radar- and computer-guided Gatling guns, and sophisticated Soviet electronic warfare capabilities. We had the potential for having whole strikes wiped out if they ever went into combat against a well-defended target using then-current tactics.

A glaring need that also had to be dealt with was the failure of the system for tactical development and training to take full advantage of existing intelligence. Enormous investments that the United States had made in satellite and air-based intelligence-gathering and computerized fusion of the latest intelligence had been largely untapped by the naval aviation community. All the information was available in the major fleet intelligence centers, but the operational units simply were not asking for the product in a useable form. Nor did the squadron and air wing have sufficient well-trained intelligence personnel to synthesize the intelligence into forms usable by strike planners and squadron aviators.

The solution to these problems was the creation of the Navy Strike Warfare Center, or "Strike U."

In May 1984 I signed the order creating "Strike U" and directed the reprogramming of $200 million over five years to equip the site. We chose the existing training base at Fallon, Nevada, and funded major improvements to procure a computerized training range that could handle thirty-six aircraft simultaneously with a theater that could handle an entire air wing for playback. We funded sufficient real and simulated equipment to provide actual-threat radars and missiles to establish an environment equal to the most challenging target conceivable.

To bring the enormous resources of intelligence product to the tactical doctrine and training, we set up an intelligence fusion center at "Strike U" to gather from the intelligence community the latest and most highly classified intelligence bearing on tactical aviation and to apply it with proper safeguards to the development of tactics and evaluation. Equally important was use of this intelligence fusion to train air wing leaders to know what to ask for and how to use what they could get. We also funded a competitive program to provide each air wing and eventually each squadron with a desktop computer and software able to do rapid route planning, strike planning, and tactical evaluation by fusing all inputs of threat intelligence, geography, environment, and weather.

Jim Watkins; Vice Admiral Robert "Dutch" Schultz, the deputy CNO for air; Roger Duter, my special assistant for tactical programs; Captain Joe Prueher, the first commander of "Strike U"; and Dr. Roger Whiteway, first director of training, deserve enormous credit for achieving the most rapid doctrinal and budgetary turnaround I have ever witnessed in government. By September 1984 we had a building at Fallon operating, with the first class entering. As of this writing it has taken over the role we had envisioned. Today every air wing must go to Fallon for a three-week period of daily flying and tactical training and evaluation. It is done on the fully instrumented range against real, active threats, dropping real ordnance that is scored very accurately. Each strike or flight is recorded and played back before the aviators and their staffs. If the bombs did not get to the target, this is exposed to all. Even more attention-getting are the missiles that fly on the computer screens and blow up those jets using inadequate tactics. Now we know what works and what does not work, and there is a source to promulgate the do's and the don'ts and the proper tactics for all squadrons throughout the fleet and the fleet marine force. "Strike U" is now the single authoritative source for this tactical development. Every use of tactical aviation around the world is watched carefully, and experienced aviators from friendly nations come and share their tactical lessons. We are now training a generation of aviators who understand what the technical intelligence and the national intelligence collection capabilities can produce of use to them, how to get it, and how to use it. The "Strike U" staff is also asked for an annual evaluation of the proposed navy budget priorities for tactical naval aviation. Usually they have very significant disagreements with what the bureaucrats in Washington are proposing in the budget, and still more with what the summer interns on the Hill are writing into the legislation.

Training

The December 4 raid revealed two things about our training. First, it was based on inadequate tactics; second, it was not producing what on paper it looked like it was producing. The creation of "Strike U" would correct the first problem through its development and dissemination of proven tactics to each of the aircraft type-wings. But the second problem required a new approach to ensure that the training concentrated on those tactics and skills that "Strike U" had validated and not simply what was the most fun. Chief among the least-fun things that jet aviators do is fly at night. And, while the requirement for night qualifications always has been maintained, there is a big difference between being able to take off and land safely at night, at which all carrier aviators are proficient, and being able to fly against an enemy threat at night and put weapons accurately on targets and still survive. Flying night interdiction tactics very close to the ground at high speed over all terrain and in all weather is every bit as demanding as landing on a carrier at night. If air crews don't do it frequently, they will not be able to do it when they really have to without killing themselves.

We initiated a complete reorientation of our training syllabus. We abolished the ORE alpha strike as the final exam for each air wing and instead concentrated on a syllabus requirement of certain kinds of training missions that had to be done with a certain frequency, such as night terrain-following; and "nap"-of-the-earth navigation and standoff bombing. As a result, today the training of the air wings is far more realistic, is derived directly from the most likely missions required, and is based on the tactics validated by "Strike U."

Equipment

Because of the light-attack force structure that Vietnam had bequeathed to naval aviation, there was a large mismatch between the types of aircraft in the navy inventory, the types of weapons for all the aircraft, and the types of missions that the theater commanders now required of them against a threat that was far more sophisticated than any faced in Vietnam. In the navy and the marine corps, we had forty squadrons of light-attack A-7s and A-4s, but only seventeen of the much more capable night all-weather A-6s.

The huge inertia of the Pentagon system bequeathed tactical air munitions from the Vietnam-era and even World War II. These were primarily conventional iron bombs delivered by World War II dive-bombing and lay-down fly-overs of the target. Such equipment and weapons are effective if nobody using very sophisticated equipment is shooting back at you. As we saw in Chapter 8, the Argentines used these A-4s to put iron bombs into twenty British ships in the Falklands, but as we also saw, the Royal Navy had only pre-Vietnam era defenses. Where a target area is defended by modern-technology air defenses, such as the Soviet ZSU-23-4 radar-guided guns, and heat-seeking and radar-guided missiles of supersonic speed, light-attack aircraft with conventional munitions simply cannot survive. The Israelis found this out the hard way in 1973, taking horrendous losses in the first week before calling off use of such aircraft against defended targets.

The equipment answer to today's sophisticated threats lies in sophisticated weapons that can be fired from outside the most heavily defended target area yet give accuracy measured in feet. But even for the delivery of standoff weapons, one needs aircraft more sophisticated than A-7 and A-4 aircraft, because of the need in most cases to keep either data link or laser contact between the delivery aircraft and the standoff weapon and the target. In most combat situations there is some potential aircraft threat from every direction, if only from small-arms fire, but 90 percent of the defenses are in and around the high-value target itself, whether it be a headquarters, a tank formation, or an enemy ship. Against such defended targets it is a losing game to come within three to five miles of operating defenses at night.

In daylight an attacking aircraft has the dilemma that the higher he goes the more vulnerable he is to radar missiles, whereas the lower he goes the more he eliminates the missile threat but vastly increases the gun threat. The United States in Vietnam and Israel in the Yom Kippur War lost over 60 percent of their aircraft losses to guns. One Israeli pilot told me in 1973 that flying at four hundred knots at a hundred feet over the battlefield, he saw a Syrian soldier raise a pistol and shoot as he flashed over him. The bullet hit the hydraulic line, and the Israeli had to eject.

The obvious answer for the survival of tactical air over the battlefield is to do the missions at night. Not only are all human beings less effective at night, but also 90 percent of the current threat to our aviation depends on visual acquisition by the antiaircraft operators, especially including the highly effective heat-seeking missiles. This is clearly the way to go when you can pick and choose the time of attack. Unfortunately, however, armies tend to fight during the day, and, land or sea, wars do tend to go on twenty-four hours a day.

Low-cost, single-pilot aircraft have difficulty in both environments. Controlling an aircraft against multiple threats is a full-time job, and adding to it controlling laser-guided or other precision munitions to precise targets is more than one human being can reliably handle unless defenses have been suppressed.

Using night to advantage requires flying very low to the ground, which eliminates the air-defense radars and radar-homing missiles, which are equally effective night or day. But flying low to the earth at high speed at night is very dangerous and takes a sophisticated aircraft with terrain-following radar and use of the fullest concentration of a well-practiced pilot. Therefore, all such aircraft today and probably indefinitely into the future require more than one crew member. As the pilot concentrates on not hitting the ground, the copilot navigates and operates the defensive and offensive weapons systems. There is simply too much to do for one human being, no matter how well trained and equipped.

When attack missions must be carried out in daytime against a modern sophisticated defense network, there is no alternative to a highly integrated systematic approach to suppress the integrated air defense system of the target area. This requires a careful rolling back of the defenses through electronic warfare, and jamming and destruction of warning and fire-control radars and missile sites by radar-homing missiles and other precision munitions. This defense suppression must be done before attacking aircraft can come into the target area without suffering unacceptable loss rates.

But to carry out such a defense suppression (SIAD—suppression of integrated air defenses) successfully requires a great deal of very sophisticated high-tech equipment in the form of on-board jammers, standoff jammers, and other electronic warfare measures; very expensive radar-homing missiles and stand-off precision munitions; and highly effective technical intelligence-gathering to avoid surprises. It cannot be done on the cheap, and it cannot be done by cheap, simple aircraft.

After the 1973 war the Israelis rejected further procurement of cheap, low-mix, light-attack aircraft and procured instead the most sophisticated high-tech aircraft, jammers, and other equipment necessary to develop a SIAD approach. Thus we saw in the Bekaa Valley campaign of the Israelis the change in equipment and tactics that applied a systematic rollback of Syrian defenses with nearly 100 percent effectiveness. It is this integrated approach differing between night and day tactics that has now been validated on the instrumented ranges of MAWTS and "Strike U" and that is now the foundation of naval tactical aviation doctrine and training.

Unfortunately, however, we had in 1983 a huge mismatch between the kinds of aircraft that had been procured and indeed those that were in the pipeline. Even with the many extra light-attack squadrons, we had many more light-attack aircraft than even they could use. Congress had continued to add light-attack aircraft to navy budgets throughout the 1970s, long after the Vietnam War was over. The navy gave away or sold off at tiny prices hundreds of A-4s and A-7s but still had to put many of them in storage at David Monthan Air Force Base in the desert.

As recounted elsewhere, the ideological devotion of the OSD staff to the cheaper-is-better theory had created the F/A-18 program, against navy opposition. Thus in 1981 we inherited a navy plan drawn up by the OSD that required us to procure 1,366 lightweight F/A-18s to replace the recently procured A-7Es, but no A-6s nor any replacement for the A-6s and very few jamming aircraft and no new electronic intelligence aircraft.

Having been forced to accept the F/A-18 by the OSD, the navy in the 1970s quietly added more and more capability and sophistication to it as it was being developed so that by 1981 it was in fact a dandy aircraft for its daylight mission.

The F-18 is a magnificent airplane to fly, with a better than one-to-one thrust-to-weight ratio and eye-watering maneuverability. It is thrilling and satisfying to fly it in its daylight maneuvers with pop-ups, roll-aheads, jinking, and switching back and forth from air-to-air to air-to-ground modes. But it is not fun to do this at night; in fact, it is very scary. Neither is it fun to be placed in a subordinate position as one part of an integrated SIAD, as the F-18s were forced to do in the Libyan air strike while the A-6s did the bombing. Because of the dominant numbers of members of the light-attack community within naval aviation, there remains still a strong resistance against moving too far away from the Vietnam style of ground attack.

Because of the speed and agility of the F-18, its advocates raised the cry that the answer to the increased threat environment is "speed is life." By going faster and jinking harder, one could joust with the SAMs and guns and beat them. That macho argument is valid if your only task is to survive. Obviously, the shorter time you are in the threat area the better off you are; and against the older Soviet SAMs it is possible to turn harder and faster than the missiles. There are, however, two fundamental flaws with this argument. First, the faster you go and the more you jink, the less possible it is to deliver weapons accurately. And if you do not deliver them accurately, there is no point in being there in the first place. Second, the modern generation of Soviet and Western missiles are supersonic, have a 40-G turn rate capability, and can outfly any aircraft known to man. If they have locked on to you it makes no difference whether you are going five hundred knots or twelve hundred knots—you cannot outfly them. Third, to maneuver at high speed at low altitudes it is necessary to use afterburner. In afterburner, fuel consumption rates increase by ten times, and the brilliant heat source negates entirely the use of defensive flares against heat-seeking missiles.

Based on the operations analyses and the data from the instrumented ranges, we documented what common sense had told us, that while supersonic speed was essential for air-to-air mission capability, it was downright counterproductive for the attack mission. Far more important was the ability to fly safely at very low level and deliver weapons reliably with precision measured in feet, and to do all this at night and in foul weather. Based on this we accelerated a program for an entirely new advance tactical aircraft (ATA) for the night all-weather attack mission. It would be a highly maneuverable subsonic two-man aircraft with major new technologies for survivability. For the interim we contracted to integrate all the new technologies developed for the F-18 in new computers, radars, engines, and survivability into the basic A-6 frame. We committed to continue to procure the F-18s so we could have sixteen to eighteen of these highly versatile and reliable swing fighters in each carrier air wing and equip all the marine fighter squadrons with it. We accelerated the EA-6 electronic jamming aircraft and invested in a substantial upgrading of its capabilities. We increased the procurement of the E-2C early-warning aircraft and started a new program to procure a replacement for the thirty-year-old EA-3 electronic intelligence aircraft.

For weapons systems we put into immediate production a great program called the Skipper, which was developed at our China Lake navy lab, inventor of the Sidewinder missile. The engineers at China Lake took a laser-guided thousand-pound bomb and stuck a missile motor on the back, giving the fleet a seven-mile standoff missile with a huge thousand-pound payload and a ten-foot accuracy. It cost only $25,000 apiece and could be procured immediately. As a result the navy and marines now have thousands of Skippers throughout the fleet and crews that are able to fire them in training because of their low costs. The Skipper was the first used successfully in combat by an A-6 to sink an Iranian frigate in the Persian Gulf in 1988.

We funded other major standoff programs, such as the infrared-homing version of the Maverick standoff missile and a laser-homing version of the same missile. We improved the Harpoon antiship missile and developed a new version called SLAM for use against land targets. We also joined with the air force in two advanced standoff weapons programs.

Aviation Career Policy

Another problem brought into clear view by the Beirut air strike was the inadequacy of the command structure in the carrier air wing, and the career planning and assignment system in support of it. The command organization that had evolved after World War II and had been cemented during the Vietnam War was headed by the battle group commander, a rear admiral. The carrier air wing, normally composed of eight to ten squadrons, was commanded by a senior commander in rank who reported directly to the carrier skipper. He was called the CAG, from the old title of the wing as the carrier air group, and the squadron commanders reported to him. Normally about thirty-five to forty years old, the CAG was given no special training but moved directly to command of a wing after squadron command, with about a year of staff duty between. His only training for the job was a two-week tactics school, and qualification in two or three of the different wing aircraft. The emphasis was on hands-on flying leadership.

This system, inherited from World War II, was also adequate for Vietnam, where the tactical situation and the missions were straightforward and unchanging for most of the ten years. Since the Vietnam War, however, use of the carrier air wing in crisis situations has taken on a far more important and complex role. As in Beirut and Libya, employment of the air wing has come to be the chosen instrument of the president of the United States, carrying the gravest implications and involving the focus and judgments of the entire world. The wing itself uses systems far more complex than before, in a far more technically complicated environment, facing a far more sophisticated defense.

In Beirut it became painfully obvious that we were placing de facto responsibility for successful use of the air wing on the shoulders of men who were not given the requisite training and experience to carry out the job in the most demanding circumstances. This inadequacy was not just discovered in Beirut but also had concerned many battle group commanders years before. The Beirut raid, however, crystallized the issue, and we moved to change the situation.

Jim Watkins was at first a bit skeptical of my determination to make major changes as a result of the Beirut lessons learned. He did not attend the air board meeting at Nellis, but he went along with my plan for "Strike U," which resulted from it. But as 1984 progressed he was more deeply involved with the JCS in formulating contingency plans for possible action in the Mideast. He expressed to me increasing frustration with the strike plans that our navy CAGs were sending in. They were much less imaginative and thorough than those submitted by the air force. We had long discussions about the causes, and together we formulated plans for change. Jim suggested we pull together a group of aviators from commander to one-star admiral, including Mel Paisley, a World War II fighter ace, and have a day brainstorming at the new "Strike U." We did this on February 22, 1985. It was a crackling, no-holds-barred free-for-all in which Watkins, a submariner, was superb. My proposals were argued, challenged, and re-formed. Out of it came our agenda for changing the wing commander's role and the entire system of training the carrier air wing.

The system we now have in place puts the air wing under the command of a senior experienced captain who has been given extensive training in battle group employment, tactics, and strategy, and extensive introduction to the intelligence community and training in the uses and calibration of intelligence. In addition to squadron command, the senior captains will have had at least one Washington tour to enable them to understand (to the extent it is possible) how the national security system works so they appreciate what is really intended by orders given from Washington.

Instead of reporting to the captain of the ship, he is an equal of the captain of the ship and reports directly to the admiral. The captain of a carrier when it is under way must be on or near the bridge twenty-four hours a day and has his total attention consumed by the operation and housekeeping of the ship itself, the air wing commander is subordinate to the captain, but the captain has no operational authority over the air wing commander's strike planning and employment of the air wing. This new senior air wing commander is called "super CAG" and has a deputy who is a former squadron commander who will be selected for super CAG if he has a successful tour as deputy. The deputy now does the flying and leads the air wing from the cockpit. The air wing commander now has the principal responsibility for the intelligent employment and tactical operation and planning of the air wing itself. Thus, on April 18, 1988, the deputy led the successful strike against the Iranian frigates while the super CAG remained with the admiral aboard the *Enterprise*.

Equally important, we changed the rote system of working up the air wing prior to deployment, by deriving the training syllabus from contingency plans based on tactics developed and validated by "Strike U." For the first time we had rationalized the process to hone the carrier as a tool of the theater commander, the "CINC." The CINC establishes the mission; "Strike U" develops and validates tactics to execute the mission; the super CAG trains the air wing (including three weeks at "Strike U" to master those tactics); the super CAG and battle group commander plan and execute actual missions as ordered by the CINC.

Unlike under the prior arrangement, the super CAG now controls all his squadrons when the carrier is not deployed and the squadrons are dispersed to their functional air wings. He writes the fitness reports of the squadron commanders, controls the training money, and supervises the tactical development and training of his squadrons. He becomes the critical operational link that ties together the validated tactical doctrine developed at "Strike U" and combines it with the proper equipment through appropriately rigorous training to make the air wing a fully efficient military tool.*

On a different level, we finally set up a new career path called aviation duty officer (ADO), providing the opportunity for outstanding aviators who do not wish to become bureaucrats and compete for flag to stay in flying jobs for their full careers.

The fighter community, those aviators charged with the responsibility for maintaining air superiority against enemy bombers, fighters, and cruise mis-

*A great many admirals opposed this new career path. They did not realize the major drawback of the old system in that a would-be flag candidate had to pass through so many jobs (executive officer of a squadron, commanding officer, a CAG, executive officer of a carrier, commander of an oiler or supply ship, command of a carrier) so quickly that little time was left to improve the system or question assumptions. The resulting carrier admirals had a profound faith in the existing arrangements—perfectly understandable but a major reason why an ossified carrier aviation community practiced tactics twenty years out of date.

siles, was not in need of reform. As a result of the heads-up tactical approach that has been established with the Top Gun school at Miramar, the fighter community had very innovative and effective tactics and doctrine standardized throughout the fleet and was staying well ahead of the potential threat. We had an excellent fleet air defense system in the F-14 and E-2C, a new development to upgrade the F-14 using F-18 avionics and new General Electric engines, and we had a memorandum of agreement with the air force to develop a naval derivative of their advanced tactical fighter for the next century.

The technological and doctrinal modernizations under way in the specialized aviation worlds of the other carrier aircraft communities in antisubmarine warfare, electronic warfare, command and control, and airborne early warning, gave us a solid confidence that we were on top of the problems of the future. Now that we had used the lessons of Beirut and other inputs to correct the glaring inadequacies of the carrier air wing attack community, we had put the carrier itself back on track. It would remain the key element of national power necessary to maintain command of the seas into the next century. "If it ain't broke, don't fix it" is a pretty sound management philosophy. As a result of the Beirut raid, we found something that was indeed broke, and we fixed it.

Chapter 12

Dealing with Qaddafi

American failure in Beirut would be partially redeemed by success against a pirate in Tripoli.

Muammar Qaddafi is a living monument to the weakness and indecision of the West. On more than one occasion, this foremost practitioner of state-sponsored terrorism has been vulnerable to overthrow, only to be spared by European or American vacillation. When Washington finally was driven by his outrages to strike, it offered a case study of how difficult it had become to deal with the obvious.

Qaddafi ascended to power in 1969 under peculiar circumstances. As Libya's economic prospects brightened, its political system disintegrated. The Americans and the British, both of whom retained military bases in Libya, had helped King Idris I onto the throne when Libya gained independence in 1951. As Idris aged, however, he and his heir fell into a bitter quarrel. When Dick Allen and I were sent to Libya by Henry Kissinger in April 1969, Tripoli was full of rumors about coups against the king. Both the monarch and the crown prince were preparing to depose each other, but when a coup was launched on September 1st, it turned out to be that of the unknown, though British-trained Qaddafi. With the old king infirm, ineffective, and conveniently out of the country, the coup succeeded.

Libya's new master lost little time announcing that he was a disciple of Egyptian president Gamal Abdel Nasser. Qaddafi, a devout Muslim and fierce anti-Marxist, was by no means a Soviet puppet. Yet, like Nasser, his anti-Western proclivities propelled him to seek Soviet assistance.

We of the West have a hard time dealing with terrorism, perhaps because we do not really understand the terrorist's aims. He knows that he cannot win

an open test of strength. His objective instead is to paralyze our will to act—
to pit our regard for individual life against our instinct for self-defense. So every
terrorist action has a political purpose—to get us to change our policy to save
innocent lives. Democratic leaders here and abroad have found it very difficult to resist this pressure, especially when it is amplified by sensational TV
coverage, even if it means that other innocent lives may be put at risk later.

Qaddafi first used terrorism as part of the effort to force the United States
and Western Europe to reduce their support for Israel—an effort that began
with airline hijackings. Beyond the Arab-Israeli conflict, Qaddafi also sought
to make of himself a world power through terrorism. By the early 1970s, as
Western Europe reeled under the Munich massacre, airline hijackings, mur-
ders, and mayhem, Qaddafi's oil money was financing a terrorist interna-
tionale: the PLO, the IRA, the Red Brigades, the Japanese Red Army, even the
Moro Muslim guerrillas in the Philippines. The Soviet Union and its Eastern
European allies were happy to provide arms and training to these various "freedom fighters" in exchange for desperately needed hard cash. The result was a
horrifying paradox: In purchasing Libya's oil, the West was financing Qaddafi's
attacks . . . on the West.

The United States itself was mercifully free of many incidents on its own
territory, although Americans abroad were often targets. When Iran's Ayatollah
Khomeini turned to open terrorism, however, the issue transformed American
politics. America's inability to come to grips with state-sponsored terrorism
helped to seal the doom of President Jimmy Carter's bid for reelection. The
Reagan administration hoped to do better.

Qaddafi had made himself a target not just because he blatantly supported
terrorism but also because he had expanded his operations into outright international aggression.

Against international law, Libya had laid claim to the entire Gulf of Sidra (or
Sirte), a large indentation in the North African coastline that was flanked by
Libyan territory but was far deeper than the twelve-mile limit. This normally
would have been treated like the dozens of other unlawful claims that we do not
recognize. But the Gulf of Sidra was the only place in the Mediterranean that was
free of any major sea lanes or airways—for decades the U.S. Sixth Fleet had
depended on it for periodic live fire exercises. Qaddafi's new prohibition gave the
Sixth Fleet a training problem. The chief of naval operations, Admiral Holloway,
strongly recommended that the Sixth Fleet continue its exercises and be prepared
to defend itself. The Carter administration, however, received firm intelligence
that Qaddafi was prepared to fight. (There was indeed strong evidence that in

1979 at least one of his MiG fighters actually fired a missile at an Air Force EC-135 aircraft.) The Carter administration had no desire for any such confrontation with Qaddafi, and the navy was prohibited from deploying any of its ships or aircraft below the 32 degrees, 30 minutes north latitude line—the "line of death," as Qaddafi called it—thus bowing to the master terrorist's power play.

With Reagan in office the navy put forward a new request to resume operations in the gulf below the line of death. It was swiftly approved, and the Sixth Fleet proceeded with its plans for a major exercise in that area. In August 1981 the fleet crossed the line of death, and the Libyan Air Force, now grown to several hundred late-model MiGs, SU-22s, and Mirages, rose to meet it. Qaddafi had bought far more aircraft than he had pilots able to fly them, and there were Syrian, North Korean, North Vietnamese, and East German "volunteers" manning his force. In the first few days of the exercise Libyan aircraft attempted to get into firing positions on U.S fighters protecting the fleet. In every case they were unable. The high-tech F-14s, with two-hundred-mile radars, were able to maneuver into firing position long before the Libyans ever saw them. Very often the Libyans first noticed the F-14s when they were just a few feet off their wings. Finally, in circumstances that are still unclear today, two SU-22s were suspected of firing on a flight of two F-14s launched from *Nimitz*. The outcome never was in doubt. The F-14s had the Libyan planes locked up in their fire-control radars while the SU-22s were still on the runway in their takeoff roll sixty miles away. The Tomcats splashed them each with a single missile.

This was not the end of America's involvement with Qaddafi.

On June 14, 1985, TWA flight 847 was seized, forced to Beirut, then flown to Algeria and, before our antiterrorist units could act, returned to Beirut. The pattern proved familiar. The terrorists found an American—in this case, navy diver Robert Stethem—and murdered him. Their courage fortified, the killers then demanded that Israel release Shiite prisoners taken from Lebanon as part of the Israeli withdrawal. There were dramatic scenes of helpless Americans held at gunpoint. Finally, though no overt American pressure was proved, a deal was reached to release the Shiites.

This incident angered the Reagan White House. It was followed in October by a similar incident, but this time with a better ending. On October 3, 1985, the *Achille Lauro* cruise ship departed Genoa, Italy, for the Middle East. Careless security let four Arab gunmen board the boat despite Latin American passports and lack of luggage. Their original mission was probably to infiltrate Israel on one of the ship's port calls, but a steward discovered them oiling their guns while moored in Alexandria, Egypt.

The pirates then seized control of the ship and forced it to sail for Syria, but the Syrian government refused to receive them, and the Israeli government rejected the terrorists' demand for the release of fifty Palestinian prisoners. True to form, the terrorists then murdered an American. This time Leon Klinghoffer, a New Yorker confined to a wheelchair, was the victim.

Upon their return to Alexandria, the terrorists were set free under terms negotiated by their leader, the particularly vicious Palestinian Abu Abbas, with the support of the Egyptian government. The Italian and West German ambassadors, but not the United States, agreed formally to these arrangements, which were to send the terrorists to freedom.

But when the White House confirmed on Thursday, October 10th that the terrorists, despite Cairo's claims, were still in Egypt, an operation began that will always redound to the credit of Bud McFarlane, who orchestrated a daring plan to intercept the terrorists and force them to land at a NATO air base in Italy. The instrument would be the Sixth Fleet, commanded by Admiral Frank Kelso. He had experienced with me the extreme frustration of seeing the bloated chain of command bring on tragedy and paralysis in Beirut, and he had learned the lessons well. Kelso's battle group commander, Rear Admiral Dave Jeremiah, launched six F-14 interceptors, two A-6 tankers, and two E-2C radar aircraft from the carrier *Saratoga*. They had to fly five hundred miles in the pitch darkness to the point where they hoped to intercept the terrorists preparing to fly to Tunisia on an Egyptian aircraft.

The Egypt Air 737 from Al Maza Air Base took off for Algiers at 10:10 P.M. Cairo time, only ten minutes after the president made his final decision to intercept. While intelligence had provided the type of the aircraft and its side number, there were more than sixty airliners in the air over the eastern Mediterranean at the time. Thanks to the quality of the radars aboard the E-2Cs and F-14s, the number of potential targets was narrowed, but visual inspection had to be made of four different aircraft before the correct side number was found. In each case the F-14s had to fly silently right up next to the unsuspecting aircraft and read the side number with a flashlight. One of those aircraft inspected turned out to be the American C-141 carrying General Steiner and his commandoes, who had been ordered to Akrotiri, Cyprus, in hopes of apprehending the pirates in the event of the successful interception and was now returning to Sigonella, Italy. While the aircraft was in the air, intelligence learned that Abu Abbas, the mastermind of the plot, was himself aboard the Egyptian airliner, along with some Egyptian commandoes.

When the F-14s found the right airliner, there was a problem of communications in that they were equipped only with military UHF radios, and the airliner had a civilian VHF radio. They communicated, therefore, through one of the E-2C planes, more than a hundred miles away (the E-2C had both radios). One of the controllers aboard the E-2C spoke to the Egyptian pilot, pretending he was one of the F-14 pilots. After making initial contact, the F-14s suddenly turned on all their lights and, to the amazement of the Egyptian crew, they were surrounded by four F-14s. The initial reluctance of the Egyptian Air pilot to change course to Sigonella was soon overcome by threats of dire consequences. He changed course and was escorted some four hundred miles to Sigonella by the F-14s. On approach to Sigonella, the Italians denied the Egyptian plane landing permission, and only when he declared an emergency was he given permission to land. The E-2C controllers had ordered him to make a left turn off the runway over to the American side of the base, but at the last minute the Italian tower reversed instructions as to which runway to use, so when he turned left, it was onto the Italian side of the field rather than the American side. General Steiner and his commandoes landed right behind the Egyptian airliner and followed it off the runway. They immediately surrounded the aircraft and sought to take custody of the pirates. Italian *carabinieri*, however, arrived and surrounded the airliner and the Americans. A tense standoff followed until General Steiner agreed to turn the pirates over to the Italians. In the meantime, once the F-14s saw the aircraft safely on the ground, they returned the five hundred miles back and trapped aboard *Saratoga*. The terrorists were eventually released by the Italians.

On November 23rd an Egyptian flight was hijacked after leaving Athens; this time a U.S. Air Force civilian was murdered. Sixty passengers were killed when the Egyptians botched the rescue. The next day a U.S. military shopping mall in Frankfurt was bombed, wounding twenty-three Americans. A month later, on December 27th, the Rome and Vienna airports were struck: five Americans, including an eleven-year-old girl, were among the dead; more than a hundred people were wounded.

Clear evidence of Qaddafi's complicity in these attacks finally persuaded Washington to do what it should have done years before. Economic links were broken; the fifteen hundred Americans in Libya were ordered to leave immediately; and Libya's actions were described by executive order as an "unusual and extraordinary threat to the national security and foreign policy of the United States." Libyan assets were frozen ($2.5 billion worth), and at last the president declared that Qaddafi must end support and training camps for terrorism.

Qaddafi had reached an advanced stage of delusion with respect to American intentions. Choosing to interpret the European reaction as a rebuff to Washington, he pursued fresh terrorist plans. Once more, these were covered by "dialogues."

This time Washington would not be put off. In March, the Sixth Fleet prepared to cross the "line of death." The exercises began just north of 32/30 but did not cross it, their purpose to give our F-14s and F-18s a good idea of Libya's air force. Hundreds of their MiGs and Mirages attempted intercepts, but there was no shooting.

In the second week of March, just after these events but before the crossing of the "line of death," I flew out to the Mediterranean to meet with Kelso to discuss upcoming operations and visit the fleet and see firsthand how ready the men were. Kelso settled in aboard *Coronado*, an amphibious assault ship, which had been modified to serve as his flagship. After the Beirut fiasco, Admiral Watkins and I had decided that the commander of the fleet belonged at sea, not on land. He reviewed the plans and the rules of engagement. The fleet was ready.

There were some light moments. As we departed, the bo'sun piped us over the side, and the traditional two bells rang through the ship, "*Ding, ding,* Navy departing, *ding, ding,* Sixth Fleet departing." We went down the ladder and through a double row of side boys in full dress. There was a delay in the arrival of the admiral's barge, so we stood on the float by the side boys, awaiting its arrival. I noticed there were swarms of fish, each about a foot long, all around the flagship, so while we waited I asked the admiral what kind of fish they were. Frank did not know and asked his aide, who also did not know. Frank then asked if anybody among the dozen or so officers standing there knew what kind of fish they were. All shook their heads in the negative. Then one of the young side boys said in a very nervous voice, "Excuse me, sir, but I know what kind of fish they are." The admiral said, "Well, sailor, tell the Secretary what kind of fish they are." The young sailor, still at attention, said, "Sir, they are called shiteaters, sir."

Aboard the carrier *Coral Sea*, whose keel was laid when I was two years old, everyone was spring-loaded for their next visit down to Libya. *Coral Sea, Saratoga,* and *America* were all loaded to the gunnels with every kind of missile and ammunition, and each with ninety days of spare parts. Here was the payoff from the six-hundred-ship navy and the Reagan buildup. What was especially satisfying to me was to see the tremendous change in tactical thinking that "Strike U" had brought about in each of the three air wings. The lessons of Beirut had been applied.

In the third week of March, the fleet assembled for the third time for a massive exercise in the Gulf of Sidra. This was to be the full challenge below the "line of death." There were finally enough ships to satisfy even the most cautious bureaucrat. Kelso had under his command the three aircraft carriers; two Aegis cruisers, *Ticonderoga* and *Yorktown*; and 122 other American ships. On March 22nd the first ships and aircraft crossed below 32/30, and Qaddafi's response was immediate. During the earlier exercises there had been more than 160 attempts by the Libyan Air Force, now grown to more than 500 MiGs, Mirages, and Sukhois, to intercept American aircraft or ships. Not a single sortie ever got into a firing position on an American aircraft, thanks to the superb coordination of our Aegis cruisers, E-2C radar aircraft, F-14 interceptors, and F-18 strike fighters. Only one Libyan aircraft, a MiG-25, ever got a visual sighting on a U.S. ship, and he was under escort by F-14s when he did so.

Qaddafi's air force was intimidated. He ordered all his aircraft away from the fleet. Not one took to the air over water. But as soon as the first F-14s were within range of the Soviet-built long-range SA-5s Qaddafi gave the order to fire, and a pair of SA-5s were launched. I reviewed the printouts from the *Aegis* cruisers following the engagements, and there on the computer paper is the trace of the SA-5s locked up in the *Aegis* cruisers' fire control radar, streaking toward the U.S. aircraft, which were immediately warned. Our planes were able to counter the missiles. These highly deadly supersonic weapons exploded harmlessly at high altitude.

Jim Watkins and I were sitting in the Navy Command Center in the Pentagon when we heard Kelso give the order to attack the SA-5 missile site. We then heard the A-7 pilots report missiles away. Within a few minutes Kelso reported that the missile sites were off the air. They had been hit by the Harm antiradiation missile that for years had been the target of military reformers in Congress who claimed it wouldn't work. In the following hours, three Libyan fast missile boats attempted to engage the fleet. These were the ships that armchair strategists had declared would easily defeat large aircraft carriers and surface combatants. In each case the Libyan patrol boats were easily destroyed by A-6s from the carrier. By dawn of the following day, not one Libyan ship or aircraft would venture outside the twelve-mile limit, and not one ever did after until Kelso left the Sixth Fleet.

Kelso's plan called for approaching closer to the Libyan coast, staying outside of the twelve-mile limit, but increasing the pressure to the point where Qaddafi would have to launch his Air Force. It was Kelso's expectation that a massive turkey shoot would follow, perhaps dealing a mortal blow to Qaddafi's prestige and leadership. To our consternation and astonishment, however, the entire exercise was called off early, and the huge armada withdrew on March 27th. Internal Pentagon politics had prevailed.

While Kelso had executed the operation flawlessly, its fullest effect was frustrated by premature termination. Qaddafi seized upon the withdrawal of the Sixth Fleet to proclaim victory. He then began a new round of terrorism against civilians. Beginning on March 27th, the intelligence community received evidence of almost daily new orders for the initiation of terrorist attacks on American and other Western targets by Qaddafi's "people's bureaus." Because of good intelligence, nearly every one was thwarted, but on April 5th, the La Belle disco in West Berlin, favored by American soldiers, was bombed, killing two Americans and wounding more than fifty others. On April 8th a TWA flight from Rome had a midair explosion that took four American lives, including that of one little girl.

Following the Berlin bombing, for whatever reason, a flood of leaks from the White House, the State Department, and the Defense Department filled the media with stories that the president was now really going to clobber Qaddafi and that a retaliatory strike against him was imminent. It was, as a journalist remarked, the least secret operation in history. It was all true; Oliver North's working group was selecting targets. Five were finally selected, two in Benghazi—a commando/terrorist training camp, and the military airfield—and three in Tripoli: a terrorist/commando naval training base; the former Wheelus Air Force Base; and the prime target, the Azziziya barracks compound in Tripoli, which housed the command center for Libyan intelligence and that also contained one of five residences that Qaddafi used. (The attitude in Pentagon was that if the Libyan leader proved to be a casualty of the raid, so much the better.) These were all difficult targets, located in built-up areas where the danger of civilian damage was great.

The raid could have been executed by the twenty A-6 aircraft aboard *America* and *Coral Sea*, supported by an additional forty F-18 and A-7 light attack aircraft from the same ships, but it was decided that the air force should be included. Kelso welcomed the inclusion of eighteen additional bombers to his force. If he was to have but one raid on Libya, as Washington decreed, it might as well be the heaviest he could mount. Once more our European allies were put on the spot in testing their will to confront terrorism. All but the steadfast British failed utterly. The French in particular refused to allow even overflight of their territory by our air force.

The stream of leaks beginning on April 6th about the imminent raid greatly distressed the fleet. It had the effect of putting the formidable Libyan air defense on full alert status. But as days chased days without any raid, the fleet began to see the Libyan defenses relax, despite the media. At 1:30 A.M. on April 15th, when the raid was launched, the city lights were still on in Tripoli.

By coincidence, the air force unit chosen for the strike was the same tactical fighter wing of F-111s at Lakenheath RAF Base in England to which I had been assigned for two years as a reservist while attending Cambridge University. Because of the political cowardice of our allies, they had to fly twenty-seven hundred miles around Gibraltar, refueling four times in the seven-hour flight. In perfect coordination, *America* and *Coral Sea* launched a large, integrated support package for the air force 111s, consisting of EA-6B jammers, EA-3 intelligence aircraft, EA-2C radar aircraft, A-7 and F-18 antiradar missile shooters to suppress the antiaircraft missiles and guns, and F-14 and F-18 fighter cover.

Without any voice communications, the three sections of six F-111s rendezvoused with their navy support aircraft within three seconds of the appointed time and launched into the target area. Simultaneously, the A-6s from *America* and *Coral Sea* picked up a separate support package from the two carriers and launched into their target area around Benghazi, 450 miles to the east.

Six minutes before the first F-111 hit its target, navy jammers and antiradiation-missile shooters began their suppression of Libyan defenses. The air defenses around Libya and Benghazi are among the most sophisticated and thickest in the world, operated under the direction of 3,000 Soviet air defense technicians. Using the navy EA-6 jammers, which could jam ten different bands simultaneously, and the air force EF-111 jammers, the early-warning-surveillance and fire-control radars were rendered inoperable. The F-18s and A-7s were able to fire Shrike and Harm missiles down the throats of any SAM sites that came up operational.

The F-111s went "feet dry" west of Tripoli and flew into the desert well south of Tripoli, then turned north to attack their targets from landward. The F-111s assigned to the Azziziya barracks put their bombs on target. Apparently Qaddafi had gone to his underground command center and escaped harm. An aboveground headquarters was destroyed and his family injured from the blast. An adopted daughter was killed. The F-111s assigned to hit the air base put their bombs precisely on the target and destroyed a great many Russian-built Ilyushin jet transports and helicopters. The F-111s assigned to the commando training site in the port city of Sidi Bilal, near Tripoli, put their bombs generally on the target as well. One F-111 dropped its bombs nearly on the French embassy, damaging it badly. This caused the most civilian casualties; its target, narrowly missed, had been the Libyan External Security building, a reputed headquarters for terrorist operations. Because of malfunctions in their bombing systems, four of the F-111s did not drop their bombs because of the stringent rules to avoid collateral damage. One F-111 was seen by navy A-7 pilots to hit the water and explode just offshore while exiting the area. Most probably, it simply flew into the water. The first F-111 hit the target at exactly 2:00 A.M., and the last one cleared the beach at 2:11 A.M. Tripoli time.

Simultaneously, 450 miles to the east, the navy began its attack on the Benghazi complex. At 1:54 A.M. Tripoli time, the suppression aircraft, the jammers, and the Shrike and Harm shooters launched their attack at the defenses, in exactly the same way as was done against the Tripoli defenses. At 2:00 A.M. the first section of A-6s, led by VA-55 skipper Rob Weber (a former flight instructor of mine at Kingsville) crossed the beach at two hundred feet and five hundred knots. Eight A-6s hit the Benghazi air base and destroyed more than 20 MiGs, utility aircraft, and helicopters. Six A-6s put their bombs precisely on a target that looked on radar exactly like the commando training base but was in fact a civilian building. Thirteen minutes later the last A-6 was clear of the beach. All returned safely to *America* and *Coral Sea*.

After clearing the beach, the F-111s immediately rendezvoused with their tankers to begin the long seven-hour flight back to England. When one was reported missing, the navy commenced a search-and-rescue operation that lasted into the next day, with no result. The huge Libyan Air Force, supplemented by aviators from Communist bloc nations and Syria, was so intimidated by their experiences with the F-14s and F-18s in the earlier fleet exercises that they refused to take off to defend against the American attackers. Not a single Libyan aircraft rose in opposition.

From a military standpoint the Libyan operation would stand as a model for years to come. Qaddafi got the message and terrorist attacks on Americans ceased after the destruction of the Pan Am aircraft at Lockerbie. Other terrorist sponsors, Syria, Iraq, and Iran went to ground, and Americans abroad were to enjoy nearly a decade of security as a result. Qaddafi remains unwilling to risk direct confrontation with the U.S. to this day, although he has resumed financial support to terrorist organizations.

Lessons Learned

The Libyan strike was an overwhelming success and contains some obvious lessons. Although Qaddafi was not brought down, his standing and power were severely diminished. He lost the confidence of his people and of his military in his inability to prevent such an effective retaliation. The raid began a series of setbacks for the Libyan leader, who avoided support for terrorism until recently.

On the military level, the wisdom of the foundation of our naval buildup based on high technology rather than the "cheaper, simpler is better" arguments of the congressional reformers was validated for all the world to see. It was precisely those ships, aircraft, and weapons that had been ridiculed during the early 1980s by the antinaval reformers in Congress and their academic camp followers that performed so brilliantly: the Aegis cruiser, the F-14, the F-18, the A-6, the F-111, the Harm antiradiation missile, and the Harpoon antiship missile. The Libyan fast missile boats were destroyed with no difficulty and never posed a threat to a U.S. ship. There is, of course, a real role for the small-ship navy so beloved of congressional reformers, and we hope to see a great many more of such ships—in the Libyan navy and the Soviet navy.

An even more salutary effect occurred where we least expected it. Both the Libyan and the Syrian governments were given a thorough dressing down by Moscow for providing "the imperialists the excuse of terrorism." The Soviets made clear that on this issue, their clients could not expect much help. In Damascus tension on the Israeli-Syrian border had been growing since the February maneuvers, fueled by Syrian complicity and terrorism. Assad expressed his fear that there had been a division of labor, with the United States taking Libya and Israel preparing to take him. He hastened to signal Washington and Jerusalem that he did not intend war. Before the year was out, Syria, too, had substantially reduced its open support of terrorists.

One battle against terrorism had been decisively won for a change, but obviously not the war.

Another obvious and strong lesson was the destruction of the myth of interservice rivalry. One can argue whether the inclusion of the air force was necessary, but when called upon to participate, it did a truly superb professional job. And the flawless integration of the naval and air force strikes demonstrated the real cooperation, integration, and sharing of tactical training and knowhow that is the real relationship between and among our armed forces. Since that goes counter to the trendy Washington wisdom, however, it is an aspect of the strike that has gone unreported.

Above all, no one can count the many lives that may have been saved by discrediting and intimidating Qaddafi and deterring other would-be terrorists. He was powerless to stop us, and we can come back again.

Finally, the raid demonstrated that the United States can deal effectively with terrorism if it has the decisiveness and the wisdom to use the capacities at hand. It now has a military that, when freed of the overwhelming layers of joint military and civilian bureaucracy, is as fine and effective as we have ever had in our history.

Chapter 13

The Pacific Frontier

Nowhere are the postwar changes in our world better illustrated than in the Pacific. If we could resurrect somehow the statesmen of the 1950s, they would find themselves on familiar ground in much of Europe. Except for the unprecedented prosperity of the Western Europeans, the strategic realities of their day are little changed there today. In the Pacific, however, they would rub their eyes in disbelief. No other region of the world has seen so much economic, military, and political transformation.

Consider the economic developments that have changed forever the image of the Pacific nations as slowly developing societies mired in the transition between traditionalism and modernization. Between 1970 and 1985, U.S. trade with this region grew tenfold, and since 1980, East Asia and the Pacific has surpassed the European Economic Community as our primary regional trading partner by more than 50 percent. The American economy is deeply interwoven with the Asian Pacific economies.

While this exciting story of economic progress unfolded, equally important military changes occurred, especially during the years after the American failure in Vietnam. At the very time when the most prosperous and populous nations of the Pacific were looking toward the United States, our naval power suffered a steady decline. In a dramatic contrast, the Soviet Pacific fleet enjoyed a relentless expansion.

Today's Soviet Pacific fleet is that nation's largest, encompassing more than 400 surface combatants and 130 submarines, second only to its northern fleet in capabilities. It is far larger than the U.S. Seventh Fleet, its potential adversary in the region. In fact, in terms of full load displacement—that is, the number of tons a fleet displaces when fully loaded out on a combat footing—the

Soviet Pacific fleet is more than twice the size of the combined U.S. Seventh Fleet and Japanese Maritime Self-Defense Force.

Both the prosperity of the Pacific and the changing balance of military power there must be placed in the political context of the historic reopening of American relations with mainland China. Since the Nixon administration began to reclaim Beijing from its anti-American stance, a substantial economic relationship and a quite remarkable political evolution has occurred. In addition, during the Reagan administration important military cooperation has begun on a service-to-service basis with China, with significant implications for the military balance in the Pacific.

Thus, the political map of the Pacific has been fundamentally altered, making the once trendy notion of American retrenchment outdated. The growth of the Soviet military threat in the 1970s, the aggressive actions of Moscow's Vietnamese ally, and the remaining dangers of North Korea make American involvement and commitment to the peace and stability of the Pacific essential. Above all, five of America's eight mutual security treaties are with Pacific nations: Japan, South Korea, the Philippines, Thailand, and Australia.

These economic and security realities in the Pacific require that the United States build and sustain sufficient naval forces to deploy simultaneously to the Pacific as well as the Atlantic theaters. During the Reagan administration, these forces were joined to a new coalition diplomacy that, unlike that of the Vietnam era, did not displace or overwhelm local initiative. Clearly, an American military capability that could not count on allies would be crippled at the outset. But, by the same token, we cannot count much on our allies if our military plans call for them to be abandoned for the sake of another theater.

U.S. Navy in the Pacific

The Seventh Fleet is our forward western Pacific fleet, which meets our commitment to Japan, Korea, the Philippines, Australia, and Thailand, and in the critical straits of Southeast Asia as well as in the Indian Ocean. In wartime we would need to deploy five carrier battlegroups, two battleship surface action groups, and four underway replenishment groups to the Seventh Fleet. In peacetime we now average over the year the equivalent of one and one-third carrier battle groups in the western Pacific. That, of course, helps us maintain a peacetime fleetwide operational tempo that provides for at least 50 percent time in home port for our people and their families.

We do not have a separate fleet for the Persian Gulf and Indian Ocean. In peacetime we maintain the Middle East Force in Bahrain and now deploy one carrier battle group at all times, usually provided alternately from the Sixth and Seventh fleets. In 1987 we deployed a battleship battle group to the area for the first time.

The U.S. Third fleet has responsibility for operations off Alaska, the Bering Sea, the Aleutians, the eastern Pacific, and the mid-Pacific region. In wartime there would be considerable overlapping and trading back and forth between the Seventh and Third fleets, as was done in World War II. To cover the vast area, we must assign two carrier battle groups and one under-way replenishment group, the task force of supply and logistics ships.

Just as in the Atlantic, our ability effectively to deter the Soviets with American forces is entirely dependent on a web of alliance treaties and political relationships with nations of the Pacific Basin. Forward bases are particularly important in the Pacific region because of the vast distances.

In carrying out our new coalition strategy for the Pacific, in addition to increasing the size of the fleet to provide the necessary American contribution, we undertook five initiatives of historic importance.

Reemphasis on the Northern Pacific

Our new dependence on Alaskan and Canadian oil shipped to the United States by sea through the northeastern Pacific brought a new strategic importance to those waters. The Soviets recognized it in the seventies and began to study the geography and oceanography of the region and to carry out submarine exercises and regular deployments off the American and Canadian Pacific coasts. Their interest, of course, was heightened by our establishment of the strategic submarine base at Bangor, Washington, on Puget Sound. Late in the 1970s the Soviets began to operate their submarines regularly under the Arctic ice pack and took an increasing interest in the Aleutians. They began also to build air cushion vehicles able to move large numbers of troops and armor rapidly across the polar ice. Our Alaskan oil fields at Prudhoe Bay are less than six hundred miles from major Soviet military bases, so these new Soviet capabilities could not be ignored.

The other side of that coin is that Soviet geography on the Pacific is very inhospitable and militarily disadvantageous. The eastern Soviet Union is connected to the industrial West by only two rail lines, and much of its commerce and resupply must therefore come by sea. Its principal ports at Petropavlovsk-Kamchatski and Vladivostok are relatively ill defended and are heavily impeded by winter ice and island choke points. Until 1981 these Soviet strategic vulnerabilities had been totally ignored in our myopic fixation on the

THE NAVY IN ACTION

European central front. We never exercised in those harsh northern latitudes, and we had very little capability to operate effectively there.

Beginning in 1981 we set out to correct these problems and take advantage of the strategic opportunity afforded by geography. We began that year and have continued every year since to operate major naval and marine exercises in the northern Pacific, from Alaska to Siberia. Under the leadership of Pacific Fleet Commander Admiral Ace Lyons, the U.S. Air Force was integrated into northern Pacific operations on a permanent basis. F-15s from Alaska were redeployed for exercises in the Aleutians in support of the fleet, and Air Force AWACS radar aircraft and KC-10 tankers were built into the regular operating plans of the carrier battle groups in northern waters.

Just as we exercised multicarrier battle groups in the Norwegian Sea for the first time in twenty years, so we learned the hard lessons of operating ships and aircraft in ice and Arctic storm. We also signaled to the Soviets that if they attacked NATO Europe they could expect us to be coming at them in the Pacific.

To meet the vacuum of American naval power in our Pacific Northwest, we made the decision, based on our strategic home-porting study, to base a full carrier battle group in Puget Sound. We moved the aircraft *Nimitz* from Norfolk, in 1987, with fifteen more ships to follow in the next five years. We also began to operate the Second Fleet in Alaskan waters and began regular port visits to Anchorage, Alaska.

A New Role for Japan in Pacific Strategy

A major accomplishment of the Reagan administration's Pacific strategy was reaching agreement with the government of Japan on the role of the Japanese Self-Defense Force in Pacific strategy. The Japanese agreed with the American proposal that Japan assume full responsibility for the security of its sea lines of communications out to a thousand miles from Japan. Japan has naval and air self-defense forces that are among the most professional and effective in the world. Its naval force consists of some fifty modern frigates and destroyers and twenty-two modern diesel electric submarines. Its air force consists of F-15s and E-2C radar warning aircraft. That force is sufficient in size to back up to the policy of the thousand-mile defense, but Japan must spend considerably more than it is now spending to give it in-depth war-fighting sustainability and qualitative modernization. This they have pledged to do. It would be politically unwise, however, to press the Japanese to expand their armed forces further. Neither the Japanese nor the other nations in the area want to see Tokyo become an Asian military superpower. Nor can the Japanese play the role now fulfilled by the United States. Beyond the thousand-mile defense in areas of their vital interest, such as the Persian Gulf, Tokyo's contribution should be substantial monetary support for regional security arrangements.

The New Role of China in Pacific Strategy

The historic reopening of U.S. relations with the People's Republic of China during the Nixon administration was brought to an entirely new level of military cooperation by the initiative of Al Haig and Cap Weinberger in 1981 and 1982. Based on their initiatives, Admiral Liu Hua Qing, head of the People's Liberation Army Navy, invited me for an official visit to begin negotiations for substantial navy-to-navy cooperation. I traveled to China in August 1984, following the route through Pakistan made famous by Henry Kissinger in 1970. In Pakistan I spent a fascinating evening over dinner with the late President Mohammed Zia ul-Haq. His grasp of world politics was impressive indeed, and his courage in confronting the Soviets in Afghanistan should stand as an example to the rest of the world. His advice on dealing with the Chinese and his realistic assessment of where American and Chinese mutual interests lay were full of insight. What I heard there, echoed elsewhere by experts on China, is worth repeating for its sensitive understanding of how to manage this crucial relationship.

The Chinese, he said, dislike diplomatic circumlocution and could be expected to respond directly. Be bold and straightforward—tell them exactly what you want and what you expect. They are tough negotiators but usually put their final position on the table and then don't budge. When you finally reach agreement with them, it will be met with certainty. Their culture and bureaucracy combine to make execution often excruciatingly slow. But once the agreement is implemented, you can count on their fidelity.

Above all, he warned, avoid giving the Chinese any impression that the United States sought to play off the Chinese navy against the Soviet navy.

President Zia and I got on so well that he spontaneously urged me to extend my visit and accompany him personally to the National Day celebrations in Rawalpindi the next morning. The event took place at the former palace of the British viceroy and was a colorful occasion. Unfortunately, it was cold and rained torrents throughout. As part of the President's party, I found his enthusiasm and excitement infectious, but after the third hour of stirring speeches in Urdu as I sat shivering in the downpour, I had enjoyed about all I could stand.

By the time we got to Beijing, I was down with a bad case of the flu. Admiral Bill Narva, a good friend and an excellent navy doctor, gave me medicine and warned me to spend at least three days in bed. Poor Narva was himself recovering from root-canal work he had to get done by a missionary dentist in Rawalpindi just before we left Pakistan.

The head of the Chinese navy, Admiral Liu Hua Qing, came by to visit me in the Diao Yu Tai State Guest House, where I occupied the same grand Russian gothic suite occupied by Khrushchev and Nixon. Admiral Liu brought with him the head of Chinese naval medicine, who gave me the same diagnosis as had Bill Narva. But he gave me some herbal tea to drink every four hours and said next day I would be good as new if I faithfully drank the tea. Unfortunately, I couldn't wait until the next day because I was guest of honor at an official dinner in the Great Hall of the People. Though weak with fever, I went to the dinner. It was magnificent. While Great Hall itself is also of Soviet Gothic architecture, each of its rooms is decorated in the art of one of the Chinese provinces, and many of these rooms are quite beautiful.

The meal itself was an awesome thirty courses, including camel-foot soup, sea slugs, tree fungus, whole fried little birdies, and things whose identity I wouldn't dare ask. I love Chinese cooking, and this was superb. But between each course there was the inevitable toast with mou-tai, the horrific 140-proof liquor that would dissolve tungsten steel. The first was a truly fulsome welcome from Admiral Liu followed by "*Gan Bei!*," which means "Down the hatch!" in naval English. I replied with a very warm and optimistic toast to our new naval relationship—another "*gan bei!*" By the last mystery course, we had put twenty mou-tais "down the hatch" and were slightly overrefreshed.

Back at Diao Yu Tai I collapsed in bed, dosing with herbal tea as directed. During the night the fever peaked and broke, and next morning I was in good form. Chinese herbal medicine has clearly made a convert of me!

The remaining meetings in Beijing were fascinating and productive. In a clear signal that our naval cooperation had the highest sanction, the prime minister, Zhao Zi Yang, received us for a full hour at Zhong Shan Reception House. After the obligatory five-minute speech on Taiwan, we talked about the geopolitical balance in the Pacific, and I explained to him the objectives of our naval discussions, that it was in our American interest to see that China could defend her home waters effectively. Our cooperation was aimed against no one but would deter any attempt to use Soviet naval power to intimidate China. I made a strong pitch for an early visit to China by U.S. Navy ships to symbolize the new relationship.

Zhao's view of the Pacific balance was realistic and perceptive. There was no hint of ideology or posturing, and while making no commitments he said that our coming naval discussions had the full support of the Chinese leadership.

That afternoon we had a working lunch with Zhang Ai Ping, the minister of defense. It was in another part of the Imperial Park at Diao Yu Tai. It was a magnificent teahouse that had been a fishing lodge of the emperor. The setting could not but impress the visitors with the refinement and artistic beauty of an ancient culture. It was the first of many examples of the great lengths the regime has gone to since the Cultural Revolution to restore and preserve the incomparable treasures and beauties of the Middle Kingdom.

The views of the defense minister were equally sophisticated and a degree more enthusiastic toward our military cooperation than the prime minister's. The defense minister was a bit more explicit about the potential military threat from the Soviet Union and our mutual interest in maintaining freedom of the seas. His views of the Pacific balance were in complete harmony with our own. Once again, there were thirty courses of superb food and twenty *gan beis*, with ever more flowery toasts. I soon learned to cheat and take only a sip, or I never would have survived the trip. In all, we had sixteen thirty-course banquets in ten days. I even acquired a certain taste for the purple quivering sea slugs, though Barbara did not. She was not the only one.

Every once in a while I noticed my military assistant, Paul Miller, with jowls like a chipmunk. I found that he couldn't bear to swallow the sea slugs but occasionally had to put them in his mouth under the watchful eye of his counterpart. There in his jowls they would stay until he could find a discreet moment to slip away. We had many a good laugh over that and indeed many other things throughout our travels. On that trip, as on nearly every trip, we worked hard, but we really had great fun.

These meetings set the stage for very productive negotiations on specifics with Admiral Liu and his naval staff. After two full days of negotiations we reached agreement on a framework of specifics for moving forward on real naval cooperation.

The overall approach originally set by Haig and Weinberger that continued to serve as the framework for our negotiations was straightforward and pragmatic. America's national interests are served by a stable China that contributes to the peace of the region, and improvement of our relations, including military cooperation, will substantially advance that process. China is a friend, not an ally. Our military cooperation must be based on common security interests, not on a formal military alliance. That requires that we be clear about our purposes and realistic in our expectations. As President Reagan put it, "Our intention is to provide China with a capability to defend itself more effectively against the common threat to the region." We must also recognize that China's long-term modernization program should emphasize economic growth rather than increased defenses. To quote the president again, "The U.S.-PRC military relationship helps develop and maintain China as a force for peace and stability in the region and the world, while not posing a threat to other U.S. friends and allies in the region."

The United States and China share a common sea in the Pacific, and we share common interests in safeguarding the Western Pacific from Soviet aggression. Based on these principles, an agreement was reached during my visit on four lines of cooperation.

First, we agreed on a continuing series of high-level visits and discussions to follow my visit. Admiral Liu made a return visit in the following year and there have been numerous visits by other naval delegations since. Admiral Liu was one of the veterans of the Long March and is a very impressive man. He personally guided me through the military museum in Beijing, walking me through the experience of the Long March in 1934. He discreetly bypassed the section of the museum filled with war souvenirs and pictures from the Korean War. After Beijing I visited the North Fleet headquarters at Dalian, and the East Fleet headquarters at Shanghai. During both visits the Chinese were totally open and allowed me to tour all their ships, including one of their nuclear attack submarines. The Chinese have a very large navy of some 270 destroyers and frigates, more than 70 diesel submarines, and a few nuclear submarines. Except for the latter, nearly all of their ships are based on twenty- to thirty-year-old technology but for the most part are quite professionally operated.

When Admiral Liu came on his return visit to the United States the following year, we gave him similar treatment and access to naval facilities all over the country. I hosted him to a final negotiating session in Key West, where he was especially impressed in visiting with Mel Fisher and his just-recovered treasure trove from the Spanish galleon *Atocha*.

This was followed by a succession of extensive visits by Admiral Watkins, Assistant Secretary Paisley, and General Kelley.

The second initiative we agreed on was to begin working-level exchange visits and small-scale exercises. These have now developed into a steady range of exchanges both ways, and we had our first exercise between units of our two navies in the South China Sea in 1986.

Our third initiative was to exchange naval ship visits, with the first to be a visit of American ships to a Chinese port for the first time since 1949. After many diplomatic delays on both sides of the Pacific, the historic visit took place in October 1986, when Admiral Lyons led a flotilla of destroyers and a cruiser into Qing Dao Harbor for a very successful visit.

While symbolically the visit to Qing Dao was the most significant of the agreements we reached in Beijing, by far the most functionally important was the fourth and final agreement, to undertake a program to modernize Chinese destroyers and frigates with modern technology, enabling them to carry out effective antisubmarine warfare. Turning the Chinese surface fleet into an effective antisubmarine force will do more to deny the Soviets the possibility of dominating the western Pacific in wartime than any other single action. Much of this initiative is now under way, with agreements having been concluded to sell and provide technical assistance for LM-2500 gas turbines of the type that power our most modern surface combatants, new technology Mark-46 torpedoes, sonar communications, and other equipment, along with the technical assistance to integrate these systems into the Chinese ships.

In the four years since this naval agreement was reached, we have confirmed a clear common interest. Both we and the Chinese recognize the reality and the significance of the Soviet navy's postwar expansion, oriented to interdicting the sea lines of communications. Both of our navies operate almost daily in close proximity to Soviet naval forces in the western Pacific, and that has bred a common perspective of concern and respect for Soviet capabilities. It has served as a strong impetus to greater navy-to-navy ties on both sides.

The greatest credit for the success of this historic navy-to-navy initiative goes to Rear Admiral Dave Ramsey, the most masterly diplomat-warrior ever to be attaché in China. He began the initiative in Beijing and kept it on track until he left. He was succeeded as naval attaché by brilliant young commander, Phil Midland, who continued the tradition.

Although the Chinese acknowledge and object to our continued relations with Taiwan, they have not allowed this to interfere with their own best interests. Nothing we are doing with the Chinese navy will in any way increase the potential threat to Taiwan or to any other of our Asian allies. On the contrary, as the web of functional relationships between our navies develops, the likelihood of converging perspectives with regard to naval matters throughout the Pacific increases.

Afterword

The Falklands War has had far-reaching effects. In Argentina the discrediting and removal of the ruling junta has resulted in a considerable liberalizing of Argentine politics. In Great Britain the victory gave Margaret Thatcher a base which enabled her to carry through the most extensive reforms of modern British history, transforming "the sick man of Europe" into one of the most prosperous nations in Europe. The war of course saved the Royal Navy from reduction to an insignificant force. While smaller than at the time of the Falklands War, the Royal Navy today, in addition to its ballistic missile submarines, has some of the most modern and effective attack submarines and surface ships in NATO. In a final legacy, Britain is now embarked in the design and construction of a new full-scale nuclear aircraft carrier.

But the most important legacy of the Falklands was its strengthening of the web of deterrence that ultimately brought about the peaceful end of the cold war. Leadership of the eastern bloc was taken aback that a supposed decadent member of NATO had the fighting will to carry out a war on principle and to carry out a military campaign with superb war-fighting effectiveness. It was another weight on the scale.

The island of Grenada has long faded from the headlines and returned to a peaceful and somewhat more prosperous Caribbean existence. The flow of economic development assistance promised when it was a potential cold war arena was reduced to a trickle when the cold war ended. But the legacy of democracy and stability restored by the military operation endures.

What did not endure were all of the lessons from the mistakes made in the military operation. Not long after the battle Congress passed the Goldwater Nichols Act, which significantly reorganized the military command structure. The theater commanders gained a much needed strength and authority, particularly in bringing the service components together for truly joint training— a major lesson from Grenada that was in fact learned. But with the legislation also came orthodoxy that, as in Grenada, every operation *must* be joint with all services taking part. The operation carried out in Haiti when two army divisions were transported and put ashore from two navy aircraft carriers—with their army helicopters able to operate from those carriers—was a testament to the learning of a major lesson of Grenada. The theater commander, Admiral Paul Miller, had been able to ensure the training of the army and navy units so that proper communications, and the proper hardware, had been put in place to carry out what was a flawless joint service operations.

Seventeen years after our withdrawal from Lebanon in abject failure, the country has become a vassal of Syria, and Israel has another hostile state on its northern border.

The lessons to be learned from the tragedy of the marine barracks are well documented in the Long Report and have been entirely ignored ever since.

The layers of staff bureaucracies between the decision makers in Washington and the units in the field have increased not decreased. The terrorist attack on the U.S.S. *Cole* in 2000 was very similar in motivation, and the same failures of intelligence and obfuscation by the many and large staffs in interpreting intelligence and applying rules of engagement were almost exactly repeated in the *Cole* tragedy and will be repeated in the future.

While state departments in every administration want to treat naval ships like so many cost-free chessmen, in recent years the profligate willy-nilly deployments have been running all of the services into tatters. During the Reagan years of cold war activism, the navy was deployed to crisis areas beyond ordinary deployments an average of 5½ times per year, which fully stretched a navy of nearly 600 ships. Over the same time span in the Clinton years, the navy deployed out of the routine 12¼ times per year with a fleet that has been slashed to only 318 ships. This has not only pummeled morale, retention, and family life, but it also has exposed a less-ready, thinned-out fleet to many more hazardous duty stations.

As the navy learned at Okinawa, where 35 ships were sunk by kamikazes, it is impossible to protect completely against suicide attacks. The only defense is good intelligence and the will to retaliate against the source.

Since the air strikes against Qaddafi and the Lockerbie attack, Colonel Qaddafi seems to have ceased conducting direct terrorist operations and limited his terrorist support to large financial subsidies to their organizations.

The aircraft that conducted the strike, the F-111s and A-6s, have both been retired. The strike today could be carried out by B-1s and B-2s or F-15Es from the air force, but the A-6 replacements for the navy deep-strike mission, the A-6F and the A-12, were both canceled. In future years navy carriers will have a more limited precision strike capability with the F-18F.

Because of the budget cuts and OSD policy changes over the last decade, the naval aviation plan outlined in chapter 11 has been replaced with a very bleak outlook. The Defense Department has canceled most of the modernization programs outlined in the chapter including the upgraded F-14D and A-6F and the A-12. There is no replacement on the drawing board for the navy deep-strike mission nor for any of the support aircraft, the E-2C surveillance, EA6-B jammer, S-3 ASW, and P-3 maritime patrol aircraft and SH-60 helicopters. Naval aviation today is living off the fat of the Reagan buildup with the average age of its airplanes at eighteen years.

The entire future of carrier aviation lies with the F-18E and F-18F, an improvement over the older F-18 models but with performance still well short of the F-14s and A-6s that they will replace. There is also the Joint Strike Fighter program that OSD hopes will not repeat the sorry history of the McNamara TFX program, the last failed effort to provide one aircraft program to cover the disparate requirements of the marines, navy, and air force.

Naval aviation personnel policy has changed enormously since this book was written. The traumatic witch hunt following the 1991 Tailhook affair led to the forced or voluntary departure of more than 300 experienced naval aviators. Retention rates for aviators have been far below requirements ever since. The navy is now short almost 3,000 pilots. One unfortunate response of planners to this problem has been to lengthen the obligated service for pilots to nine years from the start of flight training. This has led to a quite noticeable shift in the mix of people going into naval aviation. The extreme political correctness imposed during the Clinton years resulted in the unfortunate removal of Admiral Stan Arthur from the promotion list for the sole reason that he approved a decision down in the training command to remove a woman from flight training.

Marine aviation is in far better shape today with nothing like the navy morale and retention problems and with new aircraft like the V-22 Tiltrotor coming in to the force. F-18s, Harriers, and Cobra attack helicopters are an excellent combination for their close air support requirements in the future.

Since this book was written the navy participated in the Persian Gulf War in 1991. The Gulf War was a land war with an adjacent support base in Saudi Arabia containing 35 airfields designed to American specifications. The air force and army rightly got enormous credit for a brilliantly conducted campaign to eject the Iraqis from Kuwait. But the navy played a vital supporting role. The pre-positioning ships built during the Reagan years and based in Diego Garcia in fulfillment of the Carter Doctrine provided the critical early blocking force that prevented the Iraqis from moving into Saudi Arabia. The aircraft carriers provided the immediate deterring air power while the U.S. Air Force deployed its power. Once again 95% of all of the weapons and supplies came to the theater in ships chartered or operated by Military Sealift Command and protected by the U.S. Navy. Once again the battleships *Missouri* and *Wisconsin* proved invaluable in pulverizing Iraqi coastal defenses with their 16-inch guns and in tying down the Iraqi strategic reserves by maintaining the credible threat of a U.S. Marine amphibious assault. Also, along with the *Aegis* cruisers and submarines, the battleships provided the massive air assault of Tomahawk cruise missiles against precision targets in Iraq.

The pre-positioning in Diego Garcia has been maintained and is now being modernized, and, along with the continuing naval presence in and around the

Gulf, including an aircraft carrier, our naval commitments in the region remain undiminished.

Much has changed also in the Pacific Basin since the book was written. The painstaking initiatives to improve military relations with China were severely set back by Tianenman Square. The Chinese government has moved steadily to fill the military vacuum created by the withdrawal of both the Soviet and American fleets from their former, very active presence in the western Pacific. The U.S. Navy has lost its forward Pacific base in the Philippines and now must operate from some 1,700 hundred miles farther east with a fleet now reduced almost by half. Thus it is rare today to see a major American combatant in the great ports of the Pacific. Managing relations with China and the role of a naval balance in that relationship looms as one of the greatest foreign policy challenges of the next ten years. There is no ideological or geopolitical reason why China and the United States should be enemies. Certainly the issue of Taiwan is difficult, but a long-term peaceful relationship with China should be achievable in a way that was inconceivable with the Soviet Union.

September 1, 2001

PART IV

A Summing Up

Chapter 14

"Ninety Thousand Ants on a Log Floating Down the Mississippi, with Each One Thinking He Is Steering"

Leaving the best job in the world is not easy, but I was determined not to stay too long, which meant staying until my goals were reached and no longer. By 1985, the navy's confidence and morale had been restored, the maritime strategy was in place, and the management philosophy was established. We had added fifty ships to the fleet and had over a hundred more under construction. The management disciplines that we had in place assured that we could maintain the six-hundred-ship navy with only 1 or 2 percent real growth per year, much less than the growth of the GNP.

Months afterward, while unpacking my memorabilia I came across a copy of a letter written by Theodore Roosevelt when he was assistant secretary in 1896. In it, Roosevelt recommended that the navy test a "flying machine," believing that it could hold great promise for revolutionizing naval warfare. On researching further, I had found that Roosevelt's prophetic recommendation had been dismissed with contempt by a board of admirals soon after he left. They said that the flying machine could be of possible interest to the army but had no applicability at all to the navy.

The episode seemed to me fair warning for current times. During the Reagan years, we had spent billions in a mighty effort to close the gap between our commitments and our forces, and to restore the health and respect of the military. After six years of unprecedented success, however, the old congressional-military-industrial complex was in danger of rejecting the new and falling back into its old familiar patterns: Congress chopping huge amounts out of the defense budget; the Pentagon bureaucracy chopping navy force structure; voices in industry and the bureaucracy urging the return to cost-plus, sole-source contracting; the uniformed services succumbing once again to the lust to fiddle, change, and goldplate systems; and, of course, a procurement scandal in which the dishonesty of a few becomes the cover for many to argue that the older ways were the better ways.

Dishonesty in the Pentagon or in the defense industry is intolerable. While the incidence of fraud in the defense industry is well below the industrywide statistics, the public sector should be held to a higher standard. Still, the real issues today are not fraud. Professor Robert Higgs, who has studied the ebb and flow of Pentagon reform movements, wrote this conclusion: " . . . fraud has never been, and is not now, the major problem. For every dollar diverted by fraud, there may be a hundred wasted by congressional patronage and micromanagement, military intransigence and inefficiency, contractor mismanagement and cost padding, and pure bureaucratic bungling at the Pentagon."[1]

Simply put, the major problem at the Pentagon is that we are not getting what we need: the right forces at the lowest cost. Too frequently, we are not getting the right forces at all. And sometimes we are getting the wrong forces at the highest cost.

The worst possible approach to this problem would be to repeat the errors of the past: a multiplying bureaucracy overseen by congressional micromanagers, justified as necessary to prevent "waste, fraud, and abuse"; another cascade of laws and regulations giving birth to another swarm of consultants and ex-officials "in the know"; severe cost cuts to "punish" the Pentagon. Equally self-defeating would be blanket judgments that contractors, consultants, and procurement officers are dishonest ipso facto. All of these things *will* change the defense business but not for the better.

My experience tells me something else. By applying common sense, direct-line instead of staff management, and restoring incentives—carrots and sticks related to performance—the system can be much improved. That means more competition, less gold-plating, halving the bureaucracy, and boosting career incentives.

A New Era and A New Approach to Managing Defense

If I had been present at the creation of the Department of Defense, I would have made some helpful suggestions. The list of things obviously wrong with the way we provide for our common defense would be very long. In deciding how to fix the Pentagon, we must first realize that some of its most fundamental inefficiencies cannot or should not be corrected. The Founding Fathers were apprehensive about the prospect of an efficient, powerful military establishment and deliberately divided responsibility between Congress and the president to prevent either the parliamentary tyranny of a Cromwell or the executive tyranny of a George III. Another "inefficiency" we should accept and indeed welcome is that caused by freedom of the press and freedom of speech. There are other categories of problems, such as fundamental civil service reform and politics, that are complex, difficult areas. Setting all those inefficiencies aside, we nonetheless have a list of manageable problems that can be fixed and the correction of which *can* make tremendous difference.

The Defense Department is much too big. In rough book value, it equals the top thirty companies on the Fortune 500 list combined. It buys, builds, repairs, or provides virtually every product, service, and skill that exists in our economy. The navy alone is larger in budget and employees ($100 billion and 1.2 million employees) than all cabinet agencies combined except the Department of Health and Human Services and the Department of the Treasury. (See figure 8.) And yet the Pentagon is organized like a 7-Eleven store, with all decision-making drawn up to a centralized office. The board of any corporation one-thirtieth the size of the Defense Department that allowed the company to be organized in such a nonsensical fashion would undoubtedly be committed to an asylum.

Imagine a learned professor at the Wharton School proposing that, to gain efficiency, the top thirty companies be merged under a huge centralized headquarters staff, with all procurement under a one-man "czar." Even in academia such an idea would be met by laughter, with the professor himself put under clinical observation.

Of course, decision-making in the Pentagon is not really centralized at all. It is the classic allegory of the ninety thousand ants on a log floating down the Mississippi, with each thinking he is steering.

Ironically, it is the pretense of centralized management decision-making in this vast sea of bureaucracy that prevents harnessing the defense services and agencies to a common policy direction.

The 1947 National Security Act, creating both the National Security Council and the Defense Department, was a sensible step. Later modifications, however, went down the wrong path and created the grotesque illusion we have today. Instead of strengthening the NSC as the forum to integrate defense and foreign policy and keep service rivalry from becoming counter-productive, subsequent legislation went the other way and created more and more centralized bureaucracy in the Pentagon and left the NSC to languish as an occasional forum for strong NSC advisers like Kissinger and Brzezinski, but never to become a real integrator of defense policy.

There is no integrated defense policy. Thanks to three decades of reforms, the vast Pentagon bureaucracy is occupied almost solely with programming and budgeting, and is currently based on sheer repetitive momentum. The origin of defense PPBS derived from the assumption that behavior is determined by economic forces—i.e., budgets. Thus nearly every office in the Pentagon, whether charged with dependents' schools, nuclear research, or guerrilla warfare, spends 95 percent of its time on the endless meetings concerned with the annual budget preparation and presentation to Congress.

One small group of bureaucrats drafts a "front end" planning document called the "Defense Guidance." In the Reagan administration that was very well done by Under Secretary Fred Iklé. But real policy integration must be done every day by senior officials relating budgets to objectives and integrating daily decisions and crisis events to larger policy. In today's Pentagon that cannot be done. The huge JCS staff churns out its papers, the OSD staff theirs, and the military departments still others. Nowhere are they brought together except in a procedural sense of staffing paperwork. The nearest approach comes once a week when the secretary of defense meets with the JCS in the secret "tank" (a secure meeting room used by the JCS).

The answer lies in *stronger centralization of defense policy-making and major decentralization of the day-to-day management and operations* of our $300 billion-per-year defense establishment.

There must be a strong secretary of defense, and he should be located, with the secretary of state, at the White House, available every day to walk back and forth to consult with the commander in chief. His chain of command for the operational forces should be through (not to) the chairman of the JCS to the combatant commanders, bypassing the service secretaries and the service chiefs. For all other matters concerning the military department, his chain of command should go directly to the secretaries of the military departments.

The position of deputy secretary of defense should be abolished. Instead, when the secretary of defense is traveling or incapacitated, one of the secretaries of the military departments would become acting secretary of defense. Which one would be determined by a rotational schedule, with each assigned a three-month period of each year to be on call. This would ensure that all the secretaries would keep a broader cross-service perspective and would remind a president that those selected to head the military departments should be of a caliber able to assume the duties of the secretary of defense.

The secretary of defense's executive committee of policy and decision-makers should be the existing statutory Armed Forces Policy Council, composed of the secretary of defense, the secretaries of the military departments, the chairman of the JCS, and the chiefs of staff. It should meet several times per week and should be the forum for all decision- and policy-making, budget issues, and crisis management.

The office of the secretary of defense should be cut in half and redirected to truly cross-service budget and policy issues, leaving line management to the military departments.

The vast and sprawling defense agencies—accountable now to no one—should be gathered into a military support department equal to each of the three current military departments.

Within the military departments themselves, subsidiary departments should be created around existing functions such as shipbuilding, aircraft development procurement and maintenance, medical services, and the like. Operating like wholly owned subsidiaries in a civilian company, each of these subsidiary departments should have a civilian secretary, with full executive authority, who would report directly to the secretary of the military department. The title and authority of each civilian secretary should be that of a CEO. They should be men and women of demonstrated accomplishment and experience and loyalty to the president's agenda.

The JCS should stay essentially as it is, but its huge bureaucracy should be at least halved. The unified commanders should stay the same, though some could be eliminated. Their views should continue to carry great weight, but their bloated staffs should be halved. Similarly, the numbers and size of the subsidiary unified and component staffs under the CINCS should be halved, and the operational chain of command shortened and streamlined. The current absurdity of Persian Gulf naval operations being run by a thousand-person bureaucracy in Tampa, Florida, speaks for itself.

Bureaucratic bloat must be reduced. This is a phenomenon that afflicts all aspects of our defense establishment. Counting all defense department agencies, military staff, and appendages, there are more than ninety thousand bureaucrats in the Washington, D.C., area alone.

The layers and size of bureaucracy should be cut by as much as half. We proved in the navy that it can be done without firing people. Normal attrition in the military and civil service is about 8 percent per year, so careful use of hiring freezes brings about a rapid natural shrinkage. Increased opportunity for voluntary early retirement with pensions or large severance payments would enable a new administration to cut the Pentagon bureaucracy by 30 percent in three years without firing a single person.

Civilian control should be restored. With total control of operational forces now in the hands of the unified military commands (except for the secretary of defense, there is no civilian authority over or in the unified command), the principle of civilian control of the military—so critical to the Founding Fathers—has been severely diluted. But in 1988, under congressional pressure, the secretary of defense agreed to give the chairman of the JCS primary responsibility for selecting admirals and generals for promotion to three- and four-star rank in all the services. Civilian control has now effectively been brought to an end. Without responsibility for promotion and assignments, the service secretary and any other civilian official below the office of secretary of defense has little authority. All military officers must now obey and please the unelected chairman, for he alone—or, more accurately, his staff—controls their fate. The sole exception is the slender thread of one soul, the secretary of defense.

This is not a healthy situation for a democracy. In peacetime, it makes the operational forces essentially immune from management, and in war it could lead to very grave developments. Historically, this loss of civilian control is a result of the postwar drive for unification and "jointness."

The solution lies partially in restoring the Armed Forces Policy Council as an effective body, partly in putting the unified commands under the management authority of designated subsidiary departments of the appropriate military department, and finally in restoring civilian authority over flag promotions.

Congressional anarchy must be curtailed. The post-Watergate disintegration of Congress as a coherent legislative body has brought special chaos to the Pentagon. Instead of four oversight and appropriating committees to deal with, the Defense Department must now deal with more than sixty committees and subcommittees. They write thousands of pages of legislative directives—much of it contradictory—each year. By actual measurement in July 1985, legislation, regulations, and case law governing defense procurement alone cover 1,152 linear feet of shelf space. With every member on so many subcommittees, most legislation is written by staffers of minimal experience.

Socialist philosophy still prevails. Our current military-industrial complex is the product of the total government mobilization of World War II. In that all-out war effort the U.S. government built factories and paid for tooling to arm the forces in the kind of state socialism that democracies tolerate in war. But then the rapid development of the Cold War, Korea, and Vietnam kept this military-industrial socialism in place as a permanent relationship.

Robert McNamara poured a new cement on the structure with the management theories of systems analysis and PPBS. These empirical doctrines shared many of the behavioral assumptions of Marxist determinism; the state (Pentagon) should own the tools of production; human (military) behavior is determined by economic factors (budgets); and all reality can be quantified and empirically analyzed.

Caspar Weinberger is the first secretary of defense who actively challenged the socialist orthodoxy of the Pentagon system. Currently the career military and civilian bureaucrats in OSD are the "priesthood" of the entrenched system and have resisted the new philosophy and its reforms. Their power derives from the control of the PPBS system, the system analysis and should-cost studies, and the cost-plus, sole-source procurement system. In this they have strong allies in the less efficient contractors who cannot compete but who seek the protection of monopoly. The circle is completed by the military staffs who want only cost-plus procurement so they can change design and add bangles to ships, tanks, and aircraft without interference.

The impenetrable complexity of the vast bureaucracy, combined with the capricious and political micromanagement by congressional committees, has created over the past forty years a huge industry of defense lobbyists, lawyers, and consultants. Overwhelmingly they are honest men and women of integrity. They are salesmen, marketers, intelligence gatherers, influence peddlers, and technical and political advisers. In that trade, the distinction between what is proper and legal and what is not remains ill-defined and cloudy. When a company has invested millions in a program that is subject to change by a dozen different bureaucracies in the Pentagon and forty-six subcommittees in Congress, the company wants as much information as it can get, and also wants all dozen bureaucracies and all forty-six subcommittees to hear its pitch for the program. The company hires law firms, lobbyists, and consultants to do those tasks, and sometimes they may cross the line. The allegations of criminal activity involving these kinds of activities revealed in the massive fraud investigation begun eight months before I left office have brought cries for reform. Whatever crimes may prove to have been committed should be used to spur reform. In all human activity, there will inevitably be a small number of dishonest people, but it would be a terrible injustice to the vast majority of dedicated military, civilian, and industrial members of the defense establishment to base new legislation on a presumption of dishonesty. Reducing the bureaucracy and restoring coherent line management will greatly reduce the opportunity for abuse, but the greatest source of opportunity for abuse comes from the capriciousness of the legislative micro-management and pork-barrel politics inflicted on the Pentagon by Congress.

Of course, inevitably the defenders of the old cozy military-industrial complex have blamed the source of the abuse on the reforms we introduced requiring fixed-price contracts and dual-source competition. That is like blaming muggings on the victims.

The answer is a firm commitment to change the procurement philosophy and the system from socialism to capitalism and to increase disciplined competition. But it should not be used as an excuse to accelerate the evil trend of recent years toward the criminalization of policy differences between the branches. As Madison warned of the fearful tendency of Congress in "drawing all power into its impetuous vortex," this shift has drastically altered the balance of power between the branches. Since Watergate, Congress has done away with the two-hundred-year practice of executive privilege, created special prosecutors who have convicted former Executive officials of what former congressmen do freely every day, created "independent" inspectors general in each Executive agency who report to Congress and created a "gestapo" system of hot-line numbers encouraging anonymous harassment of Executive officials. From each of these limitations on the executive branch Congress has exempted itself.

Diminished quality of civilian managers. Another aspect of the post-Watergate domination of the Executive branch by Congress has been the steady beggaring of Executive branch officials through a pay cap that has reduced their real compensation by some 40 percent over the last ten years, and the steady addition of nonfinancial obstacles to the recruiting and holding of talented people. Imagine any successful corporation in which no official could be paid more than $77,000 per year. Unlike congressmen, they are not permitted to accept speaking fees or to earn outside income (senators are allowed to keep speaking fees of up to 40 percent of their salary), and unlike congressmen, Executive branch officials have no accountable slush funds from PAC contributions. Such a salary level in the Washington area dictates a standard of living for career and noncareer civilians that is dramatically below the normal standard of living for even modestly successful professionals in business and academia. Add to that the inevitable harassment of civil litigation and the Orwellian atmosphere now created by the anonymous hot-line system, and service in the Executive branch of government appears highly unattractive. In the first two years of my tenure as secretary of the navy, we lost a quarter of our best career civilian talent each year to the private sector. The senior presidential appointees now average less than two years in the government before they return to private life.

In a system that transacts 15 million procurement actions every year, there always will be some wrongdoing, and there must be an effective policing system. The Naval Investigative Service began the investigation that uncovered the abuses revealed in June 1988. But because of the lynch-mob atmosphere created by a few sensational stories, Congress has erected a system that now assumes that *all* Pentagon officials are venal and felonious. It has created an atmosphere in which any disgruntled bureaucrat or private citizen can pick up the phone and defame any Pentagon employee, military or civilian, and subject him or her to investigation. Procurement officials are constantly being put under investigation and subjected to time-consuming depositions and demeaning interviews by various investigative agencies and services. Many are subjected to frivolous and malicious lawsuits.

An effective and highly professional inspector general staff and investigative services to deal with the inevitable instances of waste, fraud, and abuse are essential. The Naval Investigative Service, for example, has done so vigorously in the most recent cases. The current renegade inspector general system and its gestapolike hot line, however, must be forced to act with integrity and due process and be put under responsible judicial review.

It is past high time to take the advice of the Presidential Commission on Executive Compensation. Executive branch officials need increased compensation decoupled from the congressional salary level (which congressmen are allowed to augment). Post-employment restrictions should be retained on direct selling to, information-gathering for, or representing a client back to one's former agency, and there should be a complete prohibition on talking to anyone about postgovernment employment until the official has actually left. In consideration of this prohibition, however, departing officials should be given severance pay proportionate to their length of service—for instance, two months' salary for every year served. The quality of Pentagon management can be no better than the quality of the people we attract and hold to manage its policy and business.

The wrong mix prevails in our uniformed services. By every measure of statistics and intuition, we have today the highest-quality uniformed services in our history. The restoration of a good living standard and high pay, along with the resurgence in patriotism and national self-confidence, have made military service once again respected and sought-after.

But the very success of the overall volunteer force and the Reagan military buildup have brought about changes in the world military balance and the nature of our specific military requirements. The military structure that was drawn up and recommended ten years ago, which became the Reagan platform and then the blueprint for the successful military buildup, now needs substantial modification, with regard particularly to the mix of forces between active and reserve, between officer and enlisted, and between unskilled and technical.

Balance should be maintained between active and reserve forces. The current force structure in each of the armed forces today is about right. The army has 28 divisions, the navy will soon have 15 carrier battle groups and 4 battleship battle groups, the air force has 37 fighter wings, and the marine corps 6 division equivalents and 4 air wings. Each of the services, however, has too much of this force structure on full-time active duty. We do not need 18 active and 10 reserve army divisions; the ratio should be the reverse. Instead of a 600-ship navy of 550 active and 50 reserve ships, the ratio should be 450 active and 150 reserve. We do not need two-thirds active wings and one-third reserve wings in the air force but, rather, closer to half and half. Instead of 5 active division equivalents in the marine corps (officially there are only 3 divisions) and 1 reserve, the ratio should be 2 active and 4 reserve.

Each of the military service bureaucracies will tenaciously resist changing the existing ratios. The reasons always given are that there are insufficient training facilities available to expand the reserves and that each service is having enough trouble recruiting to fill current reserve billets without expanding them. These arguments are illogical and easily refuted. If there are fewer active forces using the training facilities and ranges, more would be available for the reserve. It would require shifting some of the reserve to the effective system used by many of our European allies. Instead of monthly weekend drills of limited utility, there should be one two-week to one-month annual training periods, using the best equipment on the best training ranges. Answering the second argument, obviously if you are able to recruit for full-time active duty, you can certainly recruit for part-time active duty. To do so effectively, however, pay and benefits to reservists must be increased.

The net savings to shifting the force structure in each of the services from full-time active duty to part-time trained reserve would be about a 40 percent net reduction below the cost of maintaining those units in the active force.

Optimum balance between officers and enlisted personnel is essential. The United States, like other leading industrial nations, has undergone a dramatic shift in the makeup of its work force over the past ten years. A decade ago, the ratio in the work force of college or technically educated to those with high school education or less was 1 to 6; today it is about 1 to 3 ½. In the very high-tech segments of industry the ratio was 1 to 3, and it is now 1 ½ college/technical school graduates to 1 high school graduate.

The military has undergone an even faster trend to high technology but, unlike in the private sector, there has been no shift in the ratio of officers to the enlisted except in the air force. The ratio in the air force today is currently 1 to 4 ½; in the army, 1 to 6; in the navy, 1 to 7; and in the marine corps, 1 to 9.

In both the active forces and the reserves, we should reduce the number of enlisted personnel and increase the number of officers, including the technical specialists called warrant officers and senior NCOs. We simply do not have a need for large numbers of people with limited education and no technical skills. To get men and women with good skills and better education, and to hold on to them, it is necessary to provide the rank and compensation of commissioned and noncommissioned officer status. Contrary to popular wisdom, there is very little difference in the ratio requirements of all of the services. All are equally dependent on high technology and tactical initiative. The proper ratio for all of them should be about 1 to 4.

The balance in flag and general officers is also way out of kilter. To run an organization of 4.5 million employees (500,000 posted abroad), with a book value equivalent to the top thirty Fortune 500 companies, Congress permits the Pentagon a total of only 1,073 flag and general officers. That is a tiny fraction of the number of senior executives of equivalent rank (and much higher compensation) than any well run corporation would have in proportion to budget, employees, or responsibilities. There also has developed a great imbalance among the services. The army has 412 general officers while the navy and marine corps combined, with a larger budget and equivalent manpower, have only 318 admirals and generals. The air force, with fewer people than the navy and a budget equivalent to that of the navy, has 338 generals. (See table 4.)

Balance within the officer corps is also needed. As the unprecedented large standing armed forces of the postwar period developed an ever-larger layering of bureaucracy to administer their worldwide peacetime forces, and as decades of reform legislation created more and more unified, joint, and component staffs, there has been a steady tendency in all of the armed forces to

create slots for more and more staff officers and to require more and more staff
duty at the expense of operational and tactical specialties. For instance, the air
force currently has as many nonflying staff officers—70,000—as the entire
navy has officers. And within the navy itself the requirement to fill more and
more staff billets in unified and component bureaucracies has created a hash
out of career patterns for most officers, requiring them to move constantly from
job to job. It is not uncommon for a naval officer to spend less than an average of eighteen months in any one job and to move his or her family more than
twenty-five times in a full career. In all the services this development has had
a serious perverse influence in modifying the professional values and standards
of the officer corps. So far has this process gone that now Congress requires
that all officers *must* have at least three and a half years of staff duty in a joint
bureaucracy and at least one year of a joint school even to be considered for
admiral or general. Thus it has finally become encoded in legislation that staff
duty and skills are what military service is all about; experience and distinction
in leading troops in the field, driving ships, and flying aircraft are secondary
and, judging from recent trends in promotions, even unnecessary for advance-
ment to the highest ranks in our peacetime military.

TABLE 4: 1985 FIGURES FOR EACH SERVICE

	GENERAL/FLAG OFFICERS	ALL OFFICERS	ENLISTED PERSONNEL	GENERAL/FLAG OFFICER TO ENLISTED RATIO	OFFICER TO ENLISTED RATIO
USAF	338	108,400	488,603	1:1766	1:4.5
USA	412	109,687	666,557	1:1618	1:6.08
USN	253	70,657	495,444	1:1958	1:7.01
USMC	65	20,175	177,850	1:2736	1:8.82
USN and USMC Combined	318	90,832	673,294	1:2117	1:7.413

Source: U.S. Department of the Navy, *Report to the Congress, Fiscal Year 1987* (Washington, D.C.:
U.S. Government Printing Office, 1986), p. 13.

It is well past time to reassert the primacy of tactics, strategy, leadership, and
the operations of our forces. Staff duty should be seen as a necessary adjunct
to bring the perspective of the professional war-fighter to bear on headquarters
policy and decision-making rather than the pinnacle of the military profession,
as the present system has it. If the number and size of all the joint service staffs

were at least halved to eliminate the requirement for so much staff duty, undoubtedly the entire chain of command would immediately operate far more efficiently and smoothly.

Conclusion

On April 10, 1987, I left the Pentagon for the last time. I had had the opportunity of a lifetime—to lead an effort not only to rebuild the navy but also to help restore the confidence and the strength of our country. I had been blessed with every advantage—an inspiring president, a steadfast secretary of defense, and a great staff. A few battles were lost, but in the main we succeeded in what we set out to do. We left the navy better than we found it.

The experience demonstrated that, in spite of an irrational system, the thousands of first-rate people in our defense establishment can still achieve great things when the direction is clear and when they are given the support they deserve. Indeed, my happiest days were spent with men and women of such quality and real altruism—sailors, marines, generals, admirals, civilians, and yes, even a few OSD bureaucrats. It is they who have rebuilt our military strength. However the details of this story may blur with the passage of time, my deep affection for the navy and marine corps will always remain.

Afterword

The National Security Act of 1947 created the illusion of a single unified organization called the Department of Defense. It is of course no such thing but rather a collection of hundreds of functionally independent entities with a bewildering "organization" chart and contradictory and blurred lines of authority. In addition it is deluged in its annual authorizing and appropriating bills with hundreds of new "reforms" each year. And of course it is the largest honey pot for pork barrel politics in the federal government. Reform, therefore, will always provide "low hanging fruit" for a new and determined secretary of defense.

Since this book was written, the gross inefficiencies and waste of bureaucratic bloat remain intact. To be sure successive defense secretaries, where they have concentrated on a particular issue, have made some notable savings and improvements. Perhaps the most dramatic of these since the book was written has been the successful effort to allow commercial off-the-shelf (COTS) technologies and products to be acquired.

Many bases were closed in the post–cold war initiative which has resulted in significant savings but that effort soon ran out of steam. It remains a fertile area. Nevertheless the most important reform that could be made in procurement would be to streamline the process. The cost of sophisticated programs is a function of time. I was present at the meeting that started and funded the F-22 program in 1983. It will be more than twenty years from that date when the first fully operational squadron deploys. The annual and cumulative costs have been staggering.

The problems that I have reviewed in chapter 14 and some of the solutions suggested are as timely today as when written. Nothing much has changed. Since then the sweeping legislative changes of the Goldwater Nichols bill have taken effect. Its impact has been both good and bad. On the positive side, it has significantly strengthened the hand of the joint theater commanders enabling them to have more say in the kinds of training, interservice exercises in peacetime, and a firmer control over all resources in war time as we saw demonstrated so well in Desert Storm. It is no small accomplishment.

On the negative side, it has resulted in a significant step backwards in time, imposing on the Pentagon the obsolete general staff system adopted by the European powers more than 100 years ago. The chiefs of the services no longer have frequent access to the president and National Security Council. Thus senior decision-making is presented with but one single military point of view, as was the case in Europe in World War I. It has resulted in enormous loss of civilian control over the military in the sense of significant visibility into military planning and decision-making. Civilian control with regard to operational matters resides now solely in the person of the secretary of defense.

Another bad effect has been a significant shift in the military culture. The new law requires that an officer must have served at least four years staff work before he can be considered for promotion to flag rank. There is no such requirement for operational command. Therefore, like the German General Staff, the staff officer and staff duty and the skills that go with staff bureaucracy become the dominant criterion for the officer corps; this is having a noticeable effect in the type of flag officers now moving to the top.

Much of *Command of the Seas* concerns reforms of the navy, a subchapter in the ever difficult task of managing the military overall. I had come to believe DOD needed its own "perestroika," the restructuring of a vast, overstaffed but undermanned establishment with a hopelessly complex way of researching, developing, building, and deploying our weapons.

With the enthusiasm of youth and the years of struggle as SECNAV, I thought that some of our reforms might stick. Some have—most have not. The Pentagon bureaucracy proved far more resourceful than its Soviet counterpart in preserving the *Gosplan* way of doing business. The credibility of these reforms was not helped when Assistant Secretary Melvyn Paisley pled guilty to taking payments from individuals. This was a terrible blow to the navy and to his colleagues. It was promptly seized by many contractors and bureaucratic critics who blamed the reforms and especially fixed-price competition.

Only a few years and a new administration unfamiliar with the Pentagon sufficed to turn back the clock. Through Pentagon subsidized consolidation, dual sourcing and hence competition have been largely replaced by the sole-source cost-plus contracting of the pre-Reagan era. Runaway cost escalation has of course returned with it.

Twelve years after completing this book it remains my strong view that for a significant improvement in the way we manage our defense effort, centralized policy formulation must be maintained, but the execution of decisions and the accountability that goes with it, particularly in procurement, must be decentralized and delegated as in all well run large corporations.

The key to significant improvement in the conduct of our defense will always be the service secretaries. When they have been empowered as the line chief executive officer of their services accountable to the secretary of defense, great improvements have been made. When secretaries of defense have treated them as ornaments and relied instead on non accountable assistant secretaries of defense and the OSD staff, trouble and mismanagement have resulted.

In short, if the 1980s were an era of reforming the DOD, then the 1990s were a lost decade. Once more the American taxpayer is threatened with the worst of all worlds: A more expensive but not more capable military. We fixed it once. It's "broke again."

The overriding issues, however, are how to use the navy best for some of the threats on the horizon. How can we design and build a hi-lo mix fleet of 400 ships within projected budgets? How can we protect the navy's extraordinarily sophisticated command and control systems in the era of global hacking? And the greatest challenge of all, how can we restore morale, attract a cross-section of the best young people in America, and retain them in the fleet?

Command of the seas and our nation's future depend on new answers to some timeless questions. We answered them in our day. We must answer them tomorrow.

September 1, 2001

Appendix

Contract Types

In the ship construction business the form of the contract between the builder and the customer, whether government or private, has been of three main types.

Firm-fixed price (FFP). Under this form a price is agreed to between the builder and the customer, and the builder must deliver the ship for that price no matter what it actually costs him; the customer is obligated to pay that price even if the actual cost of building it is well below that. The builder, therefore, has every incentive to keep costs as low as possible and complete the job as soon as possible to make maximum profit. The customer is relieved of the danger of cost overruns, since the basic risk of performance is borne by the builder. This contract type is appropriate for proven designs of ships that can be built without a lot of government-furnished material and can be furnished quickly, thus avoiding the uncertainties of labor and material costs over time. The benefits of this contract type quickly disappear if the customer decides to make basic design or engineering changes after the contract is signed or cannot meet the prior agreed-to contractor's schedule requirements for delivery of customer-furnished equipment. No well-managed builder will allow any changes without a modification to the contract. The customer always is at a huge disadvantage in such a situation, since construction is already under way, and he has no leverage to take his business elsewhere. Traditionally, therefore, builders have used change orders to modify fixed-price contracts greatly to their advantage.

Cost-plus-fee (CPF). Under this contract the builder is not bound to deliver the ship for any stipulated price. He is obligated only to provide "due diligence" and "best efforts" to deliver the ship for the "target price," which has no real binding force, being really only a "best estimate" or guess at actual cost. The builder's profit is fixed based on this estimate, so there is little incentive to keep cost growth under control. Most important, there is little to no risk for the contractor—he is not obligated to perform beyond the estimated ceiling price for the contract. And any change to his scope of work can result in an increase in the ceiling price—with additional profit. A variant of the cost-plus-fee contract provides a system of "incentive fees" in which the customer may award additional profit over the negotiated minimum or base profit according to progress in milestones or other mutually-agreed-on, performance-related parameters. This contract form is appropriate for a ship that is not yet well defined but whose importance is such that rapid completion transcends economies. The customer simply must have the ship and will accept the risks inherent in going forward on this basis. The crash program for the Polaris was an example where such a contract form was appropriate because of the urgency of the requirement. In peacetime, however, it should almost never be used. But it is the most favored contract form in the navy bureaucracy because it allows various offices and staffs to customize the design and make design and engineering changes without limit. Thus, in the thirty years preceding 1981, ships built under this contract form exceeded their budget price by an average of more than 100 percent.

Fixed-price incentive (FPI). Modern warships, and large, complex commercial ships now take years to build, so the disciplines of an FFP contract become too risky, because significant government-furnished materials and information must be provided through other contractors, and labor, materials, and other general economic changes bring too much uncertainty over the years of contract execution. The FPI contract form has evolved to accommodate those uncertainties yet still retain most of the disciplines of the firm-fixed price contract. The FPI contract sets a contractual target price that is supposed to be the best estimate of the builder and customer as to a fair price. There is in the contract another price also agreed to, called the ceiling price, which may be from 10 to 50 percent higher than the target contract price. This represents a worst-case price that the customer is willing to pay if costs increase. A specific fixed profit is agreed to as a reasonable percentage of the target price. In addition, there is an agreed "share line" in which the builder and customer agree on a percentage split of costs between target and ceiling. If costs go all the way to the ceiling, the builder must pay all costs above the ceiling price. When such a share line is agreed to, it is also extended below the target price, providing both the customer and the contractor with the opportunity to share in savings below the target price. Whether this compromise contract form between fixed price and cost plus is more of the one or of the other really depends on the share line and the amount by which the ceiling price exceeds the target price. The larger the share of additional cost that the builder must bear on the share line, the closer it comes to the disciplines of an FFP contract.

Notes

Introduction

1. *Armed Forces Journal*, September 1981, p. 42.
2. Normal Polmar and Thomas B. Allen, *Rickover* (New York: Simon & Schuster, 1982), p. 302.
3. Philip Ziegler, *Mountbatten* (New York: Alfred A. Knopf, 1985), p. 220.

Chapter 2

1. See Steven Coontz, *Flight of the Intruder* (Annapolis, MD.: Naval Institute Press, 1986), for a powerful novel on this theme. Coontz is an A-6 combat veteran.
2. Henry Kissinger, *Years of Upheaval* (Boston: Little, Brown & Co., 1982), pp. 72–81.
3. *The New York Times*, August 29, 1971, p. 37.
4. See *The Powers of the President as Commander in Chief of the Army and Navy of the United States* (Washington, D.C.: U.S. Government Printing Office, 1956); U.S. Congress, House Committee on Foreign Affairs, "Background Information on the Use of United States Armed Forces in Countries" (Washington, D.C.: U.S. Government Printing Office, 1970).
5. James Madison, "The First Letter of 'Helvidius,'" cited in R. S. Hirschfield, *Power of the Presidency* (New York: Atherton Press, 1968), p. 57.
6. Alexander Hamilton, "First Letter of 'Pacificus,'" cited in Hirschfield, p. 52.
7. Clinton Rossiter, *The Supreme Court and the Commander in Chief* (Ithaca, N.Y.: Cornell University Press, 1951), p. 8.
8. Joseph Harris, *Congressional Control of Administration* (Washington, D.C.: Brookings Institute, 1964), p. 255.

Chapter 3

1. Declassified Joint Chiefs of Staff papers are quoted in Rosenberg, "Oil in a Future War," *Naval War College Review*, Summer 1976.

2. JCS 1887/6, ibid.
3. *The New York Times,* November 12, 1980.
4. Bill Gully, *Breaking Cover* (New York: Simon & Schuster, 1980), p. 257.

Chapter 4

1. Elmo R. Zumwalt, Jr., *On Watch* (New York: Quadrangle Books, 1976), pp. 183, 464.
2. Harold Brown, *Thinking about National Security* (Boulder, Colo.: Westview Press, 1983), p. 174.
3. Robert N. Komer, "Maritime Strategy versus Coalition Defense," *Foreign Affairs* (Summer 1982), pp. 1132 et passim.
4. B. H. Liddell Hart, *Strategy,* 2nd ed. (New York: Praeger Publishers, 1967).
5. *Proceedings of the United States Naval Institute,* February 1987, p. 113.
6. Tom Pocock, *Horatio Nelson* (New York: Alfred A. Knopf, 1988), p. 289.
7. See U.S. Department of the Navy, *Report to the Congress, Fiscal Year 1988* (Washington, D.C.: U.S. Government Printing Office, 1987).

Chapter 5

1. The Washington Papers, vol. 6, no. 52 (Beverly Hills, Cal.: Sage Publications, 1978).
2. *Public Papers of the Presidents of the United States: Ronald Reagan, 1983, Book II: July 2 to December 31, 1983* (Washington, D.C.: U.S. Government Printing Office, 1985), p. 1142.

Chapter 6

1. Patrick Tyler, *Running Critical: The Silent War, Rickover and General Dynamics* (New York: Harper & Row, 1986), p. 312.
2. The "85-804" settlement of the massive claims brought by the navy's three largest shipbuilders in theory forced the contractors to take large losses and the navy to pay substantial claims as well. The settlement stipulated that Electric Boat would absorb without reimbursement $359 million of otherwise allowable costs. Litton was required to absorb a $200 million loss based on the projected cost at completion of the disputed contracts. Newport News was to receive a payment from the government of $23.2 million. As of October 1984, a GAO audit of the contracts indicated that Electric Boat suffered no loss but actually made a profit on the disputed contracts, and that Newport News made a substantial profit on the contracts.
3. Congress of the United States, House of Representatives, Armed Services Committee, *Hearings,* March 12, 1981 (Washington, D.C.: U.S. Government Printing Office, 1981).

4. For the Veliotis perspective, see Tyler, *Running Critical.*

5. *Hearings,* March 25, 1981.

Chapter 7

1. In uncovering the crooked books in the F-18 project, Paisley also discovered that
   as part of subordinating management to the requirements writers, the financial officer for every project worked for the project manager who wrote his fitness report,
   and not for the comptroller of the Systems Command, who reported to the assistant secretary for financial management. This violated the most fundamental management principles, and I directed it be changed immediately. There was tremendous resistance from the OPNAV staff, but Jim Watkins completely agreed. The
   reason for the opposition from the deputy chiefs of naval operations was that in reality they controlled the project managers through some ninety "commissars," called
   "project coordinators," who reported to the "barons," the deputy chiefs of naval
   operations for air, submarine, and surface warfare. Since at the time virtually all
   project managers were unrestricted line aviators, submariners, or surface warfare
   officers who hoped to get good assignments back with the fleet, they danced to
   the tune of the "barons" and not to that of the systems commanders. It took us
   nearly a year, but the system now has the financial officer and budget manager for
   each project reporting up a separate chain of comptrollers, who, in turn, report to
   the assistant secretary of the navy for financial management.

2. *The Wall Street Journal,* September 30, 1987, p. 6.

Chapter 8

1. This chapter draws on the following accounts: Alexander M. Haig, Jr., *Caveat* (New
   York: Macmillan Publishing Co., 1983); The Sunday Times Insight Team, *War
   in the Falklands: The Full Story* (New York: Harper & row, 1982); *The Falklands
   Campaign: The Lessons, Presented to Parliament by the Secretary of State for
   Defense* (London: Her Majesty's Stationery Office, December 1982); and *Lessons
   of the Falklands* (Washington, D.C.: U.S. Department of the Navy, February 1983).

2. Quoted in *War in the Falklands,* p. 256.

Chapter 9

1. Sources consulted for this chapter include: U.S. Department of State, *Grenada
   Documents: An Overview and Selection* (Washington, D.C., September 1984);
   Lessons of Grenada (Washington, D.C.: U.S. Department of State, February 1986);
   Lessons Learned in Grenada, Statement of Hon. Fred C. Iklé, Under Secretary for
   Policy, Department of Defense, Testimony to Committee on Armed Services, U.S.
   House of Representatives, January 24, 1984; William S. Lind, "The Grenada

Operation," Report to the Congressional Military Reform Caucus (Washington, D.C.: Military Reform Institute, April 5, 1984); Hugh O'Shaughnessy, *Grenada: Revolution, Invasion and Aftermath* (London: Hamish Hamilton with *The Observer*, 1984).

2. O'Shaughnessy, p. 26.

Chapter 10

1. *Report of the Department of Defense Commission on Beirut International Airport Transit Act, October 23, 1983* (the Long Commission) (Washington, D.C.: U.S. Government Printing Office, December 20, 1983), p. 35; this chapter also draws on Benis M. Frank, *U.S. Marines in Lebanon 1982–1984* (Washington, D.C.: History and Museums Division Headquarters, U.S. Marine Corps., 1982); Alexander M. Haig, Jr., *Caveat* (New York: Macmillan Publishing Co., 1983); Harvey Sicherman, "Europe's Role in the Middle East: Illusion and Reality," *Orbis*, Spring 1985; Richard A. Gabriel, *Operation Peace for Galilee: The Israeli-PLO War in Lebanon* (New York: Hill and Wang, 1984); Zeev Schiff and Ehud Yaari, *Israel's Lebanon War* (New York: Simon & Schuster, 1984); and Itamar Rabinovitch, *The War for Lebanon: 1970–1983* (Ithaca, N.Y.: Cornell University Press, 1984).

2. Even the bureaucrats had begun to face reality; hostile-fire pay of $65 per month for marines and sailors of the 24th MAU had been authorized on August 31. See Frank, p. 151.

3. Long Commission *Report*, pp. 50–51.

4. Ibid., p. 46.

5. Ibid., pp. 83–84.

6. Ibid., p. 11.

7. Frank, p. 152.

8. George C. Wilson, *Supercarrier: An Inside Account of Life Aboard the World's Most Powerful Ship, the USS John F. Kennedy* (New York: Macmillan Publishing Co., 1986), p. 142.

9. Ibid., pp. 189–90.

Chapter 11

1. E. B. Potter, *Nimitz* (Annapolis, Md.: Naval Institute Press, 1976); see also E. B. Potter and Chester W. Nimitz, eds., *Sea Power and Naval History* (Englewood Cliffs, N.J.: Prentice Hall, Inc., 1960).

Chapter 14

1. Robert Higgs, "Military Scandals Again," *The Wall Street Journal*, June 27, 1988, p. 12.

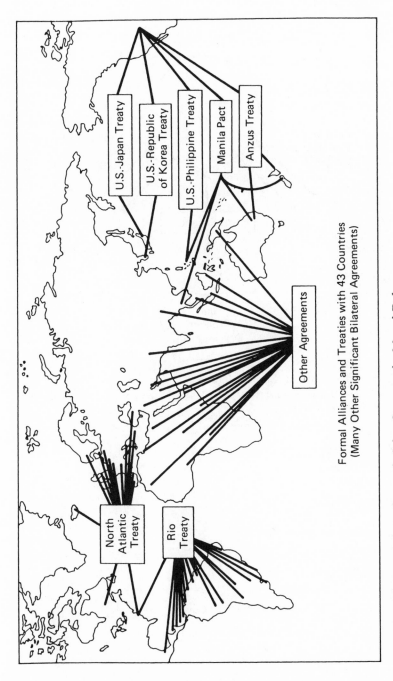

Figure 1. U.S. Treaty Relationships with Other Countries for Mutual Defense
SOURCE: U.S. Department of Defense.

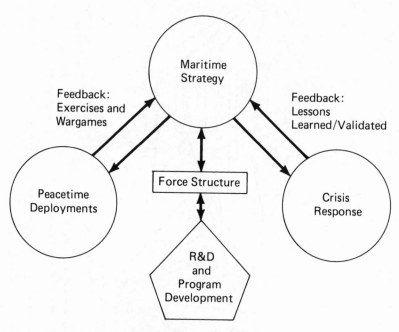

Figure 2. The Maritime Strategy Process

SOURCE: The 600-Ship Navy and the Maritime Strategy (Washington, D.C.: U.S. Government Printing Office, 1986), p. 63.

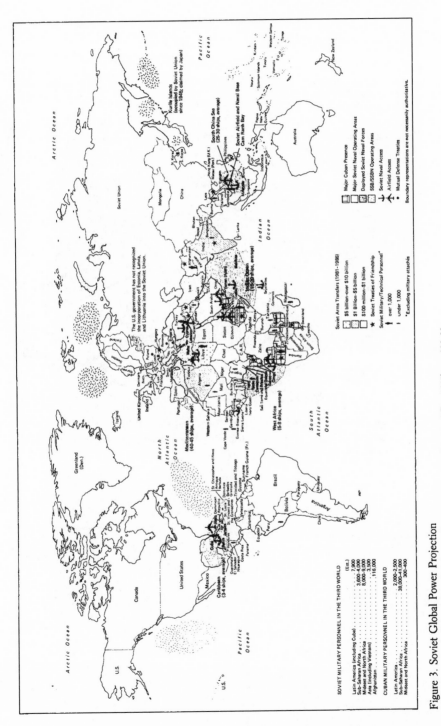

Figure 3. Soviet Global Power Projection

SOURCE: Soviet Military Power (Washington, D.C.: U.S. Government Printing Office, 1987), pp. 128–29.

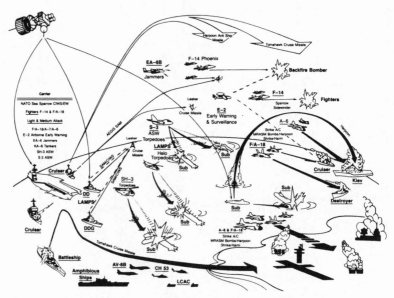

Figure 4. Naval Exercises and Air Strike Near Gulf of Sidra, 1986

SOURCE: U.S. Department of Defense, from The Maritime Strategy (Annapolis, Md.: U.S. Naval Institute, January 1986), p. 14.

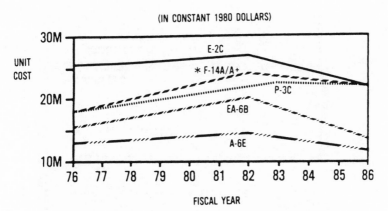

(IN CONSTANT 1980 DOLLARS)

UNIT COST

FISCAL YEAR

* INCLUDES IMPACT OF FIRST F-14 A + BUY IN FY 86

Figure 5. U.S. Navy Recurring Unit Flyaway Cost Trends, 1976–1986

SOURCE: U.S. Department of the Navy, Report to Congress, Fiscal Year 1988 (Washington, D.C.: U.S. Government Printing Office, 1987).

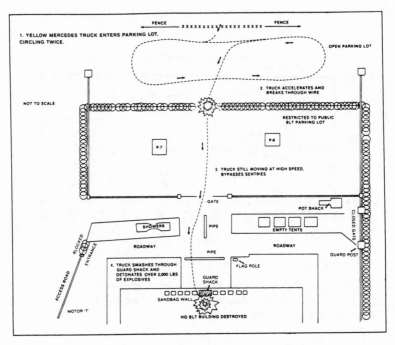

Figure 6. Sketch Map of Route of Terrorist Bombers, October 23, 1983
SOURCE: Report of the Department of Defense Commission on Beirut International Airport Transit Act, October 23, 1983 (Washington, D.C.: U.S. Government Printing Office, December 20, 1983).

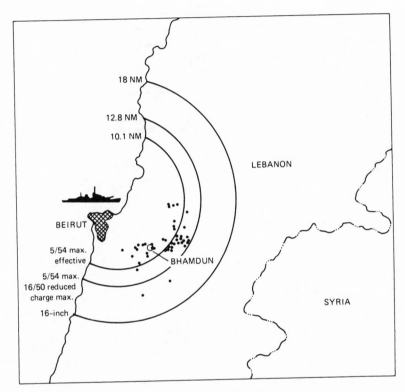

Figure 7. Range of the 16-Inch Guns of U.S.S. *New Jersey*
SOURCE: U.S. Department of Defense.

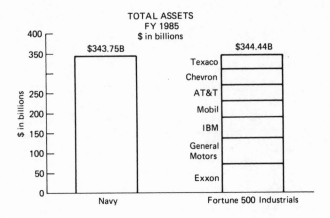

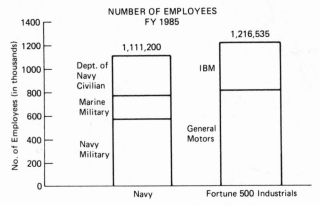

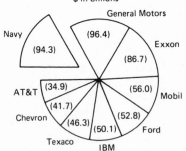

Figure 8. Comparison of U.S. Department of the Navy with Fortune 500 Companies

SOURCE: U.S. Department of Defense.

Index

About the Author

John F. Lehman is the chairman of J. F. Lehman & Company. He is also a director of Bail Corporation, Insurance Services Office, and Sedgwick Group plc. Dr. Lehman was formerly an investment banker with PaineWebber Inc. Prior to joining PaineWebber, he served for six years as the secretary of the navy. He was president of Abington Corporation between 1977 and 1981, and he served twenty-five years in the naval reserves.

Dr. Lehman has also served as staff member to Dr. Henry Kissinger on the National Security Council, as delegate to the Force Reductions Negotiations in Vienna, and as deputy director of the U.S. Arms Control and Disarmament Agency.

He holds a bachelor's of science from St. Joseph's University and a B.A. and M.A. from Cambridge University. He earned his Ph.D. at the University of Pennsylvania.

Dr. Lehman serves as vice chairman of the Princess Grace Foundation and is a director of the OpSail Foundation and a trustee of the Spence School. He lives in Manhattan and Pennsylvania with his wife and three children.